JESUS FOR LIVING

JESUS FOR LIVING

Daily Prayers, Wisdom, and Guidance

Mark Lanier

1845BOOKS

Book design by Baylor University Press

Cover design by *the*BookDesigners
Cover image: © Shutterstock/Eskemar

Hardback ISBN: 978-1-4813-1880-8
Paperback ISBN: 978-1-4813-1881-5

Library of Congress Control Number: 2022914257

INTRODUCTION

Over the millennia, the church has recognized the need for daily devotional life with God through prayer and study of Scripture. The historical church has also seen the value of a full expression of spreading the study out through an annual church calendar. The church calendar changes slightly from one denomination to the next, but most of the dates are common.

This devotional book is targeted around the church calendar. Because the Western calendar begins January 1 and runs through December 31, this devotional book is written to service a reading program that begins on New Year's Day. Unlike my other devotional books (*Torah for Living* and *Psalms for Living*), this book allows for the use of the church calendar in ordering the readings. This means that one will read Easter devotionals during the season of Easter, Christmas devotionals during Christmas, and so forth.

Since the church calendar exists independently of the Western calendar, the days do not always align. Christmas is always December 25, but Easter can vary tremendously. As a base year, I have chosen 2023, and the dates fit within that year's time scheme. If you are reading this book in a different year, you may need to make occasional adjustments.

The detail of some church calendars is quite specific, and different denominations use different calendars. With some ecclesiastical calendars, each day of the year can be a feast to someone, a time of memory of one aspect of the life of Christ, or another event important to the church. This devotional book doesn't chart every daily celebration or recognition of the most intricate calendars. It follows the major holy days of most calendars of the historical church.

A number of churches only adopt portions of the historical church's calendar, and a few churches eschew the calendar altogether. To make this devotional more useful for those, before each major section of the church calendar, I will give a short explanation for that season.

The goal of the church calendar is to give a well-balanced diet to believers. Following this calendar gives attention to each area of Christian devotion. One covers the birth of Christ, the ministry of Christ, and the death of Christ, as one moves through periods of repentance, rejoicing, focus on sin, and the victory found in Jesus.

A number of passages are used for multiple devotionals. Most, if not all, of the Bible passages will produce a multitude of ideas and teachings often from the same verse. That reality is picked up in these pages.

Of last note, the church calendar begins with Advent, those four Sundays before Christmas that anticipate the coming Christ child. This book begins with January 1, the Western start of the year. Therefore, this book begins toward the end of the Christmas season, then rapidly moves through the rest of the church calendar before "starting" in Advent.

To God be the glory.

CHRISTMASTIME

Many people think of Christmas as the day of December 25, followed by New Year's celebrations. People may sing "The Twelve Days of Christmas" and think it applies to the twelve days *before* Christmas. This is a common misperception among people who are not active in a liturgical church that adheres to the church calendar.

The twelve days referenced in the song refer to the twelve days *after* Christmas, not before. The church celebration of Christmas centers on the incarnation of Christ, and that didn't end on the day of his birth. On subsequent days, Jesus was circumcised, the wise men came, and other events happened around the infancy narratives.

So, in the Western calendar, as the new year begins, the focus in the church calendar is still on the infancy of Jesus, the incarnate God. This lasts through the day of Epiphany and the Baptism of the Lord (January 8 and 10, respectively).

JANUARY 1

And at the end of eight days, when he was circumcised, he was called Jesus, the name given by the angel before he was conceived in the womb. (Lk. 2:21)

The doctor Luke reported that Jesus' circumcision occurred on the eighth day after birth, precisely as God directed Abraham about two thousand years earlier (Gen. 17:12). The same day, he was given his Jewish name, *Yeshua* (ישוע), the New Testament-era Hebrew spelling of the name we commonly call "Joshua" (*Yehoshua*, יהושע). Most of the world calls *Yeshua* "Jesus" because the Hebrew name was rewritten into Greek for the New Testament, a collection of books and letters written in Greek. The "Y" became an "I" in Greek, which later became a "J" in English, and since the Greeks didn't have a "sh" sound, the "sh" became simply an "s." The final "s" is a typical Greek ending for a subset of nouns.

Naming was never haphazard in those days. Your name was significant and carried meaning. If your name didn't fit your character and your life, your name was changed! The name Jesus or *Yeshua* or simply Joshua, meant "Y is salvation!" "Y" was an abbreviation for the name of God, spelled with the Hebrew equivalents of our letters Y-H-V-H (commonly guessed as being pronounced "Yahweh," although many consider it blasphemous to even speak the name of God).

As the year dawns, the church historically celebrates the circumcision of Jesus, and key to that is the proclamation that the Lord God is salvation! That is a name that Jesus infused with meaning as it had never before held. God had promised his salvation from the first day of humanity's fall. Y-H-V-H announced his curse on the serpent in the garden proclaiming that a male offspring from woman would bruise or step on the head of Satan. God was bringing a solution to all sin through Eve's offspring.

God's salvation was already known, even before the events of the garden. Paul explained that we were chosen *in Christ* "before the foundation of the world" (Eph. 1:4). Jesus was no Plan B. Jesus was never a fallback option. God knew what the cost would be of endowing humanity with free will. God knew what it would cost God to redeem humanity in a way consistent with God's just character. God decided to make humanity with an ability to make choices, even though it would cost God beyond our understanding to redeem us. He didn't have to make us, but he chose to out of love. He did so already knowing the cost of his redeeming love. This is the love that awaits us this year. The question we must address is how we will respond.

The love of God moves me to love him. I learn love from him. I am touched and moved. I want to walk closer this year and learn his love in deeper ways. I want to reflect that love to a loveless world. All to his glory!

Lord, thank you for eternal love! May I learn to love you deeper. In Jesus' name, amen.

JANUARY 2

And when the time came for their purification according to the Law of Moses, they brought him up to Jerusalem to present him to the Lord (as it is written in the Law of the Lord, "Every male who first opens the womb shall be called holy to the Lord") and to offer a sacrifice according to what is said in the Law of the Lord, "a pair of turtledoves, or two young pigeons." (Lk. 2:22–24)

When I was young, my mother always made black-eyed peas for New Year's Day dinner. I really didn't fancy their taste, but Mom said that sometime during the year, I would earn a dollar for every one I ate. So, eat them I did, as much as I could stomach. I didn't like them then, and still don't like them today.

Some people live for money. Some impoverished people need more to have a decent life. Some who have a decent life, need more to have a better life. Some who have a lot, need more to sustain a life of overabundance. Money can be a huge motivator. But as students of the Bible, we should know better.

God had a pick of where he would be incarnated. God could choose the mother (Mary) and the home (her husband Joseph). God could have given Joseph great wealth, so Jesus would be born into luxury. God could have, but he didn't. Mary and Joseph were not wealthy, and we know that from today's passage, as well as later indicators from the life of Jesus.

Leviticus 12:6–8 gives the details of what a mother was to do when the time for "purification" came after childbirth. She was to bring a one-year-old lamb, and if she "couldn't afford a lamb," then she was to bring "two turtledoves or two pigeons." That is what Mary brought.

Jesus wasn't born into wealth because he was born for a purpose different than luxury, comfort, or accumulation. He was born to carry out God's work in bringing his kingdom of heaven to the people of earth. Jesus came to prepare a place for us in the presence of God. Jesus came to suffer and die for eternal reasons, not to enjoy the moment.

As this year unfolds, I ask myself where I am going to put my efforts. I want to make sure that I am concentrating on living to God's glory. If that means God places plenty at my doorstep, I know to be diligent in remembering "to whom much is given, much is expected." If God gives me little, I still want to make sure I give all of my energy and talents to his purposes. This is what this life is about. To think otherwise is to build up treasures on earth that serve no real purpose in eternity. In other words, a waste of time and effort! I don't want that this year!

Lord, please give me this year what I need this year to serve you and your plans. May I keep my focus on you! In Jesus' name, amen.

JANUARY 3

Now there was a man in Jerusalem, whose name was Simeon, and this man was righteous and devout, waiting for the consolation of Israel, and the Holy Spirit was upon him. And it had been revealed to him by the Holy Spirit that he would not see death before he had seen the Lord's Christ. . . . And when the parents brought in the child Jesus . . . he took him up in his arms and blessed God and said, "Lord, now you are letting your servant depart in peace, according to your word; for my eyes have seen your salvation that you have prepared in the presence of all peoples, a light for revelation to the Gentiles, and for glory to your people Israel." (Lk. 2:25–32)

Simeon is the Bible in a snapshot: this Jewish man whose name sounds like the Hebrew word for "heard." Simeon "heard" the Lord's promise concerning the "consolation of Israel," that is, the Messiah. For thousands of years before Simeon, God had assured humanity that God would send one who would solve humanity's major problem. That problem was that sin created a barrier in the relationship between a just God and an unjust people.

God told Adam and Eve that he would fix the problem. God told Noah that he would fix the problem. God told Abraham, Isaac, and Jacob that he would fix the problem. God told Moses and the Israelites through the Law (Torah) that he would fix the problem. Then through David, through countless prophets, and through unfolding events, God continued to promise that he would fix the problem.

Simeon "heard" that God would fix the problem, but he also "heard" something more. Simeon heard that he would not die before he saw the Messiah (the Hebrew word for "Christ"). Once Simeon saw the baby Jesus, his sight joined his hearing. What he had heard, he now saw. Simeon beheld the Christ, and with that, he was ready to die.

Simeon knew Jesus wasn't just the consolation of Israel. Jesus was never just Israel's Messiah. Jesus was the glory of Israel, but he was also the Savior of the world! The work of Jesus reached to all nations.

I like the way Simeon beheld God and his work. He heard, he saw, he touched (held), and he spoke. This was a full experience for Simeon and gives us the full Bible message. People need consolation before God. We need something to restore our relationship. God promised one who would bring that restoration. That promised one is Jesus. Jesus came through Israel, as God had assured the world he would. Jesus came for all nations and peoples. Through Jesus, everyone, Jew and Gentile alike, can walk intimately with the Lord God. And all of us who behold Jesus in this way, all who see him and believe in him, are ready to die! We have found restoration with God.

Lord, thank you for the story of Simeon. Thank you for the consolation of Israel. Thank you for Jesus, Savior of the world! May we see him for who he is, embrace him in faith, and proclaim his identity to the needing world. In Jesus' name, amen.

JANUARY 4

The beginning of the gospel of Jesus Christ, the Son of God. (Mk. 1:1)

In 1992, Disney released the animated film *Aladdin*. The film featured a theme song with lyrics by Tim Rice. The song, a duet, won both an Academy Award (for Best Original Song) and a Grammy Award (for Song of the Year). The song's title and resonating theme was "A Whole New World." In it, Aladdin takes Princess Jasmine on a magic carpet ride, promising to show the previously confined princess a life of freedom and love.

The lyrics promise, "A whole new world (don't you dare close your eyes); a hundred thousand things to see (hold your breath, it gets better). . . . I can't go back to where I used to be. A whole new world with new horizons to pursue. . . . Let me share this whole new world with you. . . . A whole new world (a whole new world); a new fantastic point of view . . . ."

I don't know where Tim Rice got his lyrical inspiration, but his ideas were reflected thousands of years earlier in the start of Mark's gospel! Mark begins with what may seem a simple introductory sentence in our Bibles: "The beginning of the gospel of Jesus Christ, the Son of God." However, if you were in the first-century Roman world, this would have spoken to you powerfully.

The language Mark chose was language already in use. The best example comes from a stone inscription written in 9 BC in the ancient city of Priene, in western Turkey. The city fathers there decided to redo their calendar to begin with the birth of Caesar Augustus. They inscribed into stone their purpose: The coming of Caesar "transcended the expectations . . . with the result that the birthday of God [Caesar Augustus] signaled the beginning of good news for the world because of him." The phrase used—"the beginning of good news"—is the same phrase Mark uses, although translated in the Bible as "the beginning of the gospel" (which means "good news").

In Mark's day, this language heralded the coming of a whole new world. This was a time unlike any before, or any anticipated to come. This was a "hold your breath" moment. It was all Tim Rice wrote of and more. But time has shown that while Caesar's birth was important, it was a dim flame compared to the bright sun of Jesus' coming. A Roman reading in Mark's day got the idea immediately: with Jesus it's a *whole new world*. Jesus present changes everything! It did in Mark's day, and it does today.

Lord, come into my life with your good news. Change me. Change who I am, how I think, how I behave, and where I am going. Make me yours! In Jesus' name, amen.

JANUARY 5

And Jesus increased in wisdom and in stature and in favor with God and man. (Lk. 2:52)

Plants need certain things to grow well. They need roots that burrow into strong soil that can bear support when heavy rain and wind might otherwise cause the plant to fall. With deep supported roots, the plant can grow fully and bear fruit as appropriate. Without its roots supported, the plant will not grow as it should.

In some ways, people aren't much different. The plant serves as a useful analogy to what we need. Consider Jesus as set forth in today's passage. The doctor Luke would have known about children growing physically. It is the natural process that moves us from infancy to childhood and into adulthood. But Jesus didn't simply grow physically. He also grew in wisdom and in favor (or grace) with God and with people. This is part of growing like a well-grounded plant.

If we just grow physically, we reach adulthood ill-equipped to withstand the storms of life. When trouble blows in, we buckle under, unable to stand up without the aids of drink, food, drugs, pleasure, or some other crutch. When stress builds up, some blow their top while others retreat into a dark hole. People don't have the tools to handle trouble and stress when they grow up physically but without godly wisdom and favor.

With godly wisdom and favor, however, growing up becomes a good maturing process. It is one that produces good fruit and withstands the hurricane forces that come in when we least expect it. Godly wisdom teaches us how to respond to crisis.

Why is godly wisdom so valuable? Part of that answer lies in *where* we get godly wisdom! It only comes from God. This means that when faced with storms in life, we learn to lean on God, a rock that withstands any storm. We live in the presence of the Almighty, held by his strong, untiring arms. He surrounds us with a love that teaches and guides us through the storms. He calms the winds.

As I grow in life, I want to grow in godly wisdom. I also want to follow Jesus and grow in favor/grace with God. The Greek word for "favor" is *charis* (χάρις), a word most often translated as "grace." In this passage the translators chose "favor" because Jesus grew in this both with God and man. Man doesn't dispense "grace" in the theological sense, so the translators did not want to stray into misunderstandings from using the word "grace." Still, our understanding of the passage is infused with meaning as we understand this sense of favor or grace. Jesus was viewed favorably not only by God as he grew but also by men.

As we grow in favor with God, as we develop in wisdom, our growth isn't lost on those around us.

Lord, please help me grow in wisdom and favor. May the world see it and give glory to you. In Jesus' name, amen.

EPIPHANY

"Epiphany" comes from a compound Greek word (*epiphaino*, ἐπιφαίνω), which conveys the idea of "appearing" or shining upon someone or something. At its root is the early church's celebration of the baptism of Christ. The celebration recognized that when Christ came forward to receive baptism from John the Baptist, Jesus appeared or shone out in his ministry as Messiah for the first time.

Later in church history, the feast was also a celebration of the initial appearance of Christ as a child, normally recognizing the time Jesus appeared to the Magi. It seemed to fit into the Christmas season well as a celebration of the "three kings," as the early church determined to have been the number and titles of the biblical Magi.

Some churches celebrate Epiphany for a short time, others celebrate it for four Sundays. Some celebrate it for the presentation of Jesus to the Magi, some for the baptism of Jesus, and some for both! Some also add in the wedding at Cana as the first time Jesus was presented as Messiah to mainstream audiences.

During Epiphany, then, the devotionals center on times when Jesus appeared as God to various peoples in various stations of life.

JANUARY 6

On the third day there was a wedding at Cana in Galilee, and the mother of Jesus was there. Jesus also was invited to the wedding with his disciples. When the wine ran out, the mother of Jesus said to him, "They have no wine." . . . His mother said to the servants, "Do whatever he tells you." . . . Jesus said to the servants, "Fill the jars with water." And they filled them up to the brim. And he said to them, "Now draw some out and take it to the master of the feast." So they took it. When the master of the feast tasted the water now become wine, and did not know where it came from (though the servants who had drawn the water knew), the master of the feast called the bridegroom and said to him, "Everyone serves the good wine first, and when people have drunk freely, then the poor wine. But you have kept the good wine until now." This, the first of his signs, Jesus did at Cana in Galilee, and manifested his glory. And his disciples believed in him. (Jn. 2:1–11)

God goes to a wedding? God alters the laws of nature to make sure that the host isn't embarrassed by underestimating the consumption of wine by the guests? Really???

Yes, really! This was the way Jesus' ministry began. This was the official launch that John characterized as God "manifesting his glory." "Glory" is a bright status, a splendor, a magnificence, an honor or prestige. Performing this miracle in this way and at this time was Jesus manifesting, or showing, the brilliance of who he was as God Incarnate!

What does this passage tell us about the glory of God? God is interested in people, not simply as a race, but as individuals. God cares about what happens to us. God's concerns aren't focused only on the awful moments when we desperately need his rescue; God also cares about the times when we just need help to get through the day. God cares about the happy times as well as the sad. God cares about rejoicing as well as mourning. God wants to be there when we dance as well as when we cry.

God is a full-interested God. He cares about us in intimate ways and in individual ways. His care is not that of an observer. He is a participant. Some think humanity is God's heavenly equivalent of a television series. He watches and at times enjoys the show. Such is not our God, however. God wants to be involved. God wants to bring us joy. God wants to meet our needs.

What is God doing in your life? Are you doing your part? As Mary said to the servants, "Do whatever he tells you." When we follow Jesus and do as he tells us, amazing things will happen in our life. God will manifest his glory!

Lord, thank you for manifesting your glory in my life. Thank you for your personal love and care. I love you. In Jesus' name, amen.

JANUARY 7

And from there he arose and went away to the region of Tyre and Sidon. And he entered a house and did not want anyone to know, yet he could not be hidden. (Mk. 7:24)

Today's passage makes most sense within its context. Jesus was busy. He was constantly surrounded by people in need. He was also inundated with enemies who wished him ill. In the midst of this life, Jesus strove for time to be able to teach his disciples necessary lessons, the lessons they would need to understand who he was and what he was doing. These were lessons that would shape and inform the ministry of the apostles and that form the backbones of our biblical gospels.

Multiple times in Mark, the notation is made that Jesus at times wanted anonymity with his disciples. In Mark 9:30–32, Jesus passed through Galilee "not wanting anyone to know" where he was so he would have time "to teach his disciples." So today's passage fits in well with this idea of Jesus needing anonymity. Jesus left Galilee and went to the adjacent land to the west, the land of Tyre.

Tyre was not Jewish. In fact, Tyre had a bad reputation to Jews. Jezebel came from Tyre (aka Phoenicia), and she was Israel's worst queen, responsible for seducing the people with wickedness and pagan gods. During the intertestamental time, Tyre sided with Israel's enemies in battle. Tyre was not where one would expect to find Jesus and his disciples.

Yet even in Tyre, Jesus "could not be hidden." The power and presence of Jesus shows his magnificence to those who are looking and those who aren't. Even people who say, "How can there be a God when there is suffering in the world?" are seeing God, even though they don't realize it. It is God who teaches them that suffering is not a good thing. It is God who shouts to the world that we should do something about suffering. The morality of humanity is a trait installed in people by God. Morality and fairness are not inherent in nature's evolution. The sharks don't feel bad about eating other fish.

So, Jesus can't and doesn't remain hidden. It couldn't happen. Even in pagan Tyre, the power and might of God in Jesus is obvious. Today's verse precedes Jesus healing the non-Jewish Syrophoenician woman's little daughter. The momma sought Jesus' help, and Jesus gave it. Jesus not only couldn't stay hidden, Jesus was found as the compassionate one he was.

This speaks to me. I wonder how good I am at showing Jesus to the world. Jesus doesn't want to stay hidden as he lives in my heart. He wants the world to see him in me. This is the way his kingdom grows. Heaven forbid I try to hide Jesus! I need him to explode from my life into the world around me!

Lord Jesus, may I live to show you in your glory and compassion. In your name, amen.

JANUARY 8

Then Jesus came from Galilee to the Jordan to John, to be baptized by him. John would have prevented him, saying, "I need to be baptized by you, and do you come to me?" But Jesus answered him, "Let it be so now, for thus it is fitting for us to fulfill all righteousness." Then he consented. And when Jesus was baptized, immediately he went up from the water, and behold, the heavens were opened to him, and he saw the Spirit of God descending like a dove and coming to rest on him; and behold, a voice from heaven said, "This is my beloved Son, with whom I am well pleased." (Mt. 3:13–17)

The presentation of Jesus at his baptism is one of Scripture's most marvelous affirmations. In his baptism, Jesus gave a real-life event and image as an illustrative point of his coming into the world. Jesus came into the world to identify with sinners.

John baptized others for their repentance from sin. Those people who were convicted of their inadequacies before God came to John, repenting of their sins and seeking God's cleansing. John had baptized many, and when Jesus appeared for baptism, John rebuffed Jesus. Although John wasn't fully clear of Jesus' role in the world, likely through God's Spirit, John declared the truth: Jesus didn't need to repent from sins and hence didn't need John's baptism.

What John didn't understand was that Jesus had come to stand with sinners. Jesus was going through a process (baptism) that would be a ritual for his church. In identification with those sinners who would subsequently enter his church, Jesus was walking where they would later walk.

The identification of Jesus with sinners is explained more fully in the text of Isaiah 53. In Isaiah 53, Jesus carries the sins of humanity being "numbered with the transgressors," even though he "bore the sin" and was the "intercessor."

This is the Jesus who is worthy of our praise. Jesus came into this world with a purpose. Jesus was going to save humanity, and do so in a way that not only complied with God's justice and character but also that fully identified with humanity. Jesus didn't sin, but he was counted among the sinners.

This speaks of the depth of God's love for us, as well as his purpose. When we come to God, we come through Jesus, one who has known us for who we are, identified with us in our sin, even though perfect. Jesus explained this in his teaching and showed this in his life. Then God the Father declared through God the Holy Spirit, "This is my beloved Son, with whom I am well pleased." Importantly, this is a two-way street. As Jesus identified with us, so we also identify with him. Here God expresses pleasure and confirmation not only to Jesus, but to all who are identified with Christ!

Lord, thank you for reaching out to me. Let my life reflect your love. In Jesus, amen!

JANUARY 9

But immediately a woman whose little daughter had an unclean spirit heard of him and came and fell down at his feet. Now the woman was a Gentile, a Syrophoenician by birth. And she begged him to cast the demon out of her daughter. And he said to her, "Let the children be fed first, for it is not right to take the children's bread and throw it to the dogs." But she answered him, "Yes, Lord; yet even the dogs under the table eat the children's crumbs." And he said to her, "For this statement you may go your way; the demon has left your daughter." And she went home and found the child lying in bed and the demon gone. (Mk. 7:25–30)

The mother was worried sick. Her "little daughter" was sick in ways that no one could treat. The details aren't known to us, but there was an unclean spirit having his day with the little girl. It wasn't the girl's fault; she was too little for personal blame. This was part of the ongoing war between the forces of light and darkness. This was the spiritual warfare that was especially intense during the time of Jesus' earthly ministry.

So the mother found Jesus, and coming into his presence, she "fell down at his feet." This isn't the first time Mark has recorded someone falling at Jesus' feet. He reported Jairus doing the very same thing just a few pages back. The similarities don't stop with Jairus falling at Jesus' feet, for Jairus also did so out of need for healing for his "little daughter." Jairus' daughter needed Jesus' touch or she was going to die. Despite all the similarities, there was also a huge distinction. Jairus was one of the rulers of the synagogue! He was no pagan woman.

Even though the daughter of Jairus died before Jesus could reach her, Jesus brought her back from death. In the story here, the little daughter hadn't reached that point yet, but Jesus' touch was necessary for her to be saved, nonetheless.

The indications are that this woman wouldn't have known the God of Israel. But the woman had faith in Jesus. She engaged in dialogue with him and kept working Jesus, knowing he was her only hope. That was the seed of faith that Jesus found. Jesus healed the daughter and sent the woman home for her faith to grow.

There is something about faith to be mentioned here. Faith isn't always great. Faith isn't only knowledge. Faith is also about trust. The woman wouldn't let Jesus deny her request, and once Jesus acknowledged her and agreed to the healing, the woman left, trusting that Jesus had healed her daughter as he had said.

I have a friend who reads the Bible and finds the assurances of God. He trusts them, even when logic says he shouldn't. My friend says, "I need to trust God's promises, regardless of whether they make sense to me." I think my friend is wise.

Lord, teach me your promises and let me be better at trusting you. In your name, amen.

JANUARY 10

Then he returned from the region of Tyre and went through Sidon to the Sea of Galilee, in the region of the Decapolis. And they brought to him a man who was deaf and had a speech impediment, and they begged him to lay his hand on him. And taking him aside from the crowd privately, he put his fingers into his ears, and after spitting touched his tongue. And looking up to heaven, he sighed and said to him, "Ephphatha," that is, "Be opened." And his ears were opened, his tongue was released, and he spoke plainly. (Mk. 7:31–35)

Today's passage follows the event when Jesus healed the little daughter of the Syrophoenician woman from Tyre. After returning to the areas around Galilee, Jesus heals a man who was deaf and had a speech impediment. This man's loved ones seem to have brought him to Jesus; Mark doesn't say that the man came on his own. The loved ones "begged" Jesus to lay his hand on him. They didn't ask directly for healing, but they were clearly hoping the blessings of Jesus' hands would help the man in some way.

Jesus touches the man, but not simply laying hands on him. Jesus puts his fingers into the man's ears and spitting, touches the man's tongue. In a sense, Jesus puts himself into the man, invests the man, and in so doing, brings the man full healing. This is the empathy of Jesus. This is Jesus relating to those he came to serve. This is the manifest love of a compassionate God.

But there is something more to be found reading the Greek text of Mark. The Greek word for the man's speech impediment (*mogilalos*, μογιλάλος) is only used once in the entire Bible. In the Greek version of the Old Testament in use at the time Mark wrote, the word is used in Isaiah 35, a prophetic Scripture about the joy of the redeemed at the revelation of the Lord in the end times.

In Isaiah 35, the wilderness and dry land are rejoicing. Lebanon, where Tyre was located, sees the glory of the Lord, something the Syrophoenician woman would certainly proclaim. And then Isaiah 35 speaks of the "ears of the deaf" being "unstopped" and the "tongue of the mute" singing for joy. The translated word "mute" is that rare Greek word Mark uses. Mark doesn't want his readers to miss the fact that Jesus is the promised one.

Seeing the link to Isaiah 35 is especially meaningful to me, for right in the midst of the discussion of Lebanon (the Syrophoenician in Mark's gospel) and the healing of the mute (today's passage) lies Isaiah 35:3–4. It is a promise that Jesus will "strengthen the weak hands" and "say to those who have an anxious heart, 'Be strong; fear not!'" That word is for me!

Lord, please be my healing God today. Strengthen my weak hands. Give strength and faith to my worried heart. By the might and in the compassionate name of Jesus, amen.

ORDINARY TIME
OR PRE-LENTEN SEASON

Church calendars vary on when Epiphany ends. Some churches have four Sundays worth of Epiphany. Others begin "ordinary time" or the days of general moral teaching after the baptism of Jesus, taking it up to the beginning of Lent.

Some churches begin a pre-Lenten season (aka "Septuagesima"), for three Sundays prior to Lent. For these churches, this time period focuses on why God came to earth in Jesus, with a consciousness of the problem of sin.

In this devotional book, the days up to Lent will be filled with "ordinary time" devotionals along with devotionals dedicated to why Jesus became incarnate as Lent approaches.

JANUARY 11

You are the light of the world. A city set on a hill cannot be hidden. Nor do people light a lamp and put it under a basket, but on a stand, and it gives light to all in the house. In the same way, let your light shine before others, so that they may see your good works and give glory to your Father who is in heaven. (Mt. 5:14–16)

Who we are and what we do makes a difference in the world, whether we like it or not! It can be a good difference or it can be a bad difference. We need to live with our eyes open and our hearts tuned into that truth.

In legal ethics, one of the principles for lawyers and judges is to "avoid even the appearance of impropriety." This ethical rule is rooted in a realization that how things appear are often as important as how they truly are. "Perception is reality!" is the saying we often hear. How people perceive something is often regarded as how something is, even if the perception isn't accurate. Therefore, lawyers are instructed to be careful about how things appear, as well as how things actually are.

This is a good admonition for the Christian as well. Christ taught his disciples that our lives are on display. Our choices and attitudes are seen by others. We can live in ways that bring God glory or we can live in ways that bring him disrepute. The world is watching, and what we do and who we are is on display.

Practically speaking, this means we need to be people who reflect God. We should be demonstrating his love and compassion. Often Christians can err, and we become more like the judgmental and self-righteous Pharisees that Jesus confronted rather than becoming more like the loving and compassionate Savior.

I want to figure this out. I want to do better at living with a full consciousness that my actions are on display. I want that vision of being a light on a hill that can't be hidden from view. I want to always, even when alone, be aware that my actions will be seen either directly or by the way they shape my character. In other words, I want to live with a full and constant recognition that my life is seen. It makes a difference in the world. I make a difference in the world!

Appearance can be reality, but I want to make sure that reality is accurate. I want my appearance to show my heart for God. I want people to see my life and see Jesus. I want to show love, even when I get frustrated. I want to show compassion even when I am angry. I want to be a light for the Lord!

Lord, please help me live fully aware of my actions, my heart, and how they appear to others. Let me reflect one who loves you and models your love for the world. In Jesus' loving name, amen.

JANUARY 12

Beware of practicing your righteousness before other people in order to be seen by them, for then you will have no reward from your Father who is in heaven. (Mt. 6:1)

One of the joys of my life has been teaching a class at church each Sunday. For decades, my weekly preparation has been a source of personal learning, conviction, and life-changing study. I then get to share each week those things of God I have been learning. It is a marvelous, fulfilling part of my life.

Over many of those years, several trusted class members have e-mailed me their thoughts after class. My friend Dale calls them his "PGC's" or "Post Game Commentaries." My friend Janet simply calls them "Reviews." Those e-mails mean a lot. They can be positive reinforcements of some good point made, and they can be good reminders of ways I could teach better. My friends have insights I don't, and I can learn from them.

I have to be careful, however, that I am not teaching just to get strokes or affirmation. My motives for teaching need to be pure. Now those reading this may not be regular teachers at church, but I suspect everyone has the same temptation I write about. We all have areas where we are tempted to do well, to perform a good or noble deed, and do so to get the affirmation of others.

Take a self-test. When you do something nice for someone you love (parent, spouse, friend, etc.) do you want to make sure that person knows it was you? Is that because you want them to feel loved (a good thing) or at least a little because you want them to be impressed with you? Do you find that some of your best deeds have a bit of selfishness about them? Can you join me in the ranks of "affirmation junkies" who like to hear people say, "Well done!"

Passages like today's challenge me. They make me examine my motives. Am I living to impress others? Are my actions ones that are seeking to boost me in the eyes of others? Or am I concentrating on doing right and pleasing God without regard to whether others see it and are impressed by it?

I want to get better at this. One way I can do that is by making sure each day I find ways to do right without anyone knowing! I will show my wife love by cleaning up without pointing it out! I will serve my friends (and enemies) in some way and not sound the trumpet to announce my good deed. I will honor God with actions that no one else will ever see or hear about. I want to live focused on God, not me!

Lord, help me to live for you and not for the attention and affirmation of others. May my soul be satisfied with your love. In Jesus I pray, amen.

JANUARY 13

Beware of practicing your righteousness before other people in order to be seen by them, for then you will have no reward from your Father who is in heaven. (Mt. 6:1)

I read of Watchman Nee learning to ride a bicycle in early twentieth-century China. He learned to ride later in life and had a horrible problem staying upright and keeping the bike straight. After many frustrations, a helpful person asked Watchman where he was looking while trying to ride. Watchman said he was staring at the handlebars. He was working to make sure he didn't move his hands. The person told Watchman that he needed to change his focus. If Watchman looked down the road, he would keep his balance. That shift in perspective made the difference, and Watchman could ride a bike.

We often need a visual shift in perspective. Today's passage is instructive in that regard. It is a good thing to do things that are right, true, and good. It is good to be generous. Likewise, it is good to be kind and loving. Being reliable is a virtue as is being trustworthy. But if we are doing those things because we want the praise and honor of others, then our actions—however right they may be—do not proceed from the best motives.

Jesus taught us that our perspective should be centered on God, not on ourselves. When we are doing things to be seen by others, we are really doing them for selfish reasons. If we do things to be seen by God, then God becomes the center of our attention, our affection, and our desires.

This may seem a subtle shift in perspective, but it isn't. It is the difference between night and day. At the root, it reflects our deepest love and desire. Do we care most about how people perceive us so that we get the honor and glory or do we seek to do right to give God the glory and honor?

You may not think that your life is one where people even take notice. I suspect, however, most everyone lives a life where others take notice. Each of us will experience the difficulties that come from living under the microscope of another's eye. The temptation will be to live in ways that please, impress, or draw positive attention from those observing. We need to change our perspective.

Just as Watchman Nee had difficulty riding a bike when his focus was faulty, so will we fall when we live for others rather than the Lord. It can be subtle and may seem okay ("What's wrong with being righteous?"), but it isn't the right focus!

Lord, teach me to retrain my eyes. Let my life be about you, and not me. Teach me righteousness so I live true and right before you—to your glory. In Jesus, amen.

JANUARY 14

Thus, when you give to the needy, sound no trumpet before you, as the hypocrites do in the synagogues and in the streets, that they may be praised by others. Truly, I say to you, they have received their reward. But when you give to the needy, do not let your left hand know what your right hand is doing, so that your giving may be in secret. And your Father who sees in secret will reward you. (Mt. 6:2–4)

I was riding a Peloton bicycle with an instructor barking commands about how fast to go, when to stand up on the bike, when to sit back, and what posture to maintain. At one point she told us, "When you breathe, try to breath in through your nose and out through your mouth." She didn't say, "If you breathe . . ." She took for granted that we would be breathing.

In like manner, Jesus taught his followers how to go about giving to the poor and needy. Notice Jesus never said, "If you give to the needy . . ." He took for granted that we would be giving to the needy.

Before we consider *how* we should give to the needy, we need to take note *whether* we give to the needy! Our temptation is not to think about such things because we pay taxes and the government is charged to use our taxes to help the needy. Or maybe we give to the church, and we can send the needy to church.

To the contrary, Jesus assumed that his followers would be giving to the needy. Doing so is a part of being a follower of Jesus. Jesus was God Incarnate; he came into the world to give salvation and love to a needy and desperate people. It is only right that those of us who say we follow Jesus also live a life committed to helping the needy and desperate.

When we realize that when we are helping those in need we are like our Lord, then we find the second part of this admonition. Our actions are for the Lord, not for aggrandizement before others. We don't give to the needy so people will think us generous. We don't help the helpless so people will admire us.

This is all part of Jesus' radical idea that in the believer's life, everything revolves around the Lord. We do because of who he is and what he wants. We seek to please him and him alone. We are concerned with the things that concern him. We focus on the matters that he draws to our attention. This life and all we are rotate around God.

This is a transformation from the way of the world. It is the way of Jesus and should be our way as well.

Lord, I confess my life rarely rotates around you alone. Forgive me and help me to do better. Much better. In the holy name of Jesus, my example and Savior. Amen.

JANUARY 15

And when you pray, you must not be like the hypocrites. For they love to stand and pray in the synagogues and at the street corners, that they may be seen by others. Truly, I say to you, they have received their reward. But when you pray, go into your room and shut the door and pray to your Father who is in secret. And your Father who sees in secret will reward you. (Mt. 6:5–6)

One night when I was a preteen, we went out to eat as a family. Our food came, and we began eating. I asked Mom and Dad, "How come we pray before every meal at home, but when we go out to eat we don't?" Mom's answer was the first time I heard and had any insight into this passage of Scripture. Mom had always taught us the importance of prayer, but prayer was never to be for show. It was a deeply personal and private conversation we had with our Lord and Father.

We lived at the time and in a place where praying in public before a meal would stand out as a glaring display of showy religion. Over time, I have found myself living in different places and the times have changed. It became more common to see others praying in public before meals. To do so was not an awkward spectacle but simply an acceptable practice of folks who chose to do so.

When I became a father, I realized I had responsibilities for teaching my children how to pray privately and publicly. This changed how I prayed in public vis-à-vis this passage. I now will frequently stop and pray before eating in public.

That said, I would love to say I am a pious fellow who *always* stops and prays publicly before each meal, but I'm not. It's not that I don't care sometimes, or that I am ungrateful to God for the bounty we enjoy at mealtime. It is that sometimes it seems to feel like a show or spectacle, while at other times it doesn't.

When I am by myself, I can pray without anyone knowing. When I am with others, I can acknowledge God's graciousness without an overt prayer. It is easy and right to say to those who join you in a meal, "I am thankful to the Lord for this meal and for a chance to eat with you."

Today's passage isn't just about meals. I use mealtime prayers to demonstrate that we are to take the passage practically and seriously. We need to be aware that our prayers are never for show. Our prayers are true, heartfelt communication with the Creator of the universe, who also happens to be our Father in heaven.

Lord, thank you for prayer. Thank you for listening to the cries of our hearts. Thank you for loving us. Forgive us when we lose focus on you. In Jesus' name, amen.

JANUARY 16

And when you pray, do not heap up empty phrases as the Gentiles do, for they think that they will be heard for their many words. Do not be like them, for your Father knows what you need before you ask him. (Mt. 6:7–8)

When I first started working as a lawyer, one of my bosses was an exceptional writer. He urged me to get and read *The Essential Elements of Style*, a book on writing by William Strunk Jr. and E. B. White. The book is small, and it gives a minimal number of simple rules to use in writing. I remember the first rule: Omit needless words. I loved that rule: three simple words that couldn't be reduced further.

Some think that there is power in using numerous words. Often, however, using many words when a few would do simply becomes showy or reflects thoughtless speech. Jesus taught his disciples to pray in simple terms, communicating to God from their hearts and minds.

The Gentiles didn't speak plainly and directly. Instead, as Jesus explained, they spoke in "empty phrases." The Greek word for "empty phrases" (*battalogeō*, βατταλογέω) is an onomatopoetic word, meaning it means much as it sounds. The onomatopoeia is the "batta" sound. ("Logeo" is "to speak.") "Batta" is a babbling noise in Greek.

In fairness to the Greeks, they were never certain their gods were listening to their prayers. They needed certain incantations to invoke the attention of their gods. They also would speak repeatedly in hopes the gods might listen at some point. Jesus explained that God was starkly different. God wants our conversation. He desires our hearts and minds to turn to him for help, in praise, and through all of life.

We don't have magic phrases that command God's attention. We don't need to wake him up so he will listen to us. We needn't think that we have to catch him at a good moment. God is more than 24/7. God exists fully attentive in every moment, and he wants to hear our prayers. We have the marvelous opportunity to come into the presence of Almighty God and speak directly to him. This is the door that was opened to us by the death of Jesus. Jesus himself paved the way for the imperfect human to speak openly to the perfect God.

Jesus didn't want prayer to be a time to babble through phrases that we've memorized and mindlessly deliver. Prayer is something more. It is genuinely speaking to God. We have no need for "needless words." Let our prayers be thoughtful and to the point.

Lord God, thank you for hearing my prayers. Teach me to pray better. I pray through the righteousness from Jesus, amen.

JANUARY 17

Pray then like this: "Our Father in heaven, hallowed be your name. Your kingdom come, your will be done, on earth as it is in heaven." (Mt. 6:9–10)

Why does Jesus teach his disciples to pray? Isn't prayer at its basic level, just a conversation? Did they not already know how to have a conversation? Is a conversation with God so different that we need to learn how to do it? If Jesus is teaching prayer mechanics, shouldn't he be addressing how to stand, sit, or kneel? Wouldn't we expect Jesus to say, "Eyes shut!" or maybe "Eyes open and looking to the sky!" Jesus wasn't teaching his disciples the physical rules to prayer. Jesus was teaching his followers about the content of prayer.

Jesus doesn't give a "wordy" prayer. His concern was not about repetition of words and phrases. He doesn't have magic formulas to be recanted in order to command God's attention or channel God's power. Jesus taught his followers some very basic guidelines in speaking to God.

Jesus had his disciples address God as their heavenly Father. This wasn't because the followers of Jesus were all one family, all one race or ethnic group (though those listening were all Jewish). This is because anyone who follows Jesus has God as their heavenly Father. It is an address rooted in the reality of a relationship with God. Without a relationship with the Almighty, we have no place to approach him in prayer or dialogue.

Jesus then teaches that prayer is first and foremost about God. It is about declaring him "holy" or "hallowed." It is knowing that our first wish and desire in this world, that which we bring before him immediately, is the declaration and recognition of God's greatness. This should be first in our prayers and first in our life choices. Our lives should align with our prayers in bringing glory to God.

Jesus immediately adds prayers for the advancement of God's kingdom and achievement of God's will. A theological interest to this is that such would need prayer at all. Isn't God's kingdom guaranteed? Who or what could stop God's will? Why would we need to pray such things? Jesus taught that people don't exist as mere pawns or actors in a cosmic drama. We are actual participants. We help write the script. When we pray, God acts. Humans were put in charge of this world at creation, and God never took that responsibility away. We need God to achieve what must be achieved and hence we pray for his will and his kingdom. Then we act to find it and express it in life!

Heavenly Father, may we bless your name as we seek your kingdom and will in our lives and our world. Through Jesus our Lord, amen.

JANUARY 18

You call me Teacher and Lord, and you are right, for so I am. If I then, your Lord and Teacher, have washed your feet, you also ought to wash one another's feet. (Jn. 13:13–14)

When I was in college, one of my good friends and I began having regular devotionals in our dorm. My friend Steve was legally blind, but he could read with the assistance of a strong and massive machine that would make each word and letter almost the size of a sheet of paper. What Steve lacked in sight he made up with insight. I think reading slowly heightened his perception of what he read.

When we studied this verse, Steve noticed the noun change Jesus made. Look at the verse again. Do you see it?

Jesus pointed out that to his followers he was first a Teacher, and second their Lord (or Master). That was how his followers saw him. They weren't wrong in seeing Jesus in both roles. Jesus was indeed their Teacher, and it was a title that he readily used for himself. Similarly, Jesus was their Master or Lord. He was the one they not only learned from ("Teacher"), but that they also followed ("Lord").

The shift that Jesus made in the nouns was in their ordering! Jesus should not be seen as "Teacher" first and "Lord" second. Jesus is first our Lord and then our Teacher. The reason that Jesus' life and words should instruct and teach us is because he is our Lord and Master. It is who Jesus is that makes what he has to say important and relevant to our daily lives.

Over the decades since these dorm-room devotionals, I have been challenged by Jesus' shift in positioning these words. I do not believe it accidental. Jesus had a habit of changing the ordering of things for emphasis. This is just one example. But it is an example that challenges me.

To many in the world, Jesus was a great teacher. He was a worthy example of virtue and wisdom. He gave valuable life lessons that can make the world a better place. To love our enemies, to turn the other cheek, to live with honesty and integrity, these are valuable admonitions worthy of our attention. But those who see Jesus as simply a teacher worthy of following are missing out on the key point.

The key point is that Jesus is Lord. He is worthy of our allegiance and devotion. We properly see him as more than a moral teacher. We see him as one to whom we will give our lives.

Lord, I give you my life and devotion. Teach me daily what that means. Amen.

JANUARY 19

Then the Pharisees went and plotted how to entangle him in his words. And they sent their disciples to him, along with the Herodians, saying, "Teacher, we know that you are true and teach the way of God truthfully, and you do not care about anyone's opinion, for you are not swayed by appearances. Tell us, then, what you think. Is it lawful to pay taxes to Caesar, or not?" But Jesus, aware of their malice, said, "Why put me to the test, you hypocrites?" (Mt. 22:15–18)

I write these devotionals as an older fellow in his early sixties. I grew up in the 1960s and '70s—the era of "peace and love." We were products of the Vietnam War and the Civil Rights movement. We grew up wanting to make sure that the battles we waged were ones of value and worth. The millennial generation, those coming into adulthood in the twenty-first century, has a somewhat different focus. They have grown up with the internet, where in a matter of moments, you can find someone who will say almost anything. Arising with this is a healthy dose of skepticism, a recognition that the news we get might be "fake."

The millennial generation has developed an appetite and yearning for authenticity. The importance of genuineness cannot be overrated. It gives a fuller shine and luster to understanding the events unfolding in today's world, but also today's passage given above.

Jesus' fame and influence were growing. Many in power didn't like that. They wanted to bring Jesus down a few notches. They sent some of their stronger folks to try and trap Jesus and get him into trouble. These folks brought with them "Herodians," some of the people responsible for collecting and using taxes. The line chosen to set Jesus up dripped with false flattery. "Teacher," they called him, pretending they were at his feet to learn. They set Jesus up as one who would teach the way of God truly, without regard to what others thought. Then they asked Jesus whether or not it was appropriate to pay taxes to the pagan Roman emperor Caesar.

They thought this the perfect trap. If Jesus said, "No," then the Herodians could seize him as a rebellious instigator. If Jesus said, "Yes," then the nationalistic Jews would see Jesus as a sellout. If Jesus refused to answer, Jesus would be seen as a coward who wouldn't stand up to Caesar.

Jesus stumped the instigators by showing Caesar's face on a coin and telling them to give Caesar what belonged to him but give God our hearts. But before outsmarting their inquisition, Jesus pointed out the hypocrisy of those asking. Their flattery was fake, and their calling Jesus their "Teacher" was bogus. In twenty-first-century speak, they were not authentic. I want my life to be authentic, especially as I relate to the Lord. He knows the difference.

Lord, help me to live authentically before you. May I never fake who I am. In your name, amen.

JANUARY 20

And James and John, the sons of Zebedee, came up to him and said to him, "Teacher, we want you to do for us whatever we ask of you." (Mk. 10:35)

Whoops! Those words have escaped my lips many times in life. Since high school, my life has revolved around speaking. In school I took debate every year, along with every other speech class I could find. I took a degree to preach, and another to try lawsuits. I have spent my adult life teaching, lecturing, and speaking in front of judges and juries. True confessions: Over the years, I have stuck my foot in my mouth more times than I can count. I have said things that as they left my lips had me thinking, "Why on earth am I saying *that*?" I have said things that sounded right at the time, but on reflection I realized, "Ugh!!!"

For me, today's passage might be one of those "foot-in-mouth" moments that I would rather forget, at least if I were James and John. Look at what they said! They went up to Jesus and asked him to write a blank check. They wanted Jesus to commit to them to grant their request sight unseen. Without telling Jesus what they wanted, they wanted Jesus to ensure that their wish would be granted. They were treating Jesus like a genie in a bottle, just with one wish instead of three.

I suspect at the time, it seemed a possible way to get what they wanted, but looking back, it must have made them sheepishly embarrassed. After all, the proper question should never be "Jesus, will you do whatever we want you to?" Rather we should always be asking, "Jesus, what do you want us to do?" We should be doing whatever Jesus asks!

To make things even worse, James and John began their request by calling Jesus, "Teacher." They certainly had need of a teacher at the moment!

I am not judging James and John, for I have made many worse gaffes. I am actually taking solace in their faux pas. I love that Jesus dealt with them seriously and didn't start laughing. Jesus was gentle as he explained that they were asking something outside the realm of propriety.

I read this with a chuckle. I have suffered from foot-in-mouth disease often, and I know I will again. When I do, when I say things I shouldn't, I am glad I have a merciful Savior. I need that more than I need a wish-granting genie. I need someone who can help me apologize if I've said something offensive, help me try to right whatever I have set wrong, help me overcome a tongue that gossips, and help my words be holy and pure.

Lord, please forgive me for words rashly spoken. Help my words be seasoned with grace and fit for a student of yours! In Jesus' name, amen.

JANUARY 21

And one of the scribes came up and heard them disputing with one another, and seeing that he answered them well, asked him, "Which commandment is the most important of all?" Jesus answered, "The most important is, 'Hear, O Israel: The Lord our God, the Lord is one. And you shall love the Lord your God with all your heart and with all your soul and with all your mind and with all your strength.' The second is this: 'You shall love your neighbor as yourself.' There is no other commandment greater than these." And the scribe said to him, "You are right, Teacher. You have truly said that he is one, and there is no other besides him." (Mk. 12:28–32)

Mrs. Kingston, Mrs. Jarrett, Mrs. Smith, Dr. Floyd, Dr. Baxter, Ken Dye, Joe Barnett—I have had many great teachers in my life. The list could go on and on. What made them great? Some of it was undoubtedly their style. They made learning fun and accessible. But it also centered on content. They had material that was important, useful, and interesting. It resonated with who they were as people and it made sense in my life.

I think of them as I read today's passage. The passage reflected the insights of a fellow who was watching Jesus and his disciples. This fellow was a "scribe," one trained in the law and able to read and write it. Doubtlessly he had spent his life trying to decipher and better understand what God had instructed in the Torah (the Jewish "Law," better known to many today as Genesis-Deuteronomy). This scribe was intrigued and even impressed with Jesus' dexterity with the Law and so he asked Jesus to isolate the most important law of all.

Jesus readily responded by quoting Deuteronomy 6:4–5, what is known in Hebrew as the "*Shema*" (Jewish for "hear," the first word in the passage). It was God's firm admonition that everyone is called to love the one true God with all of our heart, soul, mind, and strength. Jesus then gave the scribe a bonus! In addition to giving the most important law, Jesus added a second as well. It was from Leviticus 19:18 and it instructed all to love those in their lives as much as they loved themselves.

After hearing this, the scribe gave Jesus the title, "Teacher." The scribe saw that Jesus was worthy of that appellation. Jesus wasn't just spouting off random ideas, he was giving substance worthy of learning. Jesus had something to say.

I am thankful for the great teachers in my life. I am especially thankful for Jesus as Teacher. From him I can learn of God, life, others, and myself. He was, and is, the greatest teacher. His insight is genuine. I will learn from him today, and I will seek to love God and my neighbor better than I did yesterday!

Lord, help me grow in my love for you and for others. In Jesus' name, amen.

JANUARY 22

Jesus answering said to him, "Simon, I have something to say to you." And he answered, "Say it, Teacher." (Lk. 7:40)

I really *really* like today's passage. The verse itself is tremendous: Jesus has something to say to Simon, and Simon is ready to hear it. But beyond the verse the backstory is fantastic. Then if we add in what seems to be a habit of the author Luke, we have an amazing one-two-three-layered lesson.

The first layer is simply the passage. Jesus isn't isolated from our lives. He isn't a Himalayan mountaintop sage who we must hike to so we can ask our questions. Jesus seeks us out. Jesus *wants* to speak into our lives. Jesus has things to say to us. Our job is to listen! We are to have open ears and open hearts so we can hear the voice of God spoken into our lives. This is a key reason behind daily devotionals and daily quiet time with God. We read from passages of his word and ruminate on what they mean. We try to hear what God is saying.

The second layer involves the backstory. Simon had invited Jesus to be a dinner guest in Simon's home. While they were reclined and eating, a "sinner" (likely a prostitute) came into the house and with tears flowing down her cheeks, gave Jesus a ceremonial foot washing putting ointment on Jesus' feet. Simon should have been embarrassed that no one in Simon's home had seen to this common courtesy for Jesus. Instead, however, Simon was thinking something harsher and more judgmental. Simon's thoughts were that Jesus must not be all he was rumored to be. If he was, Jesus would have known that the woman touching him was a "sinner." Jesus read Simon's mind and called him out over the affair. Jesus pointed out that the woman had done what Simon should have done. Yet Simon judged the woman when he should have been judging himself!

The third layer involves perceiving how Luke wrote his gospel and the book of Acts. Luke did his research. He traveled throughout the Holy Lands to make sure he had the right story. When Luke wrote up events, he didn't always name names. He would name those who were famous or whose story tied into well-known events. But he would also name people he interviewed. These were by and large those who had come to faith decades later when Luke was researching and writing. In this story, Luke calls Simon by name. I suspect this indicates that Simon listened to Jesus. Simon's life changed. Luke could have written stories of Jesus getting his feet washed in Bethany (John), or in the home of Simon the leper (Matthew and Mark). But Luke chose this incident instead. Luke documented the road to faith that began with one man listening to Jesus.

I want to listen.

Lord, speak to me and give me ears to hear what you say. In Jesus' name, amen.

JANUARY 23

While he was still speaking, someone from the ruler's house came and said, "Your daughter is dead; do not trouble the Teacher any more." (Luke 8:49)

This is one of the devotionals I am writing while in the middle of a several-months-long trial. Most lawyers in trial have little time for anything that isn't absolutely crucial. I don't either. But my devotional life *is* absolutely crucial to making it through each day, especially when the day is intense and the stakes are high. So, during trial I find some of my best chances to reflect on the Lord, his word, and what he says to me. Today's passage speaks to me and should speak to all of us who live in a hectic world where things are often beyond our control.

There was a ruler in Israel who had a very sick daughter. The doctors were no help, and the father was desperate. He sent his trusted servant to see if the rumored teacher Jesus might be able to come help. After all, if the stories were true, this carpenter turned teacher/rabbi was able to heal folks who were beyond hope. Jesus was his last hope.

Before Jesus was even reached, the man's daughter died. Burdened with grief, the father sent another servant to inform the first that there was no point in bothering Jesus. The girl was now dead. The father didn't understand who he was dealing with. Neither did the servants. Jesus was a "teacher," as addressed by the man, but Jesus was much more than that. The man wasn't just dealing with a miracle-working teacher. The father was dealing with God. Bothering the teacher might have been pointless once the child died. But God is a whole different matter! A grieving father with a deceased daughter needs God like never before.

Jesus knew this. He disregarded the message, "It's too late," and he went to work! Jesus raised the girl from the dead and restored her to her family.

When I was young, I remember being blown away by Paul's comment to the Ephesians that God is "able to do far more abundantly than all that we ask or think." I can think and ask for a lot! Of course, we need to remember that God will not answer those prayers or desires that might be counterproductive to his overarching plans and will, but we shouldn't be wanting such prayers answered anyway.

So, I continue to work today in my trial. But I do so knowing that I have a friend in Jesus who is not only a teacher, but is God. And God is able to meet my needs today and every day, in ways that exceed my meager imagination. You may not be a lawyer, but you likely go through trials of your own kind. Don't lose sight of your God!

Lord, I look to you. Please take care of today. All of my needs I know and those I don't, I set before you eagerly anticipating your hand in my life. In Jesus' name, amen.

JANUARY 24

Someone in the crowd said to him, "Teacher, tell my brother to divide the inheritance with me." (Lk. 12:13)

I love a well-written line in a good song. Some artists/poets have a way of turning a phrase that brings a larger idea to mind. One of my favorites in this regard is Bob Dylan. From an early age I remember being impressed with one of his lines from "Stuck Inside of Mobile with the Memphis Blues Again." Dylan sings of a character who tells him, "Your debutante just knows what you need, but I know what you want." I always liked the important distinction between what we need and what we want.

Passages like today's reinforce for me the importance of seeking from God what we need, and not what we want. Jesus was going about his day when an anonymous person shouted out to him, "Tell my brother to give me my fair share of my inheritance!" I am sure that to the fellow shouting, this was of major importance. Look at it from his perspective: This was his money. He was entitled to it. He just wanted his fair share. His brother was withholding it wrongfully. His brother was in the wrong. Jesus was a man of great authority. Jesus should be able to weigh in and his brother would have to listen to Jesus.

What the man failed to discern was the difference between what he wanted and what he needed. This man needed a priority adjustment, not Jesus to step in as arbitrator in an inheritance dispute.

Jesus told the man as much. Jesus told him that he wasn't there to play arbiter. Jesus had something much greater to offer the man. Jesus instructed the man to consider his motives. Life is about more than what you have. When our desire for things trumps our desires to have our hearts right with God and others, we have lost sight of what matters.

Jesus didn't give the man what he wanted. Jesus gave the man what he needed. I read this and reflect on my life. What are the things I ask of God? With all there is in the world, where do I place value such that it commands the attention of my prayers? Am I seeking God to bring about his will? His kingdom? The praise of his name? Those are the *first things* Jesus taught his disciples to ask for in prayer. Then the disciples pray for personal needs. Again, though, those are needs, not wants! "Daily bread," "forgiveness," "deliverance from evil"—these are needs!

I want to focus on refining what I seek from the Lord.

Lord, you know my heart, please purify it. You know my needs, please meet them. You know my desires and wants, please don't let them skew my priorities before you. I pray in Jesus' name, amen.

JANUARY 25

Judge not, that you be not judged. For with the judgment you pronounce you will be judged, and with the measure you use it will be measured to you. (Mt. 7:1–2)

Today's passage makes me nervous. I am *really good* at seeing mistakes and problems in others. It is a gift of mine. I can see where people fall short, and if anyone wants to know about it, I could quickly tell them.

This passage gives me insight, however, into why I can be so good at seeing problems in others. It is because I have the same problems myself. I may not realize it, but this is true. The problems we see in others are so recognizable because we have the same problems ourselves.

I remember in my preteen years when someone at school would call someone else a name, an oft-heard reply was, "It takes one to know one!" Those words were truer than we realized! Often it does take one to know one. This is the point of today's passage, but the passage doesn't stop there.

When we judge others, we are actually judging ourselves, without realizing it. Helpful here is understanding the Greek word for "judge." It is *krinō* (κρίνω). It can refer to a judicial proceeding and what a judge might pronounce. But it also can reference being critical or judgmental toward another. It is used in this sense in today's passage. When we criticize others, we are setting ourselves up for the same judgment. We should be admonished by the old adage, "People who live in glass houses shouldn't throw stones."

Looking at today's passage makes me want to do the very difficult thing of turning my gaze inward and asking myself where I need God's help and mercy because of my own shortcomings. Then I want to see others with the same eyes of mercy as I seek from God.

Am I a gossip? Do I speak of others in ways that I wouldn't if they were present? Am I short-tempered or harsh at times to others? Do I see this trait in others but fail to address it in myself? Am I short on self-control and self-discipline? Do I see others who fail to do what they should simply for lack of willpower and judge them for it? Do I wallow in self-pity? Do I see others who seem to feel sorry for themselves, and when I do, do I have no mercy on them?

The odds are quite strong that what I see in others is something I would see in myself if my visions were true. I need to work on this!

Lord, help me to be kinder and gentler in my dealings with others. Forgive my judgments and help me to be a better person. In Jesus' name, amen.

JANUARY 26

Do not give dogs what is holy, and do not throw your pearls before pigs, lest they trample them underfoot and turn to attack you. (Mt. 7:6)

As a creature of habit, I picked up phrases as a young man that have stuck with me for decades. One that I inherited from my father was opening the door for another and saying, "Age before beauty" as I urged them to go in before me. The saying generally merited a chuckle, but I remember one time opening the door for my friend Edward Fudge. I said, "Age before beauty." Edward didn't miss a beat. He walked in before me and proudly said as he did so, "Pearls before swine!"

If for no other reason, today's verse is one I have ruminated on at length. In the context of the Sermon on the Mount, it doesn't make clear sense. It causes some commentators to stumble, trying to figure it out. The terms are clear enough. Dogs and pigs were "unclean." That was clear from the Torah, the Jewish Law books and Scriptures we today call Genesis through Deuteronomy. But practically, what was Jesus referring to in this passage?

Even in the early church, the passage was considered hard to apply. Just what did Jesus mean? In the *Didache*, an early instruction manual for Christians (likely written within a hundred years of the death of Jesus), this passage was interpreted as speaking to closed communion. In other words, the Eucharist or Lord's Supper was not a meal open to the unsaved. But it seems odd to me that Jesus would have been speaking of that years before he instituted the Lord's Supper.

I think the key to understanding this passage is found in the many injunctions in the Torah, the core Scriptures at the time of Jesus. Over and over in the Law, we read the injunctions emphasizing the importance of keeping clean things clean. The clean and unclean were not to mingle. This applied to foods, clothing, work, and play.

God has always emphasized the importance of cleanliness. "Clean" is a metaphor for the righteousness we should have in our lives. "Unclean" is a metaphor for sin. We should never mix the two. Unclean has no role in the life of a follower of God, any more than pearls have a role in a pig sty. No one should take the holy bread God had set aside for priests (in Jesus' day) and give it to unclean dogs.

I think the application of today's passage is not as hard as many make it. I think it is rather simple. Jesus is telling us to be careful what we watch, what we hear, what we read or look at on the internet, and so forth. We are to be holy and clean. No uncleanliness has any place in our lives. We should heed this.

Lord, please make me conscious of what I put into my life. In your name, amen.

JANUARY 27

And the Word became flesh and dwelt among us, and we have seen his glory, glory as of the only Son from the Father, full of grace and truth. (Jn. 1:14)

One of the most frustrating parts of trial is facing a witness who won't admit the truth, regardless of how obvious it is. Juries and judges find these witnesses as frustrating as I do. I can show a document that says the sky is blue, and these witnesses won't just say, "That is true." They will fight over it in some uneventful way. I frequently ask these witnesses, "Did you ever take a true/false test?" When they answer, "Yes," I then ask if they passed those tests by answering something other than "True" or "False."

For most twenty-first-century people in Western civilization, the idea of "truth" means the opposite of "false." When we say something is "true," we often mean it is "accurate." If we limit our ideas of "truth" to this concept, we miss out on much of the import of the New Testament Greek word for "truth," *alētheia* (ἀλήθεια). The Greek idea included something being truthful or accurate, but especially in the New Testament the word also conveyed the idea behind what is "true." This includes being reliable, dependable, or upright. In the Greek version of the Old Testament in usage when John wrote his gospel, *alētheia* was the Greek word used for the Hebrew *emet* (אֱמֶת) or "faithfulness."

Jesus came into this world as an expression of God. When we see Jesus, we see not only what is real or valid, we see God's faithfulness. We see in Jesus the dependability of our upright God.

I need this Jesus in my life. I need to understand God as one who is not only real but is reliable. I can entrust Jesus with my eternity, and I can entrust Jesus with my here and now. God is not a distant uncle who visits occasionally. Nor is he a deity who wears blinders and is unconcerned for my life. He doesn't see me as one out of eight billion people on the planet. God has a special interest in me. Everyone can say that. God has a special interest in each of us.

So, as I face today, I want to face it with truth. I can depend on Jesus to be with me. He will strengthen me and give me direction. He will provide what I need. He shows me God's faithfulness in a real and tangible way.

When we doubt, grow weary, get a bit lost, worry and fret, grow scared about what lies ahead, imagine all sorts of problems, or face the unknown, we need to remember a truth—Jesus. He has gone before us, goes alongside of us, and has prepared a place for us. He is truly faithful.

Lord God, may we praise your faithfulness in Jesus. Amen.

JANUARY 28

For the law was given through Moses; grace and truth came through Jesus Christ. (Jn. 1:17)

Every time a witness takes the stand in trial, the process is the same. The court authority has the witness hold up a hand and swear or affirm to tell the truth, the whole truth, and nothing but the truth. It is the bedrock of the American judicial system. Law without truth is injustice.

John wrote that Israel had law through Moses (the "Torah"). It was in Jesus, however, that grace and truth were most clearly manifested. What is the distinction that John is making between "law" and "grace and truth"? Surely John is not saying that the law of Moses was "false," for that law also came from God on Sinai. No, the law was truth, but the truth of the law was as an expression of what God expected from his people. It was a law code of behavior to guide individuals as well as the larger Israelite society and nation. The law was a magnificent gift from God, but it was based upon human effort at keeping it.

John's contrast between law and grace and truth is found in the source of the ideas. If we understand that "truth" is also "faithfulness" and "reliability," we see that the grace and truth that came through Jesus looks to God's character and God's actions, not those of you and me.

Here we see and understand John's contrast. The law of Moses was a code of human effort, fraught with all the shortcomings we humans know too well. As perfect as the law might be, human imperfections will always leave something undone, or something done wrong. You and I are useless at being perfect! So, in Moses we got a code we couldn't keep, even though the code was worthy of keeping. Jesus brought something altogether different. Jesus brought us grace and truth. These aren't human actions. These are actions of God. God is the God of grace who delivers mercy. God is also the God of "truth" in John's full usage of the word—one who is reliable, faithful, and dependable.

We need to be reminded daily that while we try our best to walk holy before God, thankful that he has taught us right from wrong, he has guided us in ways that will bring prosperity to our lives and bring about the greatest good. Still, we will fall short. When we do, we are uplifted remembering that God is also at work. He hasn't merely given us instructions while he watches what we do or where we fail. He is faithful and full of grace. He is there for us to pick us up and follow through when we are inadequate on our own. What an awesome God we serve.

Lord, thank you for your grace, your faithfulness and your mercy. In Jesus' name, amen.

JANUARY 29

Jesus said to him, "I am the way, and the truth, and the life. No one comes to the Father except through me." (Jn. 14:6)

Truth is important to John. Now you may be thinking, truth is important to everyone, and it is. But the translated word "truth" is especially important to John. Matthew uses the noun once. Mark and Luke use it three times each. John uses the noun twenty-five times in his gospel and another twenty in his short epistles.

What makes this word so important to John? For John, truth isn't a list of facts. Truth isn't simply "reality," although he will use the word in that sense occasionally. Truth is the character of God. John knew "truth" is who God is at his core. This idea of truth is found in the Old Testament Hebrew words אֱמֶת and אֱמוּנָה (*emet* and *emunah*). They are translated frequently as "faithful."

John stood at the foot of Jesus' cross when Jesus called out his final words, quoting Psalm 31:5, "Father, into your hands I commit my spirit!" (Lk. 23:46). Had I been John, I would have run home to look the verse up! Reading it fully, we would see, "Into your hand I commit my spirit; you have redeemed me, O LORD, faithful God." The redemption promise would have meant the world to me, especially once the resurrection occurred and I saw how literally true it was! But the Psalm claimed by Jesus doesn't simply speak of God's redemption, it adds, "O LORD, faithful God." The Hebrew word for a "faithful" God was rendered into Greek before the crucifixion by Jews who used the same word as John, where it is translated "truth."

John knew that Jesus' cry to the redeeming God was a cry to the God of faithfulness. God is a reliable God. God fulfills his plans as certain as the sun rises from the east. God not only promised redemption, he brought redemption.

John loved the idea of "truth as an attribute of God." As Bob Dylan sings, "God don't make promises that he don't keep!" ("When You Gonna Wake Up?"). God's faithfulness is a theme that John repeats over and over. God's faithfulness is an ultimate truth. It is as necessary to my life as air and food. Without the faithfulness of God, I would truly be lost.

Take a moment and think about how God has been faithful, even when we're not. God's hand might discipline, his road might not be easy. We struggle, we fall, we vacillate between hot and cold, yet in it all, we have the faithful, reliable, redeeming God. That is our hope and confidence.

Lord, thank you for your faithfulness. Forgive my sins and inadequacies. Wash me clean in Jesus and lead me in your paths for his sake and in his name. Amen.

JANUARY 30

So, Jesus said to the Jews who had believed him, "If you abide in my word, you are truly my disciples, and you will know the truth, and the truth will set you free." (Jn. 8:31–32)

"Freedom" is a marvelous word deeply rooted in Western civilization. Freedom was the basis for the American Revolution as well as many other political movements. Freedom forms the basis for most human rights: freedom from tyranny, oppression, slavery, and more. Freedom was the cry of the American Civil Rights movement, as Martin Luther King Jr. on August 28, 1963, declared, "When we allow freedom to ring—when we let it ring from every city and every . . . state . . . we will speed up that day when all God's children . . . will be able to join hands and sing in the words of the old Negro spiritual, 'Free at last, Free at last, Great God Almighty, we are free at last.'"

The Israelites had freedom entwined in their roots as a people. For hundreds of years, the people of Israel were enslaved to the Pharaoh and the Egyptians. Their liberty and freedom finally came through God's mighty works through Moses. Yet interestingly, in their conversation with Jesus, they deny ever having been in slavery. Lest we judge them too harshly, we should recognize that we often don't see where we are enslaved.

We can identify mistreatment in society. But where we often miss it is in our enslavement to sin. Sin is awfully addictive. Sin is sticky. It ensnares us and holds us captive. Think about the snare of some all-too-common sins:

- Gluttony—or as Paul spoke of it, living where our "god" is our "appetite" or "belly" (Phil. 3:19).
- Sexual immorality and its twin sensuality—some of the evil things that Jesus said come "out of the heart" (Mt. 15:19).
- Lover of money—a love that Paul said was "a root of all kinds of evil" (1 Tim. 6:10). Paul also speaks of this as a "craving" that has caused some to wander from the faith.

All sins that enslave us find redemption and release from Jesus. Through Jesus we are empowered to walk in victory, released from the slavery of this sin. We can find the right place for the cravings that are wrongly expressed in sin. Released, we learn to eat for sustenance, and even enjoyment, but in moderation. Set free, we can find holy and proper expressions of love and affection. In Jesus, we find that our possessions are not meant to own us, but they belong to God and are given to us as stewards to use for his purposes. Jesus calls us to find in him freedom from sin. We are free from its hold. Our key is to walk in his victory on our behalf. When we stumble, we confess our sin and begin again.

Lord, forgive my many sins. Set me free in Jesus to follow you better each day. Amen.

JANUARY 31

So, Jesus said to the Jews who had believed him, "If you abide in my word, you are truly my disciples, and you will know the truth, and the truth will set you free." (Jn. 8:31–32)

The history of education charts with the history of ideas and advances in science and technology. As education became mandatory, the literacy rates escalated. Shortly on the heels of these advances came the extended growth into high school education, college education, and even post-graduate learning. People pursue education to different degrees, and many do their best learning in the school of life, but regardless of where it is obtained, compared to most of history, we live in an "educated time."

What we know can be important to our success in life, but what we know pales in comparison to who we know! At first glance, today's passage may be indicating that there is some body of knowledge Jesus was calling "truth." That if we learn or know that body of knowledge, we will find freedom. But one doesn't have to read far into the Gospel of John before learning that the "truth" that Jesus referenced wasn't a body of knowledge, but a body incarnate! Jesus was the "truth" (Jn. 14:6). To "know the truth" is to "know Jesus."

The academic idea of knowledge ingrained in us through modern education might leave us wondering at the idea of "knowing" Jesus. Does it mean that we have an intellectual awareness about Jesus' existence? His work and mission? His death and resurrection? Well, yes and no!

The Greek word for "know" (*ginōskō*, γινώσκω) can indicate an intellectual awareness of whatever may be the subject, but the full semantic range of the word is much brighter. The Greek word "know" includes grasping the significance of something. "Know" includes its usage as a euphemism for sexual intimacy. The Greek translation of the Hebrew Scriptures at the time John wrote used this word for Genesis 4:1, "Now Adam *knew* Eve his wife, and she conceived and bore Cain." Similarly, Matthew used "know" to speak of Joseph not being intimate with Mary until after the birth of Jesus (Mt. 1:25).

What does this say for us? Jesus taught his disciples that knowing Jesus, having an awareness of who he was and what he was about, grasping his purpose and ministry, and then having a deep intimate walk with him was the core to finding freedom with all that entails. Jesus was asking a fallen world to take an intimate walk with the Creator God, through his incarnate Son Jesus. As we embrace Jesus, as we walk with him following him as our Lord, Savior, and friend, we experience the freedom from sin and all its implications—eternally and in the here and now.

Lord, please walk with me. I call on you as Lord, Savior, and friend. In your name, amen.

FEBRUARY 1

And Jesus said to them, "Follow me, and I will make you become fishers of men." (Mk. 1:17)

When I was in ninth grade, my school required all students to take a career aptitude test. This was about an hour long, multiple choice, computer graded test that told us what career areas were most suited to our interests and skill sets. My score came back strong in three areas: trial lawyer, preacher, and politician. I hit two out of three!

The aptitude test was great at assessing one's interests and abilities. The test missed out, however, on one very important aspect of decision-making: what does God have in store for you? God has sculpted each of us for work and tasks that he has prepared for us to do. This is true not only in our career but also on a day-to-day basis.

Because God is calling each of us to tasks, we should try to hear his voice and look to do what he calls us to do. In today's passage, Jesus called Simon, whose more common name is Peter, and his brother Andrew away from their day jobs as fishermen and into a new role as fishers of men. Peter would be taken from the waters of Galilee to the big city of Jerusalem, and ultimately to the capital of Rome itself, where this Galilean fisherman would die a martyr's death for the cause of Jesus.

As I consider today's passage, I am convinced of several things. First, I need to live today for Jesus and his purposes, not my own. Jesus didn't simply direct Peter and Andrew to make career changes. He wanted them to follow him immediately. They had specific tasks to do that day that they were to do for Jesus. The next verse says that they "suddenly" or "immediately" left their nets and followed Jesus. I don't think God is asking me to change careers today, but in my job, I meet people, and each time I do, I need to meet them in the name of Jesus, asking what Jesus would have me do for them, how I should treat them, and how I should interact with them. The tasks and opportunities that confront me today are in the path that God has called me to walk.

I also note that Jesus makes a careful play on the word, *"halieus"* (ἁλιεύς), the Greek word for one whose occupation is catching fish. Jesus says they will be in the same occupation, but they will catch people instead! God gifts us with the skills we need to do his work. Together with those skills, he gives us direction, inspiration, and strength. We can do the tasks he gives us each day and over a lifetime simply by following his daily instructions.

This determines my mission to live today and every day listening for the master's voice. I need to acknowledge that today is about him and his mission. My life should be more than an aptitude test. I should live my aptitude with direction from God!

Lord, give me direction today. In little and big things, may I live for you. In Jesus, amen.

FEBRUARY 2

And rising very early in the morning, while it was still dark, he departed and went out to a desolate place, and there he prayed. (Mk. 1:35)

Watch a two-year-old child. She or he will imitate those nearby. Watching our granddaughter Ebba at that age was like watching a mirror. She would imitate sounds, repeating what she heard. She would duplicate someone's hand motions. She would walk where others walk, sit where others sat, and learn by doing.

That isn't exclusive to two year olds. When I was a young trial lawyer, I would go to court and watch the experienced and seasoned lawyers. I would see how they prepared, see how they argued, watch their cross-examinations, and work on imitating them. I would find what worked for them and figure out how it would work for me. Professional basketball players have told me they spend hours watching other players, learning moves and gathering insights to improve their games.

It isn't just watching someone that teaches us. It is watching and doing. That is the key to a child's or a professional's success. We see others do and then we imitate it. We try to do the same. We practice and practice until we get it down.

Understanding how learning through doing works, consider today's passage. Jesus—God Incarnate—rose up early before everyone else, and he went out to a quiet place and had alone time with God. In prayer, he sought out and communed with God before joining with others.

In the context of today's passage, it is notable that the prior day had been chock full of "others." Jesus had started the day teaching in the synagogue. He then went to Peter's home where Peter's mother-in-law was sick. Jesus healed her. Word spread around town quickly, and by the evening, everyone near and far who was sick or infirmed gathered at Peter's door. Jesus spent the day healing and serving others.

Jesus had to have been exhausted when he finally went to sleep. Yet Mark makes the important point that even in the crazy business, or perhaps *because of the crazy business*, it was important to Jesus to wake up early, to leave everyone else behind, and find a quiet place of solitude to spend time alone with the Lord.

If we all learn by imitation, how does this passage inform us about life? I see a trait in Jesus that needs to be in my life. Each day, I need quiet time to be alone with the Lord in thought and prayer. From that time, I write these devotionals. From that time, I live these devotionals.

Lord, please infuse me today with your direction and strength. In Jesus, amen.

FEBRUARY 3

And a leper came to him, imploring him, and kneeling said to him, "If you will, you can make me clean." Moved with pity, he stretched out his hand and touched him and said to him, "I will; be clean." (Mk. 1:40–41)

One of the instructions judges give juries in every case is not to let bias, sympathy, or prejudice affect their decisions. This instruction is important for many jurors. This is especially important in cases I have tried where a tragedy has befallen my client. Before jurors are even allowed to sit on a case, the judge and lawyers ask each potential juror whether she or he can put aside any pity or sympathy she or he might feel.

Sometimes lawyers think that if a juror has sympathy or pity for the victim in a case, that person is unsuited for jury duty. Having sympathy, however, isn't the test. The test is whether someone can set aside that sympathy when deciding what happened. While there are plenty of people who are not moved by pity or sympathy at all, it would not be a fair and reflective jury if anyone with empathy was banned from jury duty. We can't have only hard-hearted people on juries and expect the jury to be fair.

I find this an important distinction not only in the courtroom but in life. Jesus was not a stone-hearted individual. Jesus was one who was moved by pity and sympathy. In today's passage, the leper came to Jesus. Many in Jesus' day would have recoiled from the very presence of a leper. The Jewish law said that lepers were outcasts. Lepers were to have no contact with the non-leprous, lest the disease spread. Lepers were not only not to be touched, they were to live in isolation from the non-leprous. Yet this leper came to Jesus, imploring and begging Jesus for help. The leper even knelt before Jesus. At a moment when most Jews would have run from the kneeling leper, Jesus did the extraordinary.

Jesus actually extended his hand and touched the leper! This would never be done. Lepers were charged with shouting, "Unclean!" as they walked down the street lest anyone come within close proximity of the leper. Touching a leper? It would never happen.

Jesus did so, being "moved with pity" or "sympathy." Jesus' heart of compassion overflowed with love, causing Jesus not only to heal the leper but to show him a heart full of love. He touched the leper, something the leper likely hadn't experienced since the onset of the disease.

This is our Jesus. This is our God. He cares for us. He has compassion for us. He sees our needs and yearns to touch us. He wants to heal us. He wants to show us he cares. I am thankful for our caring God and hope to become more like him.

Lord, thank you for your love, your care, and your touch. I need you. In Jesus, amen.

FEBRUARY 4

And when he returned to Capernaum after some days, it was reported that Jesus was at home. And many were gathered together, so that there was no more room, not even at the door. And he was preaching the word to them. And they came, bringing to him a paralytic carried by four men. And when they could not get near him because of the crowd, they removed the roof above him, and when they had made an opening, they let down the bed on which the paralytic lay. (Mk. 2:1–4)

I've worked with a lot of people over my decades as a lawyer. Some of the most successful people are those who won't take "no" for an answer. These people will hear "no," but in their minds it simply means, "Find another way!" or "Ask me again!" It amazes me that two different people can be in the exact same position faced with a closed door, and one will walk away saying, "The door is closed" while the other will kick the door in or climb through a window.

In today's story, a paralyzed man needed heeling. He and his friends knew that Jesus was his best chance. Jesus had already been in the town (Capernaum) and had healed many of the people there. The paralyzed man's friends thought that if they could get him in front of Jesus, then Jesus might heal him. Unfortunately, the house where Jesus was staying was chock-full with visitors. The men had no chance of getting the paralytic through the door.

Having the hope of help, but faced with the reality of a closed door, many might have told the paralytic, "Well, at least we tried!" But his friends were not so easily dissuaded. They took their friend to the roof of the house, and they cut through the thatch, lowering the man down on a stretcher. Jesus and the crowd were amazed. Jesus healed the paralytic, forever changing the future for him and those close to him.

I read this story and am encouraged to be more deliberate in working for important things. My family, my friends, my job, my clients—all of these are worthy of my best efforts. In all of these areas, I don't need to be deterred from success through a lack of effort. Those areas of life are important; however, I need to realize that nothing is as important as being touched by Jesus.

For some reason, we don't see the imperative of giving 100 percent of our best efforts in our pursuit of Jesus' touch in our lives. At times we ignore Jesus. Other times we seem to run from him, as if he will put a crimp in what we want to do. The truth of this life is that we need to pursue Jesus. We need to work through any obstacles in our lives and be touched by him. Jesus doesn't say "no," but there are other obstacles in our lives that keep us from his touch. We need to be people who insist on meeting Jesus.

Lord, please help me set aside anything that inhibits my relationship with you. I need your touch in Jesus, amen.

FEBRUARY 5

When Jesus saw their faith, he said to the paralytic, "Son, your sins are forgiven." Now some of the scribes were sitting there, questioning in their hearts, "Why does this man speak like that? He is blaspheming! Who can forgive sins but God alone?" (Mk. 2:5-7)

I received an e-mail informing me of ten "facts." Fact number one was that you cannot see your ears without a mirror. Fact four was that you cannot breathe through your nose with your tongue out. Fact five was that you tried to do fact four. Fact six was that you figured out fact four was wrong. I fell for it, and it stuck in my memory as fairly clever. The fact is, however, that we cannot see our ears without some mirror's or camera's help. I have ears. I can feel them. I use them. But if you were to put my ears in a line up, I'm not sure I could pick them out as mine. I do better at seeing others' ears than I do my own.

Why this diatribe on ears? Because it illustrates an important point. We are always better at seeing traits in others than we are in seeing them in ourselves. This is especially true of our often-harsh judgments of others. Consider the events surrounding today's passage.

Jesus healed a paralyzed man proclaiming him forgiven of his sins. When Jesus did this, some of the learned Jews sitting nearby began internally judging Jesus. These were "scribes," meaning they were well trained in the law of Moses. They were able to transcribe the law. They probably figured they knew blasphemy when they heard it. The problem is *the scribes were the ones blaspheming, not Jesus.*

The Greek word for "blaspheme" is *blasphēmeō* (βλασφημέω). The verb in Greek was used for speaking disrespectfully of another. It was speaking in a demeaning or denigrating way. It was showing disrespect. *If* Jesus had no authority to forgive sins, then perhaps Jesus was showing disrespect to God by usurping God's role. If that had been the case, then perhaps the scribes' judgment would have been correct. The problem was, Jesus *did* have authority to forgive sins. Jesus was and is God. Jesus is the one who *can* forgive.

This means that when the scribes were indicting Jesus for blasphemy or speaking disrespectfully of Jesus, they were actually committing blasphemy! The scribes were denigrating and showing disrespect to Jesus. They were so tied up in their judgment, they couldn't see their own sin. Their sin was as plain as the ears on their head. But they needed a moral mirror to see it.

I read this passage and I wonder where I am not seeing my own shortcomings. I fall short of God's holiness, and I need to do better at addressing my sins and not judging others.

Lord, forgive my harsh judgments of others. Purify me in Jesus and for his sake. Amen.

FEBRUARY 6

When the Spirit of truth comes, he will guide you into all the truth, for he will not speak on his own authority, but whatever he hears he will speak, and he will declare to you the things that are to come. (Jn. 16:13)

A Christian university asked Becky and I to speak to the Board of Regents at their annual retreat. They wanted our presentations to include our thoughts on how to present truth to a generation that all too often values tolerance over truth. Their concern was how do we teach truth when it can mean one thing is okay and another is not. Yet many collegiates believe that saying someone is doing something wrong is one of the few things that they believe to be wrong!

I believe one of the keys to teaching truth, even at the expense of valued tolerance or acceptance of others' choices, is found in today's passage. Jesus tells us that his followers do not have to find truth out on their own. It isn't me placed in the maze of life bewildered and lost while searching for the exit. The followers of Jesus have been assured that they aren't alone. Jesus, the one who by his own words was "the truth" (Jn. 14:6) assured his followers that the "Spirit of truth" would come from the Father and would guide the followers into truth!

I believe wholeheartedly in what Jesus said. I have experienced it. In my life, the Holy Spirit has brought me into wonderful truths that I would never have found on my own. He has convicted me of sin I was too blind to see. He has brought me to my knees when I was unknowingly walking in haughty pride. He has helped me grow in understanding the depths of God's love and mercy, as well as the holiness of God's righteousness.

The key for me, and for any generation or individual, is to follow Jesus, with all that entails. It is the constancy of a relationship based on love. His love for us stirs up our responsive love to him. We seek his involvement in all we do. We deliver up our wants and desires to embrace his. We trade our plans for his plans. His priorities become our priorities. We seek to be like him in thought and deed. We pledge ourselves to follow him on mountaintops and in valleys.

As we walk with the Lord in this way, his Spirit guides us in truth. We have that assurance. We can teach that to others. It is a promise. I want my family and friends to know, "Walk with Jesus. That is what changes life. The Holy Spirit will trump any of our thoughts of accommodation or tolerance. He will guide us in truth."

Lord, I commit my way to you. Work in my heart and in my life. Teach me your will. Teach me the truth. Let nothing stand between me and your will for me. In Jesus, amen.

FEBRUARY 7

And he rose and immediately picked up his bed and went out before them all, so that they were all amazed and glorified God, saying, "We never saw anything like this!" (Mk. 1:12)

Have you had some rare encounters that are stamped into your memory? I remember the first time I had lunch in chambers with Supreme Court Justice Antonin Scalia. It was just the two of us sitting in his office at a small round table. The tablecloth was pure white, and the china was Supreme Court finery. The cutlery was heavy and the food was served by a well-dressed butler carrying a silver tray. I was stunned by the opportunity to have this lunch and had been quite curious over what food would be served. As I looked up to the server with the silver tray, I noticed atop the tray were four red and white take-out containers of Chinese food. Justice Scalia explained, "I just love this take-out Chinese restaurant right around the corner. I hope you enjoy this!" I won't forget that encounter.

You can stack up all the rare opportunities you and I have had to meet people and add them all together. In doing so, we will find that the sum of our encounters would not rise to the level of a true encounter with Jesus Christ.

In today's passage, an overcrowded house of folks kept a paralyzed man from being able to come in the door to seek healing from Jesus. So the paralytic's friends hacked through the thatch roof and lowered the man down into Jesus' presence. Jesus healed the man and though he entered on a stretcher through the roof, the man walked out the front door! This left the people amazed. They were praising God for the miracle. The people readily said, "We've never seen anything like this before." They were right.

That is how it is to encounter God. As a college student, I remember going to church and seeing people who seemed to experience God in ways I never had. These good folks had aspects to their relationship with God that made mine seem narrow. I remember sitting in church prayerfully asking God to give me a greater understanding of him, his work in Jesus, and the role of the Holy Spirit in my life.

Over the next few days, weeks, and months, my walk with the Lord grew exponentially. I more fully understood the work of Jesus on Calvary. I learned deliberate worship was not simply singing the songs everyone sang but coming into the presence of God. I found growth in my holiness. My encounter with Jesus was amazing! I had never seen anything like it before or since. (Not even lunch in chambers with a Supreme Court justice!) Something profound happens when you encounter Jesus. I heartily recommend it for all, even Christians!

Lord, give me a fresh encounter with you. Teach me anew the wonders of your love in Jesus. Grow me through your Holy Spirit. For his name's sake, amen.

FEBRUARY 8

He went out again beside the sea, and all the crowd was coming to him, and he was teaching them. And as he passed by, he saw Levi the son of Alphaeus sitting at the tax booth, and he said to him, "Follow me." And he rose and followed him. (Mk. 2:13–14)

My wife and at least one of my daughters are queens of the checklist. They are always prepared for almost anything because they make note of what they need when they need it. I'd like to be that way, but unfortunately, I'm not. I have surrounded myself at work with people who are good at bringing the things I forget. My job is much easier when I have what I need.

The followers of Jesus had a marvelous chance to hear his teachings. The very Son of God speaking forth on life and truth was an immense opportunity for life-changing insight and learning. Many of those listeners, and even the apostles, thought that Jesus would be setting up an earthly kingdom. They had no clue that Jesus would teach for three years and then return to the Father's side until the end of time. After the crucifixion and resurrection, Jesus made clear that he would return one day, and the earliest believers thought that day was imminent. They had no idea it would be thousands of years later. (Similarly, I think Abraham must have thought that the promised one from his offspring would be a generation or two away, never imagining that God would wait for two thousand years.)

Jesus knew, however. God was planning from the beginning to have his kingdom brought to completion in good time. God knew that would not be immediate. So we have passages like today's. Jesus is teaching. Crowds are showing up to listen. But what is missing for the long-term church? We needed a notetaker there! God was prepared. He called Levi (also called Matthew) who was a tax collector!

Why a tax collector? They had good language skills and were able to converse with others in Aramaic, Hebrew, Greek, and likely Latin. They also were good notetakers and record keepers. They could read and write, had the ancient equivalent of pen and paper, gave tax receipts, wrote up their progress for their bosses. They were careful scriveners. Jesus drew Matthew in, and the church received some writings of Jesus' teachings. The early church writer Papias wrote of Matthew as the one who kept a record of Jesus' teachings in Hebrew. You and I have them available in our gospels in the Bible today.

God has always been prepared. He has thought through tomorrow from before the beginning of time. He is no less prepared for our life today. Whatever we face, he has the supplies ready to meet it. Our day in his hands is exactly what it needs to be!

Lord, please help me walk in your will today. Meet my needs as only you can, and may I give you all the glory. In Jesus, amen.

FEBRUARY 9

Now there was a man of the Pharisees named Nicodemus, a ruler of the Jews. This man came to Jesus by night and said to him, "Rabbi, we know that you are a teacher come from God, for no one can do these signs that you do unless God is with him." Jesus answered him, "Truly, truly, I say to you, unless one is born again he cannot see the kingdom of God." (Jn. 3:1–3)

Most everyone has a thirst for answers. We might differ on what questions we want answered. Sometimes they are big questions: What job should I take? Where should I live? Whom should I marry? How can I help my loved one in trouble? How do I parent? How can I get out of this bind I'm in? Why am I so discouraged? What do I do about my worries concerning *xyz*? (I put into the "small" category questions like, "What should I do about dinner?" "What should I wear to a certain event?")

Of course, really big questions also loom in life. Sometimes we ask them; other times we avoid them. Why are we here? Is there any purpose to life? What is life's purpose? How can I make sense of the big picture? Does God know I am here? Does he care? Who or what is God, anyway?

For many of life's questions—small, big, or really big—the answers aren't always obvious. That is why the questions plague us. To use a modern expression, on many things, we find ourselves "in the dark." In truth, though, "in the dark" isn't a modern expression! It is one we find John using two thousand years ago when writing his gospel.

One of John's major themes is that "Jesus is the light." Each time John writes about "light" or "darkness" in his gospel, the words are worthy of reflection. In today's passage, Nicodemus, an influential Jew, comes to Jesus speaking positively. John adds that Nicodemus came "by night." Many think that John added the timing because Nicodemus was embarrassed and didn't want others to know he came to see Jesus. Others think it showed Nicodemus was considerate, since Jesus was so busy during the day it was often difficult to even see him, much less talk to him. Those are certainly possible reasons, but another important theory to consider is that Nicodemus was coming to Jesus out of darkness, seeking the input of Jesus, the light.

We all live in the dark about many things. The key, as John and the other New Testament writers constantly affirmed, is that we are to bring all of our concerns, questions, worries, anxieties, issues, problems, and so on to Jesus. We are to seek his light in our darkness. We find the answers to our questions in him. He answers questions, big or small, as we commit our ways to him. He doesn't write answers on the wall, but we learn his values, his priorities, his nature, and in these lessons, we find our answers.

Lord, give me insight into life. Bring light to my darkness. In Jesus' name, amen.

FEBRUARY 10

Do not lay up for yourselves treasures on earth, where moth and rust destroy and where thieves break in and steal, but lay up for yourselves treasures in heaven, where neither moth nor rust destroys and where thieves do not break in and steal. For where your treasure is, there your heart will be also. (Mt. 6:19–21)

In the West in the twenty-first century, we often compare matters of the head to matters of the heart. Matters of the head are things we know. Matters of the heart are things we feel.

Relationships are a breeding ground for divisions between head and heart. Some don't "feel" in love with their spouses anymore. Some "feel" in love with the wrong person, being stuck in one relationship while their heart lies in a different one. This is a bad situation not only on a human level but also on the level of our relationship with God. Many make a mental and intellectual commitment to God, but then wake up one day realizing the ardor of that first burning love has smoldered into warm ashes. Their passion for God is gone.

What can be done about these situations? We humans are good at fixing matters of the head. If we don't have enough information, we learn more. If we don't have enough self-discipline, we go to work on developing better habits. If we need to make decisions, we make them. Matters of the head get fixed, but people are often lost when it comes to solving matters of the heart.

For many, matters of the heart are those over which we have no control. Almost by definition, matters of the heart are those that logic and thinking don't fix. We hear the pleas, "I know it's wrong, but it's just the way I feel." Or, "I don't want to love this person, but I can't help it." Also we hear the opposite, "I want to love my spouse, but I just don't anymore."

In today's passage, Jesus taught a profound principle of human nature that addresses matters of the heart. He taught the reason for our wandering affections. The principle is simple: where you invest your treasure is where you find your heart. Jesus doesn't mean to speak only to investing money. Our treasure is our time, energy, resources (including money), and more. Jesus explained that wherever or to whomever we choose to give what we value is where our heart will be.

So when we don't feel we love someone we should, we need to invest in that person and relationship. The heart will follow. This is true for our walk with God as well as our spouses. The corollary is true: if we invest in relationships that should be out of bounds to our love, we will soon find our love there anyway. We need to use our heads to control our hearts!

Lord, please help me direct my treasures to where they belong, beginning with my walk with you. In Jesus' name, amen.

FEBRUARY 11

The eye is the lamp of the body. So, if your eye is healthy, your whole body will be full of light, but if your eye is bad, your whole body will be full of darkness. If then the light in you is darkness, how great is the darkness! (Mt. 6:22–23)

My mom did an amazing job of teaching our children the message in today's passage. Our preteen girls wanted to see a trashy movie that their friends found hilarious. The movie trailer was on the television, and it made the movie seem like one you shouldn't miss. Yet a review of the movie's content showed it to be a vehicle for sexuality and deviancy on a level that no preteen should see.

My mom had the girls over to make brownies. She had them reading the recipe and getting out the ingredients for mixing. As they recounted what was needed, she told them to go get a cup of dirt out of the backyard. As the kids quizzed her why, she explained that they were going to add the dirt to the mix. My girls recognized that it would ruin what was otherwise going to be a marvelous treat. They explained, "Mimi, that will ruin the brownies! We aren't supposed to add dirt!" She then explained that brownies are like our brains. When we feed our brains dirt, it can ruin our minds. You can't just decide to get the dirt out of the brain once you have mixed it in.

Jesus knew and taught that what we see affects who we are and what we think. We don't "unsee" things. The eye is even more powerful than we might think. Sometime do an internet search for the "McGurk effect." You will quickly find a BBC piece, or some similar piece that shows something rather stunning. The McGurk effect takes place when you watch a person saying "bah bah bah" and it makes perfect sense. However, if the person changes and begins making the mouth gestures for saying "fah fah fah" while the overheard sound is still "bah bah bah," the human brain will think it is hearing "fah fah fah," even though it isn't. It is a bizarre effect. You fall for it, even knowing it is there. This is the power of the eye. What we see will trump what we hear, even if we are hearing the truth.

So where does this leave us in an era of visuality? We have visuals everywhere. The current generation is sometimes called "Screenagers" because they grew up with screens everywhere—on phones, watches, in elevators; even many billboards have screens that change messages every few moments.

We need to be "watchful," careful what we see. It will affect who we are and how we think. It becomes mixed in our souls the way dirt can mix into brownies. We should follow Job's advice and "make a covenant with our eyes" (Job 31:1).

Lord, give me the wonders of your love to gaze upon. Let me see things that are true, honorable, right, and pure. Give me the discipline to avoid the dirt. In Jesus, amen.

FEBRUARY 12

Therefore I tell you, do not be anxious about your life, what you will eat or what you will drink, nor about your body, what you will put on. Is not life more than food, and the body more than clothing? (Mt. 6:25)

Webster's thesaurus lists a number of words as synonyms for "worry." The words include agitation, anxiety, anxiousness, apprehension, apprehensiveness, care, concern, concernment, disquiet, disquietude, fear, nervousness, solicitude, sweat, unease, uneasiness. Today's passage speaks of being "anxious." It is the Greek word *merimnaō* (μεριμνάω). It similarly references a state of apprehension or worry.

Have you ever experienced any of that? Jesus tells us that as we worry, we need to retune ourselves to see things in a new light. That begins with putting life into perspective. Life is about more than what we are eating for lunch or what we are wearing when we leave the house. Life is about aligning ourselves with the Creator God and seeking his purposes in our lives.

Of course we all realize that we need food. We need clothing. We need shelter. God knows we need those things. Jesus doesn't tell us that such things have no place in life. He tells us that those things should never take priority over the perspective of living in service to God. When we serve God, we can be assured that such needs will be met. Those things we worry about will be taken care of by one who is greater than any need.

The biblical assurance doesn't turn life into our lucky lottery existence. The teaching doesn't indicate that God will magically put a hefty deposit into our bank accounts. Rather the lesson means live your life aligned with God and his teaching and everything will work out for the best. The same Scripture that teaches us not to worry, instructs us to work hard (2 Thess. 3:10 "If anyone is not willing to work, let him not eat."); teaches us not to live lives of self-importance (Phil. 2:3-4 "Do nothing from selfish ambition or conceit, but in humility count others more significant than yourselves. Let each of you look not only to his own interests, but also to the interests of others."); and urges us to put our worries before God in prayers that thank him for his work in our lives (Phil. 4:6-7 "Do not be anxious about anything, but in everything by prayer and supplication with thanksgiving let your requests be made known to God. And the peace of God, which surpasses all understanding, will guard your hearts and your minds in Christ Jesus.").

As we live under the guidance of God, we will find that we have no need to worry. God gave us instructions with the assurance that he will meet our needs. We need not worry! We need only to live faithfully before the Lord.

Lord, help me with my worries [list them]. Thank you for your loving care in Jesus, amen.

FEBRUARY 13

Blessed are you when others revile you and persecute you and utter all kinds of evil against you falsely on my account. Rejoice and be glad, for your reward is great in heaven, for so they persecuted the prophets who were before you. (Mt. 5:11–12)

Is it bad for me to admit that I don't like today's passage? When I come across it, I read it fast. I don't dwell on it. There are several reasons why.

First, I am not a fan of persecution. I want everyone happy and feeling good. I want people smiling and trouble free. I don't want people hurting physically or emotionally. This passage speaks of persecution. It specifies a verbal persecution. That kind of persecution can be some of life's most hurtful. We take medicine for aches and pains, but when someone speaks ill of us there's no antidote for the pain. Big pharma hasn't found an answer for the consequences of people attacking and disparaging you.

A second reason I don't enjoy reading today's passage stems from the fact that Jesus assumes that his followers will be persecuted "on his account." I think on this, I suffer from "survivor's guilt." I learned this term when I was trying a case for twenty-two women with ovarian cancer. Six had died prior to trial, and of those who had survived, they told me they feel guilty that others had died but they hadn't. Survivor's guilt is there for cancer survivors as well as soldiers returning from war, and many others. I don't want to make light of those people by claiming I have survivor's guilt, but there really is some level of analogous guilt when I think about how many have suffered on account of their faith and I really haven't.

Jesus relates the suffering he is speaking of to that of the prophets in the Old Testament. I've read the Old Testament. I know about the prophets who were stoned, thrown into wells, blinded, chased, and killed. Even in my worst days, I have suffered nothing similar for the cause of Christ.

So today, as I dwell on this passage that troubles me so, what do I perceive that is useful? Much! For starters, I need to be thankful for the manifold blessings God has given me. Heaven forbid (literally), that I not thank God for this marvelous life he has given me. Additionally, I know that I should be living fully for the cause of Jesus. If I am not persecuted because my lot in life is extraordinarily easy then "thank you, Lord." But if I am not persecuted because I refrain from lifting up the name of Jesus when I should, then shame on me! Then when I do suffer slightly because of my walk with the Lord, I need to have my eyes on my Lord, and thank him that I am counted worthy to be part of his family, with all that the world can throw at him and his followers.

Lord, I confess discomfort over today's passage. Thank you for my life. Thank you for your blessings. Help me to show your love to others less fortunate. In Jesus, amen.

FEBRUARY 14

This is my commandment, that you love one another as I have loved you. Greater love has no one than this, that someone lay down his life for his friends. (Jn. 15:12–13)

Valentine was a common name in the early centuries of this era, and at least two Valentines were Christian martyrs, Valentine of Rome (a priest in Rome who was martyred in 269) and Bishop Valentine of Interamna (modern Terni in central Italy), killed for his faith in 273. Both saints are honored by many church traditions on February 14.

Most every kid has some type of school celebration for Valentine's Day. Today, however, those celebrations are not marked by memories of the martyrs. Only since Chaucer (c. 1340–1400) do we know of a romantic association for the date. Rolling into the 1800s Valentine cards began becoming popular, and in 1868, Cadbury began selling heart-shaped boxes of chocolates for gifting on the day. In 1929, a gang shooting on that day in Chicago gained fame as the "Saint Valentine's Day Massacre"—not an act of love.

Both the massacre of 1929 and the romantic celebration of the last six hundred years do not associate so readily with the origination of Valentine's Day, yet there is an eerie thread that runs through them both. That thread is rooted in today's passage.

Jesus is about to die. His betrayal is less than twenty-four hours away, and he is having his last dinner with his apostles. Jesus instructs them to love each other. That is the instruction he wants seared into their memories. Whatever life throws at them, they should exhibit love. However they are treated, they should have love. When the world examines their lives, the world should see love. This love should be for each other but should also be characteristic of their lives at large.

Jesus made it clear: he wasn't talking about a convenient love. To quote the songstress Sade, "This is no ordinary love." Jesus tells them to have the same love for each other that Jesus had for them. And lest there be any doubt about the level of love Jesus had, they should know that laying down one's life for a friend is the exhibition of the greatest love possible. Jesus would soon be doing that for his friends.

Here is the other common thread between the martyrs of the 200s, the romance of the centuries, and even the massacre of 1929: love and sin. Humans can act horrendously. Yet Christians should model the faithful love of Jesus, even when that might mean a martyr's death. Jesus was the first Christian martyr, and he did it out of love. He wants us to have that same love. That is harder, yet more important, than a card, roses, or a box of chocolates.

Father, give me a heart to love as Christ loved. In Jesus I ask, amen.

FEBRUARY 15

Either make the tree good and its fruit good, or make the tree bad and its fruit bad, for the tree is known by its fruit. You brood of vipers! How can you speak good, when you are evil? For out of the abundance of the heart the mouth speaks. (Mt. 12:33–34)

We live in a time where people prize authenticity. Being genuine is esteemed. Fakery and phoniness are deplored. In spite of the appreciation for being real, often we encounter people who are not what they appear. We have expressions for such people. They may be "two-faced" or people who "speak out of both sides of their mouths." If they are dangerous, we may label them a "wolf in sheep's clothing." Such people aren't new to our age.

In today's passage, we read of Jesus' ironic encounter with people who weren't what they claimed to be. Jesus was healing and working miracles among those in need. A group of self-righteous Jews were trying to slander Jesus and take away from his amazing works of compassion. The best these Jews could come up with was an accusation that Jesus must be a worker of Satan, doing the deeds and casting out demons aligned with the evil one.

The absurdity of these people faking their own righteousness by slandering Jesus was not lost on Jesus. Jesus confronted them, calling them a "brood of vipers." That is Bible language. In everyday language, Jesus called them the "offspring of venomous snakes," or more colloquially, "a snake pit!" These were fairly harsh words, but well deserved.

Genesis 3 tells the story of the serpent in the garden deceiving Adam and Eve into open rebellion against God. The Jews slandering Jesus were following in that original serpent's "snake tracks" (the snake equivalent of footprints). Jesus wasn't following the serpent, and he wasn't from the serpent's camp. Jesus was destroying the work of the serpent.

Jesus made the plea for authenticity. Jesus explained that trees bear fruit. If the tree bears good fruit, it is a good tree. If the tree bears bad fruit, it is a bad tree. Jesus used this as an analogy for authentic living. Our focus for authenticity is on the walk, not the talk. Too many people claim to be Christians or godly, yet their lives show something quite different.

This passage makes me examine my life prayerfully and with repentance. Mistakes? Of course, we all sin. Yet I want to make sure that I never use the fact that everyone sins as an excuse to do as I want. Instead I want to grow good fruit. I want to work on being the kind of person that God wants me to be. I don't want to be a part of the snake pit!

Lord, please forgive my many sins. Grow me in your love. Help me to become all I can be in your name. May I be genuine in my love and commitment in and for Jesus, amen.

FEBRUARY 16

Do not think that I have come to abolish the Law or the Prophets; I have not come to
abolish them but to fulfill them. (Mt. 5:17)

My wife and I have a running joke. She loves coffee in the morning,
and I have never been a coffee drinker. She likes a full cup, but she also
adds milk and sweetener. I noticed early in our marriage that she pours the
milk in until the cup is almost overflowing. It seemed that each time she
got her coffee, at least when I was looking, she had to immediately drink
some because she had overfilled the cup adding the milk. I began offering
to get her coffee, but she would graciously say no, noting that I didn't know
how much milk to add. I told her, "Yes, I just add milk until the cup overflows!" It can still bring a chuckle.

The image of Becky's cup overflowing is a marvelous picture for understanding today's passage. As Jesus relates the above passage to his students,
he does so immediately before recounting various laws of Moses by which
the Jews lived. Jesus is about to change the emphasis dramatically, from
an outward act to an inward attitude. Jesus will tell the Jews, "no longer
should you simply not murder, but you aren't even to hate!" And, "no longer
shall you not commit adultery, but you aren't even to lust!"

Some might view these "new" teachings of Jesus as abolishing the law
of Moses, but they aren't. Jesus was "fulfilling" the law of Moses. The Greek
word "fulfill" (*plēroō*, πληρόω) means to do what Becky does to her coffee
cup! It means to take what is already there and add it until it is filled up.

The instructions for life that Jesus gives us, the instructions that take
the commands of God and teach us to have attitudes that are appropriate
to those commands, are important. God isn't about just making sure we dot
the i's and cross the t's in life. God is about transforming the ways we think
and feel about things. God wants our hearts, not just our actions. Obedience
isn't something grudgingly given or an act of obligation. God wants our
desires to be pure. He wants our hearts to be molded into his heart. He
wants us to be good trees that produce good fruit, not harsh trees with good
fruit taped onto their branches.

As I look at my life, I want to change my heart. I want to follow the
Lord's instructions out of a loving desire that knows God and seeks to be
like him. My concern isn't just the outward actions, but the inward heart!
There I see Jesus overflowing and fulfilling the law.

Lord, please change my heart. Make me more like you. Help me grow so I can not
only follow you in deed but in thought and motive. Thank you for making me a better
person in Jesus! Amen.

FEBRUARY 17

Then Jesus was led up by the Spirit into the wilderness to be tempted by the devil. And after fasting forty days and forty nights, he was hungry. (Mt. 4:1-2)

When one of our daughters was first in high school, she was competing in a speech event that required her to give an extemporaneous speech on "the agenda of the minority party in Congress." Fresh out of middle school, our daughter didn't understand that the "minority party" was a reference to the political party that had less than the majority of seats in Congress. (That year, it happened to be the Democratic party.) Our daughter gave her speech thinking that the "minority" reference was to gender, race, and sexual orientation. She thought the topic asked about the female agenda, the Hispanic/African American agenda, and the gay/lesbian agenda. By fortuity, the agendas aligned with those the Democrats were talking about, and so she did quite well in the round, even though she didn't fully understand the idea of "minority party."

We often misunderstand things in the Bible because we read them as people living in the twenty-first century, and not with the ancient mindset. As a result, even though we often get the main ideas right, we still miss important things. Today's passage gives us a good example.

In antiquity, numbers were not simply for math and counting. They represented ideas. The number one represented isolation. The number two represented strength. Three was a divine number. Four was a number representing the earth. (There were four directions or points of a compass—north, south, east, and west; four winds; four corners of the earth; four elements—fire, water, earth, air; etc.). The ancients would use ten as a multiplier to make a number complete (i.e., Jacob would complain he was cheated in his wages "ten times," meaning "constantly" or "always" [Gen. 31:7]).

So, when we read that Jesus was led into the wilderness to fast and be tempted for forty days and nights (four = earthly and ten = fully), our minds should register the number given for something beyond merely how long. It references Jesus being tempted fully in earthly matters, yet without falling to temptation. It also should remind us of the forty years the Hebrews were in the wilderness, falling to temptation right and left. Similarly, the early church chose forty days of Lent to be a time of devotion and fasting as a full period of time.

That Jesus was tempted as we are, yet was without sin, is important for a number of reasons. The early church sermon called "Hebrews" in the Bible says that Jesus being tempted means that he sympathizes with us (Heb. 4:15). He helps us in our weakness (Heb. 2:18). Jesus sought to identify with us as much as he could without actually sinning. Driven by love, he wants to help us in every way he can.

Lord, forgive us our sins. Teach us to live holy before you. For Jesus' sake, amen.

FEBRUARY 18

From that time Jesus began to preach, saying, "Repent, for the kingdom of heaven is at hand." (Mt. 4:17)

Rule one of public speaking, of courtroom lawyering, and much of life is to "start strong." As one of my friends says, "You never get a second chance to make a first impression." How we begin should reflect our emphasis. It should show what is important. It should reflect our focus. Because of this, I find it interesting to see how Matthew relates the beginning of Jesus' ministry. Having overcome Satan's temptations in the wilderness, Jesus launched into ministry in northern Israel, around the region of Galilee.

From the very start of his ministry, Jesus taught his disciples to "repent." This was core to his message. It wasn't a simple place to start; it was the central place to start. By definition, repentance entailed the sinfulness of people that necessitated the coming of Jesus. It showed that Jesus and God were confronting unholiness, calling people to find a righteousness that they hadn't previously known.

The Greek verb used for "repent" (*metanoeō, μετανοέω*) conveyed one changing one's mind. It included an idea of remorse for what happened before the change occurred. The Greek word was used for a Hebrew idea of being sorrowful over an action (*nicham,* נחם). This repentance is one that calls us to abandon our pursuits of the world for our sake (for our pleasure, comfort, significance, prosperity, etc.). Instead, we are to turn from the world and pursue God and God's agenda. Then we work for the Lord, not for worldly gain. Then we treat others as we should for the sake of sharing and living the gospel, not out of ego, pride, or selfish desire.

The implications of repentance run deep. They are intricately tied to understanding the role of God in our lives. We acknowledge his holiness and his Lordship over our hearts and minds. We dedicate ourselves to him and his will, to living for his kingdom, instead of what we selfishly desire. We find ourselves looking to him for his mercy and care as we see ourselves in need of mercy.

Try as I might, I haven't yet arrived on the holiness train of perfection. I am still struggling daily, after seeking the Lord for the better part of five decades. It brings me to a daily reminder of the need to repent. Every time my mind wanders, I need to turn it back to God. I need to understand true godly sorrow over sin and the joys of holiness. I need to repent!

Lord, I confess my sins to you. Many are unconscious acts of selfishness that come from losing focus and getting caught up in the world. I repent. Please give me mercy for Jesus' sake, amen.

FEBRUARY 19

And getting into a boat he crossed over and came to his own city. And behold, some people brought to him a paralytic, lying on a bed. And when Jesus saw their faith, he said to the paralytic, "Take heart, my son; your sins are forgiven." And behold, some of the scribes said to themselves, "This man is blaspheming." But Jesus, knowing their thoughts, said, "Why do you think evil in your hearts? For which is easier, to say, 'Your sins are forgiven,' or to say, 'Rise and walk'? But that you may know that the Son of Man has authority on earth to forgive sins"—he then said to the paralytic—"Rise, pick up your bed and go home." (Mt. 9:1-6)

Sin can be paralyzing! It hampers our ability to live and enjoy life. Sin inhibits our ministry among others. It limits how we care and love others. It even affects our "walk" with the Lord.

Jesus knew this, and so did Matthew. It is one reason today's passage reads as it does. The man was paralyzed and unable to walk. Matthew doesn't give the medical reason for the man's paralysis, but he does make clear that Jesus showed the way sin can paralyze us. Jesus did this by not simply healing the man, telling him to stand up and walk, as Jesus did so many others. Instead, Jesus pronounced a forgiveness of the man's sins, an even greater accomplishment than helping the man walk. Doctors can heal paralysis, at least of certain sorts, but no human can forgive sins. Sins are committed against God. They aren't forgiven by a human.

Jesus has the power to forgive sin and deliver the sinner from the consequences of sin. Jesus can take away sin's paralysis on a person. We need no longer fret in guilt over our inadequacies. We confess them to Jesus and trust him to forgive them.

Scripture teaches that God deals with his children in mercy and love by forgiving sins, but he also does so in integrity and justice. Jesus' forgiveness is rooted in his taking on the responsibility and sins of his children while dying on the cross. This fulfillment of the prophetic promise of Isaiah 53 includes our full healing that comes from his sacrifice. "But he was pierced for our transgressions; he was crushed for our iniquities; upon him was the chastisement that brought us peace, and with his wounds we are healed."

As the sacrificial lamb, Jesus rightly can forgive sins and heal us from all our sin has produced. Our role is to look to him in faith, and then hear and follow his voice to walk on, but sin no more!

Lord, I confess that I have sinned, in thought and deed. I have been hurt by that sin and I have hurt others. I repent, and ask for your healing touch. Teach me and strengthen me to live more holy before you, all to your glory. In Jesus' name, amen.

FEBRUARY 20

Judge not, that you be not judged. For with the judgment you pronounce you will be judged, and with the measure you use it will be measured to you. (Mt. 7:1–2)

This is one of the verses that echoes in my brain. It echoes often, but not often enough. Like most people, I have this uncanny ability to see my sins most clearly when the sin is on display in someone *other than me!*

On the morning I am writing this, my concern is on full display. Let me explain. A friend e-mailed me complaining about a politician "A" who said some fairly rough things about other politicians. Politician "A" called a number of other politicians "garbage." My friend sent me an article saying that the true "garbage" is politician "A," not the others labeled by politician "A" as garbage.

My first reaction was the hypocrisy of the article indicting politician "A" for slinging mud and calling others "garbage." Then the article says the real garbage is politician "A." The irony of calling someone "garbage" because that person called someone else "garbage," made me chuckle.

My second reaction was that the writer of the article needed a healthy dose of today's passage. That writer needed to be admonished that Jesus taught people not to judge others because what we judge in others will likely be found in us as well. Our judgment of others condemns ourselves. I thought, "If only these writers understood this. These writers are *wrong*, even if I might agree with their criticisms of politician 'A's' policies."

Only then did my third reaction register in my brain. I was being so critical of the writer's failures to check their judgments of the character and actions of politician "A," that I was guilty of the same sin I had seen in them!

Please understand, I am not saying that we shouldn't address ideas critically, that we shouldn't fail to point out erroneous thoughts and debate opinions. But there is a line of judgment where we must be cautious. I will always tend to see my own sin on display most clearly when it is exhibited in the lives of others.

This truth should move me to hesitancy in my judgments as well as more careful consideration of my own shortcomings. I need ready confession and dedication to being and living better before the Lord.

Lord, I confess to you that I am a chief of sinners. My eyes too often look outside of me at the sins of others and fail to acknowledge my own. Please forgive my harsh judgments and give me a loving spirit. In Jesus, amen.

FEBRUARY 21

Are not two sparrows sold for a penny? And not one of them will fall to the ground apart from your Father. But even the hairs of your head are all numbered. (Mt. 10:29–30)

Life rarely goes the way I script it. Surprises lurk around every corner of my day. Some of the surprises are small, and I barely notice and regard them. Other surprises loom large and abruptly change what I have planned. To be fair, I can add that sometimes the surprise is delightful, bringing fresh good news. But other times, the unexpected is something I'd never have chosen on my own. It threatens the peace in my heart, and it produces foreboding. When that happens, I need an attitude adjustment!

Today's passage speaks to me about life's surprises. In two simple verses Jesus communicates an important truth: God is never surprised. God knows when a single bird falls to the ground. Jesus underscored the significance of this knowledge of God by noting how insignificant birds can be to people. In Jesus' day, two sparrows were sold for a penny (actually for an *"assarion,"* a Roman copper coin worth a relatively small amount). Jesus explained that cheap birds, so plentiful they were almost insignificant to people, were known and monitored by God.

Recently I had a very important meeting in Dallas. This pertained to a lawsuit that had been pending for years, and it was finally reaching resolution. I needed to be at that meeting and had planned accordingly. I had older Christian brother with me, also a lawyer, and we had woken up long before dawn to fly to Dallas for the 7 a.m. meeting. We sat on the plane longer than one expects, chatting away about how we would handle the meeting, when the pilot informed us, "The left engine won't start. This is not a quick fix. Everyone off the plane!"

My immediate thought was, "Oh no! There is no other flight to get us there on time. I am about to miss a most important meeting!" Before I could think of much more, my brother Skip looked at me and asked, "Do you think God was surprised when that left engine wouldn't start?"

That question has changed me. It was rhetorical; of course God wasn't surprised! But the question spoke to my attitude in the midst of the unexpected. The question was a gut-check reminder that God was in control of each day, not me. God can handle each thing that surprises me. God has the resources, the foreknowledge, and the attitude to make sure that this world works out to the ultimate good for his kingdom. We have the assurance that the ultimate good for his kingdom includes the ultimate good for us as well. I need to see surprises differently.

Lord, thank you for the blessings of today—those I expect and those I don't! May I see all things through the eyes of faith. For the sake of your kingdom and Son, amen.

LENT

Lent is the season that begins forty days before Easter. It draws its name from the English word "lenten," which comes from the Germanic word for "long," like the English word "lengthen." Many scholars believe the name came from the fact that during the season of Lent, the days are getting longer.

The season is forty days long in memory of Jesus being in the wilderness to be tempted by Satan for forty days. It is during this buildup to Easter that Christians in many churches either fast for some portion or give up something dear to them for the season.

The season begins with Ash Wednesday. This day is honored in many churches by a service of repentance, where ashes are applied to the forehead in the shape of the cross. The ashes are to remind one that "you are dust and to dust you must return" (Gen. 3:19).

During this season, the devotionals will focus on the tempting of Jesus, the sin of humanity, and the need for repentance.

FEBRUARY 22

And Jesus said, "Father, forgive them, for they know not what they do." (Lk. 23:34)

Today's passage comes from Luke recording eternity-changing words that Jesus uttered from the cross. These words were expressed at a pivotal point in human history. Before these words and the cross of Christ, the world lived under the curse of sin, with God's promise of redemption, but no showing of how God's forgiveness could justly and rightly be given. After the cross of Christ, forgiveness is real. It is a fait accompli. Sin is finished, and with it, death has lost its sting. Eternity is opened for a redeemed people to live in harmony with a perfect God.

Forgiveness can be a difficult concept for many to grasp. Some fail to embrace it because they feel so overwhelmed with personal guilt that they think God's forgiveness likely might not extend to them. Others fail to embrace it because they don't think they need it. They figure God likely judges on the fairness system, and in the scale of deeds, their good deeds outweigh their bad deeds. Both of these camps need to spend time meditating on today's passage.

For those burdened by guilt, the forgiveness of Jesus should be the best of news. Jesus paid the price for all sin, not just the soft ones, the light ones, the ones that others have, or the ones that proceed from ignorance as opposed to a stubborn, willful and defiant nature.

The Christian monastic Isaac of Nineveh (c. 612–c. 700) spent a great deal of his life living a prayerful solo existence in the wilderness around modern Iran. His long periods of meditation, study, and prayer produced a number of marvelous insights and images. One of my favorites is, "As a handful of sand thrown into the great sea, so are the sins of all flesh in comparison with the mind [and mercy] of God." Isaac gives a spectacular image that we should embrace when we feel the burden of our sins. The sin is lost in the sea of God's mercy, in the forgiveness wrought by Christ.

For those who see little need for God's forgiveness, even though they may not vocalize it in that way, the words of Jesus should ring out reality: We all need the full forgiveness of God. Christianity is not a religion of fairness where God weighs out our deeds and then lets those whose good deeds outweigh their bad deeds slide. God is 100 percent pure, and any sin, no matter how small or soft, must be reckoned and accounted for. Good deeds don't outweigh the bad.

During this Lenten season of repentance, I need to be reminded that sin is destructive. But I also need to remember that Jesus paid the price for that sin, and in him is forgiveness.

Thank you, Lord, for the forgiveness of sin in Jesus. I confess that I sin. I wish it were otherwise. I trust in Christ's death for your forgiveness. Thank you for it. In Jesus, amen.

FEBRUARY 23

And this is eternal life, that they know you, the only true God, and Jesus Christ whom you have sent. (Jn. 17:3)

School is mandatory for most everyone at different times of life. Often children start school before ever stepping foot into a kindergarten classroom. In the United States, most people at least attend school for thirteen years (K–12). Some attend less; some attend more. Many attend *lots* more. The purpose of school includes teaching children to be sociable, good citizens, but even more so, it provides children a basic education. School should ensure a population that can read, write, and do basic math. By having an educated citizenry, the social scientists believe that productivity increases, crime decreases, and civilization moves forward.

People often speak of "knowing" in the sense of being able to pass a test. In school, children memorize lists and dates as well as formulas and procedures. This was so they "know" what is needed for tests to move forward in school.

But in the time of Jesus, and in the time when John wrote these words of Jesus, "to know" meant something other than having intellectual knowledge about something. "To know" (the Greek word is ginōskō, γινώσκω) had a range of meanings. It included our idea of acquiring information, but it also spoke of understanding that information. If you "knew" something or someone you had an intimacy with it, her, or him. This same word was used to convey sexual intimacy between a husband and wife. The word is in Matthew 1:25 where it reads that Joseph "knew her [Mary] not, until she had given birth to a son . . . Jesus."

Understanding this sense of "knowing" puts today's passage into an important light. Jesus didn't say, nor did John record, that knowing *about* God and Jesus is eternal life. The passage says "knowing" God and Jesus *is* eternal life. I can know about God, but never have an intimate relationship with him. I remember being stunned to learn that a number of the world's great scholars about Jesus and the Bible don't even believe in God, much less have an intimate walk with him.

Jesus calls forth a relationship. He wants his children to not only know him but to trust him. Jesus seeks intimacy. Intimacy with God is far beyond what we know. I want that intimacy. I know that being in an intimate relationship with God is eternal life!

Lord, I want the intimacy with you that Jesus spoke of. Give me the wisdom to walk that way. Give me the love and discipline to find a deeper walk with you. In Jesus' name, amen.

FEBRUARY 24

Then Jesus was led up by the Spirit into the wilderness to be tempted by the devil. And after fasting forty days and forty nights, he was hungry. And the tempter came and said to him, "If you are the Son of God, command these stones to become loaves of bread." But he answered, "It is written, 'Man shall not live by bread alone, but by every word that comes from the mouth of God.'" (Mt. 4:1–4)

What are your priorities today? I am a list guy. I generally function best when I make lists of things I need to do. The lists give me a visual cue of what needs to be done first as well as a clear indication of when I can cross those things off my list to move on to other things. Today's passage teaches the believer that the most important thing on anyone's list is always to listen to God and follow his instructions.

In the passage, Jesus has gone into the wilderness. Matthew says Jesus fasted for forty days and nights, and those numbers are important. The number 40 had a range of meaning in that day and culture. "Forty" could mean "40," as in the number between 39 and 41 (see, e.g., the number of silver bases made in Ex. 36:24–26). Forty could also mean a significant time, without the precision of twenty-first-century counting (see, e.g., Moses describing how long he lay on his face before the Lord in Deut. 9:18, 25). For Matthew, however, this number is an echo of its use in Moses. Moses also fasted in the wilderness before the Lord for "forty days and nights" when he received the Ten Commandments (Deut. 9:9). This echo becomes important in light of Jesus' declaration that people should live by "every word that comes from the mouth of God."

After this extended and long fast, Satan (the name given in verse 10), who is also called the "tempter" (verse 3) and the "devil" (verse 1), comes to Jesus in a seemingly kind way. What could be kinder than offering a starving man bread? Also echoing a story from the life of Moses, Satan suggests as the Son of God Jesus get bread from the stones. (The manna God gave Israel was picked up daily from the ground as one might pick up a stone [Ex. 16:14–16].)

Jesus knew that his highest priority was not taking care of himself. First and foremost, Jesus was to follow God's instructions and plans. As Jesus did that, Jesus would be taken care of in God's plans, not his own. The tempter said, in effect, "You have needs—real needs! Take care of those! Then we can figure out what God wants or doesn't want from you." Jesus replied, "No! First, I must figure out what God wants from me. I have no greater need!"

This helps me with my lists of to-do's today.

Lord, may I focus on you, your instructions, and your agenda today. In Jesus' name, amen.

FEBRUARY 25

Then the devil took him to the holy city and set him on the pinnacle of the temple and said to him, "If you are the Son of God, throw yourself down, for it is written, 'He will command his angels concerning you,' and 'On their hands they will bear you up, lest you strike your foot against a stone.'" Jesus said to him, "Again it is written, 'You shall not put the Lord your God to the test.'" (Mt. 4:5-7)

Our family had gathered in a city for an important family funeral. Sisters and brothers, cousins, aunts, and uncles, we had all attended a visitation and reception the night before the funeral. Afterward, a clump of us (fifteen or so) who were staying in the same hotel decided to walk a few blocks to get some late dinner. As we went into the somewhat empty restaurant, I noticed the manager working behind the counter had a funny look on his face. We quickly learned that the restaurant had technically closed twenty minutes before we got there, and the staff was just finishing its nightly cleaning. The manager's thoughts were etched on his face. He was weighing the question of whether he would order the kitchen to reopen to serve us. I told him if he was willing to let us order, we would gladly clean up our own tables when we were done. He reopened the kitchen, but he refused to let us bus our own tables. He explained that we were customers. The staff would wait on us. We would not wait on ourselves.

That night, we were blessed. The restaurant made it about us. In our lives, however, that is not our relationship with God. God does not exist to serve us; we exist to serve him. We often lose track of this because, in part, God is so loving that he seeks our best at all times. But our best is never what we should be seeking. We should be seeking to love the Lord and serve him.

In today's passage, Satan gave Jesus a chance to bring God into his service. Satan knew that if Jesus were to throw himself off the temple's high spot, that God would be required to intervene and save Jesus. This could make Jesus dictate what God does, rather than Jesus pursuing God's will. Satan even quoted Scripture to try and make his proposal seem right! But the proposal was wrong. Jesus put a stop to any notion that he would dictate God's actions. We don't test God. We don't instruct God. God doesn't exist to serve us.

As I examine my actions today, I want to draw a distinction between the restaurant staff and God. I want to be the one willing to reopen my life and my plans in service to my king, rather than seeking God to build his day around me. This life and this world are not about me. They are about his kingdom. We pray, "Thy kingdom come, thy will be done," not my will be done.

Lord, I give you today. Let me live for you. Forgive me for making life about me rather than you. I want to serve you better. In Jesus' name, amen.

FEBRUARY 26

And a ruler asked him, "Good Teacher, what must I do to inherit eternal life?" And Jesus said to him, "Why do you call me good? No one is good except God alone. You know the commandments: 'Do not commit adultery, Do not murder, Do not steal, Do not bear false witness, Honor your father and mother.'" And he said, "All these I have kept from my youth." When Jesus heard this, he said to him, "One thing you still lack. Sell all that you have and distribute to the poor, and you will have treasure in heaven; and come, follow me." But when he heard these things, he became very sad, for he was extremely rich. Jesus, seeing that he had become sad, said, "How difficult it is for those who have wealth to enter the kingdom of God! For it is easier for a camel to go through the eye of a needle than for a rich person to enter the kingdom of God." Those who heard it said, "Then who can be saved?" But he said, "What is impossible with man is possible with God." (Lk. 18:18–27)

In today's story one sees two different reactions to the teachings of Jesus. Both reactions are important to anyone interested in eternal life.

First comes the somewhat arrogant, or at least self-righteous, ruler or leader of the people. This wealthy individual came quizzing Jesus on what more the ruler could do to earn his eternal life, in other words to walk fully pleasing God. Jesus properly focused on what the *man himself* must do to earn God's eternity. The man needed to live without sin, to follow the law perfectly. The rich man was poor in his self-assessment, for he believed he was already doing that! No doubt the man was "holy" in the eyes of people, but what humanity perceived as "good" was not "good" on God's level!

Jesus put a sharp focus on where the man was falling woefully short of the law. The man was failing to love his neighbor as himself, accumulating and retaining resources that could have really helped others. Rather than falling on his knees seeking help, the man left Jesus, more concerned about what he had than what he would miss.

The second reaction comes from those who stayed with Jesus. After hearing Jesus recount the difficulties that come with money, the people were at a loss. They couldn't understand how anyone could ever do as Jesus taught. It was apparent that no one was able to do that which would earn them their eternal life from God. Was life therefore futile? Jesus gave the answer that foretells the gospel. While no one can earn their eternal life through sinlessness, God can give eternal life nonetheless. God can do what humanity can't. Our role is to be in that second group, calling on God for his mercy rather than walking away from Jesus to a life on our own.

Lord, I need your help today. I need your holiness because I don't have it on my own. I can't rely on what I have, who I am, or what I do in efforts to win this life. So I fall instead on your love and mercy found in Jesus. In his name, amen!

FEBRUARY 27

He also told this parable to some who trusted in themselves that they were righteous, and treated others with contempt: "Two men went up into the temple to pray, one a Pharisee and the other a tax collector. The Pharisee, standing by himself, prayed thus: 'God, I thank you that I am not like other men, extortioners, unjust, adulterers, or even like this tax collector. I fast twice a week; I give tithes of all that I get.' But the tax collector, standing far off, would not even lift up his eyes to heaven, but beat his breast, saying, 'God, be merciful to me, a sinner!' I tell you, this man went down to his house justified, rather than the other. For everyone who exalts himself will be humbled, but the one who humbles himself will be exalted." (Lk. 18:9-14)

Today's passage has troubled me. My problems come from the day I found myself in the story in an unexpected way. I had grown up fairly responsive to God and spiritual things. I went to church, said my prayers, and behaved rather sensibly, following the instructions and teachings of my parents. I didn't like to say it out loud, for it would surely sound haughty, but I relied and believed myself a good person before God, "righteous," although I wouldn't have used that term.

I knew this story of Jesus. I knew about the self-righteous fellow who "attempted" (and appeared) to give God credit for my life, when I really wallowed in self-righteousness. If you had asked me whether I "treated others with contempt" by comparing myself to them, I would have said, "Of course not! I have read Luke 18, and I know that to do so would be wrong! I am not like that Pharisee in the story! I am like the tax collector!!!"

Then one day the irony struck me. I was reading today's story where the proud man was thankful he wasn't like the sinner, and my response was to say with pride to God, "I am thankful I am not like the Pharisee (whom I termed the sinner), but am righteous like the other man." In that, I was living out the very story, but doing it from the wrong side.

Our self-righteousness and any proudness that comes from our deeds is to be shunned. As we more carefully focus on God's greatness, as we more deeply appreciate our sinfulness, as we seek out his forgiveness and mercies, we will grow before him to become more who we should be. Then we can remember the prayers of the Keith Green song, "And when I'm doing well, help me to never seek a crown. For my reward is giving glory to you!"

Our lives need to focus on God in his beauty and holiness. Then who we are will be laid bare and we can seek his merciful love.

Lord, I confess too often I am the Pharisee in this story. Please forgive me a sinner. I need your grace and mercy. In Jesus, amen.

FEBRUARY 28

After saying these things, Jesus was troubled in his spirit, and testified, "Truly, truly, I say to you, one of you will betray me." . . . A disciple, leaning back against Jesus, said to him, "Lord, who is it?" Jesus answered, "It is he to whom I will give this morsel of bread when I have dipped it." So when he had dipped the morsel, he gave it to Judas, the son of Simon Iscariot. Then after he had taken the morsel, Satan entered into him. Jesus said to him, "What you are going to do, do quickly." . . . So, after receiving the morsel of bread, he immediately went out. And it was night. (Jn. 13:21, 25–27, 30)

I was trying a case where the defendant company had sold a product [baby powder] that had asbestos in it. Asbestos is a known causer of cancer. Doctors and scientists do not know of any level of asbestos that does not have health risks. The company had an alternative way to make the product with corn starch. Studies showed that corn starch worked just as well, but the profit margins were smaller.

When the company's witness was on the stand, I asked her: "Someone has two doors in front of you. You are asked to go through one of the doors. On the first door is a sign that says, '100% safe.' On the other door is a sign that says, '50% chance this has a cancer-causing ingredient.' If all other things are equal, which door will you go through? Which door will you take your infant through?" The answer seems obvious.

In life, we have choices. We can choose to follow Jesus and walk in the light. Or we can choose to reject Jesus' leading and retreat into darkness. Judas had that choice as reflected in today's passage. Jesus even called out Judas' betrayal before it happened. In a book where John is repeatedly speaking of Jesus as the light that came into a dark world, and where the night is repeatedly associated with the darkness of sin and rebellion, we read that Judas not only spurned Jesus' warning, but that he went out to do his dirty deed. John says, "And it was night," emphasizing that Judas was working in the darkness of his soul, even as he worked in the darkness of the moment.

I can be stunned at Judas. I can see the two-doors illustration at trial and consider the choice obvious. Yet in fairness, I must confess that I am guilty of sometimes taking the light that has come into my life through Jesus and instead retreating into darkness. I, like all humans, at times make choices to sin. It is stupid. It is nonsensical. Yet it is real.

As I sin, it is important to turn back to Jesus and confess the sin, bringing it under the forgiveness found in the blood of Jesus. I need to seek Jesus' strength and live in the power of the Holy Spirit as I seek to do better. Sin always breeds trouble, pain, difficulty, and heartache. I should know better. Why choose darkness over light?

Lord, please forgive my sins. Give me strength and wisdom to live in your light. In Jesus, amen.

MARCH 1

Do not think that I have come to abolish the Law or the Prophets; I have not come to abolish them but to fulfill them. For truly, I say to you, until heaven and earth pass away, not an iota, not a dot, will pass from the Law until all is accomplished. Therefore whoever relaxes one of the least of these commandments and teaches others to do the same will be called least in the kingdom of heaven, but whoever does them and teaches them will be called great in the kingdom of heaven. I tell you, unless your righteousness exceeds that of the scribes and Pharisees, you will never enter the kingdom of heaven. (Mt. 5:17-20)

Uh oh. I don't mind saying that even on my best days, I could be in trouble with this teaching. Read today's passage once more. The scribes were specialists in the "Law" (what we call Genesis through Deuteronomy). They knew each commandment of God and had become specialists at not only writing and teaching on them but also doing them. As for the Pharisees, they were a group known for their piety. They were expected to give their lives up to stop a profaning of the Law.

These were righteous people. They fasted regularly, sacrificed assiduously, avoided every type of sin: verbal, lifestyle, tithing, and more. Yet this wasn't enough. Jesus told his followers that they needed to find a righteousness that was even greater than that of the best of the best—people who seemed to top an imaginary ladder of Holiness.

This isn't the only place where Jesus emphasized the need for an impossible righteousness. Matthew later records and tells the story of a rich young fellow who came up to Jesus asking, "Teacher, what good deed must I do to have eternal life?" Jesus told him to "keep the commandments." The young fellow thought he had done so, at least for some of the more concrete commandments like "don't murder" and "don't commit adultery." Jesus then told the fellow to keep the commandment about loving his neighbor as himself, telling him, "go, sell what you possess and give to the poor." This, the man wouldn't do, going away "sorrowful, for he had great possessions" (Mt. 19:16-22).

God is a pure God. For us to live in his midst, we must be equally as pure. This purity must exceed that of the scribes and Pharisees. This purity must exceed the concrete commandments. This purity extends to actions and thoughts. This purity extends to what we do and what we fail to do. This purity is *impossible*. Once we realize that, we have two choices. We can go home in sorrow as the rich young ruler, or we can fall on our knees and pray, God have mercy. Then as God credits us the purity that is found in Christ, we arrive with a righteousness that indeed surpasses the scribes and Pharisees. We have a pure righteousness coming from God's grace as we trust him for that. This is the game changer for today, in our lives and in our deaths!

Lord, I am a sinner. Please forgive me in Jesus. Give me his righteousness. Amen.

MARCH 2

You have heard that it was said to those of old, "You shall not murder; and whoever murders will be liable to judgment." But I say to you that everyone who is angry with his brother will be liable to judgment; whoever insults his brother will be liable to the council; and whoever says, "You fool!" will be liable to the hell of fire. (Mt. 5:21–22)

I first came across this passage when I was a young teenager. I knew it was wrong to murder, and that it wasn't a sin I foresaw in my future. That happened in television shows, but not in my life. As for being angry with my brother, that could at times be a problem, but generally I wasn't an angry fellow. So that phrase in today's passage didn't bother me too much. Besides, I wasn't clear at that age as to what Jesus meant by being "liable to judgment." The third injunction from Jesus concerns insulting another. While I knew that I was guilty of insulting others, the result was not too concerning. Jesus said that those guilty would be "liable to the counsel." I didn't know what the counsel was, much less what they would do with me!

It was the fourth clause that set off warning bells. The one who says, "You fool" will be "liable to the hell of fire." Now that was something I understood. Now forty-five years later, I can still remember my early reactions to reading this passage. I scoured my memory for whether or not I ever called someone a fool. I resolved that word would never be in my vocabulary! I would have to come up with better terms to use! (I remember even trying to get someone with knowledge of Greek to tell me the Greek word, in hopes that I could just avoid using that!)

Looking back on that time is bemusing. I appreciate the bluntness of wanting to avoid hell, but somehow in the process I totally missed a major thrust of the passage! The key to the passage isn't one clause or another. It is the total package! This passage is the first of many where Matthew sets up a contrast of Jesus' where Jesus compares the teachings of others to his own. (What scholars call "thesis-antithesis sayings.") Jesus points out what others taught, "You have heard, 'Don't murder!'" and contrasts it with his own teaching, "But I tell you don't be angry, don't generally insult, and don't use a specific insult ('fool')."

Obviously, Jesus was concerned with the outward action of murder. But the concerns of Jesus went deeper. Jesus was concerned with the heart and attitudes that produced one's outward actions. Jesus wants his followers to be godly. That requires purity not only in actions but in the thoughts and attitudes that produce those actions. As a young teenager, I erred into thinking Jesus was just adding to the "Don't do this list" and failed to see that Jesus was trying to change my heart. I want and need that change of heart, even forty-five years later.

Lord, purify my heart. Forgive my harshness and grow your love in me. In Jesus, amen.

MARCH 3

And as for the dead being raised, have you not read in the book of Moses, in the passage about the bush, how God spoke to him, saying, "I am the God of Abraham, and the God of Isaac, and the God of Jacob"? He is not God of the dead, but of the living. You are quite wrong. (Mk. 12:26-27)

When I was in high school, one of my friends asked me if I ever read the Bible and laughed. At the time, I couldn't think of any examples. (I could give many today!) My friend then told me that reading this passage in Mark made her laugh out loud. I read it and didn't understand why. She said, "Come on, isn't it funny to think of Jesus saying, 'You are *quite* wrong!'" To her, it struck an almost un-Jesus chord to hear him say not simply, "You need to adjust your thinking." Or maybe, "You haven't gotten this right." She could even envision, "You are wrong." But to say, "You are *quite* wrong" seemed especially funny.

As I learned Greek, I was eager to look at this passage to see if the translators might have taken some liberty in saying Jesus said they were "quite" wrong. The translators were spot on! The Greek word Mark uses is πολὺ πλανᾶσθε (*polū planasthe*). The first word translated as "quite" conveys the idea of "much" or "many." The second word translated as "wrong" also conveys the idea of "wandering" or "astray." Jesus' phrase means "you are way wrong," or "way off track."

A few verses earlier Jesus explained why the people were so off course. He said that they knew "neither the Scriptures nor the power of God" (Mark 12:24). Both of those are important things to know. We can know the Bible quite well, but still be off course because we don't know and experience the power of God. I am always reminded of the wise men seeking the infant Jesus asking the learned of Jerusalem where the Messiah was to be born. The learned answered through Herod, "In Bethlehem!" and then went back to their homes. They knew the Scriptures but not the power of God. If they had known what God was up to, they would have said, "In Bethlehem! Follow me there! But keep up, because I can't wait to see the Messiah!!!" (Mt. 2).

Similarly, one may be intent on experiencing God, but without a firm understanding of the Scriptures, one can easily be misled. We should seek to know God as he reveals himself in Scripture as well as in life.

I don't want to be "quite wrong" or "way off track." Therefore, I am committed to spending daily time in Scripture, but also in prayer. I want to engage with God in dialogue and grow in my understanding of his power as well as his word.

Lord, I have a lot to learn. Please open my eyes to your Scriptures. Strengthen my dedication to study. Bless me with eyes that also see your handiwork. In Jesus, amen.

MARCH 4

Again I tell you, it is easier for a camel to go through the eye of a needle than for a rich person to enter the kingdom of God. (Mt. 19:24)

Prior to graduation, my high school class voted for certain things, including "most humorous." The most humorous vote boiled down to two funny guys, Kevin and Tom. Kevin's humor was based in puns; Tom's was more joke-oriented. I voted for Kevin. Tom won. To my dismay, jokes beat out witty puns as "funnier."

We often read the gospels with a preconcieved view of Jesus as a stern and non-humorous teacher. This is a mistake. Jesus was a master teacher who used humor as a tool to help teach important lessons. We miss this because humor has changed over the centuries. In Jesus' day, a popular form of humor was based in "the absurd." Today's passage is an example.

A camel can't go through the eye of a needle. It never has been able to, and it never will. The picture of it is absurd. I try to get thin thread through the eye of a needle and find that plenty difficult, but a camel? No way.

Historically scholars have gone to great lengths to try and make literal sense of today's passage. For centuries, there was an idea that a small gate in ancient Jerusalem was called "the eye of the needle" and to get a camel through the gate required unloading the camel, getting it onto its knees, and pushing it through. Even though that idea is still taught by some today, it is the ancient equivalent of an internet rumor. No such gate has ever been found or written about in writings within one thousand years of the time of Jesus.

Jesus was using absurdity in his teaching, an ancient form of humor. Those listening likely laughed at the image Jesus painted, and they certainly got the message. Our reflection shouldn't be on "What is the eye of the needle?" but should be, "What is it about having money that makes it so difficult to enter the kingdom of heaven?"

That answer is simple. Money means resources. With money, we can buy plenty of tasty food and have safe housing, warm clothes, and access to the best medical care. We can keep those around us safe and well supplied. When we have money and the resources that come with it, we can rely on that to help us through tough times.

Without money, the world is much more uncertain. Without money we much more readily turn to God. We need God to supply our food, keep us safe and help us make it from day to day. The kingdom of God comes to those who rely on God for righteousness, for life in this world and beyond. Relying on God doesn't come easy to those with the resources to rely on themselves. Hence, the truth in Jesus' humor.

Lord, may I rely fully upon you—for life, for forgiveness, for everything. In Jesus, amen.

MARCH 5

Woe to you, scribes and Pharisees, hypocrites! For you tithe mint and dill and cumin, and have neglected the weightier matters of the law: justice and mercy and faithfulness. These you ought to have done, without neglecting the others. You blind guides, straining out a gnat and swallowing a camel! (Mt. 23:23–24)

Do you enjoy eating at buffets? Instead of ordering what you want off a menu, buffets enable you to select your food from a massive amount of choices. You get to pick what you want and how much you want. If you want the fried chicken, you get fried chicken. If you want liver and onions . . . well, I'm not sure many people ever want liver and onions, but *if* you do, and if it's on the buffet, you can put it on your plate.

Righteousness is not a buffet line. Many of Jesus' contemporaries failed to see that. They found parts of the law that were handy and easy to do, and made a big show out of their performing those requirements. Jesus used the illustration of these people taking one tenth of the mint plants they harvested for tea or cooking and giving that tenth to the priests. Likewise, when they picked dill and cumin, they were quick to give a tenth. This was easy. With each of those spices, you never use more than a smidgeon anyway. To pick an extra couple of leaves is ridiculously easy.

Meanwhile, these folks ignored important requirements of God. They ignored justice. Justice is real justice when it is freely given to everyone, to those who are powerful and wealthy as well as to those who are weak and impoverished. These people ignored mercy. Mercy isn't pity; it is a choice to help those in need, especially when the needy don't deserve it. These people also ignored faithfulness. Faithfulness and mercy are two aspects of an Old Testament word *chesed*. This Hebrew word is hard to translate with one word in English or in Greek, so Jesus has two words to give the fuller meaning. Mercy, steadfast love, faithfulness—all of these traits are wrapped up in the Old Testament word. Jesus is speaking of the "requirements" that God gave his people through the prophet Micah. ("What does the LORD require of you but to do justice, and to love kindness [*chesed*—mercy and faithfulness], and to walk humbly with your God?" [Mic. 6:8].)

Jesus finishes his teaching moment with a humorous picture that bites and teaches. As he often did, Jesus used humorous images to drive home serious points. These so-called leaders of Israel were blind. They were straining out gnats from their food or drink. Meanwhile they were gulping down camels! They were going through the buffet line and choosing what they wanted, ignoring the vegetables and loading up on desserts.

Righteousness doesn't work that way.

Lord, forgive me for seeking easy ways to serve you, and grow me up in this. May I be just, merciful, and faithful to you and your work. In Jesus, amen.

MARCH 6

But to what shall I compare this generation? It is like children sitting in the marketplaces and calling to their playmates, "We played the flute for you, and you did not dance; we sang a dirge, and you did not mourn." For John came neither eating nor drinking, and they say, "He has a demon." The Son of Man came eating and drinking, and they say, "Look at him! A glutton and a drunkard, a friend of tax collectors and sinners!" Yet wisdom is justified by her deeds. (Mt. 11:16–19)

We were blessed with five children whose ages span almost fifteen years. Multiply our five by their playmates, and the countless parties and functions with innumerable numbers of kids coming into our house or at various school, church, and social functions. In the midst of so many children, we saw great variability in their social skills. Some were born socialites; others were more naturally reserved. Most were friendly, but a few never seemed to participate. A rare few would even complain, regardless of what was happening. In this regard, children haven't changed in two thousand years.

Jesus was looking for a comparison to those who sat in harsh judgment on him and his ministry. He used children and their play circles as his life-inspired parable. Even in Jesus' day, some kids were naturally antisocial. If the children were playing flutes, some children refused to dance and join the fun. These same children, if the play were less frivolous refused to join them as well.

Jesus found those children a handy parable for the complainers who were not happy with whatever God was doing. When God sent them John the Baptist, a prophet who was an ascetic, eating little and refraining from any alcohol, these people indicted him as demonic and strange. Then when Jesus came, one who would eat—often with sinners like tax collectors and prostitutes—and drink wine, the people slandered him as a glutton and drunkard (though he neither ate nor drank to excess).

Sometimes people just aren't satisfied with the work of God. We can complain that God isn't fast enough, doesn't do what we want when we want, or just seems to be on the wrong page, ignoring our pleas. Heaven help us when we display such childishness! This life is never about what we want, when we want it, and how we want it. This life is about the kingdom of God, and how God wants us to fit within his kingdom. Our salvation was never about God joining our team to do our beck and call. It was about us joining his team to do as he directs.

Children can teach us a lot. I want to be one of the well-mannered children that Jesus calls to him. I want to be obedient and follow his lead in my life.

Lord, help me be on your page, finding your song in my life. In Jesus' name, amen.

MARCH 7

And when Jesus had stepped out of the boat, immediately there met him out of the tombs a man with an unclean spirit. He lived among the tombs. And no one could bind him anymore, not even with a chain. . . . Night and day among the tombs and on the mountains he was always crying out and cutting himself with stones. And when he saw Jesus from afar, he ran and fell down before him. . . . And the unclean spirits came out. . . . And people came to see what it was that had happened. And they came to Jesus and saw the demon-possessed man, the one who had had the legion, sitting there, clothed and in his right mind. (Mk. 5:2-3, 5-6, 13-15)

A funny thing about being sick, sometimes you can have the same or similar symptoms even though the virus or bacteria causing the illness is different. I have had a runny nose, congestion, a fever, and a sore throat from a good many different viruses. Sometimes I've gone to the doctor and been diagnosed with everything from strep throat to the simple common cold. The symptoms don't always tell me the disease.

This becomes important in looking at today's passage. Jesus had crossed the sea of Galilee and found a man in the district of the Gerasenes. The man was wild, living among the tombs. Earlier he had been chained up by the nearby townspeople, but in crazed fierceness he had broken the chains. He wailed and yelled nonsense, a crazy man demon possessed. Jesus confronted the man, cast out the demons, and set the man aright, into a new life, calm and peaceful.

Today's passage reminds me of my medical discussion. I see myself in the man of the tombs story. I have not been possessed by an unclean spirit in the sense of demon possession. Nor was I physically bound. I never cut myself and cried out loud to the world around me. But I still find myself in the story. My disease was different, but my symptoms bore a remarkable resemblance. My deliverer was Jesus.

I had more than one phase in life where I was living among the dead. I walked in the death and decay that comes from not following the Lord. This enslaved me and was a life to my own detriment. I wasn't cutting myself physically, but the spiritual and emotional harm and damage I did to myself was no less real. But thank the Lord, my story did not end there.

Jesus came into my life. He set me free from the law of sin and death. He gave me abundant life and set my feet on solid ground. He gave me wisdom and direction and then provided the strength for me to walk in a new life. I was able to sit at Jesus' feet, in sound mind and body. He gave me peace and purpose.

Thank you, Lord. From the bottom of my heart, thank you for deliverance, for freedom, for peace, and for life. Thank you for rescuing me with love. In Jesus' holy name, amen.

Jesus said to them, "You will all fall away, for it is written, 'I will strike the shepherd, and the sheep will be scattered.' But after I am raised up, I will go before you to Galilee." Peter said to him, "Even though they all fall away, I will not." And Jesus said to him, "Truly, I tell you, this very night, before the rooster crows twice, you will deny me three times." But he said emphatically, "If I must die with you, I will not deny you." And they all said the same. (Mk. 14:27–31)

Some days everything seems to be going great—the days when the sun shines on life and joy seems to leap in your heart. Some days are gray, and joy is a bit more elusive. Then some days are downright dark, and joy is a struggle to find.

When things are going great, it is easy to affirm to God our love and commitment. We truly believe we are his and nothing will tear us from his love and care. We are 100 percent on the team, ready for anything! But then darkness can crash upon us, and in a flash, our commitment is shown to be shallow. We fear and fight to find our own way, worried that we are not going to make it otherwise.

It happens to all of us. It happened to Peter. It happened to the Lord's other apostles. Jesus warned them it would come, and they didn't believe him. After all, Jesus was talking to them at a high point in their lives. But Jesus' arrest was around the corner. With the arrest was the pending death penalty for Jesus, and perhaps for his band of followers too. Suddenly, in the darkness, the disciples' faith began to lag. As Jesus predicted, they abandoned him and their trust in him.

I can't say I'm glad they forsook Jesus, but I must admit, it has blessed my life. I lean on this when my days darken. I know my faith might at times soar to great heights, but at other times, it fails me miserably. When it does, I look and find Jesus. I see him loving his own disciples, all the while knowing that they would fail him. Yet Jesus still loved them, and he still loves me.

What is more, after his resurrection, Jesus made a point of coming to his apostles and letting them know things were alright. Jesus' love for them never left, even in their own unfaithfulness. Jesus' commitment for them never flagged. Jesus was in their corner every moment, including those where they wandered from Jesus.

I need this from Jesus.

Lord, I confess that I am not as faithful to you as I should be. I fear things I shouldn't fear. I worry about things that are under your control, when they are not under my control. Instead of rejoicing over the opportunity to see your hand move in my difficult times, I get scared and panic in my heart. Forgive me as you show me your love. In Jesus, amen.

MARCH 9

When he came down from the mountain, great crowds followed him. And behold, a leper came to him and knelt before him, saying, "Lord, if you will, you can make me clean." And Jesus stretched out his hand and touched him, saying, "I will; be clean." And immediately his leprosy was cleansed. (Mt. 8:1–3)

Today's story has some hidden nuggets that stand out a bit clearer in the Greek version. The passage is one best read slowly. Let's break it down.

Jesus has been teaching what we commonly call the Sermon on the Mount. When he finished, Jesus came down from the hill toward Lake Gennesaret, commonly called the Sea of Galilee. Jesus was followed by great crowds. Undoubtedly these were people awed, inspired, and even curious about this man who taught fresh truths of God so boldly. Many *followed* Jesus, but one man did something different; he *approached* Jesus.

Look carefully at my last sentence. I used italics to emphasize that the leper approached Jesus. Italics are a marvelous way to emphasize something being written. Ancient Greek didn't have italics. Other tools were used to draw the reader's attention to a point of emphasis. One way was using "signal words" that indicated that a point of emphasis was being made, not unlike the famous chef Emeril who shouts, "Bam!" when adding a spice to a dish to give the dish an extra kick.

Matthew uses a Greek word indicating emphasis a lot in his writing. It is the Greek word "*idou*" (ἰδού). It indicates, "Pay attention to what follows!" Translators are often at a loss to put that into English. Sometimes it simply gets lost in the translation. In today's passage, the translators used a common tool and translated the word as "behold."

By using the Greek *idou*, Matthew tells his readers to note the events contrasting those who follow Jesus from the man who approached Jesus. We do well to note that distinction today. Many people follow Jesus. We watch him, seek to hear him, to listen when he speaks. That is well and good. But not the leper; he doesn't simply follow Jesus. He approaches Jesus. The leper had a need and Jesus was the answer. The leper sought Jesus' intervention and help, and Jesus gave it.

I want to be the leper. No, I don't want an incurable disease, but I know I have needs that only Jesus can meet. I want to approach Jesus. I want to ask him for help. Like the leper, I want to ask Jesus if his will includes helping me. Then I want the thrill of Jesus extending his hand to touch me. I want to know the touch of my Lord in my life when I need it the most.

Lord, I am your follower, but more than that, I am one in need of your loving touch. Please help me with my needs today, as only you can. In my blessed Jesus I pray, amen.

MARCH 10

At that time the disciples came to Jesus, saying, "Who is the greatest in the kingdom of heaven?" And calling to him a child, he put him in the midst of them and said, "Truly, I say to you, unless you turn and become like children, you will never enter the kingdom of heaven. Whoever humbles himself like this child is the greatest in the kingdom of heaven." (Mt. 18:1–4)

For many people, if not most, status is very important. We want others to hold us in high regard. Many strive for popularity, success, and a measure of control, and it seems that those things belong to society's winners. Or at least those perceived to be atop society's ladder. This is the harsh truth that underlies much of human behavior.

As we consider this reality of life, however, today's passage confronts us. The disciples are concerned with status in the coming kingdom of heaven. Jesus has taught the disciples to pray, "Thy kingdom come," and they lived with an eye toward it. Then hand in hand with that prayer and expectation of a coming kingdom, the disciples were already jockeying for position. The disciples asked Jesus who was the greatest in the kingdom.

We are reading too quickly if we fail to note the real answer to the question. The greatest in the kingdom of heaven is God himself. If we wish to know what *human* is greatest, then with Jesus in their midst the answer is no less the same—God (Jesus). Yet Jesus calls out a child to set before them. Then, as now, children were considered to be the least powerful and least influential among the adult world. Jesus explained that unless the disciples were like the child, willing to see themselves as low in social status, they would not enter the kingdom of heaven. Jesus' followers are servants, not those who are served.

Jesus modeled this concept he was teaching. Jesus, the eternal God, chose to set aside his heavenly "social status" in order to come to earth as a human and serve humanity. Paul wrote about this to the Philippians using the same Greek word for "humble" that Matthew puts into Jesus' mouth in today's passage. Paul explained that we are to "Do nothing from selfish ambition or conceit, but in humility count others more significant than yourselves" (Phil. 2:3). Paul reminded his Philippian readers that this was the very attitude of Jesus who, "though he was in the form of God, did not count equality with God a thing to be grasped, but emptied himself, by taking the form of a servant, being born in the likeness of men. And being found in human form, he humbled himself by becoming obedient to the point of death" (Phil. 2:6–8).

If status is really important, what greater status could one ask for than to be like Jesus? This means becoming the servant, not the boss. I have some work to do.

Lord, help me grow in humility. May that be my social goal. In Jesus, amen.

MARCH 11

Seeing the crowds, he went up on the mountain, and when he sat down, his disciples came to him. And he opened his mouth and taught them, saying: . . . (Mt. 5:1–2)

Recently I was visiting with a successful fellow in his fifties. Most people would hold him up as someone they admire. He had a strong and happy family. His business was booming. He was well grounded and stable in his faith. His health was strong. For him, life was smooth sailing. The sun was out, and the wind was behind him.

I asked him about his life, what decisions led him to where he was, and to what he attributed his success. He told me that he had few regrets. He had seized on the good opportunities that were presented to him. Many people, he believed, are not looking for blessings in life. Many are reticent to reach out and take advantage of open doors, either through fear or lack of faith. He had a couple of isolated examples of his own failure to achieve through hesitancy or fear, but he learned from those failures early on.

The Christian life is one that is best lived when one is looking for the blessings God has in store. We shouldn't simply wait for God to pour blessings into our life; we need to seek him out. We should seek out what he has to teach us and how we can apply it in life. If we do so, we will not be disappointed. We will be transformed.

Today's passage is a setup for what was to follow. But the setup is important, and it should not be ignored in an effort to plumb the depths of Jesus' teaching. Jesus saw the crowds and so placed himself where the crowds could access him and where he could teach them. After Jesus went up on the hillside, having sat down, "his disciples came to him." That is a key phrase.

We should be seeing where Jesus is going and what he is doing. We should be seeking him out. We should be coming to him. We should strive to hear his words. With open eyes, sharp hearing, and obedient hearts, we should prepare ourselves to hear the words of the Savior.

What does this mean practically to me? First, I am going to find a measure of time each day to open the word. The Word of God (Jesus) speaks through the word of God (Scripture). The Bible isn't going to climb into my brain. I am going to need to open it up and read it (or have it read to me). Second, as I spend time with the Lord in his word, I am going to do so prayerfully. I speak to God, and I do so with a heart listening for what he has to say to me. Finally, as I read and hear, I am going to do! What use is it to learn the words of Jesus, if I don't do them?

Lord, please honor my time with you. Give me a heart to seek you. Give me the strength to obey you. In Jesus' name, amen.

MARCH 12

Blessed are the poor in spirit, for theirs is the kingdom of heaven. (Mt. 5:3)

How do you see your circumstances in life? Do you see yourself fortunate and happy? Or do you look at life and wonder if you could return it for one that works better? Jesus had a lot to say about what makes one's life privileged or fortunate. It isn't what most people suspect!

At the time of Jesus, the Greek language had a word for someone who was "fortunate" or "happy" with life's circumstances. That word was *makarios* (μακάριος). In today's passage *makarios* is translated as "Blessed . . ." That one would speak of or teach about being happy and fortunate with life's circumstances is not surprising. What is surprising, however, is what Jesus said *is* the circumstance leading to this happy state.

Jesus pronounces the one who is "poor in spirit" as one whose circumstances lead to happiness and a fortunate life. The phrase "poor in spirit" is not some mystical phrase that might make one say, "Aha! Of course, that makes one happy!" The phrase means something that most people wouldn't associate with joy.

The Greek word translated as "poor" (*ptōkos*, πτωχός) is well represented by the English word "poor." Its core usage was for someone who was economically disadvantaged, someone needy and reliant on others for support, someone who was *poor*. But Jesus wasn't referencing income. He was referencing poorness in "spirit." Jesus' idea behind the human spirit is the personality, that immaterial part of a human that gives life to the body. It is what makes us breathing beings, rather than dying corpses.

Jesus says that for those who are down in their hearts (using a modern reference), who need help and support in facing life, who are distressed and feel defeated and ill-equipped to handle what is being thrown at them, who are suffering internally and emotionally, those people are actually the ones who can rejoice and be happy! Those people, desperate for help, are the fortunate ones! Why? Because theirs is the kingdom of heaven!

God comes down to rescue the brokenhearted. The ones who don't have what it takes to make it in life are the ones who will reach out to God. Pity the rich in spirit, who have no need to turn to God. They live in the arrogance of their over-sated souls, never feeling the need to find one who can bless their socks off.

So as I read this teaching of Jesus, I am reminded of my own impoverished need for his love. I will seek him out, knowing I am not in any position to bless myself!

Lord, show me my need for you. I lean on your strong arms to give me purpose and strength. In Jesus' name, amen.

MARCH 13

Blessed are those who mourn, for they shall be comforted. (Mt. 5:4)

I was trying a case in front of a stern judge. The case involved one who was hurt working on a ladder. The ladder did not meet the safety standards for ladders. It was built wrong. The ladder company had an expert engineer on the stand, and I was cross-examining him. At one point, rather than admit that the ladder wasn't built to the specifications, the engineer tried to play word games on what the code actually required. Judge West sent the jury out of the courtroom so he could upbraid the witness without tainting the jury.

Once the jury was absent, the judge blasted the witness. "You can't come into my courtroom like that! You can't pretend this is *Alice in Wonderland* where little is big and big is little. You are lying. I see it. The jury sees it. And I'm not allowing it!" Everyone was stunned at his outburst. Then he brought the jury back in and I continued to cross-examine. The witness was more forthcoming.

Today's passage brings back that memory because we see something today that at first glance almost seems to be *Alice in Wonderland*-ish. It seems opposite to say that one who mourns is one who is "blessed" or "happy" with life's circumstances (an alternate meaning of the word). Yet this is no word game. Jesus wasn't playing. He was making a true statement that is worthy of consideration.

The idea of "mourning" (*pentheō*, πενθέω) is being sad or grieving because of circumstances. It is a natural response to tragedy. We mourn at the death of a loved one. We grieve when tragedy strikes. When we relate to others in pain, it can bring us sadness.

Yet these are the very events that Jesus says can be blessings. These times can bring forth a fortunate state of life, where we appreciate things. The key to this is in Jesus' last phrase. Those who mourn in him will receive comfort.

Jesus isn't speaking of those who mourn in the world. He is talking to his followers. He is talking to those who embrace Jesus as Lord. We mourn, but not as those who have no hope. We mourn as those who know there is a God who is going to make things right. There is a God who cares for us. There is a God who mourns with us. There is a God who will bring dancing when the mourning is over. We have a God of comfort, and we see it most clearly when we are in need of his touch. This is the blessing!

Lord, when we suffer and mourn, please be our rock and refuge. Bring us your comfort in Jesus our Lord, through whom we pray, amen!

MARCH 14

Blessed are the meek, for they shall inherit the earth. (Mt. 5:5)

Translating ancient Greek vocabulary into English word equivalents is difficult. The Greek words flow from a different culture and time, and it isn't easy to find a one-to-one equivalent in English. The translation difficulty is especially notable in today's passage.

Who would we call "meek"? For many, that denotes someone who is quiet and demur, someone who is passive and weak. Yet the Greek word translated as "meek" (*praeis*, πραεῖς) doesn't convey that idea. Some find the best English equivalent as "gentle," but even that doesn't cover the fullness of the Greek word. Two stories of people called "meek" can help illustrate what is meant.

Long before Jesus taught this lesson, there was a famous Hebrew who wasn't too outgoing, yet was able to go before the ruler of the day and challenge him in front of a full audience. This Hebrew would make demands of the ruler, and when the ruler wouldn't acquiesce to the demands, would call down horrific curses on him. This Hebrew took a leadership role over the other Israelites, and for decades led them through their most trying times. When necessary, this Hebrew would lead the Israelites into battle. He would confront the Israelites when they were out of line. He had no trouble displaying righteous anger. Yet this Hebrew named Moses was "very meek, more than all people who were on the face of the earth" (Num. 12:3).

The second person was one who was full of the Spirit of God. This man performed miracles unequaled by any other. He was friends with many, and tender toward children. Yet when he found behavior offensive to God, he would call out those responsible being blunt in his judgment. He also would overturn the tables of those who used religion for their economic gain rather than true devotion to God. This was Jesus who was "meek and lowly in heart" (Mt. 11:29).

Those who are meek are those whose lives are marked by gentleness and a servant's heart. They will stand up for right and can be righteously indignant over sin, but their baseline is one of kindness and gentleness. These are the ones who will inherit the earth. The earth doesn't go to the self-seekers, the brash who push others out of the way to get what they want. It goes to the meek.

In today's passage, Jesus echoes Psalm 37:11, which gives insight into the meek inheriting the earth. The Psalm reads, "the meek shall inherit the land and delight themselves in abundant peace." Abundant peace comes to the gentle, not the hyper-aggressive!

Lord, may I seek to be gentle in my life, trusting you to deal with the consequences. Teach me to love others more fully. In your name, amen.

MARCH 15

Blessed are those who hunger and thirst for righteousness, for they shall be satisfied. (Mt. 5:6)

When I was young, way back in the '70s, I bought an album by a Christian band called The Second Chapter of Acts. One of their songs was from Psalm 63. It tuned my heart to love the lyric of that Psalm. "O God, you are my God; earnestly I seek you; my soul thirsts for you; my flesh faints for you, as in a dry and weary land where there is no water." Jesus knew the Psalms and frequently drew upon them to teach others. Today's passage is a great example.

Jesus spoke to a great human need—food and water. Without them both, we die. Jesus used this critical human necessity as a metaphor for those who strove for righteousness, wanting it as much as the air we breathe. "Righteousness" conveys the idea of being pure and upright before God and the world. It is moral holiness.

As we understand "righteousness" as being pure and right before God and the world, we might think that Jesus got it a bit wrong. Because Jesus says the ones who hunger and thirst for righteousness will be "satisfied" or "fed and filled." Yet experience tells me that someone who hungers and thirsts to be righteous leaves frustrated and depressed!

How, then, can we make sense of Jesus' statement? The key lies in whether our "righteousness" is self-righteousness or a righteousness that comes from God! If we are focused on our own ability to become what God wants, drawing out of our own strength and self-control, we will never achieve it, though we may deceive ourselves into thinking we have. That false assurance draws from pride, one of the sins God especially hates (i.e., "haughty eyes" in Prov. 6:16–19)!

But if we truly crave righteousness, it can be found. It is found in the Lord Jesus. Jesus was fully righteous, in ways no other human has ever or could ever achieve on his or her own. Jesus' righteousness is pure before God. He wasn't the slightest rebellious to the Lord. His heart was aligned fully with God. He did nothing out of vain conceit or selfishness. He then offers this righteousness to those who follow him.

Initially, it is "imputed righteousness," which means God credits it to us, the way we put money in the bank. It is God's free gift to those following Jesus. Beyond that, God begins to develop it in our lives. His Spirit works within us to grow us into the image of Christ, so we actually become purer as we live under Jesus.

Wow! Those who hunger for righteousness will be filled! Thank you, Lord!

Lord, please give me Christ's righteousness, and work in my life in Jesus' name, amen.

MARCH 16

Blessed are the merciful, for they shall receive mercy. (Mt. 5:7)

The brain is a funny thing. I would love to be able to tinker with it. Reading about medical cases where people have lost the function of part of their brain, and how it alters their personality or certain traits fascinates me. One of the aspects that intrigues me is how we can think one thing, but when under pressure, behave differently. Consider today's verse in this light.

Jesus calls his disciples to be "merciful." What precisely is "merciful"? The Greek word eleēmōn (ἐλεήμων) speaks to being concerned about people in need. It is a word of compassion and sympathy. It conveys clemency and forgiveness for wrongs.

We are called to have mercy on others, and in certain circumstances it seems easy. We can hear of and see people in such need that we are moved to pity, and we readily display compassion. But there are others who need our mercy who aren't so pitiable! This is especially true when we are under stress, preoccupied, or frustrated. Yet we aren't called to have mercy in situations where anyone would have mercy. Nor are we called to have mercy when our lives have made room and are emotionally prepared to give mercy. We are to have mercy at the core of who we are.

This wasn't a new teaching by Jesus. In the Old Testament, God is repeatedly called by the same word Jesus uses in today's passage, calling on his followers to be "merciful" (eleēmōn, ἐλεήμων). The Jewish translators of the Old Testament used another form of the Greek word to translate the Hebrew word *chesed*, a relationship word that shows marks of kindness and loyalty, calling on God's people to be people of mercy.

David explained God as one with "great mercy." "Then David said to Gad, 'I am in great distress. Let us fall into the hand of the LORD, for his mercy is great'" (2 Sam. 24:14). The Psalms agree, "Great is your mercy, O LORD" (Ps. 119:156). Therefore, as we show mercy to others, we follow the lead of a great and merciful God.

While mercy is a godly trait, the Scriptures paint the wicked and evil as unmerciful people. "The soul of the wicked desires evil; his neighbor finds no mercy in his eyes" (Prov. 21:10). Mercy is not merely a convenient thing for the godly. It is a deep trait.

So how do we alter our brains so that what we think right (being merciful) is what we do, even when under pressure? Through prayer, dwelling on his word, worship, and aligning our thoughts with the heart of God. It takes time and is a growing process. But Jesus joins the larger corpus of Scripture in teaching us that it is very important!

Lord, please help me grow in mercy! In Jesus' name, amen.

MARCH 17

Blessed are the pure in heart, for they shall see God. (Mt. 5:8)

One time when Becky, our five children, and I were by the Sea of Galilee, in an area where Jesus likely gave the Sermon on the Mount, including these beatitudes, we read them aloud. I asked each of us to speak for a moment about which beatitude we would like to be our hallmark. In other words, which beatitude would we like people to readily identify with our character. This is one that was mentioned.

For me the beatitude itself is simple and pure. In a pure manner, it draws out the value of being pure in heart. It gives the pure in heart an immeasurable reward: to see God. What could be a greater moment in life than to see God? When you read this blessing in the Greek, the word used for "see" draws you in. It is the Greek *opsontai* (ὄφονται) from *horaō* (ὁράω). It can mean simply "to see visually," but its semantic range is much larger. The Greek idea is that the one who "sees" God is one who experiences God. One who is mentally and spiritually perceptive of God. One who pays attention to God. One who beholds God.

Isn't that an amazing goal? To have a greater experience with God, where we perceive who God is in greater measure than ever before, where we have spiritual insight into God, and where our hearts are attuned to God—wouldn't that be worth our greatest efforts? To get there, Jesus told us to be "pure in heart."

Jesus' call for purity in heart as a prerequisite to this greater understanding and vision of God echoes the call from Psalm 24. "Who shall ascend the hill of the LORD? And who shall stand in his holy place? He who has clean hands and a pure heart, who does not lift up his soul to what is false and does not swear deceitfully. He will receive blessing from the LORD and righteousness from the God of his salvation. Such is the generation of those who seek him, who seek the face of the God of Jacob" (Ps. 24:3-6).

Purity of heart lies in motives as well as actions. It indicates one with integrity, one with compassion, one with the traits Jesus laid out in the beatitudes. Purity of heart involves melding one's heart to the heart of God. In this sense, we readily see why being pure in heart would expand one's intimacy with God. When we grow in purity of heart, we grow to be like God. We will understand him better, because he will be a greater part of who we are.

I want this! I am making a mental decision to grow in purity, not simply because I want to be a better person. Nor simply because I want to avoid the harsh consequences of sin. I want to see God!

Lord, teach me purity in heart. Let me see you and know you better. In Jesus, amen.

MARCH 18

Blessed are the peacemakers, for they shall be called sons of God. (Mt. 5:9)

THE WORLD NEEDS THIS! We need more peacemakers. War is found on the international stage. Acts of terrorism occur around the globe. Within nations, different people are filled with violence and hatred against other people. Races still divide people. Economic status divides people. Political affiliation divides people. Within social circles, we find destructive gossiping, backbiting, and nitpicking. In schools, bullying is a national problem. Gun violence regularly makes the news. Hate groups spew out venom in all corners of the globe. Even in families, where the protection of love should ring clear, we often hear of violence, animosity, hatred, and strife. Heavens, some people are not at peace with themselves, but rather loathe and hate who they are.

How do we make peace in the midst of this world? Artists have given us countless songs to inspire us to love. In 1965, Jackie DeShannon released the Burt Bacharach/Hal David hit, "What the World Needs Now Is Love" with the chorus, "What the world needs now is love, sweet love. It's the only thing that there's just too little of. What the world needs now is love, sweet love. No not just for some but for everyone." We hear that song and agree.

Marvin Gaye's brother returned from the violence of fighting in Vietnam only to experience alienation and fighting in the United States. It prompted Gaye's amazing work, "What's Going On." In it, Gaye sings, "Mother, mother; There's too many of you crying. Brother, brother, brother; There's far too many of you dying. You know we've got to find a way; To bring some lovin' here today. Father, father; We don't need to escalate. You see, war is not the answer; For only love can conquer hate; You know we've got to find a way; To bring some lovin' here today." We hear that song and agree.

But hearing the songs and reading the beatitude are not sufficient unto themselves. We need something more. I suggest we start with ourselves and build outward.

I first need peace in my heart. That will come only from the Lord. As I lean on his truth, on his love for me, on his complete forgiveness for all my inadequacies, on his promise to bring me into greater holiness, then I find a peace that passes understanding. That then allows me to extend true peace to others by sharing God's love for them. God's love penetrates racial divides. God didn't die only for one race. God's love penetrates hatred. God hates sin but loves sinners. God's love penetrates politics. God is neither a registered Republican nor Democrat. God's love permeates into every corner of life. We need to embrace it and share it. We need to shine his love into the darkness.

Lord, teach me your love. Help me show that love to this needing world. In Jesus, amen.

MARCH 19

Blessed are those who are persecuted for righteousness' sake, for theirs is the kingdom of heaven. (Mt. 5:10)

Once I guest lectured to a class of marvelous Christian students at Wheaton College. The topic was how to share one's faith. I began by passing out a sheet of paper to all forty-two students. I asked them to write their answer to this question: What is your biggest personal challenge to your faith? I collected the answers and grouped them. By far, the greatest number fell into a category of why bad things happen to good people. Put another way, why are the followers of God persecuted for righteousness' sake?

A one-page devotional isn't going to give a satisfactory answer to this huge question, but several things are worthy of further consideration. First, we should note that God created a world where rules apply ("laws of nature"). If I drop an apple, gravity pulls it down. This isn't a Harry Potter world where those laws are suspended by waving a wand. So if I choose to drive intoxicated, and I run over someone, this isn't God's fault. It is a bad decision I made alone.

Second, in the midst of this cause-and-effect world, God has made people with an ability to make choices, good and bad. If an evil person in power chooses to use that power to hurt people, then people can get hurt.

Third, God promised that in the end, his followers would be delivered to an eternity of fellowship with God. The world will work out where this occurs and where all who would call on the name of the Lord will be afforded that opportunity.

From these considerations, I draw several conclusions. First, for people to have choice, and yet for God's plans for this world to occur, there will likely be suffering as well as joy along the way. It is how God gets the world to finally be what it should be. It is how God gets his people in the fold. Second, when actions result in God's people suffering, it is not without God's blessing. Here we fall into the truth of today's passage. Those who suffer because of God's plans, because of being righteous and following him, will receive the kingdom—both individually and for others.

The Bible never says God's people won't suffer. Everyone suffers. The Bible says God will be with us in suffering, and our suffering isn't pointless. It will be used fruitfully for the kingdom. Knowing this gives me a measure of joy, even in the midst of suffering. It is me suffering for the cause of Christ, who suffered for us all.

Lord, thank you for the suffering Savior. May I follow his footsteps as necessary for your kingdom's purposes. May I do so with honor at being worthy to follow. In Jesus' name, amen.

MARCH 20

You are the salt of the earth, but if salt has lost its taste, how shall its saltiness be restored? It is no longer good for anything except to be thrown out and trampled under people's feet. (Mt. 5:13)

My brother-in-law Kevin ran our law firm for years. One of his managerial concerns was that people who worked for the firm take their "right seat on the bus." Some are suited to be bus drivers; others aren't. Some are suited to sit by the window; others belong on the aisle. Some work well near the emergency exit; others would panic should an emergency arise. People would perform best if they were placed properly for their skill set and disposition.

Jesus made it clear to his disciples that his followers had a particular seat on the bus in terms of the larger world around us. The followers of Jesus are "the salt of the earth." In Jesus' day, salt wasn't just something that was bought at the store and sprinkled into recipes and on food. It was used not only to heighten the flavor of food but also stood for much more. It was a way to preserve food, especially meat that would otherwise spoil in an age before refrigerators. Even beyond its function, however, we should note the role it had in Judaism.

Salt was a purifying agent that made temple incense "holy and pure" (Ex. 30:34–38). This was likely why salt was added to grain sacrifices for Israel (Lev. 2:13). Salt was used to indicate the covenantal relationship of God with his people (Num. 18:19; Ezra 4:14).

The Christian should be all these things in the world. We should heighten the flavor of life, giving the world a taste of joy that it could never know without Jesus. We should be a preservative of our culture, teaching God's values in the ways we treat others, in the way we find truth, in the families we work to preserve, in our submission to authority, and in other ways that enhance the culture of our world. Similarly, the Christian should be holy and pure before the world, just as salt filled that role in Jewish practice. Our role in modeling Christ to the world cannot be overstated. At the same time, we are demonstrating God's covenant with his people.

All of this is our seat on the bus. Modeling Jesus, preserving culture, displaying the joy of Jesus, and more. But if we fail to do these things, what use are we? If we leave our calling and live as just another piece of dirt in this world, rather than salt, how are we bringing glory to God? How are we helping others? Why are we wasting our lives?

I want to be the best salt I can!

Lord, help me find the right seat on the bus and be your salt. In Jesus' name, amen.

MARCH 21

I know your works: you are neither cold nor hot. Would that you were either cold or hot! So, because you are lukewarm, and neither hot nor cold, I will spit you out of my mouth. For you say, I am rich, I have prospered, and I need nothing, not realizing that you are wretched, pitiable, poor, blind, and naked. (Rev. 3:15–17)

What makes someone lukewarm? Why would someone know the true picture of God and what he did out of love for his children by the death of Christ and then be lukewarm in response? It makes more sense to me that someone is aflame in loving response. If we truly fathom the depth and love of God in Christ, it should stir up our response of loving devotion. After all, John wrote in his first epistle, "We love because he first loved us" (1 Jn. 4:19).

It makes less sense to me that someone might rebel against the love of God, but that is still more logical than being lukewarm! Most people I have met who deny God do so for emotional reasons rather than rational thought. This is true even for those who outright deny his existence. In my experience, for most atheists and agnostics, the true issue is a personal experience or emotional issue that then interprets the evidence in favor of the conclusion they want to reach. (This is commonly known as "confirmation bias.")

But what defies my understanding is the person lukewarm in response to God. I'm sure there are many reasons for this mediocre response, but one is referenced in today's passage. There are those whose lives are basically self-sufficient, at least in their own eyes. There is no perceived need for God. Things are going okay "on their own." Folks have money or resources, business for the day, and the idea and need for God rarely arises as an issue.

I don't want to be that way. I don't want my life to be so comfortable and content that I perceive no need for God. That would be living an illusion, anyway. Every good gift we have comes from God. So if we are so blessed, and we don't burn brightly for him, shame on us. It is clear arrogance to assume that what we have we achieved on our own.

A lukewarm response to God is also a lack of recognition of how truly dependent we are upon him. As my friend James reminds me often, "I am only two big bad decisions from living under a bridge!"

God doesn't love me and call me to a lukewarm walk. I am to burn hot for him.

Lord, please help me better focus on your love, and each day seek to burn brightly for you in this world of darkness. I thank you for your many blessings, but know that I still need you each day. Help me, Lord, in Jesus' name, amen.

MARCH 22

As he drew near to Jericho, a blind man was sitting by the roadside begging. And hearing a crowd going by, he inquired what this meant. They told him, "Jesus of Nazareth is passing by." And he cried out, "Jesus, Son of David, have mercy on me!" And those who were in front rebuked him, telling him to be silent. But he cried out all the more, "Son of David, have mercy on me!" (Lk. 18:35–39)

"Desperate people do desperate things!" This common saying doesn't always capture the truth, but it often does. Some folks crumble when desperate, but others are willing to do most anything when in dire straits.

In today's passage a blind man is sitting at the roadside begging. This is a scene still seen in many urban areas today. The man hears a ruckus and wants to know what is going on! He asks those around him about the ruckus. They tell him Jesus is coming by. The blind man had clearly heard of Jesus and called out to him, as "Jesus, Son of David," a different title than the others had said. (The crowd called Jesus as being of "Nazareth.") "Son of David" recognized the greatness of Jesus rather than the commonness of Jesus' hometown.

The crowd shushes the blind man. After all, he is one of the expendable population that doesn't contribute to the community but sucks from it, living off the charity of others. But desperate people do desperate things, and many refuse to be silent. He cried out more and more. He got louder and wouldn't be silenced.

Within that frame, there are three groups identified: the blind, expendable beggar; the crowd intent on taking in the spectacle of Jesus; and Jesus of Nazareth, known by a few to be something much more.

Jesus doesn't join the crowd in keeping on his path, trying to ignore the needy outcast. Instead Jesus stops. Jesus instructs the crowd as to its true duty. Rather than hush the needy man, the crowd was to bring him to Jesus. The crowd does so, and Jesus addresses the blind man directly. Jesus asks the desperate man, "What do you want me to do for you?" The man could have asked for money, for food, for time. But instead he asked for the unthinkable. He wanted to see! Jesus heals the man and the crowd that tried to stop the event freaks out! They are so stoked! They saw Jesus heal someone miraculously. They saw firsthand a first-rate, undeniable miracle.

I chuckle at the crowd. They were led to the glory of Jesus by the blind man who shouldn't have been able to lead anyone anywhere. That is the power of the desperate person who comes to God. God meets the needs of the desperate.

Lord, I am desperate for you. Please touch my life today. Through Jesus, amen.

MARCH 23

Judge not, that you be not judged. For with the judgment you pronounce you will be judged, and with the measure you use it will be measured to you. (Mt. 7:1–2)

Passages like today's put me on high alert. I don't want to be judged. I can't afford to be judged. Any judgment of me is likely to go nowhere good. So, what do I do with today's passage? Let everyone around me slide from whatever they are doing? No! Today's passage merits some prayerful and careful thought.

Many have a tendency to read this passage knowing that Jesus came to save the faithful from ultimate judgment and hell. Understandably, then, some have a tendency to read this and immediately translate it into what happens on judgment day. But people need to remember that Jesus was not giving a lecture about God's final judgment. In this Sermon on the Mount, Jesus was talking much more about what happens in the here and now. Jesus was giving solid, godly insight into how his followers should live each day.

Seeing this passage as daily living advice, it takes on a more focused and measured tone. It is fairly close to the modern proverb, "People in glass houses shouldn't throw stones." Too many people have a tendency to see the errors in others and fail to see their own faults, even when the personal faults exist to a much greater degree.

A great example is found in the Old Testament story of King David. David had lusted for Uriah's wife, Bathsheba, and ultimately took her and impregnated her. Caught in the quandary of a pregnant mistress, whose husband was away at the battlefield and clearly couldn't be the father of the child, David decided to have Uriah killed. Then David took Bathsheba formally as his wife. Nathan the prophet came to David to confront David for his sins. Nathan didn't point the sin out to David. Instead, Nathan told David a story. The story centered on a man who had one sheep. A neighboring man had countless sheep. When the neighboring man needed to entertain a guest, rather than slaughter one sheep of his many, he took the sole sheep of the first man and killed it to feed his guests. David heard the story of *someone else*, and David's blood boiled. David demanded the name of the man with the many sheep, declaring his life should be forfeited for such a deed. Nathan then told David that the story was a parable. That Uriah was the man with one sheep, and David was the thief. David fell in repentance.

It is so easy to see sin when it belongs to someone else, be it a spouse, a friend, or even an enemy. Yet it is so hard to see it in ourselves. Hence, we have Jesus teaching that one should be careful in judging or criticizing another. For in truth, we are more likely at fault than those we criticize.

Lord, give me insight into my life so I may live better for you. Forgive my critical and harsh tongue. Teach me patience and to pray for those in need. In Jesus' name, amen.

MARCH 24

Ask, and it will be given to you; seek, and you will find; knock, and it will be opened to you. For everyone who asks receives, and the one who seeks finds, and to the one who knocks it will be opened. Or which one of you, if his son asks him for bread, will give him a stone? Or if he asks for a fish, will give him a serpent? If you then, who are evil, know how to give good gifts to your children, how much more will your Father who is in heaven give good things to those who ask him! (Mt. 7:7–11)

Reflecting on today's passage always makes me want to pray more. The passage seems odd to some: God waits to give until we ask. God waits to show us until we seek. God opens doors when we take the initiative to knock on them. Sometimes I default into thinking that God will do those things anyway. After all, he knows what we need before we ask, so why do we need to ask?

But when I think that way, I need to self-correct. This planet was never one where God did everything for us. He made us responsible for the planet, under his care and direction, of course. From the beginning of time, Adam and Eve were given responsibility for things on earth. From naming the animals to working the garden, human responsibility is a real thing. The key is, it seems to me, that people aren't able to do those things by themselves. I need God's insight to see what needs to be done. I need God's provision and power to accomplish even the things God has given me to do. I need God's endurance to finish what needs to be done. I need God!

Seeking God's help to do God's will with my life is squarely in the center of today's passage. This isn't a passage that teaches God to be a genie in a bottle ready to grant three wishes. It doesn't pretend to portray God as the concierge at a five-star hotel, able to land reservations at the restaurant of my choice. God is about God's will. As his child, that should be my agenda as well.

Hence the passage states that God gives "good gifts" to his children. God won't give us the things that are outside his will. Fortunately, God's will includes our best interests, but I should never pretend to know what those are. There are too many possibilities, too many unknowns in life for me to know what I need and when I need it.

So I approach today's passage prayerfully. The passage goes hand in hand with the Lord's Prayer where Jesus "taught" his disciples to pray, "Thy will be done!" God wants his children to pray for his will as we seek to live it out. I can pray for his will with the assurance he will answer my prayers!

Father God, give me eyes to see your will in the big and the small things. Give me the strength to do your will with the endurance to finish what I start. In Jesus, amen.

MARCH 25

So whatever you wish that others would do to you, do also to them, for this is the Law and the Prophets. (Mt. 7:12)

Recently one of my daughters told me about a change in her plans. She was tired from work and from the lack of sleep her infant inflicted upon her several nights (months?) in a row. I was in town to visit her clan, and we had figured out a plan for dinner. I was going to pick dinner up and she could eat in her "at home" clothes. But things changed at the last minute, as things are prone to do! Suddenly, there was another guest for dinner. It was no longer feasible for my daughter to stay home in comfy clothes and get some rest. Instead, it meant she had to put on her makeup, get dressed, and go out. Talking to her about the new plan, I could hear the frustration in her voice. I asked, "you okay with this?" She replied, "Dad, I just figure this is someone God wants us to spend time with."

My daughter taught me something profound that day. She saw the dinner guest not as an interloper, not as someone thwarting her chance for the evening of her choosing. Instead, she saw the guest as someone God wanted their family to minister to and help. My daughter exemplified today's passage.

Jesus and God are always concerned not only with our relationship with God but also our relationship with each other. God cares about how people are treated. So much of the "Law and the Prophets," a shorthand rendition by Jesus to what we call the "Old Testament," deals with how people treat people. How people treat God is dealt with as well, of course, but an amazing amount of Scripture teaches people how to love others.

Importantly, Jesus put no qualifiers on his instructions in this passage. Jesus didn't say it only applies to those who are of our skin color, educational background, nationality, economic class, cultural heritage, or other divisive matter. Jesus wanted his followers to treat *everyone* well.

I wonder how my day would be different if everyone I saw became the subject of my self-examination, "How would I like to be treated by this person?" I know my driving would be different! I know my conversations would be too. I would better invest in others, seek to be kind and gentle, share the joy and love of the Lord, seek to bring others into a closer fellowship with the Lord—the list would go on and on.

Based on my typical day, I have a lot of repenting to do and a great deal of seeking to do better!

Lord, forgive me for not treating others with the care that you've instructed. Show me where I am failing and give me the strength to do better. Thank you for your care and example through Jesus. Amen.

MARCH 26

From that time Jesus began to show his disciples that he must go to Jerusalem and suffer many things from the elders and chief priests and scribes, and be killed, and on the third day be raised. (Mt. 16:21)

In today's passage, a small Greek word lurks in Matthew that, while well translated into English, can easily get lost as one reads the verse. The word is incredibly important as it describes what Jesus knew was required of him. The Greek word is the verb *dei* (δεῖ). Its English translation is "must." The word conveys the idea of something that is necessary, a compulsion, something one has to do.

Jesus explained that his imminent sacrifice on the cross was not an option for him. God dying for the sins of humanity was not just an option. It wasn't a course God chose out of some need for attention, or self-mortification. The death of Christ for the forgiveness of sin was a necessity. It was the only way. It was a judicial requirement. Paul explained this in more detail, especially in the book of Romans. That book's thesis statement is found in the first chapter, verses 16–17. Paul explained that the sacrificial death of Christ (Paul's "good news" or "gospel"—see also 1 Cor. 15:1–3) was God's "power" to save any and every person who believes.

God doesn't practice whim and fancy; he is not one who one day is just and another day unjust. God is a consistent, unchanging, perfect being who is fully and 100 percent just all the time. Justice demands that the wages of sin be paid. The wages of sin are death (Rom. 6:23). Even God can't overlook that requirement. Just as God himself is life, so something that is not of God (i.e., sin) is not life. Sin is a cancer that must be destroyed. Sin and the sinner must die.

So you and I will die for our sins. It is the just wage. Unless, someone who has no sin willingly gives their life in our stead. This would need to be another person. No goat is going to satisfy for the sins of a person. So God, the perfect one, had to become human. But not only did God have to become flesh, he also had to die. There was no other way.

Hence, we have the Greek word Matthew uses. Jesus must go to Jerusalem to die. It was an imperative. There was no other way. Only by this could God "justly" justify (meaning declare the believer right under the law) anyone. We are right under the law because the final judge of all things in the universe has declared that the penalty for sin has been fully and finally paid. What amazing news flows from Calvary.

Lord, I confess that I have sinned. Through my fault, in word and deeds that I have done and in what I have failed to do. I humbly fall before you and in faith ask you for the forgiveness found in Jesus on the cross. Through whom I pray, amen.

MARCH 27

Now a certain man was ill, Lazarus of Bethany, the village of Mary and her sister Martha. It was Mary who anointed the Lord with ointment and wiped his feet with her hair, whose brother Lazarus was ill. So the sisters sent to him, saying, "Lord, he whom you love is ill." But when Jesus heard it he said, "This illness does not lead to death. It is for the glory of God, so that the Son of God may be glorified through it." (Jn. 11:1-4)

"Lazarus Saturday" is the name given to the day before Palm Sunday. It is a day when the church often meditates on the story of Jesus raising Lazarus from the dead. The story begins with the verses set out today, and it continues through much of the chapter.

In the story, Jesus is near Bethany (right outside Jerusalem), but at least a day's journey away. Lazarus is the brother of Mary and Martha, two women who were prominent supporters of Jesus, his apostles, and his ministry. But more than that, they were friends. John's account clearly says that Jesus loved all three. When Lazarus fell ill, it was a serious problem. The sisters sent a 911 emergency message to Jesus. They had spent countless hours with Jesus, and they knew without a doubt that Jesus could heal their sick brother. But time was of the essence.

Jesus got the message quickly, and he proclaimed that the illness was not one leading to death, but one displaying the glory of God. Saying so, Jesus then delayed his departure for several critical days. Once Jesus finally set off to the house of his friends in Bethany, Jesus told his disciples that he knew Lazarus had died. It seemed to the apostles, and to one reading the story for the first time, that Jesus had wasted his window of opportunity.

But the story unfolds further, and Jesus arrives to the weeping and grieving of the sisters over their brother's death. Martha has a poignant message for Jesus, one that a few of Jesus' apostles might have also been thinking, "Lord, if you had been here, my brother would not have died" (Jn. 11:21). Jesus responded to Martha with a most important affirmation. Jesus said to her, "I am the resurrection and the life. Whoever believes in me, though he die, yet shall he live, and everyone who lives and believes in me shall never die. Do you believe this?" (Jn. 11:25-26). Jesus then goes into the tomb of the four-day-deceased Lazarus, and Jesus raises him from the dead.

With this story as the background, Holy Week begins, and Jesus begins his unstoppable march to Calvary. Jesus has a final job to do—the whole reason, really, for his incarnation. Jesus is going to do the work that will ensure not the temporary resurrection of a fallen human body, but its permanent eternal resurrection. Lazarus died, Jesus delayed, but Jesus didn't dawdle. Jesus knew he was living to the glory of God, and his role as a resurrected Lord was preceded by this account of him as a resurrecting Lord!

Lord, touch us, heal us, and give us eternity in your life. Through your death, amen.

MARCH 28

And the crowds asked him, "What then shall we do?" And he answered them, "Whoever has two tunics is to share with him who has none, and whoever has food is to do likewise." Tax collectors also came to be baptized and said to him, "Teacher, what shall we do?" And he said to them, "Collect no more than you are authorized to do." Soldiers also asked him, "And we, what shall we do?" And he said to them, "Do not extort money from anyone by threats or by false accusation, and be content with your wages." (Lk. 3:10–14)

John the Baptist is a good preacher for Lent! John was blunt and incisive. He attracted many people who came to hear his preaching. His messages were condemning, and people were clearly able to see their sins and inadequacies. John preached for the people to repent, and he baptized them to cleanse their souls as well as their bodies.

Today's passage records some of John's condemning sermons. John told the crowd to share with those less privileged. "If you have two tunics, share one with someone who has only one! If you have extra food, give to the hungry!"

John moved from sharing of tunics and food to answering the questions of tax collectors. Tax collectors were notorious for insisting people pay amounts over what was due and pocketing the surplus collected. Tax codes were not in place at the time, making this an easy thing to do. John told the tax collectors to collect only what they were supposed to collect.

Soldiers might have had the power of the sword, but even they didn't escape John's preaching. He told them to be content with their wages and not to use their position to get extra money from others.

This preaching from John was nothing more than practical illustrations of the Old Testament injunction that "you shall love your neighbor as yourself" (Lev. 19:18). Jesus gave the test a little extra direction in saying, "So whatever you wish that others would do to you, do also to them" (Mt. 7:12).

This is the challenge of daily living as one grows in Godliness. One should challenge the all-too-common modern notion of looking out for number one, of dying with as many toys as possible, of being King of the Hill, and so forth. The Christian life is to be spent focused on the needs of others. Following Jesus means to follow his servant's attitude. Jesus didn't come to get, he came to give. His followers should model that same ethos as we seek to be like Jesus. After all, "Christians" means we are to be like Christ. That is our calling.

Father, help me to be like Christ, seeking the good of others as did Jesus, amen.

MARCH 29

No one after lighting a lamp covers it with a jar or puts it under a bed, but puts it on a stand, so that those who enter may see the light. For nothing is hidden that will not be made manifest, nor is anything secret that will not be known and come to light. Take care then how you hear, for to the one who has, more will be given, and from the one who has not, even what he thinks that he has will be taken away. (Lk. 8:16–18)

We are spoiled by electricity. We can walk into most rooms, and regardless of how dark it might be, with the flick of a switch, we can make it light. This doesn't make passages like today's impossible to understand, but it does take some of the punch out them.

Jesus spoke in a time long before Edison gave the world the lightbulb. The closest thing in Jesus' day was an oil-burning lamp. The lamps might not have been as bright, and they did come with a bit of smell and smoke, depending on the oil used. But they still served the purpose of lighting the darkness.

Jesus found lamps a good analogy because of how they were used. Lamps had a cost every time they were lit. No one had a Bic lighter. Fire starters themselves were not so easily made. Oil was expensive, and without good-quality oil the lamp smoked a great deal. People had to find or buy wicks appropriate for each lamp. Then and only then could a lamp be lit.

Now, of course, no one would go through all that expense and trouble to light a lamp and hide it under a bed. The mere thought of it was absurd. If a lamp were lit, it was to serve its purpose to make the room visible rather than dark.

Jesus used the metaphor of a lamp for the way life would reveal truth. Behind the teaching is the fact that God knows everything. Nothing is hidden from God. God is actually the only one who *doesn't* need a lamp. God has 20/20 vision in the dead of night. God will illuminate the world in truth for his followers to live.

This passage comes at the conclusion of Jesus' teaching in parables. It is a call to his listeners to pay attention and seek understanding from God. The listener is being warned not to stumble in the dark but to seek God's teaching and wisdom. Light serves a purpose. In this regard, Jesus adds that God will give increase to those who listen. But those who don't listen, they will lose even what they think they understood.

This is an important lesson for this passage and all devotionals. As we read and study God's word, we should be seeking to understand it, letting it bring light into our darkness, letting it illuminate the world around us. As we do so, God will reveal more and more.

Lord, show me your way and truth. Let me learn it and live it. In Jesus' name, amen.

MARCH 30

And Pharisees came up to him and tested him by asking, "Is it lawful to divorce one's wife for any cause?" He answered, "Have you not read that he who created them from the beginning made them male and female, and said, 'Therefore a man shall leave his father and his mother and hold fast to his wife, and the two shall become one flesh'? So they are no longer two but one flesh. What therefore God has joined together, let not man separate." They said to him, "Why then did Moses command one to give a certificate of divorce and to send her away?" He said to them, "Because of your hardness of heart Moses allowed you to divorce your wives, but from the beginning it was not so. And I say to you: whoever divorces his wife, except for sexual immorality, and marries another, commits adultery." (Mt. 19:3–9)

Law can be a tricky thing. It is rarely black and white. In law school, some students get frustrated because often times there is "no clear answer" to the questions posed by the professor. Professors are notorious for finding problems in the law that have many shades of gray, but seemingly no black and white.

In the days of Jesus, the sect of Pharisees was noted for strict adherence to the law. They debated its nuances and tried to find black and white conclusions for most every situation. With this philosophy and reputation, a troop of Pharisees came to question Jesus on legal nuances. They asked Jesus whether he would endorse the most liberal legal interpretation, allowing a husband to divorce his wife for any reason. Jesus likely surprised them when he gave a legal view even more strict and conservative than that for which they proudly stood. Jesus said God's heart doesn't endorse divorce at all!

The somewhat stunned Pharisees replied, "Well, if that's the case, then why did Moses allow divorce with instructions about providing a certificate of divorce?" Jesus then gave a most surprising answer. Jesus said, because of the sinful hearts of people! In other words, God wanted love, harmony, and unity in marriage, but people left to their own devices could be destructive to each other in certain situations. In those, God allowed a divorce, but only to make the best of a bad situation. It didn't make divorce God's desire from the beginning.

I read this and am somewhat stunned myself. I am not surprised that Jesus bettered the Pharisees in a battle of the law. Jesus knew the law best. In a sense, he wrote it! What surprises me is the way God handles our sin and inadequacies. He doesn't simply condemn us and leave us to wallow in sin's destruction. God seeks to make the best of a bad situation. He gives us a provision that, while not his best will for us, helps us find a way to a better place than we would find on our own. God still amazes me daily.

Lord, I don't want to be a sinner. I know I sin, but it isn't my heart. Thank you for loving me even though I sin, and thank you for helping me in spite of my sin. In Jesus, amen.

MARCH 31

Then the mother of the sons of Zebedee came up to him with her sons, and kneeling before him she asked him for something. And he said to her, "What do you want?" She said to him, "Say that these two sons of mine are to sit, one at your right hand and one at your left, in your kingdom." Jesus answered, "You do not know what you are asking. . . ."
(Mt. 20:20-22)

Our daughter Sarah was in third grade when she asked me if she could have the law firm one day. I told her that maybe her siblings might be lawyers, and I couldn't just promise it to her. She replied, "Could I at least be Rebecca's boss?" (Rebecca was an older sibling by almost two years.) Today's passage is an ancient version of my Sarah story, but it is coming from an adult rather than an eight-year-old!

I can't blame the mother for seeking what is best for her sons (or daughters!). That is innate in good mothering. Good mothers readily give their lives for their children, and this mother was no doubt willing to do so. She readily went to Jesus, bowing in respect to make this request. The sons were not oblivious to what their mom was doing. They went along with her.

Jesus' response to the mother began with, "You don't know what you are asking." Jesus was right. The mom really had no clue what was going on. She thought that Jesus was going to set up an earthly kingdom and would be setting up his court to help him run it, much like other kings of history. But Jesus didn't come to overthrow Rome. Jesus wasn't going to supplant the Jewish government. Jesus was about the kingdom of God, which was a kingdom that the mother knew little to nothing about. Jesus was not headed to Jerusalem to be made king. He was headed to die for the sins of all people, to populate the kingdom of God with a multitude of righteous people, washed clean through his sacrifice.

This passage gives me pause. I have been praying to God my whole life. Many times he has answered my prayers with a resounding YES! Many times he has answered my prayers with a pausing NOT YET! And not too infrequently he has answered my prayers with a solid NO! I wonder how many times, if he had been standing in physical form in front of me as I prayed, would he have said, "You don't know what you're asking!" I suspect quite often.

Jesus always wants what is best to bring the kingdom of God into its fullness. Whenever my prayers run afoul of his plans, I am glad he sticks with his plans over my own. After all, I frequently don't realize what I am asking!

Lord God, thank you for your plans, and for the role I get to play in them. Let my prayers always be for your will, and not my own! In Jesus, amen.

APRIL 1

You know that the rulers of the Gentiles lord it over them, and their great ones exercise authority over them. It shall not be so among you. But whoever would be great among you must be your servant, and whoever would be first among you must be your slave, even as the Son of Man came not to be served but to serve, and to give his life as a ransom for many. (Mt. 20:25-28)

It happens in every organization. I have seen it in my law firm, and I have seen it in non-profit organizations. Over and over, I see people aggressively seeking to rise to positions of authority over others. It seems to be part of the American way. Or maybe it is part of the human way. Seeking to be the boss is much more common than seeking to be an underling. One of my workers once came and explained to me that perhaps he should even be my boss! I reminded him that since I owned the business, that would be a bit awkward. He then said that maybe he should just be the boss of everyone else.

That story and others readily come to mind in today's passage because of the context in which Jesus made the statements in Matthew 20:25-28. Jesus was nearing the end of his life and mission. His disciples were fairly cognizant something big was coming and knew from Jesus' statements that he would soon be coming into his kingdom. The disciples thought Jesus would have an earthly kingdom, throwing off the shackles of Roman occupation and delivering Israel into the government where it rightly belonged. The disciples were jockeying for position in that coming kingdom. Jesus, already feeling the weight of the suffering to come shortly, took the time to try and adjust the expectations of his followers.

Jesus explained that his kingdom and their hearts were not based on the lordship ideas of earthly relationships. They should not be seeking to be greater than another. Positions of authority were not positions in a secular king's court. Jesus was ushering in a kingdom of service. The greatest in the kingdom were not served by the lesser. The greater in Jesus' kingdom were the ones who served others. Jesus modeled that in both his life and death.

This passage speaks to me. I do not want to view this life like some ordinary person in the world. I should do better! I need to mature in my Christian walk.

I want to not only know, but appreciate the importance and value of service. I want that servant's heart. I want to follow Jesus. I want my life to be about more than me. I want the mission of Jesus to give me direction.

Lord, teach me to serve. May I learn its importance. In Jesus' name, amen.

HOLY WEEK

At some time in the 200 or 300s, the church began celebrating the week before Easter as "Holy Week." Holy Week draws the season of repentance (Lent) to a close and begins a careful focus on the events in the life of Christ leading up to Easter Sunday.

In most church calendars, the first day of Holy Week begins on Palm Sunday. Palm Sunday is the celebration of the "triumphal entry" of Jesus into Jerusalem, one of the rare events mentioned in all four gospels.

Holy Monday and Holy Tuesday are names ascribed during Holy Week for the Monday and Tuesday between Palm Sunday and Good Friday. Various churches celebrate aspects of the life of Christ in the days preceding the crucifixion.

On Holy Wednesday, most churches meditate on Mary's anointing of Jesus' feet, while dining with his disciples. Some also focus on the betrayal of Judas, and his deal with certain Jewish leaders to identify and deliver Jesus to them.

Maundy Thursday is the name given to the Thursday in Holy Week. "Maundy" is a liturgical descendant of a key Latin word found in the story of Jesus washing the feet of his disciples. When Jesus tells the disciples to do the same, the Latin word is *mandatum*, from which we have the more common English expression, "mandate." This was Jesus' order to his disciples and on Maundy Thursday, the church's focus is historically on the washing of feet narratives.

Good Friday is the church's day to focus on the crucifixion and the death of Christ. Some traditions call it "Holy Friday," "Great Friday," or "Black Friday."

"Holy Saturday," also known by many other names in various traditions, is typically one which focuses on the burial of Jesus, with an eye toward his resurrection. Some traditions also meditate on the "harrowing of Hell," the teaching that Jesus descended into hell to release the saints who had died before his crucifixion. Holy Saturday ends Holy Week as the church moves into Easter celebrations on Easter Sunday.

APRIL 2

The next day the large crowd that had come to the feast heard that Jesus was coming to Jerusalem. So they took branches of palm trees and went out to meet him, crying out, "Hosanna! Blessed is he who comes in the name of the Lord, even the King of Israel!" And Jesus found a young donkey and sat on it, just as it is written, "Fear not, daughter of Zion; behold, your king is coming, sitting on a donkey's colt!" (Jn. 12:12–15)

Palm Sunday. That is the label the church has given to the Sunday before Easter. This Sunday was described in John as the day Jesus purposefully and carefully entered Jerusalem, sitting on a donkey's colt while the people took palm branches to meet him.

Several things should strike us from these verses. First, the people went out to meet Jesus. Jesus makes it clear that he has come to meet with them. He was incarnated into humanity because "God so loved the world" (Jn. 3:16). He comes to the door of our hearts and knocks seeking to come into us and dwell (Rev. 3:20). Yet on Palm Sunday, while Jesus journeyed to Jerusalem for us, the people nonetheless went out to meet him. I need to be one who seeks Jesus, having his assurance that what I seek, I will find (Mt. 7:7). For Jesus is not playing a game of hide and seek. He is not hard to find. He journeys to meet us.

Second, in John's account, John specified that "Hosanna" was among the shouts of the people. The greeting of the people was an Aramaic phrase that consisted of two words in compound. The Aramaic "*hosha*," which means "save!" and "*na*," which means "please" or more directly, "we pray." The words come from the Psalm quoted by the people and is translated, "Save us, we pray. . . . Blessed is he who comes in the name of the LORD!" While there is no indication that the people had any concept of what Jesus was coming to do, and hence, in many ways their shouts were prayers of ignorance, still, their prophetic cry was going to be answered quite directly! God was about more than they had even remotely imagined. Unknowingly, the people made a blessed announcement of Jesus' royal entrance and mission, fully unaware of their role.

I have no doubt that as I live, even as I seek to live for God, I stumble into many of his plans unaware. I want to be used by him to further his kingdom, and my prayer aligns with this wish. But it seems to manifest itself in ways far beyond my comprehension. If I had been one of those who had announced Jesus' entry with such a prophetic voice, and if I had later come to Jesus in faith, believing in him once Pentecost had occurred, I suspect I would have looked back on Palm Sunday in awe. I would have rejoiced that I hadn't stayed home. I would have appreciated God's power to put my feeble life to work for him!

Lord, give me sensitive eyes to see Jesus as savior and king. May my shouts of praise be genuine and clear. I praise you for working in me and in spite of me! In Jesus, amen.

APRIL 3

Jesus sent two disciples, saying to them, "Go into the village in front of you, and imme-diately you will find a donkey tied, and a colt with her. Untie them and bring them to me." . . . This took place to fulfill what was spoken by the prophet, saying, "Say to the daughter of Zion, 'Behold, your king is coming to you, humble, and mounted on a donkey, on a colt, the foal of a beast of burden.'" (Mt. 21:1–5)

Jesus came into Jerusalem to complete God's work on the cross. Jesus was a conquering king, coming to defeat death and sin, but kings strode into cities quite differently. Most kings rode in on a stallion, or marched at the head of an army. Jesus purposely chose a donkey's colt, the ride of a man of peace, a merchant or priest, for example. This was and is Jesus' kingship at this point in history.

Jesus entered Jerusalem as a conquering king, but one who conquered through peace. Jesus the meek, Jesus the kind and gentle, Jesus the servant, Jesus who seeks and saves those who are lost, Jesus the patient, Jesus who stands at the door and knocks, Jesus the blessed Son of God seeks entry into our hearts and stands in victory over death, as a Prince of Peace.

The way Jesus entered should have spoken to the people prophetically. God had not forgotten his people or his promise. In the prophet Zechariah, one whose name literally means "Yahweh remembers," came the promise, "Rejoice greatly, O daughter of Zion! Shout aloud, O daughter of Jerusalem! Behold, your king is coming to you; righteous and having salvation is he, humble and mounted on a donkey, on a colt, the foal of a donkey" (Zech. 9:9). But Scripture doesn't end with the first coming of Jesus.

Jesus promised he would come again. And God still remembers! In Revelation 19:11–16, it is clear that Jesus' second coming will not be like his first. The king isn't riding on a donkey's colt as a man of peace. The returning Messiah rides a white horse, riding in victory until all enemies are defeated. The description is breathtaking: "Then I saw heaven opened, and behold, a white horse! The one sitting on it is called Faithful and True, and in righteousness he judges and makes war. His eyes are like a flame of fire, and on his head are many diadems, and he has a name written that no one knows but himself. He is clothed in a robe dipped in blood, and the name by which he is called is The Word of God. And the armies of heaven, arrayed in fine linen, white and pure, were following him on white horses. From his mouth comes a sharp sword with which to strike down the nations, and he will rule them with a rod of iron. He will tread the winepress of the fury of the wrath of God the Almighty. On his robe and on his thigh he has a name written, King of kings and Lord of lords."

Jesus, may I see you in peace even as I worship you as majestic king. Amen!

APRIL 4

The next day he [John the Baptist] saw Jesus coming toward him, and said, "Behold, the Lamb of God, who takes away the sin of the world!" . . . Now the passage of the Scripture that he was reading was this: "Like a sheep he was led to the slaughter and like a lamb before its shearer is silent, so he opens not his mouth." (Jn. 1:29; Acts 8:32)

Today's passage is listed as being from two places in the Bible, the books of John and Acts. Look closely, however. It actually comes from three places: John and Acts, from the New Testament, and from the Old Testament, the book of Isaiah. Like so many places in Scripture, these books, although written more than six hundred years apart, fit together smoother than the best-made puzzle.

Isaiah prophesied in Isaiah 53:7–8 that the coming Messiah would be led to the slaughter like a lamb is led, quietly and submissively. Centuries later, John the Baptist saw Jesus and testified to those listening that Jesus was the Lamb of God who takes away the sins of the world. John spoke to Jews who were steeped in the practice of regularly having animals, especially lambs and goats, sacrificed as a symbol of death needed to satisfy the penalties of sin. Then in Acts, the apostle Philip is traveling and comes across a eunuch who is reading the Isaiah passage, and the apostle taught him about Jesus, the fulfillment of Isaiah 53.

Isaiah 53 is important. In the verses preceding the passage quoted above, Isaiah instructs the reading world of what would unfold through the actions of this Lamb of God led to the slaughter. "He was despised and rejected by men" (verse 3). "Surely he has borne our griefs and carried our sorrows" (verse 4). "He was pierced for our transgressions; he was crushed for our iniquities; upon him was the chastisement that brought us peace, and with his wounds we are healed" (verse 5). "And the LORD has laid on him the iniquity of us all" (verse 6). *Then* comes verse 7, "He was oppressed, and he was afflicted . . . like a lamb that is led to the slaughter . . . so he opened not his mouth."

Jesus, the lamb that was led to the slaughter. If you ever see the *"agnus Dei,"* you get an important insight into this through art. *Agnus Dei* is Latin for "Lamb of God." It is often depicted in pictures as a lamb with one foot raised. This is meant to symbolize the voluntary nature of Jesus' sacrifice. He wasn't dragged to the cross, kicking and screaming. He went willingly and even deliberately.

Lord, your foresight, planning, prophetic words, and fulfilling actions stun me. That you did all of that as a pursuit of love leaves me speechless. I fall at your feet in amazement, gratitude, and love. May I live in ways that show the world the redemption I have in Jesus. Amen.

APRIL 5

And he said to them, "I have earnestly desired to eat this Passover with you before I suffer. For I tell you I will not eat it until it is fulfilled in the kingdom of God." (Lk. 22:15-16)

When I was young we would sing a song in youth group, "This world is not my home, I'm just a passing through. My treasures are laid up somewhere beyond the blue. The angels beckon me from heaven's open shores, and I can't feel at home in this world anymore." Now that I have aged, I find some great truths in that song (as well as a few things I would like to tweak or perhaps totally change).

The idea of this world not being the end is true. Isaiah prophesied of a "new heavens and new earth" (Isa. 65:17-19; 66:22). This was a future when the lion would lay with the lamb and the earth would be full of the knowledge of the Lord (Isa. 11:6-9). Peter would say that the heavens and earth would burn up while we "are waiting for new heavens and a new earth in which righteousness dwells" (2 Pet. 3:13). Paul would write that "the whole creation has been groaning together in the pains of childbirth" (Rom. 8:23).

Jesus knew that a better future was prepared and that he was ushering in the kingdom of God. His death wasn't simply one to get people to heaven's shores. His death was signaling the end of the age of sin and death on this earth, with a promised new Earth for his followers to inhabit in incorruptible bodies for eternity.

For the new creation, for the eternity God intended, there had to be a release from the corrupted world that held people captive. Without a release from the current condition, people are in a cycle of sin and death. But with a promised new world, comes a life that is set free from this cycle. Followers of Jesus find a freedom that culminates in the promised new heavens and earth.

Perhaps one of the greatest prophetic pronouncements of this future was the Old Testament Passover. This ritual was instituted to remember how God had taken Israel out of bondage from the land where they had dwelt for four hundred years. This liberation came at the price of death and affected all the households of Egypt, save those who dwelt under the blood of a sacrificed lamb. The emancipation wasn't a conquering of their Egyptian overlords to dwell where their homes were. It was a deliverance to a new land, a Promised Land.

Jesus was the sacrifice that would bring about the fulfillment of prophecy. Jesus affirmed this, knowing he would eat again with his people, *after* fulfilling the Passover. What an awesome God we serve!

Father, I long to see your kingdom on earth, as it is in heaven! Come, Lord Jesus! Amen.

[Jesus] rose from supper. He laid aside his outer garments, and taking a towel, tied it around his waist. Then he poured water into a basin and began to wash the disciples' feet and to wipe them with the towel that was wrapped around him. He came to Simon Peter, who said to him, "Lord, do you wash my feet?" Jesus answered him, "What I am doing you do not understand now, but afterward you will understand." Peter said to him, "You shall never wash my feet." Jesus answered him, "If I do not wash you, you have no share with me." (Jn. 13:4–8)

"Maundy Thursday," the name given to the day before Good Friday, focuses its meditation on Jesus washing his disciples' feet during the Last Supper. John's Greek account unfolds like a movie. Regrettably, the scene loses a smidgeon as it transfers from John's Greek into English.

Look carefully how it begins: Jesus "rose" (past tense) from supper. Yet in John's original Greek, the verb tense isn't a classic past tense; it is present tense. Greek scholars call John's verb the "historical present." Without a doubt, John is talking about something that happened in the past. But John used a present tense. Not knowing anything else, one would see that verb and say, Jesus "rises" from supper. The point of a historical present in the Greek is to make the story line more vivid. It casts the story as something unfolding right before your eyes. John wants the reader to feel a part of the events.

Then with careful detail, John unfolds the action. (Actually John "unfolded" the action, but I am also using an "historical present" to say "unfolds" and more closely put the reader in the scene.) Jesus lays aside his outer garments—plural, not singular. This means Jesus stripped to his loin cloth, taking the full-on appearance of a slave in that day. Jesus takes the towel, wraps it around his waist. John is giving a full visual narrative. These events are seared into his brain. Jesus poured the water in the basin, something one high in status would not do. That's the job of the lowest one present. Then Jesus begins the job of washing the feet, the job of a slave.

Needless to say, Peter tries to stop it. Jesus isn't Peter's servant; Peter thought he knew better! Peter tells Jesus, "No way! You're not my slave!" Jesus then gives the profound response, "Peter, if you won't let me serve you with my life and body, you will have no part of me." This is the purpose of Jesus. Jesus came to give his life, not save it. Jesus came to serve humanity, not be served. Jesus came to wash others clean, not be washed clean by others. The work and nature of Jesus is not what we would expect if we were God; but Jesus wasn't our perception of God. He was genuine God. John wants his readers to see that vividly. I need to change my perceptions of what is important!

Lord, I don't often thank you for serving me. Forgive me. Let me serve others for you. In Jesus' most holy name, amen.

APRIL 7

After this, Jesus, knowing that all was now finished, said (to fulfill the Scripture), "I thirst."
A jar full of sour wine stood there, so they put a sponge full of the sour wine on a hyssop
branch and held it to his mouth. When Jesus had received the sour wine, he said, "It is
finished," and he bowed his head and gave up his spirit. (Jn. 19:28–30)

I grew up in Lubbock, Texas. Lubbock is in the Texas Panhandle and
is part of the Plains in the United States. Growing up, we were fond of
saying Lubbock was "the hub of the Plains." Our picture was clear: on the
Plains, all roads lead to Lubbock!

In John's gospel, the death of Christ is the hub of all history. Everything that had happened before the crucifixion led to that event on Calvary. Everything that would happen in history after Christ's death hinges
on that moment for meaning and significance. The moment wasn't one
that simply happened to Christ. Christ controlled the events and willingly
endured them.

In today's passage, John explained that the final death of Christ didn't
occur until Jesus knew "that all was now finished." Jesus was in complete
command. He walked through the event until it was fully finished. Only
then did Christ declare, "It is finished" and give up his spirit. In the intervening moments, however, John inserts a relevant fact. Jesus said, "I thirst."
This was *after* Jesus knew it was over, but before Jesus declared it was over.
Why? Anyone familiar with the physical torture involved in crucifixion
would know Jesus would need some liquid to moisten his mouth and throat.
Jesus had something to declare with a loud voice, and he needed liquid so
he could shout.

Jesus had something to shout. He was shouting an end. Not the conclusion of his thirty-three years, not the conclusion of his ministry, not the
conclusion of the crucifixion drama. Jesus was shouting the completion of
the historical drama between sinful humanity and God. Jesus shouted the
full and final payment for sin. Jesus shouted the restoration of the broken
bond between Creator and created. For those bathed in the righteousness of
Christ, redeemed by his blood, trusting in his love, death had lost its sting.
Jesus wasn't defeated on the cross; his cry was the cry of the victor! Here
is the hub of history!

God heaped upon Jesus all the sins of humanity, those that a fully
just God had patiently "overlooked" in history as well as those that a fore-
knowing God knew would come in the future. Because the penalty for all
sin rests upon Jesus, the penalty is removed from the sinners. I can't do
anything with my sin, save take it back to the cross where it is finished. I
was saved on Good Friday.

Dearest Lord and Father, thank you seems inadequate. I thank you, love you, and
long to live for you. Through Jesus, my redeemer, amen.

APRIL 8

Since it was the day of Preparation, and so that the bodies would not remain on the cross on the Sabbath (for that Sabbath was a high day), the Jews asked Pilate that their legs might be broken and that they might be taken away. So the soldiers came and broke the legs of the first, and of the other who had been crucified with him. But when they came to Jesus and saw that he was already dead, they did not break his legs. But one of the soldiers pierced his side with a spear, and at once there came out blood and water. He who saw it has borne witness—his testimony is true, and he knows that he is telling the truth—that you also may believe. For these things took place that the Scripture might be fulfilled: "Not one of his bones will be broken." And again another Scripture says, "They will look on him whom they have pierced." (Jn. 19:31–37)

God takes care of his children. When we dig into the blessings of the cross, that truth commands our attention and should calm our fears. Of course, God demonstrated his loving concern for us at the cross, but in the events after Jesus died, God put his exclamation mark to demonstrate the confidence we can have in his care.

Look at today's passage carefully. First, is an irony that can't be overlooked. Certain Jews requested Pilate break the legs of the crucified so that purity laws would be met. (Burials had to occur within twenty-four hours, and dead bodies couldn't be touched on the Sabbath. Breaking leg bones hastened the death of the crucified, so the bodies could be touched and buried before the Sabbath.) Yet, real purity, for Jews and Gentiles, was coming from the Son of God crucified, and it would flow to those who united with his body in his death, not those who avoided touching him!

As the soldiers approached the body of Jesus, they didn't need to break his legs and hasten his demise. Jesus was already dead. The soldiers could have broken the bones anyway, or they could have walked away satisfied. But instead, one soldier thrust his spear into Jesus' side, perhaps verifying he was dead. Satisfied, the soldiers moved on.

Jesus was dead, but God was still on his throne, caring for the details surrounding each moment. God saw that the promises of Scripture were fulfilled. No bones were broken, fulfilling not only Psalm 34:20 ("He keeps all his bones; not one of them is broken."), but also the injunctions associated with the Passover lamb given in Exodus 12:46 and Numbers 9:12. In both places, God told Moses not to allow anyone to break the bones of a Passover lamb. The spear fulfilled the prophecy of Zechariah 12:10, "when they look on me, on him whom they have pierced, they shall mourn for him, as one mourns for an only child, and weep bitterly over him, as one weeps over a firstborn."

God took care of Jesus; God took care of Scripture; God takes care of me!

Lord, may I rest in the comfort of knowing your care and love. In Jesus, amen.

EASTER

In the church calendar, for most churches, the fifty days after Holy Week comprise the days of Easter. Beginning on Easter Sunday, these fifty days concentrate on the time from the resurrection Sunday until the day of Pentecost. This was the time when Jesus would appear to various groups (Paul said more than five hundred believing men at one time; 1 Cor. 15:6) teaching and explaining his resurrection.

This is a time of celebration for the church. The resurrection of Jesus is at the core of the good news. Paul would deem it a key to the "gospel." In 1 Corinthians 15, in defining the "gospel" (Greek for "great news!"), Paul said the gospel was the death, burial, *and resurrection* of Jesus. Paul and the church often speak of the death of Jesus, but never of a dead Jesus. For Jesus isn't dead; he is alive!

The celebration of these fifty days is found in this devotional through the various passages describing Jesus during the resurrection period as well as the significance of his work.

Now on the first day of the week Mary Magdalene came to the tomb early, while it was still dark, and saw that the stone had been taken away from the tomb . . . and as she wept she stooped to look into the tomb. And she saw two angels in white, sitting where the body of Jesus had lain, one at the head and one at the feet. They said to her, "Woman, why are you weeping?" She said to them, "They have taken away my Lord, and I do not know where they have laid him." Having said this, she turned around and saw Jesus standing, but she did not know that it was Jesus. Jesus said to her, "Woman, why are you weeping? Whom are you seeking?" Supposing him to be the gardener, she said to him, "Sir, if you have carried him away, tell me where you have laid him, and I will take him away." Jesus said to her, "Mary." She turned and said to him in Aramaic, "Rabboni!" (which means Teacher). Jesus said to her, "Do not cling to me, for I have not yet ascended to the Father; but go to my brothers and say to them, 'I am ascending to my Father and your Father, to my God and your God.'" (Jn. 20:1, 11–17)

The first Easter is cloaked in mystery, rich in symbolism, touching in emotion, and, most importantly, life-changing for the world.

The day unfolded with Mary coming to the tomb in the predawn. She sees the stone rolled away and hastens to retrieve several disciples. Returning, she bends over and peers into the tomb. The body of Jesus is gone, but two angels are present asking why she is weeping. As she explains, she hears another approach and ask her the same question, but then adds a second important question, "Whom are you seeking?" This is the right question for everyone facing Easter Sunday. Whom are you seeking?

Some spend their lives seeking things, not people. Others seek the right spouse, or the person who will help them get far in life. Some want simply a good companion. Others would rather be alone. But everyone who thoughtfully contemplates the purpose of life, who considers the nagging in their soul for relationship, importance, and unconditional love, should be asked that question, "Whom do you seek?" The answer, of course, is Jesus. But the Jesus we seek, should be the one we need. That is the resurrected Jesus.

The story gives more subtle details that give greater clues to this question. Mary first mistakes Jesus for the gardener! Maybe that is not strange, in that gardeners could easily be up and about early. But why does John even care to insert it? John has sculpted his gospel in many ways around the Old Testament story of creation. The creation starts with, "In the beginning" just as John starts his gospel. Creation has God working and resting for seven days, and John limits his signs and wonders to seven done by Jesus. (Although he notes Jesus did many more than those.) Then the first day of creation's second week dawns with Adam working the garden of Eden. Adam was the world's first gardener.

So here, Jesus is mistaken as the gardener, but not the first gardener of the old world. This first day of the week dawns with Jesus as the new gardener in the new world. Paul will later explain Jesus' role as the second Adam. Not in the sense of the first Adam through whom we all became sinners. Jesus is the second Adam who got it right! Through Jesus we all became righteous!

Mary didn't perceive the rich symbolism in what she was thinking as it unfolded around her, but that is often the way things are with God. Often, we miss the significance of what he is doing around us, and also through us.

Once Jesus calls out Mary's name, Mary must have looked at him closer, more carefully, perhaps in more light, and she suddenly realizes she is speaking with Jesus. Jesus is alive! She calls out respectfully, "Teacher!" and begins hugging or clasping onto him. Perhaps at his feet, perhaps his hands, perhaps his knees, we don't know where, but Jesus tells her, almost playfully, "Stop hugging me! I haven't yet gone to the Father for good!"

Jesus is letting Mary know he isn't leaving earth yet! But in that statement, the clear indication is given that Jesus would at some point be ascending to the Father. Jesus didn't say he would be dying, for Jesus had already done that. This was the resurrected Jesus. He would be ascending to the Father. He would be elevated back into the exalted throne from whence he came.

But this wouldn't happen until Jesus had appeared to hundreds of people, giving substance to their faith that he is risen from the dead. God laid the sins of the world on them, but Jesus discharged those sins and returned in glory and power, ready to take his children home. The resurrected Jesus makes God his Father, God our Father.

This is the heart of the Easter message. Jesus has set creation aright. All that is wrong in this world—all that is wrong with you and me—finds itself set aright with the risen Lord. God is our God. He exists not only as God, but in the intimacy of a *good* Father, a *perfect* Father, a Father of unconditional love who will go to any possible length to see his children saved.

The Easter question: Whom do you seek? should be a question everyone asks. Everyone's answers should have shades of differences, but everyone's answer should end up in Jesus. When I seek solace; it's found in Jesus. When I seek peace; it's found in Jesus. When I seek reassurance; it's found in Jesus. When I seek justice; it's found in Jesus. When I seek mercy; it's found in Jesus. When I seek a friend; I find him in Jesus. When I seek meaning; I find it in Jesus. If I am seeking anything not found in Jesus, I seek the wrong things!

Lord God, Father and Redeemer, I seek you. Pour your love into my life. Teach me to live for you as I journey back into your eternity.

APRIL 10

Then the other disciple, who had reached the tomb first, also went in, and he saw and believed; for as yet they did not understand the Scripture, that he must rise from the dead. (Jn. 20:8–9)

Today's passage sets two ideas in contrast to each other. Only by seeing the contrast, does one begin to understand a subtle significance John and the Bible make about the crucifixion and resurrection of Jesus.

Within its larger context, the scene is one where Mary Magdalene has found the tomb empty and she runs to Simon Peter and the "disciple whom Jesus loved" (many accord this to the apostle John, the writer of the fourth gospel who, in humility, never identifies himself by name). Peter and the other disciple run to the tomb. The other disciple gets there first but only stoops and puts his head in the tomb. Peter then arrives and goes fully into the tomb, followed by the other disciple. They see the burial clothes laying empty where Jesus had been placed, and the head cloth folded neatly next to it.

At that point, today's passage tells the reader two distinct things. First, the other disciple "believed." This is the verb form of the word commonly translated as "faith" when used as a noun (*pisteuō*, πιστεύω in the Greek). The disciple had faith! He knew there was a resurrection. Jesus was risen from the dead! Yet, even knowing the fact of the resurrection, the other disciple missed something very important.

Second, the other disciple hadn't yet understood the Scripture that Jesus *must* rise from the dead. While believing Jesus was resurrected, the other disciple hadn't yet realized the significance of the resurrection. He hadn't realized the scriptural necessity of the resurrection (the import of the word "must").

Scripture teaches that Jesus had to be resurrected for the resurrection to have any real effect on the believer. True Easter faith involves not simply an intellectual affirmation that Jesus was resurrected; it also includes an understanding of the role that resurrection plays in the life of the believer.

Because Jesus was crucified, the price for the believers' sins has been paid in full. But because Jesus is resurrected, the believer, who shares in the death and resurrection of Jesus, is also offered a new life. This isn't just a metaphor; this is reality. When one understands Scripture on this, one sees that Jesus becomes the new or second Adam. In this sense, Jesus becomes the source of a new life that begins in this earthly body but will carry forward into the fuller resurrected body the believers will inherit one day.

Lord, thank you for the death of Christ, and for his resurrection. Thank you that this new life is in me, and may I live it to your glory until you come again. In him, amen.

APRIL 11

Then the other disciple, who had reached the tomb first, also went in, and he saw and believed. . . . Then the disciples went back to their homes. But Mary stood weeping outside the tomb, and as she wept she stooped to look into the tomb. And she saw two angels in white, sitting where the body of Jesus had lain, one at the head and one at the feet. They said to her, "Woman, why are you weeping?" She said to them, "They have taken away my Lord, and I do not know where they have laid him." (Jn. 20:8–13)

How does one react to the resurrected Jesus? Some respond in faith; others in sorrow. John provides an interesting contrast of the two.

Today's passage flows from the story of Easter morning. The first to arrive at the tomb is Mary Magdalene, who had benefited from Jesus' love and caring but hadn't been as frequent with his teaching as the twelve disciples, eleven of whom would become apostles. Mary finds the stone rolled away from the tomb and, fearing the worst (that the tomb had been robbed), she ran to tell Peter and the "other disciple." Peter and the other disciple run to the tomb, where Mary had also returned. Seeing the burial clothes, Peter and the other disciple return home, believing Jesus was resurrected, but having to think about why. Mary stays at the tomb weeping.

For Mary, Jesus was missing, not resurrected. Confronted with the reality of the empty tomb, her mind conjures up ideas consistent with only human actions. She doesn't see that God was working in a most profound way. She weeps.

In the subsequent verses, the angels try to give Mary the good news. They ask her why she is weeping, but Mary's only reply is that people must have taken the body of Jesus. Mary will then be confronted by Jesus, as tomorrow's devotional will explore, but before turning to that, let's pause and reflect on Mary's immediate reaction, seeing the contrast between her and the believing disciples. The believing disciples are able to go home and consider all that is happening. They aren't yet ready to tell others, nor did they understand the full import of the resurrection. But they knew it had happened. Mary has no such belief. For Mary, insult had been added to injury. The crucified one that had shown her love and caring was desecrated in his grave.

I don't fault Mary. If Jesus was a great man, a kind teacher, a marvelous example, then Jesus died, and the story is over, then I'd weep too. This life is brief and without eternal meaning or significance. When confronted with that truth, with death, I weep. But with a resurrected Jesus, anything is possible! Death has lost its sting! I have reason to live!!!

Lord, convict me of the truth of the resurrected Jesus as well as its importance. Teach me to live to his glory. In Jesus' name, amen.

APRIL 12

Having said this, she turned around and saw Jesus standing, but she did not know that it was Jesus. Jesus said to her, "Woman, why are you weeping? Whom are you seeking?" Supposing him to be the gardener, she said to him, "Sir, if you have carried him away, tell me where you have laid him, and I will take him away." (Jn. 20:14-15)

Today's passage contains one of the many subtleties of John that cause some to say that John is deep enough for an elephant to swim and shallow enough for a child not to drown. Anyone reading this passage can find the clarity of Mary's distress—she is weeping. One can also see that Jesus is resurrected—she is interacting with him, albeit unknowingly. But beyond these clear events, there lies something more nuanced. Mary supposes that Jesus is "the gardener." Taken within the larger context of John, this detail rises to a level of theological importance.

Consider how John has carefully shaped his gospel around many facets of the Old Testament, especially the first book of Genesis. John begins his Gospel, "In the beginning . . ." just as Genesis begins. John's subtler echo of the creation is found in a full reading of John's gospel. In the creation story of Genesis 1, God miraculously creates in seven days (the seventh day as a day of rest was just as important as the days of activity, perhaps even more so as the one that was hallowed in the Ten Commandments). After the seven days, Genesis leaves the reader with the story of Adam and Eve tending the garden of Eden. John's structure subtly runs parallel. John does not include many of the miracles of the synoptics; John limits his miracles to seven, the same as the number of creation days. John even notes that "Jesus did many other signs . . . but these [seven] are written so that you may believe that Jesus is the Christ, the Son of God" (Jn. 20:30-31).

Here lies the parallel in John's version. God creates the world over seven days and then puts Adam in the garden as a gardener. John records seven miracles of Jesus, and then God resurrects Jesus, and he first appears in a garden to Mary who assumes him a gardener. These details set up a major theological truth of the Bible. Jesus is not only the resurrected Son of God. Jesus is the first of a new creation. Paul will call Jesus "the new Adam." But unlike the first Adam, Jesus doesn't sin. Then Jesus calls his believing church into his new resurrection life. Just as Adam brought death to his children and the world, so Jesus brings life. Anyone found in Christ is found *alive*, in the deepest and truest sense of the world.

It is up to the believer to trust in this reality and to live in this reality. As a child of God, I may live in the body that came from the old Adam, but it isn't who I am, and it certainly isn't my destiny. I am of Christ, a new creation!

Lord, plant the reality of the effect of the resurrection firmly in my life. In Jesus, amen.

APRIL 13

Jesus said to her, "Mary." She turned and said to him in Aramaic, "Rabboni!" (which means Teacher). Jesus said to her, "Do not cling to me, for I have not yet ascended to the Father; but go to my brothers and say to them, 'I am ascending to my Father and your Father, to my God and your God.'" (Jn. 20:16–17)

As a young reader of the Bible, I read today's passage in the King James Version. There Jesus says to Mary, "Touch me not!" I always thought this intriguingly weird. After all, what was going on in the resurrection of Jesus that would not allow someone to touch his body? What would have happened if she'd touched it anyway? I think I'd seen too many movies and *Star Trek* episodes. I was thinking back to the *Star Trek* beaming-up process where you don't want to stick your hand in a body that is reassembling!

Then I got to college. I remember the first time we read this passage in the Greek. It was like a lightbulb went off, and it left me bemused with my earlier thoughts. This isn't some mystical moment during a metamorphosis of Jesus' body. This is a simple and touching moment of reality.

(Ignore this paragraph if Greek causes your eyes to glaze over! Just move to the next paragraph!) Jesus said to Mary, *"mē mou haptou!"* (μή μου ἅπτου). The verb ("touch" or "hold") is an imperative (command) in the present tense coupled with a "negative" (which means "stop" or "quit"). In strict Greek grammar, a negative coupled with a present imperative verb means "Stop doing something," not "Don't start doing something."

In other words, Jesus wasn't saying "Don't touch me." Jesus was saying "Don't cling to me," or even, "Let go!" (undoubtedly with a smile). Jesus then adds, "I haven't ascended yet to the Father." In other words, "I'm going to be around a good bit still!" So Jesus put Mary to work, "Go tell the brothers" and assured her that he would still be around for her to see later!

Once this intrigue of the verse left me, the reality of the verse set in. Of course Mary was hugging Jesus (or perhaps falling down, was clinging to his feet)! Of course she was overjoyed and taken with the moment! She was stunned, her weeping subsided, and she was overcome with joy. I don't get to physically hug the Lord, but he resides in me as a believer. His reality is present in my heart and mind. This truth should kindle joy in me. I want to embrace my Savior's reality and resurrection with excitement, even as he puts me to work for him.

Lord, give me a true sense of your reality. Let the joy of being with you fill my heart. And Lord, please put me to work for you! In Jesus' name, amen.

APRIL 14

Mary Magdalene went and announced to the disciples, "I have seen the Lord"—and that he had said these things to her. (Jn. 20:18)

What a difference an encounter with the Lord makes! Today's passage conveys an often-missed moment that while maybe not as stark as Paul's encounter with Jesus on the road to Damascus certainly comes close.

The passage is set within a larger context of resurrection Sunday. Mary Magdalene went to the tomb to anoint the dead body of Jesus, something that had not occurred immediately after his death because of the Sabbath. Mary found the tomb empty and went to Peter and John ("the disciple whom Jesus loved" is the phrase John uses). The two men returned to the tomb, saw it empty, and believing in the resurrected Jesus, went home. Mary stood there still weeping, not believing in a resurrection, but thinking the body of Jesus was surely stolen.

Then Mary encounters Jesus! At first mistaking him for the gardener, once Jesus engages Mary in dialogue, she realizes it is indeed the resurrected Lord. Jesus speaks compassionately to the tearful Mary and charges her with a task. Mary is instructed to go give testimony to Jesus' brothers about his resurrection. While some wonder if this is the actual brothers of Jesus, who certainly came to faith early, or the disciples, the result is the same. Mary goes immediately to the disciples announcing, "I have seen the Lord!"

One should not overlook the responsibility Jesus set before Mary. By having Mary Magdalene testify that Jesus is the resurrected Lord, Jesus is rewriting Jewish culture and teaching. Under the Judaism of Jesus' day, women were not allowed to give testimony to anything of note. (This is recorded in the Talmud at Rosh Ha-Shanah 1:8.) Yet even in his resurrection, Jesus didn't let convention undermine right and wrong. Mary was the right person to have this responsibility and she handled it perfectly.

Mary's encounter with the risen Lord took her from a weepy mourner into active and joyful service for the Lord. This charges my batteries! I want to encounter the risen Lord and move into active and joyful service. For many, the question is, "How do I encounter the risen Lord?" Certainly Jesus has ascended to the Father at this point in time, but that doesn't mean one can't encounter him. When one studies with eyes of faith, when one's heart is sensitive to the truth of what Jesus has done, when one grows in understanding of the significance of the death of Christ on one's behalf, when one enters into worship, seeking to behold God in his glory and proclaim that vocally, one encounters the risen Jesus. And in that encounter, the world changes.

Lord, open my eyes and ears. Give me faith. May I proclaim your glory in Jesus, amen.

APRIL 15

On the evening of that day, the first day of the week, the doors being locked where the disciples were for fear of the Jews, Jesus came and stood among them and said to them, "Peace be with you." (Jn. 20:19)

Today's passage is one that is often read through too quickly as one follows the ongoing plot of Jesus manifesting his risen body to his disciples. Within today's verse, John sets up a contrast not to be missed.

It is the evening of Easter Sunday. The disciples are cognizant that Jesus was resurrected, but they know little more than that. They have gathered together and locked the doors, uncertain what the unbelieving Jews might do to them. After all, the unbelieving Jewish authorities had already bribed Judas into betraying Jesus, had pushed the arrest of Jesus into a death sentence, and would possibly be on a rampage now that Jesus was resurrected. The disciples feared for their safety and locked the doors.

Into this scene of fear and concern comes Jesus. The first words on Jesus' lips are "*Shalom lechem*" or in English, "Peace be with you." Jesus wishes these fearful, uncertain disciples, *shalom* peace. Now, "*shalom*" was a typical Hebrew greeting, but not one without meaning. The reason the greeting was so common lies in the depth of meaning of the word *shalom*.

Shalom has a wide range of meaning in biblical times. It referenced one at peace, but also "safety." Wishing someone *shalom* meant wishing them completeness, being uninjured, sound, of good welfare, at peace with oneself with the world and with God. It spoke to one being tranquil and content. These are the blessings that Jesus pronounced upon his believing, yet scared and directionless, disciples.

Today's passage speaks to me. There are events in my life that turn me upside down in my faith. Yes, I believe in God and I believe in his Son. Yet, some things happen that leave me a bit frightened, worried about what others might do, concerned about what may befall me, anxious about the unfolding future, troubled in my heart and mind, agitated with others, nervous about what is upcoming, in despair that I may not be up to a certain task, crippled by pain at what has unfolded . . . the list goes on and on. Into this turmoil comes the risen Jesus. Jesus speaks *shalom* peace to my heart. When I listen to him in faith, Jesus calms my storming soul. He brings a wholeness and faithful acceptance that all will be okay. The Jesus who calmed the sea, calms my chaos. Paul calls this the "peace that passes understanding" (Phil. 4:7).

I need to hear the words of Jesus and walk in his shalom peace.

Lord, please walk me through life's turbulence and give me peace. In Jesus, amen.

APRIL 16

On the evening of that day, the first day of the week, the doors being locked where the disciples were for fear of the Jews, Jesus came and stood among them and said to them, "Peace be with you." When he had said this, he showed them his hands and his side. Then the disciples were glad when they saw the Lord. Jesus said to them again, "Peace be with you. As the Father has sent me, even so I am sending you." (Jn. 20:19–21)

Have you ever been weary, tired, worn out, and in need of a long soak in a hot tub of water? I mean the long soak that leaves your fingers looking like prunes. You can close your eyes and let the hot water soak away your stress and fatigue. The bathtub analogy comes to my mind in a spiritual sense when I read today's passage. It is a passage where I want to stop and soak in it. I want to luxuriate and bask in the way my Lord works.

As one soaks in this passage, it speaks to God's peace in the midst of fear and uncertainty. Jesus twice speaks "peace" upon the disciples. Beyond that, the passage conveys the blessed way God deals with us in our human frailty.

Jesus doesn't simply appear, say "peace," and leave. Jesus showed the disciples his hands and side. He let them see for themselves that he was real. He was no apparition; he was Jesus in the flesh. Jesus did this not as the exalted Lord he was (and is). Rather John's Greek makes it clear, Jesus stood in the middle of them all.

This is the way God loves us. He comes into our distress and insecurities and stands in the middle of them. He shows his love in real ways, seeking to confirm for us who he is, what he has done for us, and his continued love and concern.

As I bathe in this passage, I am also impressed that God doesn't call us to faith and mission based on some blind faith. God gives us reasons for believing. He came in the midst of the disciples and showed them his hands with the holes, and his side where the spear had pierced, and gave solid, real reasons for the disciples' faith.

Similarly, God comes into our lives and provides rational reasons for our faith. We don't blindly believe in God, but we use our minds and consider thoughtfully the evidence for God, his love, and the resurrected Jesus. (See my book, *Christianity on Trial* for further thoughts on this.)

I love this story of the resurrected Jesus. I love the way it confirms for me that God loves me. God doesn't love me because I know enough, because I am confident enough, because my faith is solid enough. God comes to me in love to help me grow into who I should be for him.

Thank you, God. Thank you for your love. Thank you for seeking me out. In Jesus, amen.

APRIL 17

Simon Peter said to them, "I am going fishing." They said to him, "We will go with you." They went out and got into the boat. . . . Just as day was breaking, Jesus stood on the shore. . . . That disciple whom Jesus loved therefore said to Peter, "It is the Lord!" When Simon Peter heard that it was the Lord, he put on his outer garment, for he was stripped for work, and threw himself into the sea. The other disciples came in the boat, dragging the net full of fish, for they were not far from the land, but about a hundred yards off. (Jn. 21:3–8)

Recently we went to Disney World. The experience reminded me of when I was very young, and we would go to Six Flags amusement park. We would try to get there early, and we would routinely run to each ride to get in the line as quickly as possible to minimize the waiting time. I confess, at my recent Disney World trip, I didn't run one time to get on a ride. Something's happened as I aged.

I don't think I am alone. The older I get, the less I run to get somewhere. Patience comes with age. However, there are still times . . . It takes something pretty rare, but I still find myself running when something is *so exciting* I can't wait to get to it.

Today's passage illustrates this point in a touching way. Several of the apostles were, by training and profession, fishermen. In the weeks following Jesus' resurrection, several had returned to fishing. Peter and John, with other disciples, got into a boat to fish during the night. The fishing was deplorable. It was one of those nights where it seemed no fish were in the Sea of Galilee. As morning was breaking, the boat was about a football field length from shore. Jesus called out to the fishermen, "Did you catch anything?" (Something I frequently ask folks I see fishing!) A disciple shouted back, "Nope!" and Jesus told them to try the right side of the boat. They threw the net in and caught more fish than they could easily haul into the boat. At that point, John recognized the man on shore as Jesus. He proclaimed to the others, "It is the Lord!" and the rowing for shore began in earnest.

Peter was not going to wait for the boat to get rowed to shore. He got on his robe, and he jumped overboard! Peter swam for the Lord, the water equivalent of running out of joy and excitement. Peter wanted to see Jesus, be with Jesus, talk to Jesus, and not miss one minute of time with Jesus.

This story motivates me. I want to recognize Jesus in my life, and I want to run to him. I want more time with Jesus. I want to spend more time talking to Jesus. I want to be in his presence in worship, prayer, celebration, and joy. I want Jesus in the good times and bad. I want Jesus from the morning through the night.

Lord God, be with me. Show me Jesus. May I revel in your presence. In him, amen.

APRIL 18

That very day two of them were going to a village named Emmaus, about seven miles from Jerusalem, and they were talking with each other about all these things that had happened. While they were talking and discussing together, Jesus himself drew near and went with them. But their eyes were kept from recognizing him. And he said to them, "What is this conversation that you are holding with each other as you walk?" And they stood still, looking sad. (Lk. 24:13-16)

As a young man, I remember listening to the contemporary Christian band, Dogwood. They had a song called "Journey Music." It spoke of an encounter Steve Chapman had with a widow and how lonely the widow felt on the journey into eternity. The song recounted the lifting of the widow's burden as Steve sang of God's love. "Journey music," the song calls it—music to lift the soul while traveling our journey to the Father.

Luke was tuned into the "journey" motif. Both in today's passage from Luke and in Acts (the story of the Ethiopian eunuch in Acts 8:26-40), Luke tells a similar story with different characters. Today's passage recounts the two-hour walk two followers of Jesus had Easter Sunday after the resurrection. Only one disciple is named (Cleopas), but in the story line, in spite of their time spent following Jesus, the two were both rather ignorant of what Scripture had to say about Jesus the Messiah.

The resurrected Jesus joined the travelers on the road, but they didn't recognize him. Jesus probed their conversation, and the two stopped walking in sadness. Jesus then spoke to them about the Old Testament's teaching about the Messiah. Jesus patiently explained the many prophesies stating that the Messiah would come, would suffer for the sins of humanity, and die before entering into his glory. This buzzed the two disciples and, arriving at their destination, they begged Jesus to stay with them and dine. Only then did they realize who Jesus was and they got up, racing back to Jerusalem to report to the apostles.

I am nurtured by this story on many levels. The focus for me today is on the journey. These two were sad. God had been at work, but they didn't see it. God was doing the pivotal events for all of history, but they were blind to it. God was giving them eternal life and victory, but they didn't understand it. These two didn't see God's work overall, didn't see Jesus in the Scriptures, and didn't recognize Jesus on the road. They were spiritually blind, and it left them sad. Then Jesus opened their eyes. He taught them. He revealed God's love expressed in all his glory. Their sadness turned to excitement, and their lives changed forever.

When I am sad, I need to see Jesus in his glory. This is journey music for me. This is something to live on each day.

Dear Lord, I would see Jesus. Open my eyes and heart, please. In him, amen.

APRIL 19

And he said to them, "O foolish ones, and slow of heart to believe all that the prophets have spoken! Was it not necessary that the Christ should suffer these things and enter into his glory?" (Lk. 24:25–26)

Some things in life are optional; others are necessary. What I eat is optional; that I eat is necessary. The difference between what we want and what we need is often profound. Today's passage gives an eternal glimpse into this truth.

As a young man, I used to acknowledge the marvelous gift of Jesus dying for my sins. I would sing songs of gratitude and thank God in my prayers for that sacrifice. Yet, in the back of my mind, often lay this awkward doubt, "If dying for my sins was such a big deal, why didn't he just do it another way?" After all, since God is God, couldn't he just *decide* to forgive my sins?

This thought I harbored was destroyed when I learned a few things about God. Those things are inherent in today's passage. Jesus doesn't say in this passage his dying was optional. Jesus' sacrificial dying was "necessary." It had to be done. Treatises are properly written on this subject. A one-page, one-day devotional is hardly enough. But several points can still be made and meditated upon.

First, God is an ethical and moral being. God has very specific traits that center on what we as humans call "behavior." God is "good," not evil. God is "right," not wrong. God has an "other's centered love," not a "self-centered love." God is "truthful," not a "liar." In this, God is "perfect," not "sinful." Furthermore, God is not an amorphous, changing being. Neither is God an ethical amoeba, shaped ethically one way one day, and then transformed into another ethical shape the next. God is the same yesterday, today, and tomorrow. (This is a good thing. It means we can rely on God to do as he says!)

Second, humanity has a sin-based impediment to relating with God. "Sin" describes something contrary to God's ethics, something God, by definition, cannot do. Sin cannot exist in fellowship with God. Sin is a corruption, a cancer, and like cancer, must be destroyed for true life to exist. As Paul said it, "the wages of sin are death" (Rom. 6:23). The destruction of sin is synonymous with sin's death.

Third, the perfect sinless Jesus, through a divine transference, took on the sins of the world. Jesus died with and for those sins. By this, and through his resurrection, Jesus offered humanity an ability to approach a "just" and unchanging God with the "just" penalty paid for sin. For sinners to live with God, it was necessary for Jesus to die!

Lord, words escape me. But thank you for your sacrifice. With deep gratitude in Jesus, amen.

And beginning with Moses and all the Prophets, he interpreted to them in all the Scriptures the things concerning himself. (Lk. 24:27)

Someone came up to me once and, seeing a picture of my four daughters, said, "My they're beautiful!" I replied, with great sincerity, "They are as pretty on the inside as they are the outside." I meant this then and mean it today. The outside appearance comes and goes, but what one is on the inside is what really counts. I am thankful God didn't make humans simply pretty packages. God gave humans minds and wills. This allows us to make choices, to learn, to discern, to be more than a pretty puppet or computer.

God charges people to use and develop their minds. Faith and a relationship with God are calls to consciousness, not blind mindlessness. Paul spoke of the importance of "renewing" one's mind (Rom. 12:2). In the same passage, Paul tells the reader that this will enable the reader to "by testing . . . discern what is the will of God." God gave people minds to use them!

Not surprisingly, then, Jesus didn't just plop onto the scene when incarnated. The life, ministry, death, and resurrection of Jesus wasn't an unforeseen event. God had sent anticipatory prophetic indications of what would come to pass in Jesus. These date back to the garden of Eden itself.

In the garden, after the sin of Adam and Eve, upon their expulsion from Paradise, God promised that through one male offspring of woman (the Hebrew is that specific), God would undo the work of destruction wrought through the serpent and sin. As Genesis unfolded in history, in calling Abraham, God promised to bless all nations through one who would be his genetic offspring. Moses was a preeminent prophet of God, yet near his death, Moses told the people God would be raising up another prophet like himself. Over and over in the Hebrew Scriptures, it is noted that no one like Moses had yet arisen.

King David was assured that one of his offspring would reign forever and ever. This promise held, even after Israel and Judah no longer had any kings. During the ministry of the prophets, many psalms were written, many prophetic words were given that predicted and informed the discerning student when and where the Messiah would come. Even in the prophetic story of Jonah, where the prophet is "dead" in the belly of the fish for three days and nights, there is an indicator of what would happen to God's chosen.

God made me with a mind; God wants me to use it. God speaks. I should hear him.

Lord, thank you for the delicate and great way you created me. May I bring my mind and gifts to your service today. In Jesus, amen.

APRIL 21

And beginning with Moses and all the Prophets, he interpreted to them in all the Scriptures the things concerning himself. (Lk. 24:27)

I love to go to Spanish-speaking countries with my wife. Her Spanish reflects a lifetime of usage and study, including multiple college degrees. She flies through Spanish as easily as English. Left to myself, my Spanish is limited to vague memories of what I learned in eighth grade, reinforced by eating in Tex-Mex restaurants since. Left to myself, I am in the dark among Spanish speakers, but with Becky the world opens up. Becky becomes my translator, and everything makes sense. I am at home.

"Translate" is a marvelous way to explain one of the words in today's passage. Luke is writing about the journey from Jerusalem to Emmaus by two disciples on Easter Sunday. The disciples are sad and stuck on their perception of reality. They thought that Jesus would be the redeemer of Israel, but instead Jesus was killed. They were three days out from the death, and while they had heard from some that Jesus was alive, no one had seen Jesus. They may have had a smidgeon of hope, but they didn't believe it.

Jesus joins them on their journey, although at first, they didn't recognize him. Jesus hears their sad lament over what had happened and then upbraids them, calling them unthinking and slow! At that point, still unknown as Jesus, Jesus begins to "explain" or "interpret" the prophetic words of Moses and the other Old Testament prophets that bore testimony to the suffering, death, and resurrection of the Lord. The word Luke uses that the English Standard Version translated as "interpreted" is the Greek word that can be translated as "translated"! (Luke's companion Paul used the same word over and over in 1 Corinthians 14 requiring a translation of someone who speaks in tongues.)

Here is the full picture: the two disciples were in the dark. They had factual knowledge about Jesus. They knew their Old Testament. But they didn't understand it as they needed to. They needed the insight of Jesus. They needed an interpreter or translator. Paul explains some of this early in 1 Corinthians when he wrote that God's Spirit helps one understand spiritual things. Without God's insight, without God's personal translating work, one might understand the words we read, but one won't fathom the spiritual riches of God.

Everyone who reads Scripture should seek God's help in understanding what is read. It is fully appropriate in all Bible study and meditation to pray for God to open one's eyes, to soften one's heart, and to clean out one's ears! I need to read with understanding, and for that, I need a translator!

Lord, please open my eyes to Scripture. Give me wisdom and understanding to read and live the truths of what you reveal. In Jesus' name, amen.

APRIL 22

And beginning with Moses and all the Prophets, he interpreted to them in all the Scriptures the things concerning himself. (Lk. 24:27)

What transpired when Jesus spent hours explaining the Old Testament prophecies about him to the two disciples on the road to Emmaus? No one recorded the conversation, so we can't know the precise dialogue; however, the Bible is replete with teachings on this subject, so we don't have to look far to see the points Jesus likely made. This area is so important and ripe with devotional messages and teaching that I will spend several more days sitting on this passage, as I try to explain a number of messages and story lines that Jesus could have delivered.

Jesus started his explanations with Moses. Moses was born during terrible times for Israel. While the Israelites first came into Egypt as welcome foreigners, over the centuries, as the power structure in Egypt changed, the Israelites were no longer treated fairly. The Pharaohs had enslaved the Israelites, using them as an underpaid, ill-treated work force. The correct term used by the biblical writers is that the Israelites were "slaves," under the harsh ownership of the Pharaoh, forced to do the Pharaoh's bidding. The existence was miserable, but there was nothing anyone could do about it. The Pharaoh was even able to order the slaughter of innocent newborns to keep his slave force under control.

Jesus could have started his explanation during the time the Israelites were slaves because, not only was it a constant theme always fresh in the minds of the Jews, but it was also a strong metaphor for the condition of humanity before the sacrifice and resurrection of Jesus.

Paul put it this way in his letter to the Romans, "You once presented your members as slaves to impurity and to lawlessness leading to more lawlessness" (Rom. 6:19). The human condition is one of a slavery, an addiction, to sin. Sin begets sin, begets sin. Some are less obvious in their sin than others, but when one considers sins of pride, envy, selfishness, and more, there is no doubt that sin enslaves. Furthermore, there is no human who on her or his own is able to conquer this slavery of sin. I can't free myself, regardless of how hard I try. It is going to take the hand of God to free me, just as it took God to bring Israel out of slavery and into a land of promise.

As I contemplate this, I understand more fully the role that the resurrected Jesus plays in my life. Jesus has come to set me free from sin and its vicious cycle. No longer do I live under sin's death sentence or sin's control. I am set free to grow and walk in the victory of Jesus, as we will explore with more devotions concerned with this Emmaus passage.

Lord, thank you for the forgiveness and freedom found in Jesus. Help me understand how to best walk holy before you, released from sin's grip by and through Jesus, amen.

APRIL 23

And beginning with Moses and all the Prophets, he interpreted to them in all the Scriptures the things concerning himself. (Lk. 24:27)

Perhaps nowhere in the story of Moses is the prophetic picture of Jesus represented more than in the story of the Passover. The story, detailed in Exodus 11–14, is notable in many aspects.

The Passover was called for because the people of Israel were enslaved to the Pharaoh, and there was nothing anyone could do about it. Moses tried. Aaron tried. But nothing would move the Pharaoh's heart. The bondage was absolute until Passover. Paul would use similar terminology to mirror the human bondage to sin. Sin has a grip on everyone that try as one might, one can't break.

So, to counter this absolute slavery, God called forth the Passover. The firstborn of everyone (and even the cattle) in Egypt was going to die, save those who had the blood of a Passover lamb painted on their homes. The Passover lamb wasn't to be just any lamb. The lamb must be male, and it was to be as perfect as could be found ("without blemish"). The people were then to sacrifice each lamb. The blood of the lamb was to be painted on the two door posts as well as the lintel, or head bar, over the door. God said that when the angel of death visited Egypt, the land of sin, and saw the sacrificial blood of the lamb over the homes of the Israelites God would cause death to "passover" those homes. Those covered by the blood would be spared death and be delivered from slavery.

The apostle Paul would call out Jesus as "our Passover lamb" (1 Cor. 5:7) for obvious reasons. Jesus was male, without blemish, and was sacrificed so that his people could be redeemed from the slavery of sin, and so that his people would not suffer the death that results from sin. God sees the blood of Jesus, and that is enough.

As Jesus undoubtedly explained to the two on the road to Emmaus, these Old Testament passages not only illuminate who Jesus was and what Jesus endured, but Jesus' impact on all of us. With Christ dying sacrificially in my stead, I can walk each day knowing that sin no longer has a tyrannical grip on me. Am I now sinless? Of course not! Do I still struggle with sin? Absolutely! But I struggle knowing that the victory has already been won. Forgiveness has already been justly granted. He who is at work within me is greater than the sin and will be transforming me little by little each day into the clearer image of his Son. God set out a picture of Calvary over a thousand years before the events at Calvary. He set me free from the law of sin and death. And I am truly *eternally* grateful.

Lord, thank you for Christ's sacrifice. Give me greater victory over sin in him, amen.

APRIL 24

And beginning with Moses and all the Prophets, he interpreted to them in all the Scriptures the things concerning himself. (Lk. 24:27)

Jesus explained to the disciples how the story of Moses unfolded the plan and work of God in Christ. But not only Moses. Jesus also walked through the Prophets in his teaching time on the road to Emmaus. I suspect one of the prophetic passages Jesus would have explained is found in Isaiah 40:1-11.

Isaiah prophesied some seven hundred years before the death of Christ. Among the many prophetic words captured in the book of Isaiah is the Isaiah 40 passage that begins with a prophetic overview of what God would finally provide for his people. "Comfort my people . . . her iniquity is pardoned." The Prophet then announces the role and ministry of John the Baptist, "A voice cries, 'In the wilderness prepare the way of the Lord . . .'" It is then that the Prophet declares, "the glory of the Lord shall be revealed!"

Isaiah was writing early, compared to the events being fulfilled in Jesus, but Isaiah assured the people who waited for seven hundred years, "the grass withers, the flowers fade, but the word of the Lord stands forever." In other words, God was going to do this. Period. Then Isaiah calls out the word that will be heard from Jerusalem. In Hebrew, it is "*bashar*," or "good news." The Greek word used in translation by Jewish scholars centuries before Jesus is "*euangelidzo*" or what is translated in the New Testament as "gospel." Yes, Isaiah said the gospel would be proclaimed from Jerusalem in the time of the Messiah.

Isaiah then recounts that this future coming of God will be with both judgment and mercy. God will repay people for their deeds. But for the people of God, a sheep/shepherd analogy is employed. God will tend to his people as a shepherd his flock. God will lead them and feed them. Those who are too young to keep up, God will carry and nurture until they are grown sufficiently. Those burdened down, like pregnant sheep, God will lead *gently*. God will meet his people in all their particular needs and take care of them individually.

Had I been on the road to Emmaus, this would have given me great comfort. It gives me great comfort just reading about those on the road! The resurrected Jesus is the greatest news. He comes to me empowered by God to walk with me, to lead me, to feed me, to nurture me, to help me grow, giving me gentle guidance in the midst of my worries and burdens. What an awesome God I serve. How dare I ever look to another person or thing for my daily sustenance. God is assuredly all I need. In that truth, I can live today with joy.

Lord, give me eyes to follow you. Thank you for unfailing love and care in Jesus, amen.

APRIL 25

While they were talking and discussing together, Jesus himself drew near and went with them. But their eyes were kept from recognizing him. And he said to them, "What is this conversation that you are holding with each other as you walk?" . . . Then one of them, named Cleopas, answered him, "Are you the only visitor to Jerusalem who does not know the things that have happened there in these days?" And he said to them, "What things?" And they said to him, "Concerning Jesus of Nazareth, a man who was a prophet mighty in deed and word before God and all the people. . . ." And he said to them, "O foolish ones, and slow of heart to believe all that the prophets have spoken! Was it not necessary that the Christ should suffer these things and enter into his glory?" And beginning with Moses and all the Prophets, he interpreted to them in all the Scriptures the things concerning himself. So they drew near to the village to which they were going. He acted as if he were going farther, but they urged him strongly, saying, "Stay with us, for it is toward evening and the day is now far spent." So he went in to stay with them. (Lk. 24:15-19, 25-29)

Have you ever missed the obvious? I might be the king of overlooking what is plainly before me at times. But I am not alone! Today's story of Jesus' disciples gives me good company.

In this post-resurrection story of Jesus, the disciples on the road to Emmaus have no clue Jesus has joined them on their journey. They are trying to get a grip on all that has happened with the crucifixion and the reportedly empty tomb, but they are a bit clueless. Jesus asks them the open question about what happened, and in their explanation, they offered that Jesus was "a prophet mighty in deed and word before God and all the people." Of course, as they speak of Jesus, they have no clue they are talking *to Jesus*. That is critical to understanding the humorous error Luke puts into his account.

Jesus then *demonstrates* his role as "prophet mighty in deed and word" by opening up the Old Testament and explaining it in great detail, showing how God had foretold the sufferings of the Messiah, as well as the Messiah's subsequent glorification. These two disciples of the Lord got an uninterrupted lesson explaining the central work of God among humanity. Jesus taught them in words of power, and though they thought Jesus was the unknowing rube, they were the ones at that moment not seeing Jesus for who he was! The truth was staring them in the face, and they were oblivious to it.

I have a friend Rick who had spent years searching for God. I and a number of other godly folks had been speaking into Rick's heart and mind about the Lord for a long time. One day Rick said to me, "I wish God would send me a personal message about this stuff." I said, "Who do you think sent me and these others to you?" The lightbulb then went off. God is still reaching and speaking to his people today. We need to see him.

Lord, open my eyes to you. Teach me. May I see and hear your voice in Jesus, amen.

They said to each other, "Did not our hearts burn within us while he talked to us on the road, while he opened to us the Scriptures?" (Lk. 24:32)

If one goes to the drugstore, one finds many medicines for heartburn. Today's passage speaks of heart burn, but not the kind that one has with indigestion! This heart burn was for the truth of God, for the insight of Scripture, and for the implications truth and insight have on life.

The passage comes in the middle of Luke's account of two of Jesus' disciples walking to Emmaus on Easter Sunday. Unaware of the resurrection, although they had heard rumors about it, the two were in the dark until Jesus came to them on their journey. They didn't recognize Jesus, but Jesus intervened in their conversation, and then proceeded to give them an Old Testament tutorial on God's prophetic promises about the Messiah. Afterward, over the dinner meal, their eyes were opened, and they recognized Jesus for who he was. Jesus then disappeared, and the disciples made the comment above.

When I read the story to Emmaus, I pause at this point. Luke was writing on a scroll. People didn't make their own scrolls, by and large, but rather purchased them. You could buy a scroll in different lengths, not unlike buying a blank book or journal today. The largest scroll one could buy was determined by its wieldiness. Some scrolls reached a size where one just couldn't work with the scroll if it got any larger. Luke had bought that jumbo-size scroll. He wrote the longest gospel, and it fills the longest scroll that he could buy. At this point in the Emmaus story, Luke is nearing the end of his scroll. In other words, for Luke, every word counts. That is why I pause at this point in the story.

Luke didn't have to add this little verse. His gospel would have read fine without us knowing the two disciples had this conversation. But Luke chose to put it in. Luke wanted his readers to read this statement. So as I read it, I pause and meditate on it, and I believe I begin to see why it is worth the scroll space it took.

Scripture explained and understood can produce a burning inside one's heart. It is a mighty majestic matter that God would speak to humanity through his prophets. That the Creator of the universe chose particular individuals, placed his words into their minds and mouths, secured that those words would both be recorded and kept for later usage and understanding is amazing. Understanding what God has to say is an immense privilege and opportunity. It begins with reading the word, something I try to do each day. For the words of God can't burn in my heart if they aren't placed in my heart. I want to open the Scriptures more. Scriptures burning in my heart is a good heartburn!

Lord, please help me in my commitment to dwell in your word. Give me insight and understanding as I study and read. In Jesus, amen.

APRIL 27

They said to each other, "Did not our hearts burn within us while he talked to us on the road, while he opened to us the Scriptures?" And they rose that same hour and returned to Jerusalem. And they found the eleven and those who were with them gathered together, saying, "The Lord has risen indeed, and has appeared to Simon!" (Lk. 24:32–34)

Medical science has produced a plethora of medications for heartburn. Tums, Rolaids, Pepto Bismol, and more. Medical heartburn and acid reflux are not welcome by anyone. But while today's passage speaks of "heart burn," it isn't the discomforting kind. To the contrary.

The context of the heart burn is important. The events occurred on Easter afternoon into evening. Jesus was resurrected, but the disciples had only heard a rumor or two, and they didn't have confidence in the reports. While walking from Jerusalem to Emmaus, the two were deep in discussions over the events of the weekend when Jesus joined them on the road. Jesus was incognito. For reasons not given, Jesus chose to speak with them without revealing who he was. Jesus explained to the two the Old Testament prophetic messages that explained not only the necessity of the Messiah dying for the sins of others, but also the truth of the Messiah's physical resurrection. The two were enthralled. Arriving at Emmaus, they asked Jesus to join them for dinner. Jesus agreed and prayed over the meal. Only then did the two realize they had been sharing the road with Jesus. At this point, today's passage is inserted into Luke's narrative.

When the disciples said, "Did not our hearts burn within us while he talked to us . . . while he opened the Scriptures . . ." they were speaking of a good heart burn, not indigestion! Much as the expression is used in Psalm 39:3 or Jeremiah 20:9, "burning in the heart" was a way to say there was an emotional effect to the truth unfolding before their eyes.

That is the way of God exposing his people to the truths of Scripture. Scriptural truth should never be simply an intellectual exercise. When the truth of who Jesus is opens up to the believer, it creates a reaction that consumes one totally, like a fire. It begins in an often-dried heart, but bursts through the dryness into an open flame. The effect on the two was immediate.

Although night travel was inherently dangerous with unlit roads, unseen robbers easily hidden, and even beasts out for nighttime feeding, the two immediately left their destination and hustled back to where they had been earlier in the day. This stark U-turn was the fire's effect. They had their eyes opened to Scripture and then had seen Jesus. That joyful fire put any fears to rest. Excitement stirred. God was moving!

God, open my eyes to your word and to Jesus. Let me see you on the move, and may I joyfully move with you. In Jesus, amen.

APRIL 28

As they were talking about these things, Jesus himself stood among them, and said to them, "Peace to you!" But they were startled and frightened and thought they saw a spirit. And he said to them, "Why are you troubled, and why do doubts arise in your hearts? See my hands and my feet, that it is I myself. Touch me, and see. For a spirit does not have flesh and bones as you see that I have." And when he had said this, he showed them his hands and his feet. And while they still disbelieved for joy and were marveling, he said to them, "Have you anything here to eat?" They gave him a piece of broiled fish, and he took it and ate before them. (Lk. 24:36–43)

Are you familiar with the expression, "too good to be true!"? The expression is so common, it was even the title of a book written by English author Thomas Lupton in 1580. At one time or another, almost everyone struggles with accepting what is true and real when it flies in the face of expectations. Today's passage speaks to the difference between reality and expectation.

The apostles were not expecting to see Jesus. They weren't even fully cognizant of the physical resurrection of Jesus. At their best hope, Jesus might have been a spirit or apparition making periodic post-grave visits. After all, in 1 Samuel 28, the medium at Endor summoned an apparition of the deceased prophet Samuel at the behest of King Saul.

So when Jesus made his appearance recorded by Luke, the apostles were thinking it must have been a spirit or apparition. Jesus wanted there to be no mistake. He was physically present. The resurrection of Jesus was a pure, 100 percent, bona fide physical resurrection. If anyone had any doubt, Jesus offered them a chance to touch him and see that he had flesh and bones. Jesus even requested fish to eat as proof. After all, ghosts don't eat physical food! The apostles were faced with the reality of the true resurrected Lord. Yet even with the truth staring them in the face, "they disbelieved" at first. Luke explains that their joy was so great, that they marveled. It was too good to be true! Yet it was true, as they soon began to realize.

As I reflect on this, I am reminded of many things that are pure, 100 percent, bona fide truth. These are things that I might even accept in my head, but they seem to flee quickly from my heart. Many have trouble hanging onto certain truths. Do you realize that God loves you? I don't mean in a banal or trite way, or in some friendly way. I don't mean a conditional love you have earned by being good enough. I mean that God, knowing the innermost secrets of your heart and character, loves you fully. Too good to be true? Well it's the truth!

Lord, thank you for your love. It is too good to be true! I am thrilled by it. Help me appreciate it and accept it. In Jesus' name, amen.

APRIL 29

And calling the crowd to him with his disciples, he said to them, "If anyone would come after me, let him deny himself and take up his cross and follow me." (Mk. 8:34)

When I was young, we sang a song at church taken directly from this passage. We would sing it through once, and then as half of our group sang it a second time, the other half would sing a complementary part that included an overlay of "Hallelujah, he is King!" It was, and is, an important and interesting contrast.

Jesus did not have an easy end of life. We know little of his early life, but what we know gives no indication that it was inordinately difficult. He was born to devout parents. His earthly father was keen on keeping him and caring for him, despite having no role in Jesus' conception. The family made trips to Jerusalem for Passover, including one where twelve-year-old Jesus was so consumed in speaking with the rabbis that he didn't make the first leg of the trip home.

At some point, Jesus left the work and life at home for ministry on the road. This is where we get most of our information about him, and also where his life became manifestly harder. While Jesus still had a great time with his followers, enjoyed the presence of little children, took joy in defeating disease, demons, and death, he also had to endure mockery, ridicule, family strife, rejection, and attempted stoning all before those last horrid hours of betrayal, abuse, savage beating, and a most inhumane death, with nails biting into his wrists and feet.

Why? The Bible makes it plain Jesus suffered for others, not for himself. He had no personal need for suffering, nor was he powerless to stop it. But he didn't stop it because he suffered on behalf of his followers, those he loved more than life itself.

This same Jesus calls his followers to live like he did. He wants us to find a higher calling. He wants us aware that the needs of the kingdom outweigh the earthly desires of those in the kingdom. I should care more about the mission than my comfort. I should care more about his purposes than my cravings. Suffering for *his sake* and for the sake of his kingdom should not surprise me. Nor should it send me whimpering into a corner moaning, "*Why me?*" I need to be at peace with whatever God brings my way. Even more so, I need to welcome it.

I signed on to take up my cross and follow Jesus. After all, I am following the King of kings! Hallelujah, indeed!

Lord, take me where you will for the sake of your kingdom! Where you lead me I will follow. In Jesus' name, amen.

APRIL 30

For what does it profit a man to gain the whole world and forfeit his soul? (Mk. 8:36)

I love much about my country. Other countries have much to offer as well, but I like the way in the United States anyone from any social background can become president. Abraham Lincoln went from a log cabin to the White House. Anyone can.

This aspect of the United States is closely intertwined with our capitalism economy. People work for their personal gain, not simply for the whole of society. Save for taxes, capital that is generated is kept or used by the one who makes it. That can produce in some great levels of success as it fuels invention, productivity, and other marvelous things.

Yet it can also feed greed. People can become so consumer-driven that they lose sight of the important things in life. I had a lawyer friend who died recently. Only four weeks after he received his diagnosis he was dead. Two weeks before he died, he reached out to me as his "religious friend." He wondered if I had any friends near where he was hospitalized who might be able to comfort him in faith. I contacted my childhood minister who is semiretired and lives in that area of the country. My minister altered his schedule at once and went to the hospital that very day.

Over the next two weeks, my minister friend walked with my lawyer friend through the last days of his life. We had several chances to talk by phone before he died. He told me that he wished it hadn't taken his imminent death to get him to address the important things in life, but he was glad he had at least a chance to get it right, even if just for a few days.

My friend had made a lot of money in his day. My friend had spent a lot of money. He had a great family, and by the world's standards, a great life. But he was missing something money couldn't buy. He had missed an intimacy with the Lord himself. That intimacy transforms everything. It becomes the fulcrum around which one lives. It gives peace and comfort. It gives meaning and purpose.

I don't want to wait until my last week of life to find out what is important. I don't want the capitalistic drive of my homeland to distort my focus on the importance of knowing God and of having that unique righteousness that comes from the love and sacrifice of Jesus.

I could have the whole world, and it wouldn't hold a candle to having Jesus.

Lord, I give you my life. Don't let my eyes stray from you and your love. In Jesus, amen.

MAY 1

The Son of Man came eating and drinking, and they say, "Look at him! A glutton and a drunkard, a friend of tax collectors and sinners!" Yet wisdom is justified by her deeds. (Mt. 11:19)

If one wants to read the history of ancient Greek philosophy, one early source would be a Greek fellow named Diogenes Laërtius, who seems to have lived and written in the first half of the 200s AD. Diogenes is known for his work *Lives and Opinions of Eminent Philosophers.* In the fifth book, Diogenes writes of the famous Greek philosopher Aristotle (384–322 BC), who was a student of Plato and tutor to Alexander the Great. In the twentieth verse, Aristotle is asked, "What is a friend?" Aristotle replies, "A single soul dwelling in two bodies."

One Greek word for friend, from the days of Aristotle to the time of Diogenes is *philos* (φίλος). The word is still used today. A "philosopher" is a friend of wisdom (*sophos* in the Greek). Philadelphia is the city of friendship (or "brotherly love," another way to translate *philos*). The word *philos* is used in a most extraordinary way in today's passage.

The passage is quoting Jesus explaining his poor reception among many of the snooty, establishment Jews. One of their indictments against Jesus was that he was a "friend" (*philos*) to those who were considered low class, unholy, and even in many circles, outcasts. This passage has kept me from sleeping some nights. It is hard for me to fathom.

Jesus was and is God. Almighty God is beyond my comprehension. He fashioned the universe. He knows each soul on the planet, now and for all time. He knows our thoughts. He can number the hairs on everyone's heads. He is rightly worshipped by the heavenly creatures. His existence as a Triune God is unique and hard to fathom. He can intervene in the world with miracles. He is a fearsome and just God. He is a warrior God, seeking to defeat evil and to bring all things under his feet, where they belong. This awesome and, in a sense, unrelatable God, came to earth as a human and sought to be a friend to humanity. To top it all off, Jesus didn't seek to be friends only with the high and mighty, the rich and famous, or the holy Joes. Jesus sought out the outcasts, the sinners, those without the qualifications and became their friend.

Understanding that Aristotle uses the Greek word *philos* to mean that one is on such intimate and personal terms with another that it can be described as two souls in one body, then I begin to grasp the magnitude of today's passage. God wants an intimate friendship with me. Wow.

Lord, I'm not worthy of a glance from you, much less a deep and abiding friendship. But I am thankful for your love and caring. Thank you for being my friend in Jesus, amen.

MAY 2

Blessed are those who hunger and thirst for righteousness, for they shall be satisfied. . . . At that time Jesus went through the grain fields on the Sabbath. His disciples were hungry, and they began to pluck heads of grain and to eat. (Mt. 5:6; 12:1)

When one of my daughters and I first met Nora, the marvelous woman who was to become our daughter-in-law, it was over a great Italian meal at Jaime's in Oxford, England. As I was working on compiling a marvelous feast, our daughter Rebecca asked Nora, "Have you heard of the five 'love languages'?" (This phrase comes from a book that cites five basic ways different people show and receive love. They are acts of service, quality time, physical touch, words of affirmation, and gifts.) Nora had heard of them, and Rebecca then explained, "We Laniers have found there is a sixth love language—food. Especially chocolate."

Everyone laughed, but in my mind, I kept thinking Rebecca was onto something. I do love food. I love to make it, I love to serve it, and, I love to eat it. I suspect this is one reason the gospel of Matthew has a warm place in my heart. Matthew uses the word "hungry" more than a third of the times the word is used in the entire New Testament! In stories told in Matthew, Mark, and Luke, Matthew will insert the word "hungry" where Mark and Luke leave it out. (See Mt. 12:1 compared to Mk. 2:23 and Lk. 6:1.)

Hunger is a basic driving force of life. It can keep one up at night. It can motivate one to set aside other tasks in an effort to eat. It is a force to be reckoned with! Matthew knew that. I think he would have readily grasped the Lanier love language of food. This makes the first part of today's passage stand out to me.

Matthew the foodie understood the depths of Jesus' admonition that happiness would come when people hunger for righteousness. Righteousness entails holy and ethical living. It also was a judicial word reflecting someone who has right standing in a court of law. Matthew knew, and Jesus promised, that those who hungered for righteousness would be satisfied.

I take today's promise in two ways. First, when I prioritize being ethical and right in the way I live, I will live a satisfied life. I will find peace as I find myself well fed in doing right. Second, and more fundamental, when I seek to be declared right by the great eternal judge (God), then I will find myself declared not guilty by the sacrifice of Jesus. Jesus paid the price for my sins so I could be clean and righteous before God. That fact also makes it easier for me to live seeking to be ethical and righteous before others.

I want Matthew's attention to hunger, and I want to feast on righteousness!

Lord, I hunger for you. Fill me with your righteousness, please. In Jesus, amen.

MAY 3

And behold, some people brought to him a paralytic, lying on a bed. And when Jesus saw their faith, he said to the paralytic, "Take heart, my son; your sins are forgiven." And behold, some of the scribes said to themselves, "This man is blaspheming." But Jesus, knowing their thoughts, said, "Why do you think evil in your hearts? For which is easier, to say, 'Your sins are forgiven,' or to say, 'Rise and walk'? But that you may know that the Son of Man has authority on earth to forgive sins"—he then said to the paralytic—"Rise, pick up your bed and go home." And he rose and went home. When the crowds saw it, they were afraid, and they glorified God, who had given such authority to men. (Mt. 9:2–8)

I love typing in boldface. *I also love italics.* Exclamation marks are some of my favorites!!! These are just some of the ways writers today express emphasis. In the time when Matthew wrote his gospel, the Greek language didn't have these tools. No one underlined for emphasis, and emoticons were almost two thousand years in the future. Yet Matthew was not without tools for showing emphasis. One of his favorite tools was a Greek word, *idou*. This word doesn't always even get translated. Its power lies in the idea of "Pay attention to what follows!!! It is important and worthy of underlining or putting in bold print!!!"

Matthew uses this word twice in rapid succession in this small vignette. Matthew does this because he wants his readers to understand two competing emphatic ideas. First, *idou* is used and translated as "behold" in reference to the paralytic being brought into Jesus on a mat, carried by his friends. This is a scene that Matthew wants the reader to underscore. Jesus tells the paralytic to "take heart" or one could translate it, "be confident, be courageous!" Jesus then proclaims, "your sins are forgiven!"

Matthew then uses the emphatic word *idou* a second time, to draw special attention to a second presence in the story. Again translated as simply "behold," a number of the scribes present began thinking about the audacity of Jesus proclaiming the paralytic forgiven for his sins. Of course, someone can forgive another for the actions committed against the person. But no one has the right to forgive the sins committed against God! That is God's sole domain and right.

Yet that is who Jesus was and is—God. Jesus had that right, as Matthew will explain before the gospel is over. Jesus can pronounce the man's sins forgiven because Jesus will personally pay the death penalty for that man committing sins.

I want to be in the first emphasis group. I want my story to be that I came to Jesus hurt and paralyzed, and he forgave my sins and set me on a journey of service to him.

Lord, thank you for forgiveness in Jesus. May I walk in your service. In him, amen.

MAY 4

And Jesus cried out and said, "Whoever believes in me, believes not in me but in him who sent me. And whoever sees me sees him who sent me." (Jn. 12:44–45)

One of the most challenging parts of any case I try is taking an area that most jurors don't know anything about and explaining that area so that it can be understood. I have had trials with nonmedical persons on the jury where I had to explain the process of certain drugs on enzymes in the bloodstream. As I am typing this, I am picking a jury today who will need to be taught how asbestos can migrate from a woman's lungs to her ovaries. Part of my teaching generally includes figuring out an analogy or metaphor so the jury can relate the new knowledge to something they already know.

Jesus had a chance to do something similar in today's passage. We all should want to know God. We can read about him in the Old Testament, and sometimes we find that reassuring. We like the God who has love and mercy. But some of the Old Testament stories about God might leave him seeming harsh, arbitrary, angry, possessive, spiteful, or even petty. Let me add that I don't believe careful reading and understanding of the Old Testament leaves one with that picture, but at first glance, there are places that might lead one to think of God that way.

God wasn't satisfied with people wrongly thinking of him. So one reason for God sending Jesus was to show us who God is. Jesus was God in the flesh. When people saw him, they saw God. When they understood this, believing in him as God Incarnate, it helped them better understand God. God used the incarnation as a tool to help us understand God in ways we wouldn't be able to otherwise.

In Jesus the merciful, we see a God of mercy. In Jesus the kind, we see a God of kindness. In the patience of Jesus, we see a patient God. In Jesus' joy, we see the joy of God. In the quiet peace of Jesus, we understand a God of peace. In the goodness and purity of Jesus, we glimpse the goodness of a pure God. In the love of Jesus, we better understand the love of God.

After the incarnation and life of Jesus, God is no longer someone hard to know. We are no longer having to guess at his motives, cares, or concerns. In a real understandable sense, we see God at work interacting with people in loads of circumstances. We see his love for the unloved, his help for the needy, his comfort for the hurting, his instruction for the aimless, and his opposition to the proud. I can tell you about God by telling you about Jesus. Knowing Jesus is knowing God, and that changes everything.

Lord, thank you for revealing yourself in Jesus. May I know Jesus more and better each day. Be with me today, please. In Jesus' name, amen.

MAY 5

In the beginning was the Word, and the Word was with God, and the Word was God. He was in the beginning with God. (Jn. 1:1–2)

COFFEE! That's how my wife and several daughters start their day. Growing up, our house smelled of coffee in the morning because Dad's day never started without it. I was never a fan of the flavor, but the aroma brings back warm memories.

How do you start your day? With or without coffee, I suggest every day start with Jesus. Today's passage marks John's first words in his story of the Savior Jesus. John placed Jesus at the start. Not simply the start of each day, but Jesus was at the start of the first day! When things were just beginning, Jesus was there.

John writes the Greek passage in a way that gives an idea of something beyond the very first beginning of the universe. The Greek language has a "definite article," which is the grammatical label given to our English word, "the." It specifies the noun that follows. So, for example, we can speak of "the" food I ate for breakfast. English also has an "indefinite article," the label given to the words "a" and "an." These words precede nouns that aren't so specific as those preceded by "the." Greek doesn't have an indefinite article. It just has a definite article.

Why does that matter? Well, John writes today's passage *without* the definite article. Our translators put the word "the" into the translation to make it read less choppy, but John's gospel begins more literally, "In beginning was the word." We could read it as in "a beginning" or in "the beginning." Jesus is at the beginning of everything!

I think we all need to start every day with Jesus. Let Jesus be in our day's beginning. Let him be in the beginning of each of our projects, in our day's work, in our times of entertainment, in our relationships, in our thoughts, in our actions, in our study, in our conversations, in our goals, in our hobbies, in our prayers, hopes, dreams, and aspirations. Let Jesus be at every beginning we have!

What does that mean practically? We should acknowledge Jesus as ever-present. We should dedicate part of each day to prayerful reflection on how we can do all things to his glory and for his kingdom. We should seek his insight into what we are about. We should dedicate our efforts to him. We should give him the glory when things go well, and we should seek his mercy when we mess up.

Jesus in the morning. Maybe not in the place of coffee, but certainly with that first cup!

Lord, thank you for seeking a place in my life. May I place you at the beginning of all I do. In Jesus, amen.

MAY 6

When I saw him, I fell at his feet as though dead. But he laid his right hand on me, saying, "Fear not, I am the first and the last, and the living one. I died, and behold I am alive forevermore, and I have the keys of Death and Hades." (Rev. 1:17–18)

Most everyone fears something. Some fear heights; some fear flying. Some fear noises in the night. Some fear what faces them in the day, those difficult times of life everyone has to walk through. Some fear being alone, while others fear being in a crowd. Many, if not most people, fear death. What do you fear?

Today's passage recounts a day of exile in the life of Jesus' follower John. It was a day when Jesus made a physical appearance to John. By the time of this appearance, Jesus had died, been resurrected, and ascended to heaven. He had been gone from a physical presence on earth for about six decades. John had become a very old man. John was exiled to Patmos, a small island of two mountains joined by a spit of land off the coast of Turkey. On a clear day, standing on one of the mountains you could just make out the mainland, where ancient Ephesus thrived in John's day.

We don't know where John was looking, but what he saw in his exile scared him to death! John first heard Jesus talk to him, but turning saw the Savior in a way he'd never seen him before. Jesus had snow-white hair and eyes that flamed like fire. John fell to his face, petrified.

Jesus spoke words of reassurance to John. Jesus used words he had used with John and so many of Jesus' followers during his earthly ministry. "Fear not!" While Jesus frequently put his followers at ease with those words, at least one time he provided an interesting contrast for John. Less than a week before his crucifixion, Jesus came riding into Jerusalem on a donkey, a sign of an invading king who conquers by submission rather than war. Jesus quoted Zechariah 9:9 when he came in assuring the people, "Fear not . . . your king is coming, sitting on a donkey's colt" (John 12:15). In other words, Jesus conquers as we submit to him, not by force.

In the revelation vision, however, John saw Jesus in a different light. Jesus was no tame Messiah riding on a donkey. Jesus was the ruling Messiah who was about to wage war on his enemies and bring them into submission. Even as a warring God, however, John needn't fear, nor should any of Jesus' followers. For what becomes apparent is that God wars on our behalf. He isn't coming to conquer his followers but to defeat those who oppose him. Because of that, the followers of Jesus needn't fear. We needn't fear Jesus nor anyone else. We needn't fear the night or day, life or death. We have a God who is in control who can and will conquer all enemies. Fear not!

Lord, infuse my life with the assurance of who you are and how you care. In Jesus, amen.

MAY 7

Fear not, I am the first and the last, and the living one. I died, and behold I am alive forevermore, and I have the keys of Death and Hades. (Rev. 1:17–18)

The Bible doesn't use the word "trinity" in describing God. In fact, the Bible doesn't use the word "trinity" at all! The church devised the word as a way to describe the being we know as "God" who is both one and yet three. As the old hymn "Holy, Holy, Holy" proclaims, "God [singular] in three persons, blessed Trinity." This Christian understanding was formalized in the doctrine of the Trinity at the council of Nicaea in 325, but its roots go back to the pages of Scripture. Passages like today's proclaim the concept, even though they don't use the term.

Jesus is speaking to John while John is exiled for his faith on the island of Patmos, just offshore ancient Ephesus. Jesus proclaims to John "I am," which is *ego eimi* (ἐγώ εἰμι) in Greek. These are no ordinary words to John. Writing his gospel just a handful of years earlier, John quoted those words from the mouth of Jesus twenty-four times in his gospel, more than twice what is found in the other three gospels combined. These were important words. John knew that Jesus used these words to echo the voice from the burning bush that spoke to Moses over a thousand years earlier on the slopes of Mount Sinai.

Recorded in Exodus 3, God spoke from a burning bush calling Moses to rescue the Israelites from the Pharaoh's slavery. Moses asked God what he should say to Israel when Israel quizzed Moses on who exactly this God was who had sent him. God told Moses, as translated into Greek by the Jewish scholars two centuries before Jesus, "*ego eimi*" (ἐγώ εἰμι). "I am," in English. This is the passage where God identifies himself as "Yahweh" in the Hebrew. The "I am" is the one true God.

Jesus leaves no doubt about his deity as he continues to tell John that he (Jesus) is "the first and the last." This phrase God used for himself multiple times in Isaiah. For example, "This is what the LORD says—Israel's King and Redeemer, the LORD Almighty: I am the first and I am the last; apart from me there is no God" (Is. 44:6).

Jesus is God. The depths and complexities of God as a being we struggle to understand, but the historical church vocalizing it as the Trinity is rooted in the biblical truth that God is more than one super-sized human. He is a being of love, justice, mercy, truth, awe, and unlimited in power who exists in God the Father, the Son, and the Holy Spirit. We, his followers, worship him as God, Redeemer, our fervent pursuer not willing to leave us to our own devices, but bringing us into his glorious kingdom.

Lord, thank you for your love. Thank you for showing us your character. Thank you for claiming us as your own. Forgive us for failing to see and honor you as we should. Amen.

MAY 8

I know your works, your toil and your patient endurance, and how you cannot bear with those who are evil, but have tested those who call themselves apostles and are not, and found them to be false. I know you are enduring patiently and bearing up for my name's sake, and you have not grown weary. But I have this against you, that you have abandoned the love you had at first. (Rev. 2:2–4)

Larry Norman, a child of the '60s, sang, "You can be a righteous rocker, you can be a holy roller. You could be most anything. You could be a Leon Russell, or a super muscle. You could be a corporate king. You could be a wealthy man from Texas, or a witch with heavy hexes. But without love, you ain't nothing without love. Without love you ain't nothing, without love."

The apostle Paul wrote, "If I speak in the tongues of men and of angels, but have not love, I am a noisy gong or a clanging cymbal. And if I have prophetic powers, and understand all mysteries and all knowledge, and if I have all faith, so as to remove mountains, but have not love, I am nothing. If I give away all I have, and if I deliver up my body to be burned, but have not love, I gain nothing" (1 Cor. 13:1–3).

Jesus told the Ephesians through John, "You can work hard, you can endure much, you can stand against evil and stop false teaching. You can do all of it in Jesus' name. But if you have abandoned your love, you are missing it." Jesus spoke of our love for God and for each other. It is at the root of who we are, and should be at the root of all we do.

Sometimes in life, we can find that we are doing the right things, staying busy for God. The warning of the Lord in today's passage should speak to us all, even if we are working our fingers to the bone to do right and serve God. The motivation for our work matters. The attitude of our heart matters. Our efforts should stem from a responsive love for Jesus.

Jesus taught us that he had the greatest love for us. He told us that and he showed us that, leaving the throne of heaven to come in humility to earth. Then once in human form, Jesus further showed his love through acts of service in demonstration of how we should live. The ultimate display of human and divine love culminated in Jesus allowing unholy humans to exercise power over the Almighty God and put his human form to a humiliating and painful death. Jesus, out of love, was the only one who could meet God's justice for human sin. As we understand this love of Jesus, we are rightly moved to respond in love. Love to him and love to others, whom he also loves. If we lose track of that love, then all our best deeds are missing God's greatest transforming gift—love.

Lord, may I learn to love you and others. Don't let me lose sight of your love. Don't let me get lost in busyness. Keep my attitude right in Jesus. Amen.

MAY 9

The words of the holy one, the true one, who has the key of David, who opens and no one will shut, who shuts and no one opens. "I know your works. Behold, I have set before you an open door, which no one is able to shut." (Rev. 3:7–8)

I hope you are reading this in the morning. If you are, then think about what is before you today. If you are reading it later in the day, or in the evening, then think about what you have left to do this evening or what is in your life for tomorrow. Most of the time, we have things we enjoy, things we endure, and some things we'd rather skip! I suggest we can take this verse and change our perspective on such things. To do so, however, we are going to need to dig into the Greek a bit.

Today's passage has some Greek that is difficult to translate fully into English. It takes some work to dig into it, but it is well worth the effort! Jesus is speaking in this passage. Jesus is the one who opens doors no one can shut. Jesus is the one who closes doors no one can open. We need to see that in reference to our lives each day. Those things set before us to do aren't simply "chores" or "opportunities." They are open doors that we can walk through—doors opened by the Lord Jesus.

With that in mind, when Jesus says, "Behold, I have set before you an open door," the Greek has a bit more information for you and me. The word translated as "set before" you is δίδωμι (*didōmi*). It conveys the giving of a gift, the donating of something valuable. Jesus isn't simply setting an open door before us, he is *giving* us that open door. (Thanks to Wheaton College Greek Professor Gerald Hawthorne for pointing this out.) Jesus gives us open doors. Our days are filled with doors he grants to us out of his bounty.

Jesus gives us these "open doors" and the Greek for the "open" door also is important. The Greek word is a "perfect passive participle" (open) modifying "door." The word is "passive" because the door is opened by Christ. This shouldn't surprise us. He is introduced as the one "who opens." The "perfect tense" is because the door has already been opened and it remains open for us today. We also know that what Jesus has opened, no one can close!

Understanding this more fully, we can look again at what is before us today or tomorrow. These aren't things that are just happening. They aren't coincidences of scheduling. They should never be viewed as nuisances or hassles. Our opportunities in life are open doors, opened by the Lord himself. They are gifts to us to help us grow, to bring his love to others, to show mercy and justice, to teach, to model his holiness, to advance his kingdom! Thank you, God, for these open doors!

Father, forgive my failure to see your hand and gifts in things set before me. Help me grow out of my tendency to see things from my perspective. In Jesus, amen.

MAY 10

Are not two sparrows sold for a penny? And not one of them will fall to the ground apart from your Father. But even the hairs of your head are all numbered. Fear not, therefore; you are of more value than many sparrows. (Mt. 10:29–31)

Recently I got my hair cut. It had been a few months since my last cut, and I have a decent amount of hair on my head. As Simon was finishing my cut, a kind lady with a broom started sweeping up the hair on the floor. Under the broom was a massive hair ball that would have made a litter of cats envious. It was the size of a volleyball. I asked her whether all of the hair was mine, and she replied, "Yes, and there's a bit more I need to get." My mind immediately went to today's passage.

If you had asked me how many hairs were in that ball on the floor, I wouldn't be able to hazard a guess with even a remote hope of being right. I suspect I would have a better chance at winning the lottery. Yet God knew the precise number of those hairs. What is more is that if one of the hairs had been blown away from the larger ball, God would have noticed the ball was one hair short.

Wow. This God is not only beyond my ability to fathom the depths of his knowledge and awareness, but something else about him touches me. God cares enough about me to know these things *about me*. This is true for everyone reading this devotional. "Mark Lanier" isn't anything special to God that *you* the reader aren't. God cares for all of us with a deep, interested, and unending love. Heavens, he even cares for the sparrows; those small birds that aren't extraordinary count with God.

So with that in mind, Jesus asked his followers, "What are you afraid of? What worries you? What do you fear?" We can and should answer Jesus' question, but the answer is properly met with the conscious realization that God cares about us. God is interested in us. God is taking care of us. God is protecting us. God loves us unconditionally. God is going to work his will in our lives.

If you're like me, you may be thinking, "Yes, all of that is well and good, but what if *I mess things up?*" Well, the promise of God is to work in and through us. The God who numbers our hairs knows our propensity for messing up. He takes that into account. What is more, he promises to use our errors to help us grow before him. He will grow us into better people as he continues to direct our lives. In other words, add to the list of things we shouldn't fear—our own inadequacies and mistakes! God has that too.

What a God we serve!

Lord God, I can't fathom the depths of your love and concern. But I need them, desperately. So I thank you for them, and pray that I will respond in love and obedience. In Jesus, amen.

MAY 11

Pray then like this: "Our Father in heaven . . ." (Mt. 6:9)

I was very blessed to have an amazing earthly father. Dad wasn't perfect and without a doubt made errors in parenting. But he was terrific! He loved us more than life itself and worked hard all his days to best ensure we would grow up knowing God's love, knowing our dad's love, and knowing our own self-worth. He wanted us to have all we needed to be happy and succeed in this world. I know many aren't fortunate to have an earthly father like mine, and I wonder how passages like today's are received by others.

For me, however, today's passage is a source of great warmth and comfort. "Father" means a lot of caring and sincere love to me, and the idea of God as my Father carries great weight in my life.

Jesus likely used the Aramaic term "Abba" here, and Matthew translated that into the Greek word *Pater* we read in the Greek New Testament. Abba was a special term that the church adapted early, as per Jesus' teaching here. Jesus taught his followers to address God in that way, and Paul noted what an honor it is to call God, "Abba Father" (Rom. 8:15; Gal. 4:6).

Abba was a personal term for father. Little children would call their fathers, "Abba," and that has led some to think that "daddy" is a good translation of the word. I would suggest that "daddy," as is frequently used today, might be a bit *too* childish as the word we use with God. Yes, small children would use "*Abba*" to address their fathers, but so would adult children. As an adult, I (and most others I know) do not use the childish term "daddy" when speaking of my father. "Father" and "dad" are more typical.

Even if we remove the childish "daddy" from our consideration, we must not lose track of the significance that the term used to pray to God is a very familiar and intimate term, nonetheless. Through Jesus, God becomes "our Father" in a special intimate way. His love operates better than even the best earthly fathers on their best days! He works to teach us his love and care, illustrating our worth to him by his redemptive work for our lives. He prepares us to have a joyful and fulfilling walk in this world with an assured hope that he takes us into his kingdom through eternity.

My earthly father passed away almost fifteen years ago as I write this. I still miss him immensely. I am confident that I will see him again one day. But in the meantime, frequently lying in bed at night, I will start my prayers with, "Our Father." I then stop and consider it, dwelling for the moment in the midst of a deep contentment that flows from knowing God in this special way.

Our Father . . . thank you for your love and care. I rest in you. In Jesus, amen.

MAY 12

Jesus replied, "A man was going down from Jerusalem to Jericho, and he fell among rob-
bers, who stripped him and beat him and departed, leaving him half dead. Now by chance
a priest was going down that road, and when he saw him he passed by on the other side.
So likewise a Levite, when he came to the place and saw him, passed by on the other side.
But a Samaritan, as he journeyed, came to where he was, and when he saw him, he had
compassion." (Lk. 10:30–33)

I was at a dinner for speakers at a law symposium. Two seats to my left
was a law professor who, along with her husband and children, were faithful attenders of church. Toward dinner's end, she turned to me and said, "I
have a religious question." She then asked me how, if, as Jesus indicated, it
was so hard for a rich man to enter the kingdom of heaven, then how can
we live with the treasures we have? This is a great question almost everyone
should ask.

In our discussion, I turned to this parable, which came out of that very
context. Jesus was approached by a lawyer who asked him what a person
can do to inherit eternal life. Jesus responded to love God fully and love
one's neighbor as one loves oneself. The self-righteous lawyer pressed Jesus
further asking, "Who is my neighbor?" Jesus answered with the parable
in today's passage, asking afterward, "Who was neighbor to the man who
fell to robbers?" Importantly, the parable went beyond what we have put in
our reading for today. The Samaritan not only stopped with compassion, he
tended to the wounded man lovingly. The Samaritan was a neighbor.

We have all been given more than we need. We can always find people
and worthy projects around us that are in need. How we show neighborly
love, how we show godly love in those opportunities is at the core of this
parable. In illustrating "neighbor," however, we often fail to see something
very important tucked into this parable. The Samaritan found his neighbor
"as he journeyed." He was "going down the road" when he happened upon
the man in need.

We have a direct responsibility to help those in need when we come
across them, those who "interrupt our day," in a manner of speaking. That
is different than our going out into the world to seek anyone less fortunate
than we, disbursing all we have above our level of need. Now our attitude
needs to be willing to give everything, for indeed everything is God's. But
beyond our tithing, we are to give as opportunity presents. This is responsible giving as a steward for God. We don't give gullibly or simply to avoid
trying to determine if giving is the right thing. But we give or help those
we see in need.

Lord, interrupt my day with chances to be a good steward of what you have entrusted
to me. In Jesus' name, and following his lead, amen.

MAY 13

So when they had come together, they asked him, "Lord, will you at this time restore the kingdom to Israel?" He said to them, "It is not for you to know times or seasons that the Father has fixed by his own authority. But you will receive power when the Holy Spirit has come upon you, and you will be my witnesses in Jerusalem and in all Judea and Samaria, and to the end of the earth." And when he had said these things, as they were looking on, he was lifted up, and a cloud took him out of their sight. And while they were gazing into heaven as he went, behold, two men stood by them in white robes, and said, "Men of Galilee, why do you stand looking into heaven? This Jesus, who was taken up from you into heaven, will come in the same way as you saw him go into heaven." (Acts 1:6–10)

Today's passage marks Ascension Sunday, the day the church celebrates the ascension of Jesus to the right hand of the Father. The passage is notable for many reasons. First, this passage comes right before God sends his Holy Spirit to indwell the apostles. Notably, without the Spirit, the apostles were still missing core insights into the mission and work of Jesus. They still believed that Jesus had come to set up an earthly restoration of Israel as an independent political entity and world power. Until the insights brought by the Holy Spirit, they were ignorant that God was about something much grander.

Second, the ascension of Jesus wasn't significant as the end of something. The significance was what it pointed to for the future. Jesus ascending to the right hand of the Father was never because he was finished with humanity. His ascension marked a new phase in God's relationship with humanity. God was coming into people's lives not by interacting in human form (Jesus). God's Spirit would actually indwell people. This would be the time when people would get deeper insights than can come from one's own brain! As Jesus had explained to his somewhat blinded apostles at the Last Supper, "the Holy Spirit, whom the Father will send in my name, he will teach you all things" (Jn. 14:26). Core among the teachings of the Holy Spirit is the relationship with God that comes to people of faith: "In that day you will know that I am in my Father, and you in me, and I in you" (Jn. 14:20).

A third item of note lies beyond even the coming of the Holy Spirit. The angels who came to speak for God to the watching apostles had something incredible to add to the day's events. They told the apostles that Jesus would return. This return would be real; it would be physical; and it would be amazing. In the Revelation Jesus gave to John (recorded in the "Book of Revelation") is included the vision of Jesus returning in judgment on the world as he takes his people home. Jesus is pictured on a white horse, wearing the name "faithful and true" (Rev. 19:11). That is the promise of the angels. That is a part of Ascension Sunday. The Jesus we worship is here in Spirit and coming again in victory.

Lord, let your Spirit open my eyes. Give me direction as I await your day! In Jesus, amen.

Then I saw heaven opened, and behold, a white horse! The one sitting on it is called Faithful and True, and in righteousness he judges and makes war. His eyes are like a flame of fire, and on his head are many diadems, and he has a name written that no one knows but himself. He is clothed in a robe dipped in blood, and the name by which he is called is The Word of God. And the armies of heaven, arrayed in fine linen, white and pure, were following him on white horses. From his mouth comes a sharp sword with which to strike down the nations, and he will rule them with a rod of iron. He will tread the winepress of the fury of the wrath of God the Almighty. On his robe and on his thigh he has a name written, King of kings and Lord of lords. (Rev. 19:11–16)

Sometimes in life, great moments of inspiration occur. One of those moments happened in the life of Julia Howe on November 18, 1861. She was staying at the Willard Hotel in Washington, DC, and had gone to bed. She awoke the next day in the early morning twilight with lyrics dancing in her head. The lyrics would accompany a tune many were singing in her day. She decided she needed to write the lyrics down quickly, lest she forget them and the moment of inspiration evaporate.

So she jumped out of bed, found a pencil stub, and wrote as fast as she could, "Mine eyes have seen the glory of the coming of the Lord; He is trampling out the vintage where the grapes of wrath are stored; He hath loosed the fateful lightning of His terrible swift sword: His truth is marching on." The lyrics were inspired by today's passage. They formed the first verse of what is now known as the "Battle Hymn of the Republic." The chorus, "Glory, glory, hallelujah!," is also well known.

Howe was writing during the dark days of the American Civil War. She included an important verse of inspiration, "In the beauty of the lilies Christ was born across the sea, with a glory in His bosom that transfigures you and me. As He died to make men holy, let us die to make men free, while God is marching on." Howe understood that the life of Christ should inspire people of all ages to live lives of sacrifice for the good of others. Jesus said it this way, "If anyone would come after me, let him deny himself and take up his cross daily and follow me" (Lk. 9:23).

Howe's last verse stands out: "He is coming like the glory of the morning on the wave, He is Wisdom to the mighty, He is Succour to the brave, so the world shall be His footstool, and the soul of Time His slave, our God is marching on." Howe describes today's passage. Jesus will come again. His coming will mean judgment on those who oppose him, but life and liberation to those who follow him. I am going to take Howe's inspired song in my heart today and sing "glory hallelujah" to the King of kings, while I stay on mission to fulfill his commands.

Lord, thank you for the inspiration you provide. May I live for others in Jesus, amen.

MAY 15

And the blind and the lame came to him in the temple, and he healed them. But when the chief priests and the scribes saw the wonderful things that he did, and the children crying out in the temple, "Hosanna to the Son of David!" they were indignant, and they said to him, "Do you hear what these are saying?" And Jesus said to them, "Yes; have you never read, 'Out of the mouth of infants and nursing babies you have prepared praise'?" (Mt. 21:14–16)

A big question for any business centers on personnel and organization. People need to be in the "right seat on the bus." Some folks are splendid working with other people. Those folks need to be in people roles. Others aren't as comfortable with people as they are with computer terminals. Those folks need to be in front of terminals. The well-used maxim of "the right seat on the bus" comes to mind. You don't want the passenger who is a poor driver switching seats on the bus with the driver!

Our relationship with God is one where we need to remember this principal. We should make sure we are in the right seat on the bus. God is God. We aren't. As God, he has roles and responsibilities that we don't. The more readily we see this day by day, hour by hour, moment by moment, the more readily we will live in peace.

Today's passage sets this truth plainly before us, although we might miss it if we aren't attentive to "Hosanna," the Aramaic word in the passage. The events in this passage unfolded in Aramaic. Matthew wrote in Greek, but here, Matthew took the Aramaic shout of the people and sounded it out as closely as he could into Greek letters. Matthew produced "ὡσαννὰ" ("Hosana") as a Greek spelling of the Aramaic phrase hosha' na. In most English Bibles, the word is not translated, but is turned into an English spelling. Hence, we read "Hosanna."

"*Hosha' na*" was an Aramaic shout of praise, common among the people of Jesus' day. Beyond being a phrase of praise, however, this Aramaic phrase has meaning. If we translate the word rather than simply respell it into modern languages, it proclaims, "Save, I pray you!" Or more colloquially, "Save, I'm begging you!" or even, "Save!!! Please!!!"

This praise infuriated the chief priests because it gave Jesus a peculiar seat on the bus. The people were appealing to Jesus as their Savior. Some of the people likely meant, "save us from Rome," some, "save us from disease," and some, "save us from ___," i.e., whatever they found afflicting. But "save us" was their plea. Jesus termed this the "praise of [trusting] infants and babies." That is *our seat on the bus with God*! We need to praise God by coming to him in trust, seeking his saving from all afflictions.

Lord, I am afflicted. Save me, please. Hosanna! In Jesus' name, amen.

MAY 16

Then some of the scribes and Pharisees answered him, saying, "Teacher, we wish to see a sign from you." But he answered them, "An evil and adulterous generation seeks for a sign, but no sign will be given to it except the sign of the prophet Jonah. For just as Jonah was three days and three nights in the belly of the great fish, so will the Son of Man be three days and three nights in the heart of the earth. The men of Nineveh will rise up at the judgment with this generation and condemn it, for they repented at the preaching of Jonah, and behold, something greater than Jonah is here." (Mt. 12:38–41)

In this passage Jesus references Jonah when replying to the request for a sign. The Jonah story is familiar to many. God told Jonah to go to Nineveh, a pagan land to the northeast of Israel. Jonah was to preach repentance. Jonah instead went southwest! He fled God's plan on a boat. A storm set in and Jonah was chucked overboard by the boat crew. A big fish swallowed Jonah. While Jonah was figuratively dead for three days and nights (and literally dead to the world), Jesus would truly be dead for three days and nights in the heart of the earth. This sign was confirmed after the crucifixion with the resurrection for Christ as he was "brought up" by God from the grave.

The early church got this. Some early artwork (second and third century) shows the church using Jonah as a type of Christ, especially in the Roman catacombs among the Christian burial sites.

The illustration Christ gives goes a bit further though. Not only is Jesus similar to Jonah in the three-days-and-nights aspect, but Jesus is truly greater than Jonah, and so the people should consider Nineveh and repent! Jonah, the fugitive from God, never really had God's heart for the foreign people. Yet he was effective nonetheless as the people of Nineveh repented.

Jesus was *not* a fugitive from God. He was *not* recalcitrant in his mission. Jesus is *not* a parallel to Jonah (even though he would suffer death for three days as Jonah did figuratively). Jesus was fully on mission with God to preach to those whose sins had risen before the Almighty's face. Moreover, Jesus was not simply preaching to Nineveh; he was laying down his own life *for* Nineveh. The sadness is that even in the face of this reality, the Ninevites were more responsive to God than the scribes and Pharisees listening to Jesus.

I want to make sure I hear the cry from Jesus and the empty tomb. I want to hear the call for repentance as I seek God's mercy each day.

Lord, please tune my heart to hear your call. I repent of my sins, and I seek your mercy. Thank you for the forgiveness through Jesus my Lord. In whom I pray, amen.

MAY 17

Then Jesus said to the crowds and to his disciples, "The scribes and the Pharisees sit on Moses' seat, so do and observe whatever they tell you, but not the works they do. For they preach, but do not practice." (Mt. 23:1-3)

Ouch! Today's passage is a hurter! It's one thing for me to say, "Practice what you preach!" It's another thing to hear the words of Jesus say, "They don't practice what they preach." I don't mind that so much from another human being. After all, most everyone has the same problem, and the one who is pointing it out in another likely has a level of hypocrisy themselves. But Jesus? He has ZERO hypocrisy when he says it.

Jesus indicts those who "sit on the seat of Moses." The idea of "sitting in the seat of . . ." means to emulate, or be as someone else, here Moses. The wording is the same as that of Psalm 1:1, which says one shouldn't "sit in the seat of scoffers." Jesus notes that people sit like they are Moses, the law giver, the judge, the answer for Israel, but their actions betray them as something altogether different.

Hence Jesus can say, "Do what they say, but not what they do." Jesus gives a number of examples in the larger passage from which I took this summary. Jesus spoke of the heavy loads that the scribes and Pharisees put on others, while doing nothing to help others with those loads. It is the opposite of what Paul instructed the Galatians when he said, "Bear one another's burdens, and so fulfill the law of Christ" (Gal. 6:2). So Jesus says, teach people right living but also *help* people live rightly.

Another example Jesus gives is that these nonpracticing preachers do their deeds to be seen by others. Jesus knew righteous deeds are important. Disciples of Jesus are to do those righteous deeds. But never because they want to be seen by others. As Jesus had taught on the Sermon on the Mount, righteous deeds are to be done because God taught us so (Mt. 6:1). We do them for God, not for others. An obedient heart seeks to please God, not people.

Still another example Jesus gives is the love these nonpracticing preachers have for being called "rabbi" and being recognized as teachers. Jesus wants his followers to teach as helping instruction for others to better understand and walk with God. Teaching should never be about the teacher but about the Lord, the One who is taught.

Today's passage has a sting, but the sting is best felt by me looking at myself, not others. Jesus rightly could tell others to practice what they preach. I need to tend to that for me. I need to be helping others bear their burdens. I need to teach others about God, rightly. This passage is for me!

Father, forgive my failures. Help me practice what I preach. In Jesus, amen.

MAY 18

After this the Lord appointed seventy-two others and sent them on ahead of him, two by two, into every town and place where he himself was about to go. And he said to them, "The harvest is plentiful, but the laborers are few. Therefore pray earnestly to the Lord of the harvest to send out laborers into his harvest." (Lk. 10:1–2)

Today's verse has always struck me as instructive in its oddity. The verse oddly tells us that we are to pray to God to send laborers out into *his* harvest. Does that strike you as odd? If it is *his* harvest, shouldn't *he* be sending out the laborers? Furthermore, we can surely determine that sending out laborers is in his will. After all, he wants his harvest gathered.

This oddity is what makes this verse so instructive to me. God has made this world and placed humanity in charge of taking care of it. As early as the garden of Eden, God gave Adam and Eve charge for working and understanding creation. This was true in the days of utopia. The world was just what it needed to be, and Adam and Eve were not marred by sin. Yet, "The LORD God took the man and put him in the garden of Eden to work it and keep it" (Gen. 2:15). Working the garden (Heb. *avad* - עָבַד) included things like tending to grapevines and other general chores of agriculture. "Keeping" the garden (Heb. *Shamar,* שָׁמַר) includes inspecting the creation or observing it for what it needs and what it does.

Adam and Eve had responsibilities. God gave them abilities and authority to take care of the earth. The fall came into the picture, and the work of people got much rougher. Suddenly the work was no longer done in Eden but among the thorns and thistles of the sinful world. But the responsibilities of people never changed. That means you and I are charged by God with seeing that this world is used in ways that bring glory to God.

In the words of Jesus, we are to seek God's kingdom on earth as it is in heaven (Mt. 6:10). This includes the important task of praying for God's will to be done. It isn't that God can't do his will. It is that it is our responsibility to seek it. We are to pray for God to enact his will.

This radically transforms prayer. No longer am I praying simply for my own needs. I am praying for God's will. My time and energy are spent trying to discern what God seeks in my life and in the world at large. Then with prayer, I am to ask God for those things. Then armed with God's power and answers to prayer, I am to go out and do as he commands and wishes.

Father, may I understand your will, seek your will, and do your will. Give me discernment, motivation, and strength. I want to be what you want me to be. In Jesus, amen.

MAY 19

And the scribes of the Pharisees, when they saw that he was eating with sinners and tax collectors, said to his disciples, "Why does he eat with tax collectors and sinners?" And when Jesus heard it, he said to them, "Those who are well have no need of a physician, but those who are sick. I came not to call the righteous, but sinners." (Mk. 2:16–17)

Do you remember when the T-shirt was going around that said, "Been there, done that"? Today's passage reminds me of it. Why? Because I read the passage and I think, "I was *there*! I am in this passage! This story has MEEEEEEE."

The passage is in the context of Jesus early in his ministry having dinner with tax collectors and sinners. I suspect that we often forget how reprehensible these groups were to the religious of Jesus' day. The distaste and disapproval ran deep because it wasn't as simple as "they aren't good people." Many religious folks thought that these sinful Jews were causes for God's displeasure. After all, the Jews remember with mourning God's judgment that came upon Judah, taking them to Babylon hundreds of years earlier. The deportation was because the Jews were living sinful lives.

Similarly, less than two-hundred-plus years before Jesus, the effort to paganize Judaism by Antiochus Epiphanes was met with a Jewish rebellion that effectively liberated Judea until Roman occupation. The Jews would have argued that Jewish sinfulness was the cause of God's harsh judgment on the nation. To eat dinner with sinners and tax collectors was tantamount to condoning those who would see Judea destroyed, or at least see God's restoration and liberation of the nation from Rome put off.

Jesus didn't see things that way. Jesus was not entertaining sinners and tax collectors because he condoned their lifestyle. To the contrary, Jesus ate with them because he viewed them worthy of his healing and saving touch. Jesus sought to bring them to the truth. He is a transformer, and he wanted to transform them into holy children of God.

This is where I find myself in the story. Jesus said, "Those who are well have no need of a physician, but those who are sick. I came not to call the righteous, but sinners." He came for the sick and the sinners! That is me! I am both sick and sinful.

I wish I was different. I wish I could get my mind and life where it should be. How incredible would it be to have the discipline I need. I wish I had more of a loving heart. I wish I didn't struggle with sin. As Paul said, why do I do what I don't want to do and fail to do what I want to do? I am sick and sinful! Yet Jesus came for me! He dines with me! He saves me! This is glorious news. I am glad to be in this story!

Father, thank you for coming for me. Save me, make me well to the glory of Jesus, amen.

And this is the judgment: the light has come into the world, and people loved the darkness rather than the light because their works were evil. For everyone who does wicked things hates the light and does not come to the light, lest his works should be exposed. (Jn. 3:19–20)

Have you ever taken a personality test? There are lots of them. One popular test gives you an Enneagrams test to learn if you are a 1, 2, 3, . . . 9, then personality types are assigned to the numbers. Another prominent test is the Myers Briggs Type Indicator test. These tests are supposed to help you better understand yourself by giving insight into how you think, feel, process, interact, and so on.

John sets up a personality examination of sorts in today's passage. John uses light and darkness in his gospel to speak of righteousness and sin. In John 1:4–13, John associates the light with Jesus. Similarly, in John 8:12, John quoted Jesus as saying that anyone following Jesus would not walk in darkness (unrighteousness) but would walk in the light (righteousness) as Jesus is light.

The personality test for John involves simple introspection. One needs to ask and truly answer certain questions, starting with, "What do I love?" and "What do I do?" If someone loves darkness, one will be doing sinful and evil works. Doing wicked things makes one a hater of light.

This will make many people search for the test questions to determine what is wicked and evil. Reading through Paul's writings reveals a tough list. In 1 Corinthians 6:9–10 Paul wrote, "Do not be deceived: neither the sexually immoral, nor idolaters, nor adulterers, nor men who practice homosexuality, nor thieves, nor the greedy, nor drunkards, nor revilers, nor swindlers will inherit the kingdom of God." Some items on that list are not a problem for many people, but some on that list bother most everyone. If that list doesn't get you, how about this one: "They were filled with all manner of unrighteousness, evil, covetousness, malice. They are full of envy, murder, strife, deceit, maliciousness. They are gossips, slanderers, haters of God, insolent, haughty, boastful, inventors of evil, disobedient to parents, foolish, faithless, heartless, ruthless. Though they know God's righteous decree that those who practice such things deserve to die" (Rom. 1:29–32).

Going through Paul's lists makes me realize that I may not live in darkness, but I do make some trips there! My personality test isn't what I wish it was. But the good news is that God will work in the lives of his children to transform our minds and improve our personalities! We just need to let Jesus sanctify us and bathe us in the light (1 Cor. 6:11)!

Father, bring me into ever-increasing light, please! In Jesus I ask, amen.

MAY 21

And when they came to the crowd, a man came up to him and, kneeling before him, said, "Lord, have mercy on my son, for he has seizures and he suffers terribly. For often he falls into the fire, and often into the water. And I brought him to your disciples, and they could not heal him." And Jesus answered, "O faithless and twisted generation, how long am I to be with you? How long am I to bear with you? Bring him here to me." And Jesus rebuked the demon, and it came out of him, and the boy was healed instantly. (Mt. 17:14–18)

What is different in one's life if one is desperate for Jesus? In today's passage, desperation drove a man to seek the help of Jesus' apostles, and failing their ability to help, to find Jesus and implore him for mercy. What drove this man to be so distressed? His son was suffering from seizures that would drive him into the fire at times, and into water at times. The boy was possessed by a demon, and Jesus' apostles proved useless in helping the boy.

The desperate father came to Jesus, and Jesus came through. Jesus exorcised the demon, and the boy was healed.

I want to be desperate for Jesus. I am not demon possessed, but I live in a world that still shudders and groans under the weight of Satan's influence. There are evil people in this world. Some are leaders of countries, some are private and secluded, but they are there, wreaking havoc. The physical world experiences evil also. I know people who have lost everything to hurricanes, people whose homes were destroyed by fire, and people who have had to endure economic ruin because of repeated crop failures driven by poor weather.

Even beyond the world, I have seen people ravaged by sin as they battled addiction, as they tried to find peace in a house at war, as they tried to find a reason to live after losing a child to cancer. These people can rightly be desperate for Jesus.

But what about the rest of us? What about the people who have a decent life, with little to no trouble? First, I am not sure anyone like that really exists. So to those who feel they are so fortunate, I say, "Just wait. It will come!" Because we all are going to be in places where we *should* be desperate for Jesus.

I want to seek Jesus like a thirsty person seeks water. I want nothing to get in the way of my daily *need* for Jesus and interacting with him. Then as the struggles come, I am ready! I can walk through the fire with my friend who has walked with me every day!

Father, I crave Jesus. I want to know him more deeply. Please, Lord. In his name, amen.

MAY 22

Are not five sparrows sold for two pennies? And not one of them is forgotten before God. Why, even the hairs of your head are all numbered. Fear not; you are of more value than many sparrows. . . . Fear not, little flock, for it is your Father's good pleasure to give you the kingdom. (Lk. 12:6-7, 32)

A consistent theme of Jesus' is that his followers need have no fear. Over and over in the teachings of Jesus, he reinforces this theme, noting only that everyone should have a healthy fear of God! But beyond that, when people place themselves in God's hands, there is zero need for fear.

I believe that most people are afraid when things seem unknown or out of one's control. As children, fear of the dark stems in part because the dark can contain that which one can't see. Some things accumulate in the imagination, growing in one's mind, even though they have no existence in reality.

Think through the list of things that frighten or worry people of all ages. Not only children fear the dark, but so do older people. Add to that the fear of losing a job, failing at a task, getting a bad health report, losing a loved one or an important relationship. I got a text once from one of my daughters who was not going to get to a certain seminal event. She said she had "FOMO." The first time I got that text, I had to reply, what is "FOMO," to which she replied, "Fear Of Missing Out." We have fears about fears!

Jesus knew and taught that God has control of every crisis. God knows each detail in our lives. What is more, he has a caring heart toward us. He isn't going to see tragedy and leave us abandoned unable to cope. As a buddy of mine who in his sixties became a new-born believer in the Lord told me recently, "You know, I have figured out that God doesn't give you more than you can handle! He might take you to the brink, but he always steps in before it's too late." My buddy is right.

When I have a loving and caring God addressing my daily circumstances, my fears should evaporate. Yet too often I see the fears are still there. Why? I suspect here is where I am seeing a lack of faith on my part. Yes, God loves me, and yes he is in control, but what if he isn't? What if he doesn't? Don't bad things happen all the time to good people?

Yes, there are still problems. Having no fear doesn't mean that all is golden. It means that we can be resolute that whatever God sends our way, he gives us strength to handle. And in the end, it will all work out, and I will be okay.

Father, give me trust in you. Grow my faith. Help me overcome fear by entrusting you in the small and large things of life. I give myself to you, in Jesus. Amen.

MAY 23

Stay dressed for action and keep your lamps burning, and be like men who are waiting for their master to come home from the wedding feast, so that they may open the door to him at once when he comes and knocks. (Lk. 12:35–36)

Back in my law school days, my buddy Curtis and I coopted the term, "Men of Action." It is a bit hard to describe what we meant by it, but at the time we might have described it as a moral James Bond. I'm not quite sure where we got it, and it was a bit of a joke between us, but we would frequently proclaim ourselves and whatever we might do as appropriate for "Men of Action." If there was a problem, we would solve it as Men of Action. If someone had a question and we could answer it, we would do so as Men of Action. If someone didn't understand what we were doing or saying, we would decry such saying, "He clearly isn't a Man of Action."

I look back on that with a chuckle but am reminded of it in considering today's passage. Jesus taught his disciples to always be people on the ready. "Stay dressed for action," he said, using a frequent Hebrew expression for "be ready for service." The literal expression is to stay with your long robe tucked up into a waist belt so that you could run, or do whatever needs to be done. Jesus puts it in the present tense because this is a permanent state of readiness.

Jesus adds that his followers are to keep their lamps burning. Again in the present tense, Jesus wants his followers constantly in this mode. Burning lamps connote being watchful. This goes hand in hand with the instruction to be ready for service. The follower is to not only be ready to serve but be looking for service opportunities.

Jesus then takes these instructions and explains them with the analogy of servants being ready for their master to return home. Jesus knew that he would leave this earth at the culmination of his service to God in his sacrificial death but also that he would one day come again in victory. Jesus expects his followers to live expectantly, knowing that Jesus could return at any moment.

This forward-looking mentality isn't simply a "Let's sit and wait for heavenly deliverance from this life." This is a practical challenge to the believer to be alert and watchful in the interim, looking for ways to serve God by serving others.

The believer should live a life looking forward to service. The believer is to be a Woman or Man of Action!

Father, give me a ready heart and alert mind to see needs and to take actions to serve. I want to be Christlike in my life as I eagerly await his coming again. In him I pray, amen.

And when Jesus had stepped out of the boat, immediately there met him out of the tombs a man with an unclean spirit. He lived among the tombs. And no one could bind him anymore, not even with a chain, for he had often been bound with shackles and chains, but he wrenched the chains apart, and he broke the shackles in pieces. No one had the strength to subdue him. Night and day among the tombs and on the mountains he was always crying out and cutting himself with stones. (Mk. 5:2–5)

The man of the tombs is a story that touches a deep spot in my heart. I can't read the story without reflecting on the heart of one so damaged that he lived among the tombs, finding his residence among the dead. He was too wild for anyone to tame. He spent his days out of his mind, cutting himself, and, not surprisingly, ostracized by the community.

The man was demon possessed, but not without a surprising grip on reality. Seeing Jesus, the man fell down and recognized Jesus as the "Son of the Most High God" (Mk. 5:7). At a time when many had no knowledge and were afraid to acknowledge who or what Jesus was, this man had insight. Jesus, the Son of God, healed the man—fully. Jesus cast out the demons and then the uncontrollable man, hateful of life and his condition, self-loathing, and self-destructing, was changed. In an instant. Some from a nearby town came out to see what was going on. They may have been among those who had tried to control the man with chains, we aren't told for certain. But we know that they knew of the man's struggles with life.

When the townsfolk came out, they found the man sitting there with Jesus. The man was clothed and fully in his right mind. Jesus brought the man peace and purpose along with his healing. Then a strange reversal happened. The townspeople were scared to death of Jesus and begged him to leave their area! Yes, Jesus the merciful was at peace with the "crazy man," as the town saw him. And that caused the town to do something crazy themselves. Rather than find out what happened, rather than bring their own sick for healing, rather than seek the blessing of the Son of God Most High, the townsfolk begged Jesus to leave!

As much as it pains me to see and say, I find myself in this story. There are times when I am the man of the tombs. I am self-destructive, choosing sin over righteousness even though I know it is wrong. Then there are times when I am the townspeople. I know what Jesus has done and can do, but I want him far removed from what I am doing or how I am living, at least temporarily.

Jesus, Son of the Most High God, have mercy on me.

Lord, I confess that I am not always very smart about life with you. You have shown me great mercy, and I am not worthy. Please forgive me and help me. In Jesus, amen.

MAY 25

And Jesus said to them, "A prophet is not without honor, except in his hometown and among his relatives and in his own household." (Mk. 6:4)

The familiar expression is, "Don't take it for granted!" (Or as I said when a child, "Don't take it for granite!") The expression is common because the human tendency is to take the obvious or commonplace for granted. The grass is greener on the other side of the fence because I've been eating my grass for so long, it is ordinary.

Jesus was taken for granted. Today's passage comes from a time when Jesus was in his own hometown. Jesus taught in the synagogue, and even though his teaching was masterful, the people were offended. After all, they didn't see Jesus as the Son of God, he was just Jesus, the son of Mary and Joseph, the brother of James, Joses, Judah, and Simon. Jesus was the local carpenter who had a career change and started appealing to the masses as a teacher/healer. The locals were having none of that. Jesus was Jesus. No more. No less.

Today's passage makes me wonder where I take Jesus for granted. No, I don't see him as the local carpenter who grew up in my community. But I also fail to always see him as the divine Son of God he is. That may sound like a rough admission to make, especially for someone writing a devotional book, but it is the harsh truth. If I consistently saw Jesus for who he truly is, my life would be different.

If I didn't take Jesus for granted at times, I would be more faithful day in and day out. I would have a clearer focus on helping the helpless. I would more readily seek to serve rather than to be served. I would not worry over things, but I'd deliver them over to his shoulders. I would seek first his kingdom, not my wants and desires. My words would consistently be more kind. My prayer life would be more deliberate and intimate. My thoughts would be more holy. I would be a better husband and father. The list could go on and on.

But I take Jesus for granted. I assume he will always be there. I know he will always care. I can talk to him at my convenience based on my schedule, not his. I choose when to read about him and when to think about him. My thoughts tend to revolve around what is comfortable to me.

I need to change. I need to see Jesus for who he is. I need to let the real Jesus change my life. Of note, the story of today's passage concludes with Jesus leaving his hometown doing very little there because of their unbelief. I don't want that to be me.

Lord, I repent of taking you for granted. Please illuminate my heart and work in my life as I seek to be more diligent in my appreciation and walk with you. In Jesus, amen.

And wherever he came, in villages, cities, or countryside, they laid the sick in the market-places and implored him that they might touch even the fringe of his garment. And as many as touched it were made well. (Mk. 6:56)

Confession: I love things in excess. The wholesale stores that sell in bulk are made for me. My wife says I need to start a twelve-step program for those who buy in bulk. I like to pile food on my plate. If I find a pair of socks I like, I want to buy two. If I am going to collect something, I like to collect it all. I need to learn moderation in everything. It doesn't come naturally to me.

Because of my flaws of excess, I am touched by the passage today. Jesus is going around in his public ministry and everywhere he went, people set down the sick before him. Jesus was a healer, and people knew that he could do what the doctors could not. That makes sense to me. If I had a loved one who was sick, I would travel long and far to get that person before one who could heal miraculously.

Yet in the passage, there is a note that some people were hopeful that they would get to at least touch the fringe of Jesus' garment. They didn't have to have Jesus in excess. They discovered that even a little of Jesus can change the world.

This goes against my excessive gene. Importantly, it isn't to say that we shouldn't seek more and more of Jesus. There is no such thing as having too much Jesus. Yet we are not being fair to his power if we don't realize that Jesus can do what he needs to do in our life without *him* being excessive with us. This passage speaks to Jesus being able to be Jesus without Jesus being excessive.

In other words, Jesus can help me today, without being physically present. Jesus can teach me without verbally instructing me. Jesus can hear my prayers without having to stop listening to someone else. Jesus can meet my needs without having to sacrifice the needs of others. Jesus can grow me up spiritually without others losing out.

Jesus is God, and he has God's resurrection power coursing in him. Jesus has God's creation at his beck and call. Jesus knows my thoughts. Jesus has written my destiny. Jesus can and will answer my cries for help. Jesus might not be physically walking through my neighborhood, but I don't have to journey to find him. He stands at the door of my heart and knocks. He awaits my invitation. He will answer when I cry out to him. And with Jesus, even the fringe of his garment is enough to change my world.

I don't need excess, I need Jesus.

I repent of my own selfishness and pray for the touch of Jesus in my life. Amen.

MAY 27

Hear me, all of you, and understand: There is nothing outside a person that by going into him can defile him, but the things that come out of a person are what defile him.
(Mk. 7:14-15)

Consider this story. There was a man who was meticulously careful about certain aspects of driving his car. This man would always buckle his seatbelt *before* inserting his key in the ignition. He would always check to make sure his door was fully closed. The man would make sure his car was clean, inside and out. Then this man would get in his car and drive 30 miles per hour *over* the speed limit, weaving in and out of traffic, at least when he stayed on his side of the road! He changed lanes with no regard to his blind spot. He ran red lights and never found a stop sign he didn't roll through. But if you asked this man about his driving, he would tell you only about how careful he was to buckle his seatbelt before starting his car.

My feeble attempt to find a modern parallel to today's passage likely falls woefully short. But sometimes we miss much of what Jesus was teaching the public. In speaking to a Jewish audience, Jesus considered their particular rules that they believed set them apart from the non-Jewish world. The audience thought that because they were meticulously careful about not eating any unkosher food, they stood apart from ordinary people. They were a cut above those who would eat as dictated by their taste buds and budgets.

Jesus explained that what one ate didn't dictate whether they were especially set apart for God. Jesus used the word "defile." The Greek word Mark wrote was koinoō (κοινόω). It conveys the idea of making someone or something "common." Jesus was saying that it wasn't what one ate that denoted whether they were common, as opposed to holy in the Lord. It wasn't what went into a person, it was what came out of the person!

Jesus went on to detail lots of things that made one "common," like those who didn't follow God. These unholy things that came *out* of a person included evil thoughts, sexual immorality, theft, murder, adultery, coveting, wickedness, deceit, sensuality, envy, slander, pride, and foolishness. Jesus listed important matters.

Was Jesus saying to ignore the laws of Judaism? Not necessarily. People need to fasten their seatbelts. Yet if we are bragging that we drive safely because we fasten our seatbelts but speed and drive recklessly, we are fooling ourselves to our own detriment.

I need to focus on what comes out of my heart. I may not have all of the problems listed by Jesus, but if I read the list carefully (and I urge you to do read it carefully now), then I have a lot of which I need to repent!

Lord, forgive me for majoring in minor things and ignoring major matters. In him, amen.

ORDINARY TIME

The days following Pentecost have traditionally been, for much of the church, considered "Ordinary time." This is a time where the church focuses on the common, everyday importance of the life of Christ.

The devotionals during these days are those that speak of the daily events of Jesus' life, with application for us today.

MAY 28

Enter by the narrow gate. For the gate is wide and the way is easy that leads to destruction, and those who enter by it are many. For the gate is narrow and the way is hard that leads to life, and those who find it are few. (Mt. 7:13–14)

Life is full of choices. I get to choose what to eat for breakfast, or even whether to eat breakfast. I can choose where I live, where I work, where I go to school. I choose who I hang around, and what we do. Today, I will get to choose how I treat people, how I respond to the things that arise, and how I spend my spare time. We are not the first generation that made choices. It is part of being human.

Jesus spoke to his followers about choices. Jesus gave them three sets of two choices. As Jesus explained life, people could choose between two gates that were traveled by two sets of people and that had two results. The gates couldn't be more different. One was narrow. Few made it through that gate; it wasn't an easy path. But at the end of the path was "life."

Many have a tendency to read this passage only in reference to eternity, but while that is a part of the passage, the context renders it also important in daily living. The narrow gate is a more deliberate and careful life. Using that narrow gate isn't always the easy path, but it is important to follow anyway. For example, when I consider how I treat people, it is easy for me to treat them out of self-interest. What works best for me? What satisfies my desires? What makes me happy? The road that asks for God's will and for the ultimate good for those I encounter is much more difficult. Yet the assurance of Jesus is that walking the difficult path through the narrow gate leads to LIFE!

This narrow gate differs significantly from the path most people tread. The wide gate holds the masses who just seem to go along to get along, flowing with the crowd, living for self-interest and not giving true life much thought. This is the gate that means I just live with my own appetites. I don't have to focus on much beyond me and what I do. Jesus taught that this narrow gate leads to destruction, not life.

I have choices today and every day. I want to make those choices carefully and fully informed of the consequences. I want to follow God's lead, and I have no doubt that he will lead me to life. Who wants to live a life, and at the end look back and realize the destruction and loss of so much meaning because of poor choices?

So as I face today, I want to do it deliberately. I don't want to react to things, I want to act!

Lord, please give me the presence of mind to live thoughtfully today. I confess I don't always do that. Help me to focus on what is important to you. In Jesus, amen.

MAY 29

During supper, when the devil had already put it into the heart of Judas Iscariot, Simon's son, to betray him, Jesus, knowing that the Father had given all things into his hands, and that he had come from God and was going back to God, rose from supper. (Jn. 13:2–4)

The bizarreness of it all! Jesus is headed to the cross. One of his own, Judas, is going to betray him. Jesus will be hauled before Roman and Jewish authorities. They will abuse him and mistreat him. Jesus is about to lose control over everything . . . and John starts the story by noting that Jesus WAS in control of EVERYTHING!

Look carefully at today's passage. As John sets up the final forty-eight hours of Jesus' life, a time of turmoil, suffering, and catastrophe, John makes a point of saying that Jesus entered those hours "knowing" that the Father had given all things into his hands. The verb "knowing" is emphatically placed at the beginning of John's statement, a Greek way to <u>underline</u> or **bold print** the word so that it would be given emphasis by the reader. We can do the same in modern English if we write it, "Jesus, **knowing** that the Father had given all things into his hands."

Jesus *knew* he was in control. Jesus *knew* God was in control. With that, Jesus could get up and go about finishing his earthly life as planned.

We live in a world where things seem beyond our control. That is because things are beyond our control! One of the biggest arrogances of humanity is to think we have control over what happens. We don't. But God has control. He always has and he always will.

That doesn't mean bad things don't happen. This world is not the utopia of Eden. The world has yet to experience the second coming of Christ with all that entails. But the Sovereign God has shown with clarity that he is able to work through all the negative, bad, and even evil in this world to secure his ultimate purposes and good. He did that with the betrayal of Jesus, and he did that on behalf of humanity. No one should doubt God's ability to work through the messes of today to bring about his ultimate good.

As I face today, as I consider what seems to be under control and what doesn't, I need to remember that God is sovereign. I don't live today by myself. I am never living in isolation. I am living with my God. And that means everything is going to work out in the end. With that, I can smile and find joy in the journey.

Dear Lord, thank you for showing me how to live in faith, knowing you are in control, even as my life (and the world) seem out of control and topsy-turvy. Please give me wisdom in this life to better trust you. In Jesus, amen.

MAY 30

The apostles returned to Jesus and told him all that they had done and taught. And he said to them, "Come away by yourselves to a desolate place and rest a while." For many were coming and going, and they had no leisure even to eat. And they went away in the boat to a desolate place by themselves. (Mk. 6:30–32)

Wait, did I read this passage right? Does Jesus teach that sometimes people *need* a vacation or at least some time to recharge their batteries? Do God's children need a time out away from work and the hustle and bustle of life? Absolutely!

Jesus had sent his apostles out for field work. The apostles went in pairs to teach and call the people to repentance. They healed those who were sick and sought to minister to families, house by house. Without a doubt the work was rewarding but also challenging. This was not a "get in a car or airplane" to travel to some predetermined spot where folks had prepared an agenda of work. There were no meals planned, no rallies set up, nor was this planned in advance.

The apostles returned to Jesus exhausted physically, emotionally, and spiritually. Jesus recognized their exhaustion and told them to take a break! Were families still in need of the gospel message? Of course. Were the sick still needing a doctor? Without a doubt. Yet even with the need all around, Jesus saw the importance of rest and restoration for his apostles.

No one should be shocked by this. God made you and me. God knows that everyone needs times of refreshment. God saw to this in his instructions to Moses for the Israelites when God told them to keep the Sabbath. Every week, the seventh day was to be a day of rest, family, and freedom from work. This wasn't a byword tacked onto a list of "to do's." Keeping the Sabbath was one of the Ten Commandments!

Jesus would explain that the Sabbath was made for people (Mk. 2:27). People need the rest. No one is at their best for God if they aren't in good health and good spirits. Science teaches the importance of sleep for restoring the mind. Getting a good night's sleep, finding times to recharge one's batteries, recognizing that no one is at one's best if she/he tries to be constantly "on" is crucial.

As with so much of everything in life, the key is balance. God doesn't call anyone to slothfulness or laziness. In fact, Scripture strongly teaches against that. The believer, through prayer, counsel, and experience can work out the details. But when you are in rest mode, don't feel guilty. God ordered it!

Blessed Father, thank you for teaching us how to live our best life. Give us wisdom for balance and strength for the day! Through Jesus, amen.

MAY 31

When he went ashore he saw a great crowd, and he had compassion on them, because they were like sheep without a shepherd. And he began to teach them many things. (Mk. 6:34)

Sometimes God's Scriptures are clever beyond words. The layers of meaning and symbolism run so deep that lifetimes of study wouldn't plumb the depths of significant passages. Consider today's verse.

Jesus climbs out of the boat on the shores of the Sea of Galilee (a huge lake about thirteen miles long and eight miles wide at its greatest width). There are masses of people awaiting him. Mark's gospel doesn't simply tell the narrative of Jesus teaching. Mark adds that "Jesus had compassion on them, because they were like a sheep without a shepherd." This wasn't a metaphor Mark made up. Mark is referring back to a metaphor found in the Old Testament.

In the book of Numbers, chapter 27, God tells Moses to go up on a mountain and see the Promised Land that the Israelites will get to inhabit. Moses is not being allowed to go into the land with the people; his time on earth has drawn to a close. Moses asks God to "appoint a man over the congregation" as a leader so that "the congregation of the LORD may not be as sheep that have no shepherd." God appoints Joshua as the shepherd. Through Joshua, God leads the people into victory.

The metaphor Mark engages in today's passage is one that comes straight from the passage in Numbers. God's people need a shepherd, and not just any shepherd: they need one handpicked and designated by the Lord. Here lies another nice subtlety that can easily be lost on today's reader. We are having to parse through three languages: Hebrew, the original language of the Old Testament book of Numbers; Greek, the language of Mark's gospel; and English, the language of the text used in this devotional.

The name Jesus takes different forms and spellings in each language. Jesus' name in Hebrew is Yehoshua. When written with English letters it is Joshua. Jesus' name in Greek is Iēsous, which becomes Jesus when written in English letters. If we combine those languages, we readily see that God designated Jesus as the one to shepherd the people. (In fact, the Greek translation of the Old Testament uses the name Jesus for Joshua in this passage.)

In the midst of these subtleties, one should never lose track of the reason behind God's work. "Compassion!" Jesus felt compassion for the people. God cares. God wants what is best for us. When we realize that, we will be happier sheep!

Lord, thank you for your loving care. Help me to follow you better. In Jesus, amen.

JUNE 1

For this is he who was spoken of by the prophet Isaiah when he said, "The voice of one crying in the wilderness: 'Prepare the way of the Lord; make his paths straight.'" (Mt. 3:3)

American society is not as socially stratified as other civilizations have been in history, but that doesn't mean there is no social awareness. There is. People learn from an early age which "crowd" seems to fit their station in life. True, America prides itself on anyone from anywhere being able to do anything, but those are exceptions. A number of studies have confirmed that even teachers, who should know better, have learned to judge students' intelligence by where they come from and their socioeconomic backgrounds. Knowing this always gives me pause when I contemplate, "Who is Jesus?"

Today's passage comes in the flow of Matthew explaining the ministry of John the Baptist, a cousin and precursor to Jesus. John was walking through the wilderness of Judea preaching "Repent, for the kingdom of heaven is nearby." Matthew adds the comment that John was the one Isaiah referred to in Isaiah 40:3 when Isaiah prophesied that one would cry in the wilderness, "Prepare the way of the Lord; make his paths straight." If one reads the original Hebrew that Matthew was invoking, one discovers that the word "Lord" used is actually the name of God! This wasn't "lord" with a lower case, as in "master," or someone of high position. Isaiah spoke of YHWH God! YHWH God was coming and John was declaring or announcing that arrival.

After his resurrection, Jesus was never perceived by his followers, by those who knew him best, as an ordinary man. Jesus wasn't a "junior God." Jesus was YHWH God from the Old Testament. Jesus came not as a lowercase "lord," but as the King of kings and Lord of lords.

Paul wrote of Jesus in much the same way as Paul urged his readers to follow the attitude modeled by Jesus. Paul explained, "Have the same attitude, in yourself which was also in Christ Jesus, who, although he existed in the form of God, did not count equality with God a thing to be grasped, but emptied himself, by taking the form of a servant, *and* being born in the likeness of men. Then being found in human form, he humbled himself by becoming obedient to the point of death, even death on a cross" (Phil. 2:5–8).

The awesome recognition of Jesus' status should bring us to our knees. He is the Supreme One. As we heed the proclamation of John the Baptist, as we prepare the way of the Lord in our lives, it should come with an attitude of humility, service, and love. Jesus is Lord, and that changes everything.

Lord, in humility may I regard others as better than myself and seek to love and serve them in your name. Amen.

JUNE 2

In him [the "Word"—Jesus] was life, and the life was the light of men. The light shines in the darkness, and the darkness has not overcome it. (Jn. 1:4–5)

Take two boxes, one box filled with light and the other box filled with darkness. Then introduce darkness into the box of light (maybe open the lit box in a dark room?) and introduce light into the dark box. What happens? The light wins—every time. That is the way of light and darkness. Light shatters darkness.

Science explains what life experience confirms. Visible "light" is actually how we see waves of electromagnetic radiation pulsing through space. "Darkness" is what we have when there are no such waves. From a scientific perspective, if there are waves, there is light. If there are no waves, there is darkness. The two cannot consume the same place. We can't have no waves where there are waves.

The scientific understanding doesn't take away from what John had to say about Jesus as the light shining in the darkness. In fact, science helps us better understand John's point. Jesus is a metaphorical light that has come into the world. He is the energy by which we see clearly. He shows reality for what it is. He brings clarity to confusion. Where we find Jesus, darkness cannot co-exist.

In today's passage, John draws a direct line between the analogy of Jesus as light and Jesus as life. The analogy makes good sense! Life and death cannot co-exist at the same place and time. If I am alive, I am not dead. If I am dead, I am not alive. It is like being half-pregnant. It just doesn't work that way.

Life is something most everyone wants, especially if that life is a high-quality life. Jesus is that high-quality life. He brings it into the world that is otherwise stagnant. He takes people who may physically be alive, but are spiritually dead, and offers them a true, full, and abundant life.

We all have areas of our lives that are dark. We all have areas that are dead. These areas leave us feeling scared, alone, worried sick, inadequate for the days before us, angry, hurt, malicious, envious, jealous, and negative. These are symptoms of darkness and death—signs that we need a healthy dose of light and life. We need more Jesus.

When Jesus increasingly shines into our hearts and minds, those areas of darkness fade just as assuredly as the darkness inside a box disappears when light waves enter. Jesus is the solution for all our darkness. He will bring us a fullness of life that no darkness can stop.

Lord, please come into my life. Shatter all areas of darkness so I may experience the light of your life. In Jesus, amen.

JUNE 3

Jacob's well was there; so Jesus, wearied as he was from his journey, was sitting beside the well. It was about the sixth hour. A woman from Samaria came to draw water. Jesus said to her, "Give me a drink." (Jn. 4:6–7)

Do you ever get tired or weary? It might be physical fatigue where your body is worn out from exertion. It might be emotional fatigue where you seem to have reached the end of your rope. You feel drained, even though your body might be fine. Some reach a burn-out stage in life. For these, the lifetime journey seems to have hit a pause button, with little to no drive to continue. Today's verse speaks to those who are weary.

The gospel of John is very strong on portraying Jesus as the Incarnate Word of God. This is the writer who clearly places Jesus at creation ("In the beginning was the Word."). John gives the insight that Jesus is God's "only begotten Son" who gives eternal life to those who believe (Jn. 3:16). John writes the three chapters devoted to Jesus explaining his deity and the role of salvation he will play for all humanity (John 14–16). John gives the High Priestly prayer of Jesus for his people where Jesus stays awake all night, even as his dearest apostles fall asleep (Jn. 17). In John's gospel, Jesus performs miracles ranging from changing water to wine to raising Lazarus from the dead. John is never short on showing Jesus as the Almighty Divine One.

Yet Jesus was also fully human. As a human, Jesus would go on journeys like the one in today's passage and get tired from walking! John wants everyone to know that the divine Jesus was also the human Jesus. Jesus was "weary." So Jesus stopped, as weary folks often need to do. Jesus sat down by a well and, when the opportunity availed itself, got water.

Even in this most human moment, Jesus teaches us. We learn that weariness is no sin. We learn that there are times when we need to rest. (Of course, it was God who gave people the Sabbath, which teaches the same lesson!) Certainly, there is always more to do, but we can learn that resting is part of recharging our batteries to enable us to do more. Today's story gives that truth as well. Jesus stopped and waited for the Samaritan woman to draw water. God sets the next divine appointment for Jesus at the place where Jesus stopped to rest his weary feet! Had Jesus trudged on, insensitive to his body's needs, Jesus would not have had the encounter at the well.

God can work in all of our human frailties. When we are weary—physically, emotionally, mentally, and even spiritually—we can be assured that God can and will still work through us, even as we tend to the needs of our human bodies. What a God we serve!

Lord, give me times of guilt-free rest. Help me find your will in weariness! In Jesus, amen.

JUNE 4

A woman from Samaria came to draw water. Jesus said to her, "Give me a drink." (For his disciples had gone away into the city to buy food.) The Samaritan woman said to him, "How is it that you, a Jew, ask for a drink from me, a woman of Samaria?" (For Jews have no dealings with Samaritans.) Jesus answered her, "If you knew the gift of God, and who it is that is saying to you, 'Give me a drink,' you would have asked him, and he would have given you living water." (Jn. 4:7–10)

Law schools are famous for their teaching methods. Most teachers use the Socratic method, named after Socrates. This method uses discussion built around questions and answers to better understand the material being taught. Socrates and other early Greeks used it, and many teachers since have found it very effective.

Jesus was a master teacher. He had a similar tool in his teaching repertoire. When Jesus sat by a well, tired from his journey and wanting a drink, he waited until a woman came by to draw water. Jesus asked her for a drink. The woman reacted by challenging Jesus the Jew for asking a Samaritan woman (Samaritans were taboo to Jews) for anything. Jews weren't to talk to Samaritans. Jesus took her reaction a step further hinting at what he could give her, had she only asked. When the story is read in the whole, we learn that the dialogue continued until finally the woman awoke to who Jesus was and she learned the message he had to teach. The story ends marvelously.

Jesus engaged the woman by seeking something from her. Jesus didn't need the woman for water. He could have found another way to access the refreshing liquid in the well. Importantly, however, we see Jesus using what the woman could do for Jesus *to bring good into the life of the woman!* This approach is the remarkable way of God.

God uses this story to teach us. We can learn from the master teacher if we read and probe the implications of the story, applying the same principles to our lives. God will seek things from us—service, obedience, kindness to others, our giving when there is need, our mercy and forgiveness when we are wronged, and more. God seeks these not because God himself is in need. God seeks from us to teach us. God seeks from us to develop us into our best self. God seeks from us *for us!*

What an amazing God we serve. When we have opportunities to live in holiness, putting him and his desires first in our lives, we grow and become what we should be. We learn what life is all about. We are changed into a better reflection of him. I need to look at life a bit differently than I have before!

Lord, give me better vision about life. Help me to see your hand as my Lord, but also my teacher. Help me to live looking for your lessons and learning from your instruction. In Jesus' most holy name, amen!

JUNE 5

Jesus answered her, "If you knew the gift of God, and who it is that is saying to you, 'Give me a drink,' you would have asked him, and he would have given you living water." (Jn. 4:10)

Growing up, I always eagerly anticipated my birthday. Our family was big on birthdays. Mom would let us select our birthday meal, and whatever we chose, she made. She also made the cake of our choice. Although we didn't have a lot of spare money growing up, Dad and Mom always made sure we had super birthday presents. I still remember when I was very young, thinking through what a birthday was as I wondered, "Why don't we have birthdays more than once a year?"

Today's passage has some interesting ideas that make me think about birthdays, but ones that happen more than once a year! Jesus is with the Samaritan woman at the well. Jesus' disciples have left to go to the ancient equivalent of the grocery store to buy food. Jesus is thirsty and asked the Samaritan woman to use her implements to draw some water for him. She is stunned and wants to know why Jesus, a Jew, is willing to ask her such, because good Jews didn't interact with Samaritans. Jesus' response is telling. Jesus tells the woman that she would be acting much differently if she "knew the gift of God."

God gives gifts. (In Greek the "gift" is "δωρεά," which is a "free gift" or one given "freely.") His gifts change our lives. Knowing he gives gifts should also change our lives. What gifts does our God give? In this story Jesus gives "living water." This is an unusual phrase. The woman is at a well or cistern. It is like a pond that is still. Contrasted to this is a river or flowing water, which is what Jesus' phrase "living water" means. Flowing or living water is what Jews used for purification. This same phrase is used in the Old Testament to speak of nourishment from YHWH God. Jeremiah contrasted the "living water" of the LORD to the cisterns used by the people that forsook him (Jer. 2:13). Later in John, Jesus uses the phrase "living water" to speak of the Holy Spirit that flows in the life of the believer (Jn. 7:38–39).

Closely linked to this gift in the words of Jesus is "knowing" Jesus. Jesus said the woman failed to know both "the gift of God" and "who it is" talking to her. These two phrases are linked because knowing Jesus, in the sense of being intimate and connected to him, ties us to God in a relationship that changes everything. We receive trustworthy teaching that changes who we are and how we live. We receive his Spirit. This relationship isn't a once-a-year birthday gift; it is 24/7. The gift of knowing Jesus and having his Spirit is permanent. This is a gift worth asking for!

Lord, I come to you humbly asking for you to be Lord of my life, with all that entails. Fill me with your presence and may I live for you. In Jesus' name, amen.

JUNE 6

Jesus answered her, "If you knew the gift of God, and who it is that is saying to you, 'Give me a drink,' you would have asked him, and he would have given you living water." The woman said to him, "Sir, you have nothing to draw water with, and the well is deep. Where do you get that living water? Are you greater than our father Jacob? He gave us the well and drank from it himself, as did his sons and his livestock." (Jn. 4:10–12)

Today's passage continues Jesus' encounter with a Samaritan woman at a well. The woman had no clue who Jesus was. Jesus engaged her in dialogue and while she seemed a bit intrigued, she was clearly intent to steer the conversation away from spiritual truth and her personal life. I suspect we are all a bit like the Samaritan woman at times.

A remarkable part of the woman's encounter with Jesus was her utter cluelessness as to whom she was dealing. Jesus had made quite a name for himself at this time, although she is clearly clueless. Her ignorance may be excused because as a Samaritan she may have missed much of Jesus' ministry. Still, in hindsight it is remarkable that this woman, going about her routine daily chores, shows up to draw and haul water, doubtlessly a strenuous job that was not the highlight of her day, and she stumbles into an encounter with the Son of God. In light of all history, Jesus walked this earth in ministry for only a microscopic moment. Even within that moment, the earth is huge, and Jesus' walk was on only a smidgeon of its surface. What are the odds that this woman would encounter Emmanuel, God with us, the Holy One, the Messiah of Israel, and the Savior of the world?

The odds are infinitesimally small if viewed from a perspective devoid of God's hand and intent. But when we see God was behind this, the encounter couldn't be missed. Jesus sought out the woman. Jesus drew her into conversation. Jesus moved the conversation beyond the mundane into the important. This was a God moment that changed the woman's life for eternity.

I wonder how many people, me included, fail to see Jesus for who he is, where he is, and what he has to offer. I know that he is ever-present. While he doesn't walk the earth as the Incarnate One, he is nonetheless present in his Spirit. He still invades our mundane everyday lives, while we do the mundane everyday chores, and works to draw us into a spiritually vibrant dialogue. Jesus wants us to know him. He wants us to relate to him. He wants us to bring our sins before him for forgiveness. He wants to stir us up to good works for the sake of the Father and the kingdom of heaven. We tend to forget how stunning it is that the God of All wants to engage us in a one-on-one relationship.

Lord, I am amazed that you call out to me, that you want to sit with me, have interest in me, and want to give me a life I could have nowhere else. Thank you. In Jesus, amen.

JUNE 7

Jesus said to her, "Go, call your husband, and come here." The woman answered him, "I have no husband." Jesus said to her, "You are right in saying, 'I have no husband'; for you have had five husbands, and the one you now have is not your husband. What you have said is true." The woman said to him, "Sir, I perceive that you are a prophet." (Jn. 4:16–19)

Today's passage makes me smile. No, I'm not smiling because the woman had had a difficult time with relationships. Undoubtedly that left deep emotional scars and a trail of pain throughout her life. I feel pity and sadness for her past, even though I know the story and the emotional healing she finds. My smile comes from reading about this woman trying to divert Jesus' attention from her checkered past. I picture a toddler trying to beat Lebron James in one-on-one. I picture a three-year-old with crayons trying to show Leonardo Da Vinci how to paint the *Mona Lisa*.

Jesus is at a water well confronting the Samaritan woman who has spent the better part of the conversation trying to avoid speaking of anything important in life. Jesus draws out the woman by instructing her to bring her husband to the well. The woman says in Greek, "οὐκ ἔχω ἄνδρα." The word order is important. In English it is, "Not, I have a husband." Greek word order was very important for conveying emphasis. (The Greeks didn't have **bold** font, *italics*, or even exclamation points! So they used other emphasis tools, especially word order.) The woman was emphasizing the "NOT!" We could capture that by writing her comment as, "I do NOT have a husband!" Jesus then corrects her word order, modifying the emphasis. I wonder if Jesus didn't have a wry smile on his face as he told her she would be right to say, "ἄνδρα οὐκ ἔχω." Even if you don't read Greek, you can compare the two Greek phrases I set out here. You can see the same three words, but Jesus put "husband" first. We can pick up Jesus' reply by writing it, "Yes, you don't have a *husband*!" Jesus knew that she'd been through five husbands and was now living out of wedlock with another fellow.

So, I smile. She was intent on painting a picture of reality that was far from the real one. She thought she was going to trick Jesus? She thought she could hide the truth of her sorrow and shame? She thought she could avoid addressing the failures in her home? She thought she could address Jesus on her terms, and not his? I smile at her feeble attempts.

I also smile because I see me in this story. I know what it is to fail in life. I know what it is to have sin. I know the desire to avoid confronting the reality of my shortcomings with the majestic God. I share her desire to talk about something—anything—else. Yet Jesus draws me into honesty and gives me forgiveness. It leaves me with a deep smile.

Lord, forgive me. Thank you for your unconditional love. I need it. In Jesus, amen.

JUNE 8

Just then his disciples came back. They marveled that he was talking with a woman, but no one said, "What do you seek?" or, "Why are you talking with her?" (Jn. 4:27)

People come in all shapes, sizes, hair colors, and dispositions! Some are inherently optimistic ("the glass is half full"). Some are naturally pessimistic ("the glass is half empty"). Some are practical ("the glass is too big"). Traits are similarly variable when it comes to how we see ourselves. Some see themselves with great confidence in who they are and what they are worth. Others see themselves and wonder whether anyone could like or notice them.

Today's passage should reassure everyone that God sees them, cares for them, and wants a relationship with them. God's desires in this aren't dictated by whether we are American, European, Asian, African, or Australian. God's interests aren't determined by our gender, education level, or occupation. God cares just as much for the young as the old, for the poor as the rich, for the successful as the one struggling to make a life. If someone will engage with God, God will be there, regardless of one's station in life. The choice is always ours to make.

In this passage, Jesus had been talking to a Samaritan woman. Samaritans were a race avoided by Jews in Jesus' day, but not by Jesus. Moreover, Jewish rabbis did not voluntarily talk to women. The ancient Jewish rabbis quoted the sages as saying, "He that talks much with womankind brings evil upon himself and neglects the study of the Law and at the last will inherit Hell" (from the Mishna, Avot 1:5). The rabbinical writings in the Talmud (where the Jewish oral law from the times of Jesus was later written down) speak of a rabbi's wife chiding a Galilean rabbi for asking her, "By which road do we go to Lydda?" when it would have sufficed to say less, "Which road to Lydda?" and reduce the dialogue ("Foolish Galilean . . . did not the sages say, 'Engage not in much talk with women?'").

Jesus spoke much to this woman. Jesus turned that teaching upside down. Jesus wasn't worried about the woman's gender. His concern was her soul. Jesus befriended people not genders. Rabbi Paul would later explain that in Christ there is neither male nor female, slave nor free, Jew nor Gentile. Jesus is God's proclamation of forgiveness to all who accept him. Jesus calls everyone into a personal relationship with God Almighty. Our shape doesn't matter. Our lineage is irrelevant. Our disposition isn't determinative. What matters is our heart. Do we come to God and humbly seek his forgiveness? Or do we stride arrogantly through life, ignoring God or relegating him to a small corner of our thoughts? Without regard to our past, we can be assured in our present that God is ready to converse with us. He cares for us. He wants us.

Lord, thank you for your love. May I accept it and thrive under it in Jesus' name, amen.

JUNE 9

The woman said to him, "Sir, I perceive that you are a prophet. Our fathers worshiped on this mountain, but you say that in Jerusalem is the place where people ought to worship." Jesus said to her, "Woman, believe me, the hour is coming when neither on this mountain nor in Jerusalem will you worship the Father. You worship what you do not know; we worship what we know, for salvation is from the Jews. But the hour is coming, and is now here, when the true worshipers will worship the Father in spirit and truth, for the Father is seeking such people to worship him. God is spirit, and those who worship him must worship in spirit and truth." (Jn. 4:19–24)

Many different styles of worship can be found among the many churches in the world today. Even in a single congregation, there can be one service with "traditional worship" with another branded "contemporary worship." Those are useful labels, for they identify the types of music and other aspects of the services such that someone can find the one that seems most suited to her or him. We must be careful, however, for our language can also serve to limit our understanding of worship.

In today's passage, Jesus is speaking with a Samaritan woman who is engaging Jesus in the debate over whether one should worship in Jerusalem (as the Jews believed) or Mount Gerizim (as the Samaritans believed). Jesus responded that times were shifting and that was no longer the debate. The place of true worship, the worship that God seeks from his people, is worship that is "in spirit and truth," not in one location or another.

Jesus taught and modeled that worship was more than "attending a service." Worship was to be an intimate part of one's heart and mind. Worship is part of our everyday living, not something we do only one or two days a week when we go to our local congregation.

At its root, "worship" means to ascribe to God the worth he is due. Wrapped up in the word "worship," especially in a close examination of the Hebrew and Greek words translated as "worship," is service to God, an awe of God, expressing the wonders and glories of God, and an attitude with actions of obedience to God. These terms should be at our core every day. In all aspects of our lives, we should be in awe of God, serving God, obedient to his word.

Does this mean we don't go to corporate worship? Heavens no! But it does mean that we worship him beyond that location. Jesus told us to worship in "spirit and truth." That instruction is a call to everyday worship. We worship him sincerely with all that we are and all we do.

Lord, may my life reflect your worth. Help me grow in serving and obeying you, and in declaring awe at your greatness, at your deep and personal love for me in Jesus, amen.

JUNE 10

Meanwhile the disciples were urging him, saying, "Rabbi, eat." But he said to them, "I have food to eat that you do not know about." So the disciples said to one another, "Has anyone brought him something to eat?" Jesus said to them, "My food is to do the will of him who sent me and to accomplish his work." (Jn. 4:31–34)

Do you use the informal phrases "You are out of touch," and "You don't have a clue"? Perhaps you more readily use the "mis-" words instead—misunderstand, mistake, misinterpret, misconstrue. Pick your choice of words or phrases and apply it to today's passage. Amazingly, the apostles had spent hours, days, weeks, months with Jesus, hearing his messages, watching his life, seeing his priorities, and trying to learn and practice what Jesus taught. Yet at times, they were clueless about what Jesus meant.

Jesus was hungry and weary. He had stayed at a well to get some water while his disciples went to a nearby market to grab some food. While the disciples were gone, Jesus got a chance to dialogue with a Samaritan woman about eternal matters. Jesus was touching the woman's soul, and God was about to reap a harvest for his kingdom from not only the woman, but from those in her village. The woman had left the well to bring her fellow villagers back to meet Jesus.

The disciples gave Jesus some of the food with the encouragement, "Eat!" Jesus wanted them to know what he had been up to, and he started that conversation with a comment, "I have food you don't know about!" Jesus, of course, was mentioning the nourishment and invigoration that came from interacting with one on God's behalf, reaching them for the Lord. The clueless disciples thought they were slow back with the food. They thought someone else must have gotten Jesus food more quickly. Jesus told them he meant something less literal.

I read this and examine my life. I wonder where Jesus is working even though I am blind to what is going on. I fear I am often like the disciples, working on getting food and life's provisions, not realizing at the same time that God is at work. The disciples weren't wrong in going to get the food. Jesus was God, but he was also human. He was hungry and needed to eat. They didn't go get the food out of rebellion but out of obedience. Yet while they were doing the mundane, Jesus was doing the extraordinary. They didn't see it. They didn't understand it. But it was true nonetheless.

I will have days where I get the invigoration of sharing God with others. I will have days where I am working for bread to feed myself and others. I must not lose sight that God is at work, even when I am not as visibly involved. I may be clueless about what he is up to, but I can trust that he is working!

Father, work through me, even in my mundane tasks of daily life. In Jesus, amen.

JUNE 11

Just then his disciples came back. They marveled that he was talking with a woman, but no one said, "What do you seek?" or, "Why are you talking with her?" (Jn. 4:27)

Recently we had a high school reunion. In addition to catching up on what has happened since we last saw each other, the reunion was a time to reflect on all that has changed since we were in high school in the 1970s. Of course, politicians have changed, and not just on a national scale. The USSR has dissolved, and the Cold War is over. Technology has profoundly changed the world, and with that, our culture and even language. We carry phones, can text at most inopportune moments, and have an abbreviated language (LOL).

The events behind today's passage are almost two thousand years old. Since then, humanity's changes are vast. Empires have come and gone, the world has been explored, science has brought great understanding and technology, and culture has, in some ways, made great strides. We might look back at the biblical times stunned at some things we read, but if we read with history in mind, we see that Jesus and his followers are key people in leading our society forward in many notable ways.

At the time of Jesus, Jewish rabbis didn't speak much with women. For almost two centuries before the time Jesus was born, good Jews lived under the shadow of the deceased head of the Sanhedrin (Jewish Supreme Court) teacher Joseph ben Johanan who said, "Do not speak much with a woman." This was true for one's wife, certainly more so for a stranger. The sages after Johanan added, "Anytime a man increases conversation with the woman, he causes evil to himself and neglects the words of Torah [Genesis through Deuteronomy]; and, in this end, inherits Hell [Gehenna]" (Pirkei Avot 1:5).

Jesus turned that teaching upside down. Jesus wasn't worried about the woman's gender. His concern was her soul. Jesus befriended *people* not genders. Jesus' follower Rabbi Sha'ul (we know him as the apostle Paul) would write just a few decades later that in Jesus is neither "male nor female" (Gal. 3:28). This was radical in that day!

Some trash Christianity and Jesus as misogynist and antiwomen. These people need to read more history and Bible! Jesus and the Christian faith propelled Western civilization to realize that everyone stands equally before God. Everyone is a sinner in need of a Savior. Jesus came to save all. God made male and female in his image, and we all walk with him alike, regardless of gender, age, economics, education, nationality, genetics, or any other human distinction you can think of, including a sinful past.

In other words, God loves no one more than he loves you!

Lord, thank you for your love. May I accept it and thrive under it in Jesus' name, amen.

JUNE 12

And Jesus said to them, "Can the wedding guests mourn as long as the bridegroom is with them? The days will come when the bridegroom is taken away from them, and then they will fast. No one puts a piece of unshrunk cloth on an old garment, for the patch tears away from the garment, and a worse tear is made. Neither is new wine put into old wineskins. If it is, the skins burst and the wine is spilled and the skins are destroyed. But new wine is put into fresh wineskins, and so both are preserved." (Mt. 9:15–17)

My wife Becky may be the funniest person I've ever known. She loves almost all types of humor—puns and witty word play, satire, comic plot, and unexpected reversals. Her humor can be sophisticated, but she also laughs hard at pratfalls. Take her to a movie, have someone step on a rake, and as the handle hits their face, my wife will be laughing out loud. It is an old joke she's seen countless times, but it still makes her laugh.

Jesus had a wide-ranging sense of humor too. He used word play (calling Peter, whose name means "rock" a "stumbling block" [Mt. 16:23]), irony (telling righteous Pharisees that prostitutes will get into the kingdom before they will [Mt. 21:31]), sarcasm (accusing some of straining a gnat while swallowing a camel [Mt. 23:24]), absurdity (in the healing of a woman with persistent bleeding, when a crowd is pressing against him, Jesus proclaims, "Who touched me?" [Lk. 8:44–45]), and more to make his points. In today's passage, Jesus makes his point using a picture of the ancient equivalent of a pratfall.

Wine is fermented juice. Microorganisms, like yeast or bacteria, consume the sugars in juice and convert the carbohydrates to alcohol and carbon dioxide, a gas. When the chemical breakdown occurs, the gas puts the wine under pressure. It expands the volume of the material. In antiquity, if new wine that was undergoing this fermentation process was put into new wine skins, those skins could and would stretch as the fermentation process occurred. Once the wine skins had stretched, however, they weren't useful for wine that was going through the fermentation process. They would explode.

We don't typically have the exploding wineskin picture in our experience. For me, the better image is what happens when you take a water balloon already stretched to its limit and add even more water. Kaboom! And water goes everywhere.

Jesus knew that his ministry, his teaching, his presence—these were things that no one had experienced before. Yes, it was a serious time, but it was a good time. His followers had the joy of the Son of God in their daily midst. We don't have the physical Son of God walking with us today, but we have his presence and Spirit in our hearts. We have days of struggle and difficulty, but we should never lose the joy that comes with our Savior!

Lord, give me joy in the journey, a deep abiding joy that is there, even when the skies are dark. Thank you for your presence in me, in Jesus, my Lord, amen.

JUNE 13

Then Pilate said to him, "So you are a king?" Jesus answered, "You say that I am a king. For this purpose I was born and for this purpose I have come into the world—to bear witness to the truth. Everyone who is of the truth listens to my voice." Pilate said to him, "What is truth?" (Jn. 18:37–38)

Some people have a knack for the obvious. Others can have something staring them in the face and miss it all together. I put Pilate in the "others" category.

While scholars find this passage interesting as one that indicates Jesus was conversant in Greek (the likely language Pilate was using), the passage serves a more direct purpose in today's devotional. Pilate was going through his routine day, having come seventy-five miles from his home base in Caesarea into Jerusalem to deal with administrative matters. As the procurator over the region, Pilate was in charge of keeping the peace and administering the judgment of Rome.

Dealing with Jesus wasn't on Pilate's agenda. Jesus was an issue that had just come up. Certain Jewish authorities were quite upset over Jesus, and they wanted Pilate to deal with him. The easiest way was to paint Jesus as one leading a rebellion, one claiming to be a king in opposition to Rome and Caesar. This accusation raised Jesus to a significance that required Pilate's personal attention.

Pilate questioned Jesus, "Are you really claiming to be a king?" Jesus replied, "Those are your words. I came into the world to bear witness to the truth." Jesus added that anyone, regardless of status, placement in the Roman Empire, slave, free, male, female—*anyone*—who would hear and listen to Jesus would be part of the truth.

Here was Pilate's big moment. Pilate had a one-on-one encounter with the Son of God. Pilate had that opportunity most every atheist always demands—"If God is real, have him appear for me and tell me!" Yet Pilate blew it. He couldn't see the truth that was standing right before him. With a chance to dialogue with God, to get life right, to find forgiveness, to have a relationship with God fully restored, to do an about-face and find faith, with all of those chances and more, Pilate missed it. Pilate turned the opportunity into a hum-drum, dismissive, almost cynical reply: "What is truth?"

The ultimate truth was staring Pilate in the face, and he did nothing with it. He was too blind to see what was right in front of him. Am I? Jesus stands before me in this passage today. Do I see him for who he is? Do I seize this moment to address him as God or do I dismiss him? This is a time for resolute decisions! I don't want to miss the obvious.

Lord, I embrace you today as my Lord, my God, and the truth I need in my life. Guide me for your name's sake. In Jesus, amen.

JUNE 14

Now after John was arrested, Jesus came into Galilee, proclaiming the gospel of God, and saying, "The time is fulfilled, and the kingdom of God is at hand; repent and believe in the gospel." (Mk. 1:14–15)

My job has me traveling a great deal. Many times, I am driving to one court or another, but often I am flying around the country. Occasionally, I fly overseas for meetings and depositions. Regardless of where I go, I like to have certain things at hand. I need my computer and cell phone. I need my notebook and pens. I find highlighters useful along with Post-It Notes. It is also important to have cash in the local currency and several charge cards. These items are all important and all serve a purpose.

On those times I fail to have something nearby, I almost always find I need it. The one time I think I can survive without cash, some place will not accept credit cards. Should I fail to bring a highlighter, I find I need one like never before.

Having something important at hand is behind the teaching of Jesus as Mark wrote about it in today's passage. Jesus was just launching his teaching ministry. His daily job as a carpenter was over, and he was going throughout the countryside teaching the gospel (*euaggelion* or "good news" in the Greek). This good news was that God's kingdom was "at hand" or was "coming near." This was happening at just the right moment, when "the time [was] fulfilled."

What did Jesus mean? Jesus had been incarnated for thirty years, but as he transitioned from carpenter to rabbi, he was moving from building furniture and such to building God's house. Jesus' time had come, and that meant God's time had come. This was the fruition of a plan that God had before he built the world. God announced this plan to Adam and Eve as God dealt with the ramifications of their sin and fall from fellowship with God. (In Genesis 3:15, God told the serpent that from the offspring of woman would come one who would step on Satan's head.)

The time was right for Jesus individually and for God's overarching design of salvation. So, Jesus rightfully told people that God's kingdom was at hand, and that people should repent and trust (or believe) in this good news.

I need this today. More than I need my computer, cell phone, or even highlighters, I need the kingdom of God at hand. The fact that God has restored fellowship with me, that he wants to know me personally and be Lord of my life should be my motivation each day. It calls me to repent and turn to him in faith.

Lord, may your kingdom be the keystone in my life. I repent of living apart from you centered on myself, and put my trust in you as my Lord. In Jesus I pray, amen.

JUNE 15

Standing by the cross of Jesus were his mother and his mother's sister, Mary the wife of Clopas, and Mary Magdalene. When Jesus saw his mother and the disciple whom he loved standing nearby, he said to his mother, "Woman, behold, your son!" Then he said to the disciple, "Behold, your mother!" And from that hour the disciple took her to his own home. (Jn. 19:25–27)

My father was the protector of our family. Growing up, I never doubted that Dad would do whatever needed to be done on behalf of Mom, my sisters, and me. That's just who Dad was. By the time we grew into adults and moved into middle age, we didn't need Dad's daily protection, yet we never doubted it was there in any measure necessary. Of course, for Mom, Dad was still 100 percent her knight in shining armor.

My father suffered a stroke that left him hospitalized and unable to speak or move very much. On one of my visits I was alone with him in his room, uncertain whether or not what I was saying was registering. I told Dad he needed to get better. I explained that I wasn't able to take care of folks and the family needed him to continue being the patriarch. Dad got an expression on his face that told me both that he fully understood what I was saying, but also that he knew I was wrong. He wanted me to know I was wrong. If something happened to him, I was more than ready to handle it. I acknowledged that I understood, but still wanted him back at home. Dad died just a few days later.

My experience with my father still plays in my head every time I consider this passage at the end of Jesus' life. Jesus was abandoned by many as he hung on the cross. Four soldiers were there performing the crucifixion, and in juxtaposition, four women were there who loved Jesus—Mary (Jesus' mother), Mary's sister, another Mary who was the wife of Clopas, and Mary Magdalene. Nearby was John the apostle. Jesus was wracked with pain. His hands and feet had massive nails through them. His weight dug unceasingly into those nailed wounds as he hung from the cross. He was exhausted, thirsty, and carried the sins of the world on his shoulders. Yet with all of this, looking down from the cross, Jesus was moved to see that his mother was taken care of. Jesus told Mary that from there on, John was as her son. Jesus told John that Mary was as his mother. John was to take care of Mary. John did so.

As the apostle Paul noted when telling the Ephesians to honor their parents, "this is the first commandment with a promise." To honor a parent includes taking care of them in old age. Jesus fulfilled this commandment, along with the other ones in his life. But Jesus did it not only in obedience to Exodus 20:12. Jesus' concern for his mother was genuine and flowed from a deep love. I am touched by the love of Jesus. I need to learn from it.

Lord, thank you for your love. May I share it and show it for others. In Jesus, amen.

JUNE 16

And behold, some people brought to him a paralytic, lying on a bed. And when Jesus saw their faith, he said to the paralytic, "Take heart, my son; your sins are forgiven." (Mt. 9:2)

Some people in this world are physically paralyzed. By accident, by birth, by infirmity or stroke, or by any number of other causes, some people aren't able to fully move and function. Some people in this world go through stages where their bodies are healthy and working fully but are paralyzed in decision-making, in loving, in forgiving, or in any number of nonphysical ways. At some time or another, most people find themselves in the latter group.

The gospel story in today's passage concerns one who was physically paralyzed, but likely, also paralyzed in nonphysical ways. Reading the verse carefully, one sees that the paralytic is almost a nonactor in the event. The paralytic is brought in, understandable since he was unable to move (the nouns are masculine, so in the Greek it indicates this paralytic was male, not female). But the passage also indicates that the faith for the healing wasn't simply the paralytic's. Jesus saw "their" faith. The "their" in this sentence must include the "they" who brought in the paralytic. Does this mean the paralytic had no faith? Not necessarily. He could easily be part of the "*their* faith," but the emphasis is still on the "they," not the paralytic.

What paralyzed the man? Physically, we don't know. Emotionally, we have a clue. Jesus doesn't simply heal the man saying, as he often did, "Go, your faith has made you well!" Instead, Jesus urges the man to "take heart." This Greek (*tharseō*, θαρσέω) could be translated with a variety of English words. "Don't despair!" "Take courage!" "Don't fear!" "Be courageous!" Jesus was encouraging the man to be enheartened for a reason. The reason is wrapped in the next words Jesus said, "your sins are forgiven." Jesus freed the man from the sins that bound his soul and his body. Jesus brought the man true deliverance, and the physical healing became a sign of the true release Jesus gave.

I am not physically paralyzed, at least at the time I am writing this devotional. But I understand the paralysis that comes into life from sin and guilt, from fear, from doubt, from lack of energy, from despair, from grief, from . . . fill in the blank. Into these moments and stages in life comes our healing Savior. Into our dark and faithless moments comes the faithful one who is light. Coming into our moments is Jesus, bringing with his presence healing. Jesus can break the chains that hold one bound. I need the healing of my Jesus.

Lord, I come to you as I am today—in need, in hope, in expectation. Please come touch me with your forgiveness and healing. Free me from the fears of this life and let me live to your glory. Through your power and name, amen.

JUNE 17

One man was there who had been an invalid for thirty-eight years. When Jesus saw him lying there and knew that he had already been there a long time, he said to him, "Do you want to be healed?" The sick man answered him, "Sir, I have no one to put me into the pool when the water is stirred up, and while I am going another steps down before me." Jesus said to him, "Get up, take up your bed, and walk." And at once the man was healed, and he took up his bed and walked. (Jn. 5:5–9)

When I was a child, we sang a song in church titled "Trust and Obey." The core message in the song was that walking with the Lord linked these two concepts together. We trust Jesus, and we obey Jesus. To separate the two ideas is to rob them both of their power.

Trusting Jesus is a deep-seated decision that is rooted in believing the truth that Jesus is God, that Jesus knows us, that Jesus cares for us, and that Jesus will act for our good. If we have that trust and belief, then we will do what Jesus says. We will obey him. If we fail to obey him, how can we claim to really trust him? Only a fool would choose to trust Jesus and then fail to listen and obey him. Similarly, if we obey Jesus, but don't trust him, then our actions are really only self-interest, and not truly rooted in a confident decision that Jesus is at work in our lives and our world. That is the situation behind today's passage.

In today's passage, Jesus has found an invalid by a pool in Jerusalem. The invalid believes that healing will come to the first one in this pool's water on the rare occasions when the waters are stirred up. Jesus asks the invalid whether he wants to be healed. The invalid doesn't look at Jesus with faith. The invalid comes to Jesus with excuses. One can almost hear the whining in his voice, "I can't be healed . . . Others get healed before me! It's not fair!!!" Jesus replies with a command, not a question. Jesus orders the invalid, "Get up!" Jesus then instructs the weakened man to "take up your bed and walk!" The man got it! With Jesus' command came healing. The man didn't have to wait for some miracle water. The man had no complaint he could make. The man had only to trust and obey.

The invalid got the "obey" part; he arose and left. But the man had no trust or faith. The ruling Jews were critical of the man for carrying his mat on the Sabbath, and they pointed out his perceived error. The healed invalid blamed Jesus for his actions! At first he didn't know who Jesus was, but as soon as he encountered Jesus a second time, rather than following Jesus in faith, the man left Jesus to tell the Jews that it was Jesus who had healed him! This fellow turned his back on the Son of God in spite of all Jesus did for him. I would be more critical of him if I hadn't also failed to trust and obey often.

Lord, forgive my lack of faithful obedience. With gratitude for all you have done, amen.

JUNE 18

As the Father has loved me, so have I loved you. Abide in my love. (Jn. 15:9)

In 1991, Disney produced the animated film *Beauty and the Beast*. In the movie, an enchantress turns a cruel and selfish prince into a beast, his body bearing the truth of who he was in his core. The enchantress leaves the beast with a rose that will lose petals and her spells will only break if the beast learns to love and is truly loved by another before the last petal falls. Otherwise, the beast remains a beast forever. After struggles and much conflict, the beast is truly loved by the beautiful Belle, and, like all Disney movies, they live happily ever after.

Humanity is properly captured by true love. People are hardwired to want and need love. Many people understand their own beastly natures and can seem somewhat difficult to love. Like the prince turned into the beast, people tend to be selfish, looking to personal needs rather than seeking to serve those around them. While there isn't an enchantress to turn self-interested, arrogant, and haughty people into beasts, the result of sin has that effect, nonetheless. Selfish people may not always realize how they look to others, but loving one's self at the expense of others, seeking to live for one's self alone, makes one quite beastly.

Left to one's own devices, and given enough time, this "beast mode" becomes nearly impossible to break. It feeds and feeds itself into habits, deeply ingrained behavioral patterns, and even an illusion of reality. It might give one great personal wealth (the beast's castle and possessions), but it leaves one isolated. Even those who are around the selfish beast are seen as mere possessions (the head of the household staff turned into a clock and the valet turned into a candlestick).

The movie is fiction, but the truth behind the plot is real. Humanity is cursed by its own failures and shortcomings. People are doomed to live and die as beasts absent the intervention of true and transforming love by one most beautiful. That intervening love is found in Jesus. Jesus takes those unlovable and cares for them. Jesus' love isn't self-interested, but it is truly centered on those he loves. If one allows him to, Jesus takes one's ugly, twisted features and shapes them through an unconditional love into those of a princely nature. He transforms his people by his love.

Jesus taught his followers that Jesus loved them with God's love. Jesus wants his followers to live for him out of love, not fear. He wants his followers to understand and accept the depths of his caring love. After all, why would anyone want to remain a beast?

Dear Lord, please take my ugly and ungodly selfishness and make me a lover of others. May I shine with your love and live as your vessel today. In Jesus' name, amen.

JUNE 19

Now a certain man was ill, Lazarus of Bethany, the village of Mary and her sister Martha. It was Mary who anointed the Lord with ointment and wiped his feet with her hair, whose brother Lazarus was ill. So the sisters sent to him, saying, "Lord, he whom you love is ill." But when Jesus heard it he said, "This illness does not lead to death. It is for the glory of God, so that the Son of God may be glorified through it." (Jn. 11:1–4)

This story of Jesus is especially fitting in its message for people today. John recounts details that help people of any age find themselves in this story, to the glory of God.

Lazarus is sick, real sick. While no one knows the disease, it is clearly life threatening. His sisters reach out to Jesus, knowing that Jesus has healed many and confident that Jesus will journey to their home to heal their brother. After all, they are able to label their brother with the statement, "this is one whom you love."

Lazarus' name is given by John not only because it informs people of who is in the story, but also because of what his name means. "Lazarus" is an abbreviated form of the Hebrew name "Eleazar," meaning "God has helped." This was a situation where his name was earned! As the story unfolds, Lazarus dies before Jesus gets there. Jesus doesn't leave him dead, however, but raises him from the grave. The entire story line serves as a picture of what unfolds in the lives of believers.

Every person who sees reality is able to say, "I am ill." Sin has made us more than sick. We may feel great physically, but until we have the healing touch of Jesus, we are "dead in our trespasses and sins" as Paul wrote in Ephesians 2:1. Yet everyone is also someone that Jesus loves. His life was one given for those he loves. So Jesus comes to us in our sickened and dead state, and he calls us forth from the grave. This is to God's glory and the glory of the Son.

God's glory has never consisted in making one's life easy or in sparing one from the sufferings of this age. God's glory is shown in how he walks with us through the sufferings of life, and *in the end*, through his grace and mercy, sustains, delivers, and conquers sin and death, with all its consequences. This is the hope of every believer.

We live in a world of despair, but we are all Lazarus. God has helped each of us. Jesus knows our condition and comes to our aid. Jesus speaks into our lives and brings us forth victorious over the grave.

Thank you, Jesus!

Lord, your love for me is life changing. Let me savor it, treasure it, grow in it, and display it to others. Humbly in Jesus I pray, amen!

JUNE 20

Again he began to teach beside the sea. And a very large crowd gathered about him, so that he got into a boat and sat in it on the sea, and the whole crowd was beside the sea on the land. (Mk. 4:1)

Do you ever wonder, "Why do I spend time in the Bible each day?" Or perhaps more specifically, "Why am I reading this? What is there for me in the teachings of Jesus *today?*"

Today's passage helps inform *part* of our answer. Jesus came into this world to die for our sins, but he didn't merely show up and then head to the cross. He also came and spent three years teaching and serving through public ministry. Teaching was important to Jesus. It was so important that on days like that in today's passage, the crowds got too immense for "normal" teaching.

Jesus was speaking at a time when there were no microphones or speaking assistance. His words would not have been heard so clearly had he stayed onshore to speak. So, Jesus climbed into a boat, which would have elevated him a bit, and gave the crowd space to hear, listen, and learn. Jesus *wanted* the crowd to hear him.

The teachings of Jesus are important. They disclose to us more fully the mind and heart of God. They are the very words of God. The immensity of this is so great that I fear I don't give it proper due. The God of the universe is speaking to me! I know if most people got a call from the president of the United States, regardless of who that president is, they would take it. Or if you can think of your favorite actor or sports figure, if that person *sought you out to talk to you,* I suspect most would not only speak to the person but would get a selfie or two! Yet with God, he so wants to talk to us, he constantly has his teaching before us, and we can easily think it a good thing, yet not go into his word regularly.

Failure to routinely spend time in God's word has a detrimental effect on us. We do not become who we are meant to become without the "renewal of our minds." Paul told the Romans that the renewal of the mind was *critical* to being able to discern God's will. We have two choices, according to Paul in Romans 12:2. First, be conformed to the world, or second, renew our minds in Jesus and be able to rise above the world's wisdom. We can then discern God's will, what is good and acceptable, and even perfect.

Now that is a reason to spend time in the word each day. There we hear from the Lord who *wants* to teach us, who wants us to learn of him and his will, who wants us to have an abundant life!

Lord, remind me, teach me, and help me listen carefully. In Jesus, amen!

JUNE 21

And Jesus returned in the power of the Spirit to Galilee, and a report about him went out through all the surrounding country. And he taught in their synagogues, being glorified by all. (Lk. 4:14-15)

"How's it going?" people frequently ask. Sometimes the answer is "Fine," or "Okay," or perhaps, "Not so good." Looking objectively at life, there are some seasons when things are going great, and some okay. But some periods are real stinkers. Regardless of how a season of life seems, the believer can be confident that God is at work. God will grow the believer and his kingdom in even life's worst days.

In the sixth century before Christ was born, the nation of Judah was in deplorable shape. The leadership of the nation had failed to guide the people in the righteousness of God. The people of God indulged in idolatry rather than true worship of the true God. God sent prophets to the leadership and the people calling them to repentance. The prophets warned Judah that failing to follow God would leave them outside his umbrella of protection. The people would not only be vulnerable to their stronger neighbors, but those neighbors would destroy Judah without God's special security. Judah didn't listen to the prophets and the word of God. Instead they tortured and killed the prophets, and they walked away from the Holy One.

Apart from God, the naked truth of what the prophets had promised came to pass. Babylon and its king Nebuchadnezzar razed Judah, destroying the temple and Jerusalem, then carted off the people to Babylon. The Judahites (or "Jews" as they came to be called) were going to be in Babylon for seventy long years. The prophet Jeremiah wrote to them in Babylon and told them their stay wasn't temporary. As recorded in Jeremiah 29, he explained they were to make their homes and lives there. They should marry, give their children in marriage, pray for their new country, build houses, plant gardens, and seek the welfare of their neighbors.

This wasn't an easy time for the Jews. On the contrary, life in exile was bitter with the memories of what they had, what they lost, and what would never be. Psalm 137 laments, "By the waters of Babylon, there we sat down and wept . . . On the willows there we hung our harps." But God finally had the attention of the Jews, and God was still at work. God developed a system for the Jews to worship apart from the temple, the priests, and its sacrifices. The Jewish people developed a system of synagogues for teaching and worship. Centuries later, these synagogues would be the place where the ministry of Jesus (and Paul) seeded the church. God works, even in the worst of days.

How's it going? God is at work! Of that we can be sure.

Lord, please work in me, through me, and even in spite of me. In Jesus, amen.

JUNE 22

And he came to Nazareth, where he had been brought up. And as was his custom, he went to the synagogue on the Sabbath day, and he stood up to read. And the scroll of the prophet Isaiah was given to him. He unrolled the scroll and found the place where it was written, "The Spirit of the Lord is upon me, because he has anointed me to proclaim good news to the poor." (Lk. 4:16–18)

Never, NEVER think you will run out of things to discover in the Bible. The pages and verses run deep, and amazing things unfold before you as you study. Don't run from the study of God's word but instead grow in it. It takes discipline, thought, and careful reflection. Pray while studying for God to enlighten your heart and mind. Then enjoy the riches of what opens before you.

Today's passage is one that, for many English readers, a few nuggets of gold aren't easily seen. But to one reading Luke in the Greek in which it was written, those nuggets enrich your soul. Luke's writing has several words that have deep meaning and significance to the believer who has Greek as her or his native, or even just studied, language.

Jesus has come into a synagogue to teach. This synagogue system had arisen during the dark times of the Babylon captivity as the Jewish people sought to worship God while their temple had been destroyed. Part of the synagogue worship was the reading of a passage from the prophets. Jesus stood from his seat, took the Isaiah scroll, and found chapter 61 from which he began to read. Beginning with verse 1, Jesus read, "The spirit of the Lord is upon me, because he has *anointed* me . . ."

Luke's Greek word for anointed is the verb *chrio*. Luke's readers would know it as the verb that in noun form is *Christos*, the New Testament word translated as "Christ." Jesus was reading that God had "Christed" one to proclaim good news to the poor. This prophetic pun was also in the Hebrew that Jesus was reading. The Hebrew word in the Isaiah 61 passage is *Meshach*, the verb of the noun "Messiah." In Hebrew, Jesus was reading that God had "Messiahed" one to proclaim good news to the poor.

The phrase "proclaim good news to the poor" would also have held special significance to Luke's Greek readers. The Greek verb for "proclaim good news" is *euangelizo*. The noun form *euangelos* is the Greek word for gospel.

Jesus read the passage from Isaiah 60, written over six centuries earlier, that a Christ would come from God to bring the gospel. Jesus finished his reading and rolled up the scroll as he taught, "Today this Scripture has been fulfilled in your hearing." Jesus the Christ, bringing the gospel to those in need. That is worthy of my deepest reflections.

Lord, thank you for the deep riches in your word. Teach me. In Jesus' name, amen.

JUNE 23

And all spoke well of him and marveled at the gracious words that were coming from his mouth. And they said, "Is not this Joseph's son?" . . . And he said, "Truly, I say to you, no prophet is acceptable in his hometown. But in truth, I tell you, there were many widows in Israel in the days of Elijah, when the heavens were shut up three years and six months, and a great famine came over all the land, and Elijah was sent to none of them but only to Zarephath, in the land of Sidon, to a woman who was a widow. And there were many lepers in Israel in the time of the prophet Elisha, and none of them was cleansed, but only Naaman the Syrian." When they heard these things, all in the synagogue were filled with wrath. And they rose up and drove him out of the town. (Lk. 4:22-29)

I like things organized. Drawers with compartments, shelves for books, drawers for orderly, folded clothes—these are things that sit well with me. Packing a car is a Tetris puzzle for me. I want everything to fit nicely. But with this proclivity of mine, I need to always be careful. God doesn't fit neatly into the boxes I might make for him.

Jesus moved to Capernaum as his home base for this ministry, but this scene occurred in his hometown of Nazareth. He had gone to the synagogue on a Sabbath and gave the reading from the prophets. Reading Isaiah 61 to the people, Jesus declared that the people were alive to see the day of that prophecy coming true. It was a gentle scene, and the people were polite, if not actually charmed. One can hear them, "Ohhhh . . . listen to little Yeshua. He has all grown up! He read that so well! And his words afterward of God fulfilling his promises, what a marvelous job he did! It's hard to believe that this is little Yeshua; his parents did good with him!"

Then Jesus explained more fully who he was and what he was about. Jesus was *really* doing the things Isaiah had prophesied. Jesus was giving sight to the blind. Jesus was setting free those who were possessed. Jesus was bringing the kingdom of God. Now the folks of Nazareth might not see that from their little *Yeshua* (Jesus' name in Hebrew), but it was unfolding in other places. Just as Elijah and Elisha didn't fix all the problems in their world, but only those of the ones God put before them, so Jesus was out doing God's will where and as directed by God.

Well, this changed everything for the listeners. This man they thought of as Joseph's son was claiming to come in the mold of the great prophets Elijah and Elisha. Jesus was claiming to be the hand of God. And quickly the refrains, "Isn't that sweet, the son of Joseph all grown up" transformed into the questions, "Who does he think he is? What right has he to say this? He has lost his regard for who he is and what he should be doing."

Ugh. I need to never put God in a box.

Lord, may I follow you, not where I want you, but where you lead. In Jesus, amen.

JUNE 24

And he came to Nazareth, where he had been brought up. And as was his custom, he went to the synagogue on the Sabbath day, and he stood up to read . . . And all spoke well of him and marveled at the gracious words that were coming from his mouth. And they said, "Is not this Joseph's son?" . . . And he said, "Truly, I say to you, no prophet is acceptable in his hometown." When they heard these things, all in the synagogue were filled with wrath. And they rose up and drove him out of the town . . . And he went down to Capernaum, a city of Galilee. And he was teaching them on the Sabbath, and they were astonished at his teaching, for his word possessed authority. (Lk. 4:16, 22, 24, 28-29, 31-32)

Everyone who is confronted with Jesus is confronted with choices. How does one respond to this man? As believers, it might seem I have made my choice, but in real life, I still have that choice to make every time I have to decide whether to accept what Jesus taught or to live my life as I see fit or think will work best. Luke illuminates a fundamental truth about Jesus by setting two stories in contrast to each other.

The start of Luke chapter 4 has Jesus in his hometown of Nazareth. There, Jesus goes into the synagogue, reads the Isaiah 61 passage that prophetically spoke of his ministry, and endured the people marveling over the fine job he did as the son of Joseph. To those folks, Jesus was a carpenter who had some "book knowledge" that made a nice addition to their Saturday service. Jesus proclaims himself a prophet to the listeners, and they were incensed and drove Jesus from their midst.

In contrast, Luke then places the story of Jesus going to Capernaum, where Jesus headquartered his Galilean ministry. As in Nazareth, Jesus went into the synagogue and taught on the Sabbath. But unlike in Nazareth, the people didn't respond to Jesus as the carpenter, son of a carpenter, and young man who belonged in a nice, tidy box. The Capernaum audience heard and saw in Jesus one whose teaching possessed authority. Jesus was not only worth listening to, but worth following. Jesus was not just a man with some learning, he had what Luke called *exousia*, or "power," "control," "capability," and "might." Jesus had "authority," as the translators indicate above.

If Jesus is a good teacher, with the time and place where I am willing to listen to him, what Jesus does in my life will be paltry at best. He did no miracles in Nazareth. He left them. If, however, I trust Jesus as the authority he is, if I believe him and follow him, even when it wouldn't be the intuitive thing to do, then I will see Jesus at work in amazing ways in my life. In Capernaum, Luke recorded that Jesus worked miracles. This is the way Jesus works in my life as I trust him. He brings to pass what otherwise wouldn't be. How do I see Jesus? It makes a difference!

Lord, I want to see Jesus better. Give me strength to trust him. In your name, amen.

JUNE 25

But now even more the report about him went abroad, and great crowds gathered to hear him and to be healed of their infirmities. But he would withdraw to desolate places and pray. (Lk. 5:15-16)

Sometimes I have to get up early in the morning, and I do so reluctantly, wishing I could sleep longer. Other mornings, I can sleep, but I find myself taking pleasure in getting up unusually early. The quiet of predawn gives me uninterrupted time to think, study, and pray. It is not time where I am expected to be working, and so I remain undisturbed by calls, e-mails, texts, and immediate demands on my attention.

Often when I have these still and quiet moments, I think about passages like today's. Jesus, Son of God, the incarnate Holy One, the miracle worker, the Savior of the world, the Messiah, would embrace the crowds that came to him. He would love on them. He would heal them. He would talk to them. He would listen to them. He would serve them. He would eat with them. He would pray with them. He would teach them. He would scold them. He would laugh with them. He would watch them. But he also took time to withdraw.

Jesus, in all of his greatness, needed and sought out quiet alone times to speak with God the Father. I think it was both a need and a want for Jesus. It should be no less for me.

I need alone time to pray with God. There are important things in my life worthy of setting before God for his insight, as well as his intervention. Think now about things that need to be brought to God's attention. Do you have a loved one who is spurning God? Do you have a personal crisis? Are your relationships on secure grounds? Do you suffer from a physical or emotional ailment? Are you under a financial strain? Do you find yourself drifting aimlessly in life? Are you missing joy and instead living under a mountain of worry?

All of your needs are met in God. He gives wisdom and direction. He gives strength and protection. He gives you the might to make it through the most difficult stretches of life. He is a balm to the grieving. He is a Father to the fatherless and husband to the widow. He is the friend you need to make it through your day.

Because God is the answer, my need for time alone with him becomes also a desire to have alone time with him. Time when I don't need to worry. Time when I don't need to be pulled in multiple directions. Time when I can be 100 percent me, know I am loved, and speak to my Father who answers tenderly. Jesus withdrew to pray. I can learn from that.

Lord, thank you for this time. Draw me into your presence daily. In your name, amen.

JUNE 26

After this he went out and saw a tax collector named Levi, sitting at the tax booth. And he said to him, "Follow me." And leaving everything, he rose and followed him. And Levi made him a great feast in his house. (Lk. 5:27–29)

When I was young in youth group at church, we sang a song, "I have decided to follow Jesus. I have decided to follow Jesus. I have decided to follow Jesus. No turning back. No turning back." The melody wasn't particularly fetching. The lyrics weren't incredibly deep. But the repetition of the phrase over and over had a mantra-like effect on us as we sang. We had made a decision and saying it reinforced that decision. We were going to be followers of Jesus. No turning back!

That song still plays in my head forty-five years later when I read today's passage. Jesus approached Levi, also called Matthew, who is working as a tax collector. Tax collectors were not favored people by the Jews of Jesus' day. The tax collector had three major strikes against him. First, the tax collector was supporting the pagan Roman government. The tax collector was collecting taxes for Rome, taking them out of the coffers of the Jews. Second, the tax collector while supporting the Roman government had way too many interactions with that government. Good Jews were by and large isolationists. They maintained fellowship with other Jews, but not with pagans. The third strike arose because tax collectors were famous for overcollecting. The extra taxes the tax collector collected went straight into the tax collector's bank account.

Jesus went to Levi/Matthew and called him to follow. Levi did. He left his job, his contacts, his career path, and followed Jesus. But before departing from his lifestyle, Levi held a feast in honor of Jesus. Following Jesus was not a time of mourning. This adventure, which history records would eventually cost Levi his life as a martyr, was a cause for celebrating! Following Jesus is the most joyous decision one can make. Not because it means easy street; to the contrary, the road can be difficult and challenging. But following Jesus puts one right with God. With Jesus one finds a peace that can't be understood by the world. Life can be tough, but the worries of life are carried by Jesus.

Levi brought an interesting skill set to the small band of Jesus' most loyal disciples. As a tax collector, Levi was a notetaker. Tax collectors wrote out receipts, and Levi/Matthew would have had the first-century equivalent of a note pad, pens, and a system for keeping track of what he had written. Jesus called a notetaker to his apostles. These notes of Matthew/Levi would one day make it into the writings of the gospels as Jesus' teachings were secured for posterity. God has this way of calling us into his service to fill roles he has made for us. This makes me want to sing, "I have decided to follow Jesus!"

Lord, I want to follow you. Put me to work in your kingdom! In Jesus, amen.

JUNE 27

And Levi made him a great feast in his house, and there was a large company of tax collectors and others reclining at table with them. And the Pharisees and their scribes grumbled at his disciples, saying, "Why do you eat and drink with tax collectors and sinners?" And Jesus answered them, "Those who are well have no need of a physician, but those who are sick. I have not come to call the righteous but sinners to repentance." (Lk. 5:29–32)

Three groups of people are featured in today's passage. The first group consists of Levi (aka Matthew) and the other tax collectors and sinners at the banquet he threw in honor of Jesus. The second group isn't really a group, but a person—Jesus. The third group are the self-righteous Pharisees and scribes. I look at the three and ask myself where I belong.

The first group of tax collectors and sinners are celebrating Jesus. Levi has decided to make a career change and leave the lucrative life of tax collecting to follow a thirty-something ex-carpenter turned itinerant rabbi. He celebrates this change of life with a party to introduce Jesus to all his friends and associates. I see it as a going away party.

Attending the party is Jesus, the guest of honor. Jesus is there to minister, to show God's love, and to shine his light into the darkness of people's lives. The people there want to see and get to know Jesus. Jesus wants to be known. It is a good event.

The third group are the Pharisees and their scribes. These were the high and mighty who viewed themselves as the holy ones who protected pure Judaism and kept Israel secure. The security came about because God would see the great holiness of the Pharisees and not render Israel destroyed as happened during the Assyrian and Babylonian conquests of the Old Testament. By maintaining holiness and scrupulously following the law, these folks thought of themselves as the reason Judah would maintain some measure of independent existence even in the midst of a Roman occupation.

Because of their self-righteousness, these Pharisees placed themselves in the role of judge and jury about the behavior of others. Somehow along the way, this group crossed a line. They were no longer holy in mind and attitude. They were good rule followers, but they had become haughty and proud, comparing themselves to others. They had forgotten the admonition of Proverbs 11:2, "When pride comes, then comes disgrace, but with the humble is wisdom."

I want to be in the first group. I want to seek Jesus and celebrate his presence. I am not as holy as I want to be, and I need the Great Physician to treat my ailments.

Lord, forgive my pride. Let me seek you in true humility. In Jesus, amen.

JUNE 28

On another Sabbath, he entered the synagogue and was teaching, and a man was there whose right hand was withered. And the scribes and the Pharisees watched him, to see whether he would heal on the Sabbath, so that they might find a reason to accuse him. But he knew their thoughts, and he said to the man with the withered hand, "Come and stand here." And he rose and stood there. And Jesus said to them, "I ask you, is it lawful on the Sabbath to do good or to do harm, to save life or to destroy it?" And after looking around at them all he said to him, "Stretch out your hand." And he did so, and his hand was restored. But they were filled with fury and discussed with one another what they might do to Jesus. (Lk. 6:6–11)

I want to know God and his work, not simply have a religion of do's and don'ts. Jesus was surrounded by folks who were proud of their fanatical ability to follow rules, but who missed the heart and work of God in the process. Look carefully at today's story.

Jesus was in town on a Sabbath and attended a synagogue service. While Jesus was teaching in the synagogue, he noticed a man with a withered hand. Jesus wanted to heal the man but knew it would set off the rule followers who would swallow a camel while straining out a gnat. The rule followers weren't missing the set up. They knew that Jesus was likely to heal the deformed man. Jesus read their harsh judgmental attitudes, and so Jesus set up a confrontation. Jesus had the hurting man stand up, showing his hand to all in attendance. Jesus then asked the rule-centered people whether it was against the rules to do a good thing on the Sabbath. With no answer coming forth, Jesus added the question whether it was against the rules to save a life on the Sabbath or whether the life should be left to be destroyed.

To anyone who knows the heart of God, the answers to these questions could have been confidently announced by a five-year-old. But the sticklers among the Pharisees and scribes were silent. They would have to say, "Of course it is legal to do good and save a life." But that answer would likely be seen to condone Jesus healing the man. Silence didn't stop Jesus. Jesus told the man to stretch out his hand, and he healed the man in the presence of the rule-righteous Pharisees in the synagogue service dedicated to God.

Then the irony is set up. These self-righteous Pharisees who were so bent on their rules missed the heart of God behind the rules; they stormed out of the synagogue and began contemplating how to bring Jesus down. Filled with anger and fury, they schemed against the Holy One of God. In their blindness, they missed the irony. They refused Jesus the right to heal on the Sabbath without incurring their judgment, yet they were more than comfortable on the Sabbath to scheme and plot the demise of the Holy One. I want to follow God and not miss him because of my fanatical self-righteous hang-ups!

Lord, forgive my self-righteousness. May I seek your heart in all I do. In Jesus, amen.

JUNE 29

In these days he went out to the mountain to pray, and all night he continued in prayer to God. And when day came, he called his disciples and chose from them twelve, whom he named apostles. (Lk. 6:12–13)

When was the last time you dedicated an all-nighter to prayer? I confess my answer: Never. This passage touches me deeply as an instruction of how I need to better focus on prayer; it also touches me in the concern Jesus has for his people.

Jesus is praying through a Sabbath night (Sabbath started at sundown on Friday) in preparation for Saturday morning. That Saturday was about two-thirds through the time of Jesus' earthly ministry. It was about a year before his crucifixion. The Saturday was significant because Jesus was going to be with the multitude of disciples that had followed him over the last several years. Out of that group, Jesus was selecting the twelve who he would specially call and send out as his apostles. Saturday morning, after the night of prayer, Jesus selected and set before the crowd the twelve apostles.

I don't think Jesus spent the night praying over whom he should choose. I think he was well aware of that, and had been for some time. Jesus was praying for the apostles. I am confident he was praying for their work, for their preparation, and for what they needed to accomplish.

The apostles had a hard road in front of them. They had a year left to spend with Jesus in ministry. Then with the crucifixion, their work would take on a new phase. Indwelt by the Holy Spirit they would each (except Judas) ultimately give their lives in service to Jesus and the kingdom. They would traverse the Mediterranean world bringing the good news of the kingdom to peoples of all nations. This would not be an easy life. They would suffer persecution and history teaches that each died a martyr's death.

Jesus did not put the apostles into that position without first spending a full night in prayer for them. Of course, this wasn't the only time Jesus prayed for the apostles. John 17 records Jesus' prayers for his apostles. He prayed for their ministry, for their joy and inner peace, as well as their growth in holiness and sanctification.

The John 17 prayer adds an element that stands out to me in a personal way. In John 17, Jesus prays not just for his apostles but also for those who believe because of the apostles' work. That includes me! Jesus offered prayers for believers for all time.

I have work to do. I need to pray more and I need to walk as one empowered by the prayers of Jesus!

Lord, give me a better sense of prayer. Thank you for your love for me in Jesus, amen.

JUNE 30

Jesus of Nazareth, a man who was a prophet mighty in deed and word before God and all the people . . . (Lk. 24:19)

Jesus was trained as a carpenter. He would have known how to select a tree for wood, how to cut it down, how to strip it, and how to harvest the lumber. Some scholars believe that a carpenter was also trained in stonework. Jesus was not a trained rhetorician who was taught the ways of persuasive speech. Centuries earlier, Aristotle had written the primer on how to use logic (*logos*), credibility (*ethos*), and emotion (*pathos*) to persuade and convince others effectively. Jesus received none of that training.

Yet Jesus had a reputation of being "mighty in deed and word." Today's passage came from the mouth of Cleopas, one of the disciples who unknowingly talked to the resurrected Jesus. Jesus had interrupted the conversation of two walking to Emmaus. Jesus asked them what they were talking about and the disciples stopped and with sadness said, "Are you the only person who doesn't know what happened this weekend?" (Referencing the crucifixion of Jesus.) Jesus said, "What things?" And that is where Cleopas started explaining by stating that Jesus was a prophet, mighty in deed and word.

What made Jesus mighty in deed and word, if he wasn't trained in classic speech communication? Without a doubt the elements of Aristotle were present in Jesus, not resulting from training, but his godly understanding of human nature. Jesus had precise logic, unmatchable credibility, and was in touch with the deepest human emotions. But beyond that, Jesus had two things that were often sorely missing among many of Israel's teachers. Jesus spoke with authority and with substantive, godly content.

In other passages, the gospel writers noted how frequently the people commented on Jesus teaching "as one who had authority, and not as their scribes" (Mt. 7:29; Mk. 1:22, etc.). Even a casual reading of the rabbinical teachings from the era of Jesus and following indicates that the typical Jewish teaching would have been along the lines of "Rabbi Huna stated, 'who is a Jewish apostate? He who desecrates the Sabbath in public'; but Rabbi Nahman said, 'In agreement with whose views?' If in agreement with Rabbi Meir who holds . . .'" and on and on with one rabbi quoting another quoting another and another (see the Babylonian Talmud, Erubin 69a for my quoted reference). Jesus wasn't that way. Jesus simply pronounced in clear authoritative language what he said. Furthermore, what Jesus said was strongly imbued with powerful content. See the authority and power in, "You have heard that it was said, 'You shall love your neighbor and hate your enemy.' But I say to you, Love your enemies and pray for those who persecute you" (Mt. 5:43–44). Jesus spoke God's content. Jesus was mighty in deed and word. Why don't I do a better job listening to him?

Lord, teach me. Help me listen and do! In Jesus' name, amen.

JULY 1

Now as they went on their way, Jesus entered a village. And a woman named Martha welcomed him into her house. And she had a sister called Mary, who sat at the Lord's feet and listened to his teaching. But Martha was distracted with much serving. And she went up to him and said, "Lord, do you not care that my sister has left me to serve alone? Tell her then to help me." But the Lord answered her, "Martha, Martha, you are anxious and troubled about many things, but one thing is necessary. Mary has chosen the good portion, which will not be taken away from her." (Lk. 10:38–42)

God blessed me with a strong, intelligent wife, and four incredibly interesting daughters. They are up on current events. Each enjoyed the opportunities of school and prepared to work in various professions in our world. Even though my wife set aside her legal career to serve as a full-time mom, my wife has never stopped learning and being industrious in and outside the home. This isn't unique in my adult life. The same can be said about my mom and two sisters.

Many women today in America are like those women in my life. But that was not the case at the time of Jesus. In Jewish culture, many rabbis would not allow women to learn. Women were expected to serve men, and a woman taking a role of student was generally viewed with extreme disfavor.

Jesus was an exception, as we see in today's passage. Once Jesus entered the village, Martha, apparently the older sister, welcomed Jesus into her home. While Martha was busy serving and doing the things society expected of her, the younger sister Mary did something considered outrageous. She sat at Jesus' feet, a posture of a student, the same language used by Luke in writing that Paul sat "at the feet of" Gamaliel (in the Greek), hence Paul was a "student" of Gamaliel (as translated by the ESV).

A woman the student of a rabbi? That was as shocking in Jesus' day as Rosa Parks riding in the front of the bus in Montgomery, Alabama, in the 1960s. Martha tried to get Jesus to send Mary to work, to put her in the place society expected for her. But Jesus refused. Jesus explained that Martha's concerns and worries were misplaced. What Mary was choosing to do was Mary's choice, and Jesus wasn't relegating Mary to the back of the bus, so to speak.

Paul would embrace this unusual affirmation of women. Paul explained that in Jesus there was neither male nor female (Gal. 3:28). Jesus was ahead of his time. His concern was God's concern. It was his desire that all people, regardless of gender, race, age, or anything else that divides people in society, come to know God through Jesus. God wants you and me, regardless of what society thinks!

Lord, thank you for your interest and love. May I learn at your feet. In Jesus, amen.

JULY 2

He who enters by the door is the shepherd of the sheep. To him the gatekeeper opens. The sheep hear his voice, and he calls his own sheep by name and leads them out. (Jn. 10:2–3)

Are you like me? I find that this life often gives me mental clutter. Let me explain. I have these thoughts and emotions that seem to constantly spin in my head. Often, these thoughts are about temporary situations and transient feelings. Not all are bad, but sometimes it can be a bit much.

Here is a sample of such thoughts: What do I have to do today? Can I get it all done? I'm not in the mood to do much of it, so can I find the motivation? How will others perceive me? Am I good enough? Am I up to the tasks? Where are those I care about today? How are they doing? Am I doing what I can to help and love them? Why do I have this nagging emotion I can't get rid of? (Fill in the blank on that one—worry? sadness? weariness?) How is my health? Am I paying enough attention to my physical well-being?

These thoughts and feelings often manifest themselves in bad behavior. Will I control my eating today or will it control me? Will I control my spending today or will it control me? Will I control (fill in the blank with your personal behavioral appetite) today or will it control me? Will I control my temper today or will it control me? Will I be able to show others love today, or will today be about me?

Into all of these external questions, and all of this mental clutter, comes a passage like today's. Today's passage speaks an eternal truth. This truth exists every minute, every day, every week, month, and year. The truth is Jesus is a good shepherd who knows your name and mine. He calls us by our name to follow him. He does this out of love. (Later in this teaching of Jesus he explains that the good shepherd loves his sheep enough to lay down his life for them.)

Let the gravity of this truth weigh down deep into your soul and mind. God loves you. The God who knows you, knows your mental clutter, knows your weaknesses, knows your innermost secrets, knows the worst there is about you, knows what you don't want anyone to know, knows your struggles and worries, knows YOU—that God calls you by your name in a very personal way. He wants you to follow him. He wants you to absorb his love. He wants to teach you how to live beyond the mental clutter. He wants you to live basking in the truth that he will take care of you, even laying down his life for you.

That changes my day (though I admit, I often have to return it again each day!).

Lord, please take my clutter and replace it with awareness of your love in Jesus, amen.

JULY 3

And while he was at Bethany in the house of Simon the leper, as he was reclining at table, a woman came with an alabaster flask of ointment of pure nard, very costly, and she broke the flask and poured it over his head. There were some who said to themselves indignantly, "Why was the ointment wasted like that? For this ointment could have been sold for more than three hundred denarii and given to the poor." And they scolded her. But Jesus said, "Leave her alone. Why do you trouble her? She has done a beautiful thing to me." (Mk. 14:3–6)

Are you familiar with Gary Chapman's book *The Five Love Languages*? Chapman, a preacher by trade, put years of experience into a book that offers five different ways that people can express and receive love. Terming these "love languages," Chapman explores how different people typically fall into one category or another. Those differences explain why miscommunication can often occur in relationships whenever one person communicates love, concern, and caring differently than another. The love languages are words of affirmation, quality time, receiving gifts, acts of service, and physical touch.

People today aren't really different than people in Jesus' day. In this passage Jesus was close to his most trying time in his humanity. He was headed toward his confrontation with the religious and civil authorities, his abandonment by his friends and family, horrible physical and mental torture, and ultimately a grueling death. Jesus knew what was around the corner. He was going in eyes open. This was Jesus' act of love for humanity—the humanity that abandoned him.

Into this scene came a woman whose love language was gifts. She came bearing an alabaster flask of ointment. Alabaster is a translucent stone that is very soft and can be sculpted into a small flask as well as many other items. The vessel itself was valuable, even aside from the ointment. The ointment was "pure nard," a *very* expensive byproduct of the nard plant.

Those with Jesus (who likely didn't have the love language of gifts!), took offense that this expensive gift was given to him. They didn't understand the love she was expressing. They weren't even perceptive enough to realize what Jesus must have been thinking and feeling, knowing what awaited him right around the corner. Jesus' followers were numb to that and simply exercised a self-righteous judgment on the loving deed of this caring woman.

I am frustrated with the apostles. I am touched by the woman. I want to show Jesus my love. I want to do whatever I can to show him my deep appreciation for his care and concern in my life. I am looking for chances to do that today.

Lord, I do love you. Give me chances to show you, please. In Jesus, amen.

JULY 4

Remember Lot's wife. (Lk. 17:32)

July 4! Fireworks!!! When I was a young man, a band called Fireworks had a song titled "I Should Be a Pillar of Salt." The song was based on the story of Lot's wife. The story of Lot's wife is found in Genesis 19. Many know the story as that of God destroying Sodom and Gomorrah because of the great evil and sinfulness in those cities. That is certainly part of the story, but the story is so much more.

Lot, his wife, and his two daughters had settled into the sinful midst of Sodom. Lot was a nephew to Abraham, and Abraham had become almost a father to Lot, taking Lot on the journey into Canaan and helping him get settled. Lot would have known God, or at least known of God. After all, the move to Canaan came about because God instructed Abraham to go. One might think that knowing of God would have prevented Lot from setting up his family in the squalor of sin that was Sodom. But Sodom also had an attractiveness (sin often does) that appealed to Lot and his family. His daughters married, and life was moving right along until two angels showed up declaring that God was going to destroy Sodom. Lot and his family were instructed to leave, and leave fast.

Lot's sons-in-law thought the whole thing some mental deficit or joke of their father-in-law. So the angels pushed Lot hard, finally grabbing him by the arm and basically pushing him, his wife, and his two daughters out of their home and out of the city. The story specifically notes this was God in his mercy trying to protect Lot. One of the angels instructed Lot to hasten specifying, "Don't look back and don't stop!"

Lot barely believed what was happening. After all, he had to be physically dragged out of the city. His wife's faith seemed to be even less. She wasn't pushing Lot to leave and protect the family. Instead, she seemed to be longing for her old way of life. As God rained down destruction on Sodom and Gomorrah, contrary to the angel's clear instructions, Lot's wife stopped, turned around, and watched, "and she became a pillar of salt" (Gen. 19:26).

Jesus invoked the story of Lot's wife to teach his disciples how to live, especially as God does his work on planet earth and Jesus is revealed. Jesus said that when God is afoot, attention should be on him and what he is doing, not on what was or could have been.

The Fireworks' song begins with this lyric, "I should be a pillar of salt; I've looked back so many times." It has stuck with me for forty years. I know God is at work. He has not brought this world to consummation yet, but he is in process. My focus should be on God today and what he is doing, not on what was or could have been. God help me.

Lord, I've looked back so many times. Help me focus on your work in Jesus, amen.

JULY 5

And he told them a parable to the effect that they ought always to pray and not lose heart. (Lk. 18:1)

I love the English Standard Version (ESV) of the Bible. It is one reason I use it in these devotionals. I have friends who work on the translation and its publication, and they are brilliant scholars with a deep devotion for God and his word. Reading the ESV is smooth yet never at the sacrifice of the integrity of Scripture. I can read it with confidence in its accuracy.

Still, even with the best translations, choices have to be made when translating a Greek text (for the New Testament) into English. Sometimes those choices sacrifice some of the original punch in the Greek. Today's passage is one where my edification is greater when I read it in the Greek. I say this because of the word the translators put into English as "ought." It is clearly an important word since Luke is saying the point of a parable that he's about to write up is that the followers of Jesus "ought" to pray. But the Greek "ought" has a real force to it that *can* be lost on the English reader, depending upon how one understands "ought."

At times "ought" can mean something is advisable. Consider this sentence, "You ought to take care of yourself!" That conveys something that is sensible. It is worthwhile and prudent to take care of yourself. Knowing this is one meaning for "ought" could take today's passage and make it a nice recommendation for one "always to pray."

But the Greek word translated as "ought" has a different balance to it. The word (*dei*, δεῖ) denotes compulsion, not advisability. Reading in the Greek, the word commands immediate attention as a direction or instruction of necessity. By using *dei*, Luke is telling his reader that the parable is teaching that it is compulsory; it is essential that one pray always and not lose heart or get discouraged.

I wonder how my life would be different if I were better at following this lesson. If I saw faithful prayer not as an advisable option, but as an important necessity. Luke wants his readers to know it is important to live life in dialogue with the Creator. God is the source of strength, splendor, and beauty in this world (Ps. 96:6), and it is only right that the children of God should dialogue with him constantly.

As I continue in prayer before God today, I will not lose heart. I will not be discouraged because I can pray with confidence God is listening. God will answer my prayers. The answer may be "no." The answer may be "not now." The answer may be "yes!" But I pray anyway, confident that God will provide the *right* answer.

Lord, please [fill in the blank with a personal need or concern]. Please! In Jesus, amen.

JULY 6

Now they were bringing even infants to him that he might touch them. And when the disciples saw it, they rebuked them. But Jesus called them to him, saying, "Let the children come to me, and do not hinder them, for to such belongs the kingdom of God. Truly, I say to you, whoever does not receive the kingdom of God like a child shall not enter it."
(Lk. 18:15–17)

I love the tenderness of today's passage.

Jesus had lived as a carpenter until his brief tenure as an itinerant preacher and teacher. As a carpenter, Jesus would have worked to fell trees, harvest them for usable wood, and then sculpted and worked the wood to its final end product. Carpenters worked from tree to product in that day. They didn't simply order two-by-fours from the local lumber yard. Jesus had decades of callouses on his hands, and undoubtedly a sinewy build. Yet, here Luke discloses the callouses stopped before reaching Jesus' heart and mind. Jesus expressed a tenderheartedness to the children in his midst, not found in the heart or minds of the disciples.

Here the disciples are playing the role of "handler" for Jesus. They thought it their responsibility to filter those who tried to occupy the mind and attention of the healer, the teacher, possibly (they were unsure on this at the time) even the Messiah! Jesus' time and energy needed to be focused. The disciples tried to keep Jesus directed to the important mission of the day.

But Jesus would have none of the disciples' limited vision. Jesus had the heart of the Father. Even that description of God should give everyone pause. "Father." To God, *everyone*, from the greatest to the least, is a child! Even into my fifties, I am as a "child" to God.

So Jesus had compassion for the children. He enjoyed the children. Even with his rough and calloused hands, Jesus tenderly touched and cared for the children, as Luke says, "even the infants." That is our tender God.

I love the passage because I need to know that God isn't shunning me, my concerns, what is or isn't important to me. God knows that I am like a child, and he has tenderness toward his children. He is delighted to give me attention and affection. He relishes the chances to interact with me. He gave his all so I could come to him in confidence, assured of his love. That changes my life today.

Lord, I need your touch. I need to sense and realize your care and attention. Please affirm for me, through your Spirit and through life, that you are on your throne, but are ready and eager to be my Father, involved in my life in very real ways. In Jesus, amen.

JULY 7

And Jesus, full of the Holy Spirit, returned from the Jordan and was led by the Spirit in the wilderness for forty days, being tempted by the devil. (Lk. 4:1–2)

Most everyone has had the experience of being challenged to do the right thing but find it almost impossible to achieve. For some people, that might mean a decision to eat healthy but then grab that donut and eat it real fast so the lapse in self-control doesn't seem so bad. I had a sixteen-year-old young man come up to me after I taught one Sunday at church and ask me in a hushed voice, "I am having trouble with lust. What can I do?" He knew what he wanted to occupy his heart and mind, but he couldn't live up to that standard. I know folks who find it nearly impossible to make it through challenging situations without using a lie to help them out of the tough spot.

What do believers do with this seemingly constant struggle between who we are and who we want to be? Part of that answer is found in today's passage.

Luke is about to detail the encounters Jesus had with the devil in the wilderness. These temptations are also set forth by Matthew, but Luke does something Matthew doesn't. Luke begins his narrative by noting that Jesus was "full of the Holy Spirit." This fullness might seem obvious to everyone. After all, Jesus was God made man. But Luke adds it anyway. Luke wants the readers to know that the Holy Spirit empowered the humanity of Jesus to stand against the temptations of the evil one.

I need to know this. It is important in my life. I need to let the Holy Spirit help guide and empower me to live through the temptations that beckon me with their siren's song. How exactly does the believer walk in the Spirit? I used to think the Spirit was like an electrical outlet that I simply needed to plug into and receive the juice necessary for almost magical, certainly supernatural, strength. As I have aged, I have learned the truth is a bit more involved!

For me, this begins with spending time in Scripture. As Paul noted, all Scripture is inspired by God. It is a product of the Spirit, and my time there begins to shape my thought patterns, my values, my desires, and so much more. I combine this with prayer. When I am praying, God's Spirit is at work, helping me to pray as I should. I also try to practice what I learn from God. For example, Paul's admonition to let my mind dwell on things that are "true, honorable, just, pure, lovely, commendable" helps retrain me and gives me the Spirit's strength in the face of temptation (see Phil. 4:8). God uses his Spirit to grow me, and while I am still far from perfect, and while I still succumb to temptation, I see God changing me bit by bit, transforming me into the image of Jesus.

Lord, may your Spirit have reign in my life. Help me to live and learn a life walking by your Holy Spirit. In Jesus' name, amen.

JULY 8

Jesus said to them, "I am the bread of life; whoever comes to me shall not hunger, and whoever believes in me shall never thirst." (Jn. 6:35)

Do you live with a safety net? Do you know someone or something that will be there to bail you out when life gets to be too much? If you know Jesus, the answer is a resounding YES!

Jesus knew the Old Testament thoroughly. His many references from those Scriptures, and his many teachings from them, aren't coincidental. Jesus, the Word of God, knew those Scriptures as the words of God. They were his bulwark, and he used them in his own times of crisis. For example, from the cross, Jesus quoted from Psalm 22, "My God, My God, why have you forsaken me?" But Jesus also taught his followers to use Scripture as a resource to better understand God and this life.

In today's passage, Jesus referenced back to the Old Testament story of God providing manna to hungry Israelites wandering in the wilderness on their way to the Promised Land. The manna came every day (with a double portion on Friday so the Israelites could honor the Sabbath).

Jesus wanted his people to know; making it more personal, Jesus wanted *me* to know that Jesus is my sustenance. Jesus is my safety net. Jesus is my stronghold in times of trouble. Jesus is my strength in times of weakness. When the Psalmist wrote, "When I thought, 'My foot slips!,' your steadfast love, oh Lord, held me up," Jesus is that steadfast love. When the Psalmist continued, "When the cares of my heart are many, your consolations cheer my soul," Jesus is that consolation (Ps. 94:18-19).

How is Jesus one's consolation? How does he keep one's feet from falling? In many ways, but I want to specify one here. The entire life and ministry of Jesus centered on God's steadfast love for his people. God never incarnated as Jesus because he was bored or was looking for a vacation from his throne. Jesus emptied himself in taking the form of a man. The life of Jesus wasn't one where he was living "high on the hog" as my dad used to say. Jesus worked hard. In his ministry, he had no home. He suffered at the hands of the very humans he made. He was scorned, mocked, and ridiculed. Ultimately, he died as a punishment for sin, but it was my sin, not his own. He willingly took on my sin so that I wouldn't have to bear its consequences.

Now I ask you, would a God who does all that fail to sustain you? Would a God who does all that ignore the cares of your heart? No, absolutely not! In Jesus, my soul finds cheer, my life finds stability and purpose.

Lord, thank you for your love in Jesus. I commit all my cares to you, amen.

JULY 9

And rising very early in the morning, while it was still dark, he departed and went out to a desolate place, and there he prayed. And Simon and those who were with him searched for him, and they found him and said to him, "Everyone is looking for you." And he said to them, "Let us go on to the next towns, that I may preach there also, for that is why I came out." (Mk. 1:35–38)

Do you have a busy day in front of you? Or a busy week with lots to do? Maybe you're at a time of relative peace, but you know that time of peace will pass. Activity and work are never far away.

This was equally true of Jesus. Jesus came to earth with purpose. Each day as he ministered, he saw people needing his healing touch, both physically and spiritually. Jesus filled his days with teaching, helping the desperate, healing the sick, giving direction to the lost, fellowshipping the outcast, loving the unlovable, and finding the lost. Jesus engaged those who were oversold on themselves, trying to bring them into the reality that their self-righteous narcissism had missed. Jesus endured the temptations brought to him by none other than the Prince of Demons. Jesus had days filled to the brim with activity.

Like anyone, Jesus needed to get ready for all of that. Mark writes today's passage with a subtle Greek pun to teach his readers how Jesus prepared for all he had to do. The pun begins with verse 35, where Jesus arose *very* early in the day, while still dark (sometime between 3 a.m. and 6 a.m. is likely from reading the Greek). Then Jesus "departed and went out" to pray. Once his friends woke up, they went to find him, telling him the calendar was full and he needed to get to work! Jesus made a calendar adjustment knowing they were heading to towns for him to teach and minister, and then Mark adds the key. Jesus said that his busy calendar was why he "came out."

The word Mark uses for "came out" mirrors verse 35. It is the same word translated as "departed." Mark explains with this usage that the reason Jesus left early to pray was because he had such a busy schedule in front of him. Jesus needed to get ready for the busy day, and the way he got ready was by getting alone with God and praying.

Days can be busy. I need to learn from my Master. The key to getting ready for a busy day is first praying with my Father in heaven.

Lord, bless this day. Give me wisdom, strength, energy, direction, purpose, fulfillment, and peace. In Jesus' name, amen.

JULY 10

Jesus said to her, "Mary." She turned and said to him in Aramaic, "Rabboni!" (which means Teacher). (Jn. 20:16)

You are important to God. As I write this, I don't know who will read it, and certainly I don't know that you are reading it on this day. But I can write with full assurance, *you* are important to God. You might be reading this book as a Christian who has walked decades with the Lord. You might be a relatively new Christian. You might not have yet asked Jesus into your life to be your Lord. You might only be curious about what this book has to say. You might not fit neatly into any of the categories I just set out. It doesn't matter. I can still say without reservation you are important to God.

Look carefully at today's passage in its context. It is Easter morning. Jesus has been resurrected from the dead. The tomb has been discovered as empty, but Mary doesn't yet understand that. She thinks someone must have taken Jesus' body. Mary sees the resurrected Jesus but mistakes him as the gardener. (Some wonder how Mary could make this mistake. . . . As one who wears glasses, if I lived in the pre-glasses era, I wouldn't have known for certain either, unless Jesus was within about ten feet of me!) Mary doesn't realize the man is Jesus until Jesus calls her name.

Once Jesus says, "Mary," she turns to him and calls him her name for him, "Rabboni," which is Aramaic for "my Teacher." (John just gives the meaning of the word, "Teacher," without noting that Mary gave the form that indicates Jesus was *her* teacher.) Mary recognized Jesus when he called her name.

Two things jump at me from this passage. First, Jesus knows our name. Yes, he certainly knew Mary from having known her during his earthly walk as Jesus, but this truth runs much deeper. Jesus knows everyone by name. He knows who we are and what we do. He knows our past, the good, bad, and ugly. He knows where we have done well and where we have come up short—sometimes woefully short. Humanity is not a big blob to Jesus. Each person is an individual Jesus seeks out by name.

This brings up the second aspect of this passage that speaks to me. How do we respond to Jesus knowing us and caring for us? Mary heard his voice and recognized him. The passage illustrates what Jesus had taught as recorded ten chapters earlier in John. The sheep "listen" to the shepherd's voice; "he calls the sheep by name and leads them out . . . and his sheep follow him because they know his voice" (Jn. 10:3-4).

I want to know Jesus. I want to recognize his voice as he calls me by name. I am important to him. I want him to be important to me.

Lord, thank you for your love. Teach me your voice. I want to follow you. In Jesus, amen.

JULY 11

On the evening of that day, the first day of the week, the doors being locked where the disciples were for fear of the Jews, Jesus came and stood among them and said to them, "Peace be with you." (Jn. 20:19)

Have you ever thought about putting yourself into the shoes of the apostles after the death of Jesus? Judas blatantly betrayed the Lord, delivering him into the hands of his enemies for thirty small chunks of metal. The others weren't so bold, but they betrayed Jesus, nonetheless. Peter told his story of denying Jesus three times, and Scripture has secured that betrayal for all of history. The other apostles didn't stand with Jesus. They didn't come to his defense before the Jewish authorities. They didn't argue when Barabbas was released in lieu of Jesus. They left Jesus to fend for himself and scampered away into hiding.

As John writes of the resurrected Jesus, this account winds up being Jesus' first contact and interaction with most of the apostles. To make matters worse, the apostles were at least aware at this time that Jesus was resurrected. His body was gone. Mary had reported seeing him and talking to him outside the garden tomb. Yet Jesus had not gotten together with his close group of trusted friends. I would have wondered.

My concern would have been that Jesus was upset. I would think that perhaps Jesus was frustrated that we had, in essence, abandoned him in his hour of need. My mind would question whether Jesus had moved on and gone and found others who were better than me. I would be worried about what might happen if I should never see Jesus again. All of this would be aggravated by my concern over the Jews still perhaps wanting to stomp out any vestige of those who followed Jesus, perhaps even more so now that his body was missing.

That would have been my mindset had I been one of his disciples in the room when Jesus miraculously appeared, as detailed in today's passage. It means a lot to me that the first words out of Jesus' mouth were, "Peace be with you." The greeting of Shalom (Peace) was a typical Hebrew greeting, but it wasn't without great significance. Jesus came in peace, and wished peace, happiness, fulfillment, good health, and more to his followers. Jesus wasn't angry or bitter. Jesus was still on mission, still kind and loving, and still wished the best for others.

I am amazed at this simple story. How many convince themselves that they are beyond God's love and reach? Yet here comes Jesus, reminding us of his desires for our good, regardless of how we've betrayed him. Lord, you are too good to me.

Father God, please forgive me of my many, many sins and mistakes. Give me your peace and help me understand more deeply the love you have for me. In Jesus' name, amen.

JULY 12

The Pharisees came and began to argue with him, seeking from him a sign from heaven to test him. And he sighed deeply in his spirit and said, "Why does this generation seek a sign? Truly, I say to you, no sign will be given to this generation." And he left them, got into the boat again, and went to the other side. (Mk. 8:11–13)

Look carefully at today's passage. Some Pharisees, a well-studied sect of Jews who ardently believed they were guardians of true Judaism, came to Jesus and began to argue with him! That is a bit stunning. First, this was no chance encounter. The Pharisees actually sought Jesus out. They came to Jesus to argue with him.

The passage makes it clear that Jesus didn't come to earth to argue with people. Jesus wasn't about to provide a miracle so that he could convince them of who he was. It isn't hard to imagine the scene.

These bastions of the "true faith" hear that Jesus is nearby. They have their set of arguments taking issue with Jesus on one thing or another. It might have been over Jesus' work on the Sabbath. Or maybe the way Jesus would speak with women and treat them equally to men. It could have been Jesus loving and caring for the poor, outcast, and diseased. The gospels show that these and other habits of Jesus incensed many of the establishment. So these Pharisees seek Jesus out to argue with him. The argument quickly demonstrated that the Pharisees were blind to the truth, for reasons that aren't apparent but can be readily surmised. Everyone knows someone who holds an opinion in the face of logic.

One can readily hear the Pharisees saying, "Well, if you're right, Jesus, if you really believe this is what God has to say, then why don't you call down some miracle from God to validate your argument?" Jesus wanted nothing to do with that.

Jesus "sighed deeply in his spirit" and left with a shrug. If people's hearts aren't willing to learn, teaching is futile. If people's minds aren't open to what God has to say, God isn't going to force it upon them. Jesus left them.

I read this and wonder about my heart and mind. How often do I argue with God? I don't think God minds a good argument, but it needs to be in the right spirit! I need to be ready at the end of the day to accept that God is God, and I'm not. He doesn't need to prove himself to me, I will accept him. I may not understand something. I may wrestle with him over certain matters. But in the end, he is right. He needn't walk from me. I am going to stay with him regardless.

Lord, sometimes I need you to help me make sense of things. Please keep my heart tender, even as I wrestle with you at times. In Jesus' name, amen.

JULY 13

Now they had forgotten to bring bread, and they had only one loaf with them in the boat. And he cautioned them, saying, "Watch out; beware of the leaven of the Pharisees and the leaven of Herod." (Mk. 8:14–15)

People have a tendency to put things into categories. I know I certainly do. When I think through my actions, I can find some that seem "right" as a believer trying to live consistent with the instructions of my Lord. I can also find some that are wrong. "Lapses of sin" some might call them. (I tend to divide even my sins into categories—big ones, little ones, etc.) But as I examine my life during the day, I also find errors that I make that I don't really consider "sins" as much as just mistakes. For example, I give someone the wrong directions, telling them to take the third left when it should have been the fourth. I wasn't lying, even though I gave wrong information. I was just wrong.

I love today's passage for two reasons. First, the disciples made common mistakes also. Second, Jesus never lost a moment to teach, even if the moment arose from a mistake.

In the passage, the disciples left the lake town Dalmanutha on the shores of Galilee and traversed the lake to the other side. But the disciples forgot to bring bread! They hadn't food for the journey. I love this!!! I think about it every time I lose my cell phone. Each time I forget something at the store. Heavens, I make mistakes similar to this on a routine basis. When I see the disciples doing it, I feel better. After all, they were in charge of such things for the Lord Jesus himself and still messed up. (I can hear the dialogue now, "I thought you brought the bread!" "No, it was your turn, remember?" "No, I brought it last time!")

In the midst of this mistake enters Jesus, always the teacher. Jesus' head was in a different place. He wasn't hung up on their mistake. He was thinking eternally. Jesus went to a higher place in the midst of the error. Jesus took the moment to teach a lesson. Seemingly from left field, Jesus tells them to beware of the leaven of the Pharisees and Herod. Reading the fuller passage, one sees that the teaching moment goes straight over the heads of the disciples as they continue to argue about who forgot the bread and what they were going to do about it.

Jesus used the Old Testament metaphor of leaven representing sin. Sin, like leaven, enters a person and even just a pinch can permeate and affect the entire loaf/person. Sin is not something to dabble with; it is something to avoid. Jesus took the moment of no bread (and therefore, no leaven) to teach the disciples the importance of avoiding the sins of those around them. Bless the disciples' hearts, they missed the moment, instead debating what to do now. I need to learn from this.

Lord, please open my eyes to your teaching, even in my mistakes. In Jesus, amen.

And they began discussing with one another the fact that they had no bread. And Jesus, aware of this, said to them, "Why are you discussing the fact that you have no bread? Do you not yet perceive or understand? Are your hearts hardened? Having eyes do you not see, and having ears do you not hear? And do you not remember? When I broke the five loaves for the five thousand, how many baskets full of broken pieces did you take up?" They said to him, "Twelve." "And the seven for the four thousand, how many baskets full of broken pieces did you take up?" And they said to him, "Seven." And he said to them, "Do you not yet understand?" (Mk. 8:16–21)

"People are people," my friend Louis is fond of saying. He is right, and today's passage is a classic example.

The disciples are in a quandary. They had been at a seaside town called Dalmanutha thinking things were going swimmingly while some self-righteous Pharisees were arguing with Jesus. Seeing that the people were stubborn and hard-hearted, not genuinely seeking truth, Jesus up and left them! Gathering his disciples, they got into a boat and headed to the far shore of the Sea of Galilee.

While on the way, the disciples realized that they had forgotten to bring bread. They were unable to eat! Nor were they ready to feed Jesus, who had spent his time and energy trying to bring sense to the Pharisees. The disciples began to quibble back and forth.

The absurdity of what the disciples were doing seems totally lost on them. They were so focused on the mundane, looking down at what they had, that they failed to consider the miraculous. They had Jesus in the boat. This is the same Jesus that fed five thousand with five loaves. Extrapolate that. That means one loaf feeds a thousand. Plus, there were twelve baskets of broken pieces left! Or worst-case scenario: Jesus fed four thousand with seven loaves. Extrapolated out, that still means one loaf feeds 571 people with seven baskets of scraps left.

The disciples were in the boat wearing blinders of fear and ignorance when they should have been looking at the hand of God that was in their midst.

I would judge them harshly, but I too often find myself in the same boat. How many times do I worry over this, that, or the other, as if there is no God, or at least not one really interested in my problems? Often I find my focus on this earth rather than the one who made the earth.

I should see the miraculous, not the mundane. But then, people are people, including me.

Lord, cast my vision on you in my need. May I trust in your hand daily. In Jesus, amen.

JULY 15

And they came to Bethsaida. And some people brought to him a blind man and begged him to touch him. And he took the blind man by the hand and led him out of the village, and when he had spit on his eyes and laid his hands on him, he asked him, "Do you see anything?" And he looked up and said, "I see people, but they look like trees, walking." Then Jesus laid his hands on his eyes again; and he opened his eyes, his sight was restored, and he saw everything clearly. And he sent him to his home, saying, "Do not even enter the village." (Mk. 8:22–26)

Today's passage is unusual. It sticks out like a sore thumb within the larger context of Mark's gospel as well as in light of the other three gospels. It doesn't sit well with the common sense of many today either. Why does it take Jesus two tries to heal this man? We can't say that Jesus was having an off day. Why does Jesus have to ask the man, "Do you see anything?" Was Jesus uncertain of his healing power?

One key to understanding this passage is found in the simple phrase Mark adds, Jesus "took the blind man by the hand and led him out . . ." Mark's Greek is remarkably similar to the Greek Old Testament language of Jeremiah 31:32. In Jeremiah God spoke of "the covenant that I made with their fathers on the day when I took them by the hand to bring them out of the land of Egypt, my covenant that they broke . . ."

Mark sets up Jesus as God who took his people out of the land, giving them his covenant. The covenant wasn't the full or final picture of God's work, nor was Jesus' first touch the full view of the man's restored vision. Jesus asked the man what he saw, so that those around would hear that it was incomplete restoration. Jesus knew the answer before he asked. With the second touch, Jesus didn't have to ask if it worked, he knew it had.

Similarly, God's second covenant with his people wasn't like Sinai and the Old Testament law. The Jeremiah passage that also uses the reference to God leading his people out of Egypt explains today's passage marvelously.

Behold, the days are coming, declares the LORD, when I will make a new covenant with the house of Israel and the house of Judah, not like the covenant that I made with their fathers on the day when I took them by the hand to bring them out of the land of Egypt, my covenant that they broke. . . . For this is the covenant that I will make with the house of Israel after those days, declares the LORD: I will put my law within them, and I will write it on their hearts. And I will be their God, and they shall be my people.

Jesus came to heal his people with a new covenant. In a master stroke, Jesus showed this.

Lord, thank you for the clarity your loving touch brings. I live and pray in Jesus, amen.

JULY 16

And they were bringing children to him that he might touch them, and the disciples rebuked them. But when Jesus saw it, he was indignant and said to them, "Let the children come to me; do not hinder them, for to such belongs the kingdom of God. Truly, I say to you, whoever does not receive the kingdom of God like a child shall not enter it." And he took them in his arms and blessed them, laying his hands on them. (Mk. 10:13–16)

As of the time I write this, Becky and I have five children and nine grandchildren. I was one of three children. We have nieces and nephews, and now two "grand" nephews and a grandniece. I love children and feel I have spent my life around them. Similarly, I love this story of Jesus.

Culturally, children were not ones who would typically have made a central character in Jesus teaching on those belonging in God's kingdom. Children were socially marginalized, not held up as examples. One wouldn't insert children into the conversation with a learned and respected rabbi. Children were a distraction. They belonged at the "children's table," to use a modern expression. Children were also viewed as vulnerable. Children needed care and protecting, or they would succumb to disease, be abused by others, and so forth. Because of these limitations, children were also seen as dependent on others.

The disciples weren't being rude or rough trying to keep the children away. They likely viewed it as part of their job! Yet into this moment comes Jesus armed with compassion and teaching. Jesus took advantage of the moment to produce a shocking reality for those listening. Jesus said that the kingdom of God belongs to those who approach it like a child. No earthly king built his kingdom on children (or those like children). Earthly kings built kingdoms on the powerful, rich, or brave. Not Jesus.

Jesus sets out the dependent and socially marginalized children. Jesus uses as an example a child who generally doesn't worry about tomorrow but trusts that her or his needs will be met. (Of those children who do worry about being fed or safe, one often hears of them being robbed of their childhood. That is not the natural way of a child.)

I want to be like a child. I want Jesus to build his kingdom with me. I want to be dependent on him. I want to know that I may be marginalized in the world, but the King of kings wants me. I am not marginalized to him. I don't distract him. He calls me.

Lord, give me the faith and trust of a child. Give me childlike joy as I walk in the world and live under your Lordship. May I show your incredible love to others. In Jesus, amen.

JULY 17

And as he came out of the temple, one of his disciples said to him, "Look, Teacher, what wonderful stones and what wonderful buildings!" And Jesus said to him, "Do you see these great buildings? There will not be left here one stone upon another that will not be thrown down." (Mk. 13:1–2)

Some things are amazing. On the simple side, I am amazed at some basketball shots I've seen. Perhaps more profound, I have also been amazed at some stunning sunsets. More than a few buildings have amazed me as well. (I find architecture fascinating.) I readily confess I have been amazed at a good many things I have eaten. I am constantly amazed at the exhibition of love I have seen from my family and friends.

So when I read today's passage, I can sympathize with the disciple, but I am brought into focus by the teachings of Jesus. The disciple, whom Mark mercifully doesn't name, is with Jesus as Jesus leaves the temple. The temple *was* amazing. It was built of massive stones, which, in an era before the use of cranes, was extremely rare. (Josephus says the big white stones were over thirty-five feet long, eleven feet high, and seventeen feet wide.) The building with its courts covered about one-sixth of the entire city's geography. It had ornate trim, covered colonnades, and multiple courtyards. The disciple saw the beauty and commented to Jesus, "Isn't this incredibly beautiful?"

Jesus responded differently than the disciple expected. Rather than affirming the temple's beauty, Jesus spoke of coming disaster. Jesus told the disciple not to get too attached to the greatness, for the greatness was destined for utter destruction. Jesus constantly saw beyond the immediate into the eternal.

Reading today's passage reminds me that it is okay to appreciate the present for what it is, but I need to live with my sights firmly fixed on the eternal. What does that mean to me practically? It means that I should see God's beauty in daily life, whether in a sunset or in the work of God's creation (a beautiful building or basketball shot!). I should thank God for such things and see them as perhaps just a slim reflection of the beauty and creativity that is God. But I should also keep a great emphasis on the eternal.

Paul told the Corinthians that we should build our lives with an eternal perspective. What we do, or in Paul's analogy, what we build, can be made of wood, hay, and stubble, or of gold, silver, and precious stones. Wood, hay, and stubble are transitory. Like the temple, they are doomed for destruction. But if we live with eternity in sight, we build with things that last. I want to do that. I want to choose love over hate, service over being served, godliness over sin, and more. That will be truly amazing!!!

Lord, please give me the presence of mind to be attentive to things that will last. May I show the world your love with an eye to your eternity. In Jesus, amen.

JULY 18

And Jesus looked around and said to his disciples, "How difficult it will be for those who have wealth to enter the kingdom of God!" (Mk. 10:23)

Today's passage is a stinger for many. If you read it thinking, "No worries here; I'm not wealthy," then I urge you to reconsider! One out of every ten people in the world live on less than two dollars a day. The poorest in the world go hungry, have little to no access to education, no light at night, and minimal to no health care.

Poverty and riches are on a sliding scale. Most everyone can find someone who is poorer and someone who is richer. This is factual economics. But in today's passage, Jesus isn't giving an economics test. Jesus wasn't speaking about a certain level above which or below which salvation is more readily available. Jesus was speaking about a veritable truth of wealth.

The core truth of Jesus' comment is readily apparent if one thinks about money as a resource, and resources as wealth. Jesus knew, and life confirms, that those who have a lot of the world's resources have less of a perceived need for God. If you are struggling and worried about how to get food on the table tomorrow, you are more receptive to the idea of seeking God's help. But if you have all the money you need to buy all the food you need, the reliance you should have on God isn't readily apparent.

In this sense, everyone should realize that Jesus is speaking beyond economics and into trust and reliance. My father, who was never a wealthy man by the world's standards, used to say he was a rich man *because* of his family and faith. If people constantly rely on God, even in the midst of plentiful resources, then folks are the exception to Jesus' concern of wealth and the kingdom.

Once people begin to realize an utter dependence on God, even when resources abound, then people begin to realize the responsibility of using those resources properly. As Jesus also said, "To whom much is given, much is expected" (Lk. 12:48). God delivers resources to people NOT so people feel self-sufficient. But God gives people resources to use for his kingdom's purposes.

So, as I meditate on today's passage, I want to be sure to rely on God for my needs each day, not the resources at my disposal. Those I want to use for his purposes.

Dear Father, teach me to rely on you for everything in this life. Please give me wisdom to use those resources you've given me for you. In Jesus, amen.

JULY 19

Therefore I tell you, do not be anxious about your life, what you will eat or what you will drink, nor about your body, what you will put on. Is not life more than food, and the body more than clothing? Look at the birds of the air: they neither sow nor reap nor gather into barns, and yet your heavenly Father feeds them. Are you not of more value than they? (Mt. 6:25–26)

The spring of 2020 put a generational defining jolt through the United States and the world. The Corona virus resulted in a long time of isolation and self-quarantine for most Americans. Unemployment sky-rocketed as more than one-third of American households had someone lose a job or take a significant pay reduction. People were not prepared, and it was unlike any event in one hundred years.

Those events put passages like today's to the test. They also help illuminate what Jesus was and was not saying.

In the passage, Jesus is NOT teaching people to live cavalier lives, without any thought to what might or might not happen. He was NOT teaching people to fail to save or contemplate a wise use of money and resources. In no way was Jesus revoking Proverbs 6:6–11 that teaches, "Go to the ant, O sluggard; consider her ways, and be wise . . . she prepares her bread in summer and gathers her food in harvest. How long will you lie there, O sluggard? When will you arise from your sleep? A little sleep, a little slumber, little folding of the hands to rest, and poverty will come upon you like a robber, and want like an armed man."

People are to live wisely, seeking to be good stewards, contemplating what might happen, and seeking to be prepared for it. But there is a difference between living wisely and fretting unnecessarily about the future. When Jesus said, "do not be anxious about your life," he was speaking of being excessively worried, unduly concerned, or deeply fretful. One can be confident that God is there to provide for his children. However, that doesn't mean that God is going to quit teaching his children. The believer shouldn't expect God to quit his process of teaching his followers how to be godlier.

Being godlier includes being responsible stewards. Because the steward is a caretaker of those things under her or his authority, God wants the believer to take care of opportunities and resources. In other words, believers of all people should live deliberately and carefully. But as I do so, I have no need to unnecessarily fret or worry about tomorrow. God is in control!

Lord, forgive my lapses in judgment. Forgive my selfish choices. Help me live faithfully as a steward. And please take care of my tomorrows. Keep me from worry. In Jesus, amen.

JULY 20

Do not give dogs what is holy, and do not throw your pearls before pigs, lest they trample them underfoot and turn to attack you. (Mt. 7:6)

All four of our daughters have had dogs that have stolen a good bit of their hearts. Gracie had Kingsley, a boxer who wanted for nothing. Rachel had Sir Barks-a-lot, not his real name, but appropriate, nonetheless. Rebecca had Barney, a massive, well-trained bernadoodle. Sarah had the home Havanese, Tizzy. Each dog lacked for nothing. Our daughters would give them any and everything they wanted or needed. To my daughters, and to others like them, the New Testament culture's disdain for dogs as horrid mongrels is foreign.

Accordingly, today's passage might at first seem strange to our current dog-loving, pork-eating society. One must remember in reading it, however, that at the time Jesus gave this instruction, dogs and pigs were both considered unclean animals to the Jews. Good Jews neither ate the animals, nor kept the animals. The animals were to be shunned.

Jesus used the metaphor of the animals to speak to the wrongness of mixing the holy and the unholy. Holy things are special, and they should be treated that way. The word "holy" itself, both in the Hebrew Jesus spoke and in the Greek with which Matthew was written, denotes something that is dedicated or consecrated to God. It is not the mundane but is the special and unique. It is not the everyday but is the rare, the one-off.

Jesus was teaching his followers that some things are special and holy, dedicated to God. Those things are not to be confused with the unclean, impure, and unholy. The two don't mix, nor should anyone try to mix them.

What does this practically mean to me on a day-to-day basis? A lot! First, it means that as I try to be "holy" or dedicated to God, I need to live a "holy" life. I can't be holy and roll in sin like a pig in mud. Sin has no place in my life. I should shun it. When given an opportunity to lie about something, I should be honest. When given a chance to be greedy, I should seek to be sacrificial. When I see a chance to gossip, I should hold my tongue. When I see a chance to be selfish, I should serve. I want to be holy, and I shouldn't be casting pearls before swine!

Maybe Edward was right about me letting him go first (see January 26)!

Lord, forgive me for the times I wallow in the filth of sin. Help me to walk holy, as you are holy, caring for things as you do. In Jesus' name, amen.

JULY 21

Ask, and it will be given to you; seek, and you will find; knock, and it will be opened to you. For everyone who asks receives, and the one who seeks finds, and to the one who knocks it will be opened. Or which one of you, if his son asks him for bread, will give him a stone? Or if he asks for a fish, will give him a serpent? If you then, who are evil, know how to give good gifts to your children, how much more will your Father who is in heaven give good things to those who ask him! (Mt. 7:7–11)

Growing up in the Lanier household, I found birthdays magical. Mom would make the meal of my choice, the cake of my choice, and most incredibly, as long as what I asked for was within reason, I got the birthday gift of my choice. I have always loved birthdays.

Today's passage is not a birthday passage. If someone reads the passage in a way that makes God a genie, ready to give the gift of one's choosing, then one is going to be sorely disappointed. God is no genie granting three wishes. God isn't a hotel concierge who gets one a seat in an exclusive restaurant. God is God.

But today's passage is saying something vitally important to the believer. It informs people that God seeks what is best for his children, and that God often waits for the believer to ask, before God gives. This might seem hard to understand, and it might seem unlike how I would like God to do things, but it helps me process this when I use the example Jesus used—that of children and fathers.

Becky and I have five children and, as of this writing, nine grandchildren. There are many things I give them without their ever asking. Our children grew up in a safe home, with a roof over their heads, and food to eat. We made sure they had clothing, a home environment where they could bring their friends to play and socialize, a spiritual home at a good church, and more. Yet even as they had these things, they would still seek other things from us. They might ask to go to Chick-Fil-A for lunch. They might seek to have a movie night at home. And yes, they would almost always ask for specific birthday gifts. We would always seek to give those gifts, but only when in the best interest of each child.

God is much the same way, only better and more perfect! God gives his children many things without asking. I have so many blessings and I should be thankful for each. But God also seeks to give us gifts when we ask—as long as those gifts work within his larger plan and are for our own good. God won't let our requests stop his greater plan for his kingdom. Nor will he let our requests work to our detriment. God is a good Father.

Lord, thank you for your love. Thank you for your gifts. Give me wisdom in asking and praying, please. May I seek your will in my life. In Jesus, amen.

JULY 22

So whatever you wish that others would do to you, do also to them, for this is the Law and the Prophets. (Mt. 7:12)

Scholars trace the title "Golden Rule" or "Golden Law" back to 1604 to identify this teaching of Jesus. The Golden Rule or Law is the rule we find the most valuable or of the highest quality of ethical behavior.

The idea behind this ethic didn't originate with Jesus. At the time Jesus was teaching, the expression was already in rabbinical circles, although frequently as a negative, "Don't do to others what you don't want them to do to you." The great Rabbi Hillel (c. 110 BC–10 AD) was challenged by a Gentile to explain the Torah (the "Law" or first five books of the Bible) while the man stood on one foot. Hillel responded, "What is hateful to you, do not do to your fellow: this is the whole Torah; the rest is the explanation; go and learn" (Babylonian Talmud, Shab. 31a).

Hillel's idea is good, but Jesus makes a profound change, turning the negative into a positive. One should certainly follow Hillel's negative prohibition and not do to another something hateful. Yet Jesus takes it another step. Jesus calls on people to find things that are positive and affirmatively seek to do them to others. One could follow Hillel's teaching by simply ignoring others. Jesus' teaching calls the obedient to action!

If I am going to follow my Lord's instructions on this, I need to practically figure out ways to serve, love, help, and pray for others. This takes on a real mental effort as well as a deliberate course of action. It is common for me to think of what I want, but to think of how to care for another doesn't always come so easily.

So today, I am going to find people around me and work to ask this question, how can I best show them the love of Jesus? How can I best meet their needs? In this way, I find the root of all that is good in the Bible.

Of course, it is easy to read these words, and even echo this concern, but then something happens and the best intentions flee from my mind. I need God's help not only to keep me focused but to grow in this trait.

Lord, forgive how self-centered I can be in my life. Give me insight to see where others have needs and how you would have me help them. Use me as your tool to bring your mercy, provision, and care to others. As I do so, may it never be for my glory, but always for yours! In Jesus, amen.

JULY 23

Beware of false prophets, who come to you in sheep's clothing but inwardly are ravenous wolves. You will recognize them by their fruits. Are grapes gathered from thornbushes, or figs from thistles? So, every healthy tree bears good fruit, but the diseased tree bears bad fruit. A healthy tree cannot bear bad fruit, nor can a diseased tree bear good fruit. Every tree that does not bear good fruit is cut down and thrown into the fire. Thus you will recognize them by their fruits. (Mt. 7:15–20)

It is sad that everyone can't be taken at face value. I wish it were true of everyone that what you see is what you get. I work with a fellow who often says to me, "To tell you the truth . . ." Although I know his motives are good, I still think each time, "So, other times when you talk to me are you *not* telling me the truth?" I have also worked with and been around folks who are the exact opposite of what they portray.

So, as I approach today's Scripture, I do it in two directions. I focus on how others relate to me, but I also focus on how I relate to others.

Some people have jobs that require a good bit of interaction with and often reliance on others. It is appropriate to be measured in how one trusts another in critical situations. One should measure other folks by what the other's actions show to be their true character. If someone is a gossip, I can rest assured that the gossip doesn't stop when I come up as a subject. If someone can't keep other's secrets, I can expect that anything confidential I share will not be kept confidential. If someone says whatever is necessary to please another, I can doubt the integrity of what such a one tells me. This list goes on and on, but importantly, flows also in positive ways. If someone proves themselves worthy of confidence, I can confide in such a one. If one keeps their word, even to their own detriment, I can rely on that person.

This truth is not only manifested in the workplace, but in social circles as well. Among friends, and even family, the same truth holds. Not everyone is what they appear to be. We should show discernment and look for actions, not simply words.

The second direction for this passage is more personal, in some ways. It challenges me in my own behavior. I will also be known by my fruits. If I tell my wife I love her, but my actions decry otherwise, it will be known. If I say I will keep something confidential, but I reveal it, perhaps even saying, "I shouldn't tell you this, so don't tell anyone!" that speaks to my character. This list goes on, but the concept challenges me. I want to be someone who is what he appears to be. I want to be genuine!

Lord, help me grow in my character to be more godly. By your guiding hand, teach me to be genuine in my life, reliable to others, and truly reflecting your character. In Jesus, amen.

JULY 24

Everyone then who hears these words of mine and does them will be like a wise man who built his house on the rock. And the rain fell, and the floods came, and the winds blew and beat on that house, but it did not fall, because it had been founded on the rock. And everyone who hears these words of mine and does not do them will be like a foolish man who built his house on the sand. And the rain fell, and the floods came, and the winds blew and beat against that house, and it fell, and great was the fall of it. (Mt. 7:24–27)

Like many readers, when I was young, I was taught the song, "The wise man builds his house upon the rock. The wise man built his house upon the rock. The wise man built his house upon the rock and the rains came tumbling down. The rains came down and the floods went up. . . . And the wise man's house stood firm." The song came with hand motions, including fists at the end for the house standing firm. Then the second verse. "The foolish man built his house upon the sand. . . . The rains came down and the floods came up and the foolish man's house went SPLAT!" and with that the hands clapped and fell flat!

When I was older and started reading the Bible, I learned that this song came straight from the teachings of Jesus, as given above. But it wasn't until I entered adulthood that I begin to understand the notable implications of this for my life.

This passage emphasizes the importance of building life around the teachings, authority, and character of Jesus. Jesus is not only the model for my life, but my success will be dependent on how well I follow his teachings.

Many times young people have come to me asking what it takes to be successful. Usually they want to know how to be economically successful, thinking that if one makes a lot of money, life is good. With these young people, I try to convey two things. First, money is no indicator of success or happiness. Success in life is measured by walking in God's will, doing the good works God has laid out for us, and growing into a better reflection of his Son. When we have that success, whether it comes with money or not, we find the joy of the Lord and happiness is at hand. The second thing I try to convey is this song.

If anyone truly takes to heart this teaching of Jesus, one will find true success. I need to read the Bible, reflect on what I read, and pray regularly. I need to know the words of Jesus to build my life on his words. Then I need to DO what I know, and my house will stand firm when the rains come down!

Lord, teach me to better know and empower me to better do your words! Let me better reflect Jesus in my life and to the world. In Jesus' name, amen.

JULY 25

And he [John the Baptist] went into all the region around the Jordan, proclaiming a baptism of repentance for the forgiveness of sins. As it is written in the book of the words of Isaiah the prophet, "The voice of one crying in the wilderness: 'Prepare the way of the Lord, make his paths straight. Every valley shall be filled, and every mountain and hill shall be made low, and the crooked shall become straight, and the rough places shall become level ways, and all flesh shall see the salvation of God.'" (Lk. 3:3–6)

Today's passage is LOADED! Luke is describing the ministry of John the Baptist and uses a passage from Isaiah 40 to explain not only John's work but the important prophetic implications of what was happening. A closer look at Isaiah 40 is in order.

The prophet Isaiah lived a long life and prophesied over a long time span. The biblical book "Isaiah" is divisible into two parts: the first thirty-nine chapters reflect God's coming judgment pronounced on Israel and Judah. The rest of the book contains God's redemptive promises that will flow after the judgment is complete. So, by the time Isaiah 40 is read, one already knows that God will be bringing a harsh judgment on the nation that refuses to repent from their sin and unrighteousness. This was not inadvertent small sins here and there. The idolatry was rampant. The rich trampled on the poor. The powerful fed themselves fat while the defenseless and powerless were sacrificed.

Then as the prophet Ezekiel explained (Ezek. 10), metaphorically, God got up, left his temple, and left Jerusalem. And left to its own devices and strength, the nation crumbled and was carted off into captivity.

Into this scenario, Isaiah 40 comes with the promise that God would be returning to his people. The God who left Jerusalem and left the temple would be returning. When God came back, he would send a herald before him to prepare the road for God's journey back. That is what John the Baptist was doing. He called on the people to repent. Repentance is what the nation lacked before judgment fell hundreds of years before. But now, as John preached the repentance God sought, God was returning. God's return was in Jesus.

Jesus changes everything for me. God has come into this world to reign over his people, to defeat his enemies, to display his Godness, to vanquish the night, to give direction to the lost, sight to the blind, and purpose to the aimless. Behold the glory of the Almighty One who has come in splendor!

Why do I worry about life?

Almighty God, forgive my doubts. Give me trust in you! Blessed be your name. Amen.

JULY 26

And he rose and immediately picked up his bed and went out before them all, so that they were all amazed and glorified God, saying, "We never saw anything like this!" (Mk. 1:12)

Have you had some rare encounters that are stamped into your memory? I remember eating lunch on a hunting trip with Supreme Court Justice Antonin Scalia. Six of us were gathered around a table feasting on Italian food when Justice Scalia posed the question: "What did you like best, *Lonesome Dove* the book, or *Lonesome Dove* the movie?" He just assumed everyone had both read the book and seen the TV miniseries. The discussion quickly hopscotched into one of whether the word "prequel" properly exists in the English language! Justice Scalia found the word an offensive combination of two Latin words that had no business co-mingling! I won't forget that encounter.

You can stack up all the rare opportunities you and I have had to meet people and add them all together. In doing so, we will find that our sum of encounters would not rise to the level of a true encounter with Jesus Christ.

In today's passage, an overcrowded house of folks kept a paralyzed man from being able to come in the door to seek healing from Jesus. So the paralytic's friends hacked through the thatch roof and lowered the man down into Jesus' presence. Jesus healed the man and, though he entered on a stretcher through the roof, the man walked out the front door! This left the people amazed. They were praising God for the miracle. The people readily said, "We've never seen anything like this before." They were right.

That is how it is to encounter God. As a college student, I remember going to church and seeing people who seemed to experience God in ways I never had. These good folks had aspects to their relationship with God that made mine seem narrow. I remember sitting in church prayerfully asking God to give me a greater understanding of him, his work in Jesus, and the role of the Holy Spirit in my life.

Over the next few days, weeks, and months, my walk with the Lord grew exponentially. I more fully understood the work of Jesus on Calvary. I learned deliberate worship was not simply singing the songs everyone sang, but coming into God's presence. I found growth in my holiness. My encounter with Jesus was amazing! I had never seen anything like it before or since. (Not even lunch within chambers with a Supreme Court justice!) Something profound happens encountering Jesus. I heartily recommend it for all, even Christians!

Lord, give me a fresh encounter with you. Teach me anew the wonders of your love in Jesus. Grow me through your Holy Spirit. For his name's sake, amen.

JULY 27

And he lifted up his eyes on his disciples, and said: "Blessed are you who are poor, for yours is the kingdom of God. . . . But woe to you who are rich, for you have received your consolation." (Lk. 6:20, 24)

I have my "go to" meals. Whether in a restaurant or at home, more times than not I seek out the same things to eat. Give me a can of tuna and some crackers, and I am good for lunch. A good turkey burger goes a long way. If I am eating at Taco Villa, I am going to be getting a bean burrito with green sauce. I am a rut guy. I find something I like and stick with it!

That may be why my tendency to read Jesus giving the "beatitudes" frequently finds me in Matthew. Matthew chapter five has the Sermon on the Mount with all nine beatitudes with which I have grown so familiar. Yet there is a lesson for me when I step out of my normal "go to" and get into something different. So it is with Luke and his rendition of the beatitudes.

As a reminder, a "beatitude" sounds like it is an attitude one should adopt or behavior one should "be." Indeed, the actions are goals I should aspire to meet; the word "beatitude" refers to a supreme blessing. The word conveys the gist of the beatitudes that as one does or experiences them, one is "blessed."

Luke chooses four of Matthew's nine beatitudes. Then, unlike Matthew, Luke marries up the four with four "woes," countering the "supreme blessing" with a supreme tragedy! Today's passage gives the first of the four found in Luke.

Jesus turns the world's wisdom upside down pronouncing as supremely blessed, one who has little in the way of worldly wealth. Jesus gives the fuller picture by noting the limits on those who have their wealth in this world. The poor of the world have kingdom citizenship, something money can't buy, and something worth more than dollars and cents. But the rich seem to have all they want, and the kingdom doesn't even enter their radar.

I don't want to be the rich person whose pinnacle in life is living off the fat of the land today. I want to be a kingdom citizen. I think the key is recognizing that everything you and I have, even if we have all the riches of the world, everything is really God's. I don't have the money in my bank account, God does. I don't have the gifts and talents that make my life what it is, God does. I don't have my job opportunities, God does. I am a mere steward of what is God's. No riches for me, please. Just the kingdom! Any riches I have are kingdom assets!

Lord, please help me walk in your will today. Meet my needs as only you can, and may I give you all the glory. In Jesus, amen.

JULY 28

Blessed are you who are hungry now, for you shall be satisfied. Blessed are you who weep now, for you shall laugh. . . . Woe to you who are full now, for you shall be hungry. Woe to you who laugh now, for you shall mourn and weep. (Lk. 6:21, 25)

Once when I was teaching on this passage, I began by saying I feel I should be standing on my head to teach. Admittedly, I can't really stand on my head, and I certainly couldn't teach while doing so, but this passage seems to stand all current wisdom on its head. So it seemed fitting to try and teach it accordingly.

Consider what Jesus is saying in these beatitudes. Jesus announces a blessing on those who are hungry. He then contrasts it to those who are filled, noting the "woe" on those that are sated. This seems to stand in opposition to the desire Jesus has for people to be filled. After all, this is the same Jesus who feed thousands with just a few loaves and fishes, even though the disciples thought it best to send people home to eat. At no point did Jesus just announce to the thousands, "Now go home! And remember you are supremely blessed because you are hungry!"

Further, this is the same Jesus who turned water into wine to help celebrate a wedding feast. Jesus also constantly spoke of his kingdom as a wedding feast. Physical hunger is not the best case scenario for people. Yet Jesus uses it in today's passage.

Jesus also adds a blessing on those who are weeping. Again, this is atypical. Jesus dries tears typically; he doesn't call them forth! The promise of the coming kingdom is one where there are no tears.

What is to be done with this passage? This passage should reassure those who are hurting. For those who are hungry, not simply for physical food, but for all the needs of life, Jesus offers the comfort of knowing that satisfaction will come. God doesn't ignore those in need. Neither does God ignore those who are hurting. The needy and hurting are the focus of God's attention. No one should feel God has ignored them, or left them alone in their need.

The ones who need to be concerned from this passage are those who seem to have no need for God. Those with full bellies, those who laugh through the days, these are the ones who should hear alarms. Life will not always be so grand. Need and hurt are always right around the corner.

As Christians, we heed this counsel when we praise God for all of life. Dark times merit God's praise, as we live in trust that he will rescue. Times that are marvelous should also turn our hearts to God in praise, knowing he is there in good times and bad.

Lord, I set all my needs before you, thanking you for life and trusting you for tomorrow. In Jesus, amen.

JULY 29

Now there was a man of the Pharisees named Nicodemus, a ruler of the Jews. This man came to Jesus by night and said to him, "Rabbi, we know that you are a teacher come from God, for no one can do these signs that you do unless God is with him." Jesus answered him, "Truly, truly, I say to you, unless one is born again he cannot see the kingdom of God." (Jn. 3:1–3)

Car navigation systems amaze me. I can rent a car in a strange town, plug in the location where I want to go, and the car will instruct me through each turn. Recently, I was using GPS navigation while driving a car and I missed a turn. The system began barking at me, "Make the next available U-turn." The comment continued on and on until I finally shut the system down.

U-turns don't happen only on the roads. U-turns are a major theme in Luke's gospel. Luke begins his gospel with indications that God, through Jesus, was coming into the world to perform U-turns. In today's passage, Mary the expectant mother of Jesus, sings of God's actions as bringing down the mighty, while lifting up the low people. God will fill the hungry and strip the rich. God will be executing U-turns.

Luke signals this over and over, with references to John the Baptist being one who will "turn" many of the children of Israel to God (Lk. 1:16). John would "turn" the hearts of fathers to their children and the disobedient to just living (Lk. 1:17). Even the birth of John the Baptist is a story of a U-turn, as God takes a barren couple past child-bearing age and gives them a child.

Luke not only has God performing U-turns, but Jesus teaches his people to do the same. Jesus explained that those who want to be great, need to work on their serving (Lk. 22:26). Some who seem to be first, will be last; while some who are last, will be first (Lk. 13:30).

Undoubtedly, the greatest exhibition of God's execution of U-turns in this world happens when Luke writes up the crucifixion and resurrection account of Jesus. Death is the final keystroke in the life of everyone, but not with Jesus. Jesus dies, and God performed the greatest U-turn. He resurrected Jesus, and with that resurrection brought forth the fruit of eternity for all his followers.

God is a God of U-turns. He wants to turn my life around. He wants to take hurt and bring healing. He wants to take sin and bring mercy. He wants to take bitterness and bring forgiveness. He wants to take needs and make abundance. This God of U-turns is exactly what I hope for and need today. Thank you, God!

Lord, give me the U-turns I need in my life. Help me be what and who I should be. Also give me the wisdom to be your tool in helping others in need of U-turns. May I live for your mission. In Jesus, amen.

JULY 30

Passing alongside the Sea of Galilee, he saw Simon and Andrew the brother of Simon casting a net into the sea, for they were fishermen. And Jesus said to them, "Follow me, and I will make you become fishers of men." (Mk. 1:16-17)

I often spend my quiet reflective time in the morning, when I first wake up. I am not as consistent as my friend Jarrett who calls it his "hour of power," nor do I often dedicate a full hour to it, but there is a power in starting the day with a focus on God.

One morning, I was in a season of life where my daily walk with God was important to me, but was a bit out of focus. It seemed to consist more of trying to do right. But life was so busy that at the end of the day, when I was physically worn out, I found that much earlier in the day I had exhausted my emotional and spritual energy without having had my quiet time. I then found this verse.

At first I read over the verse in English and without much pause. But something triggered me to go back and read it in the original Greek. When I did, I felt I'd been slapped in the face. In the Greek, Jesus' command to Simon and Andrew was especially abrupt. This was something they were to do, and they were to do it NOW! The reason was an urgency in Jesus and his ministry. In the immediate prior verses, Jesus had been noted preaching that the Kingdom of God was near. God was at work. People needed gathering into the kingdom the way fish are gathered into a net. Jesus was choosing his team of fishermen.

This impressed on me the urgency of the day. Every day I have is 24 hours long. A good bit of it I usually spend sleeping. I will need, and God made us to appreciate, a bit of time for recharging our batteries, for working, for socializing, for eating, for self-preparation (studying, grooming, etc.). Yet all of this needs to be done with some measure of urgency. If I don't spend today as best as I can, then I can't hit a "redo" button and do it again tomorrow. I have one shot.

This makes my morning reflective, prayer, and study time important. It helps me get into ready mode for the day. It helps me find that right range of focus on distributing my time and energy. It gives me insight into how each part of my day can be to God's glory. I never hit it perfectly, but I find with the right preparation to the day, I do much better! Then when I go to sleep at night, I thank God and rest peacefully in his arms.

Lord, give me insight and determination to live intentionally for you today. Whether at work or play, let it be done showing your love and mercy! In Jesus' name, amen.

JULY 31

A man once gave a great banquet and invited many. And at the time for the banquet he sent his servant to say to those who had been invited, "Come, for everything is now ready." But they all alike began to make excuses. The first said to him, "I have bought a field, and I must go out and see it. Please have me excused." And another said, "I have bought five yoke of oxen, and I go to examine them. Please have me excused." And another said, "I have married a wife, and therefore I cannot come." So the servant came and reported these things to his master. Then the master of the house became angry and said to his servant, "Go out quickly to the streets and lanes of the city, and bring in the poor and crippled and blind and lame." And the servant said, "Sir, what you commanded has been done, and still there is room." And the master said to the servant, "Go out to the highways and hedges and compel people to come in, that my house may be filled. For I tell you, none of those men who were invited shall taste my banquet." (Lk. 14:16-24)

Wow. Today's parable always stuns me. I am not sure if I am stunned more by the fact that so many make excuses to avoid spending time with God, or by one man's excuse of blaming it on his wife!

Stunned as I may be, however, I can't help but internalize Jesus' message. The Almighty God has come into this world to bring an intimate fellowship with humanity. People will stand in long lines to get a good deal at a store, they will sleep out overnight to get good concert tickets, they will pay large sums to dine with leaders of government.

Yet when it comes to spending time in God's presence, people often hardly give it a second thought. I suspect this is in part because God is always available. Maybe it also is because God isn't readily visible. It may also be that many just don't really know him that well, and aren't comfortable spending time in prayer, meditation, and study of his word.

Excuses may abound, but excuses are just that—excuses. I don't want to be one who makes excuses. I want to be someone who lets nothing get in the way of my time with God. That means taking the time to read these devotionals, to pray these prayers, to expand my study beyond this book, to fellowship with others in worshipping the Lord, and in doing so much more. Times spent getting to know God, learning to trust him, and sharing knowledge of him with others are some of the richest times of life.

If I see my invitations to meet God as something as real as an invitation to meet a dignitary or famous person, I think my life would be different. I know my priorities would be.

Lord, forgive the times I take you for granted. Forgive my failure to appreciate my fellowshipping with you. May I grow in my love for you as I grow in my time with you. In Jesus, amen.

AUGUST 1

Then Pharisees and scribes came to Jesus from Jerusalem and said, "Why do your disciples break the tradition of the elders? For they do not wash their hands when they eat." . . . And Jesus went away from there and withdrew to the district of Tyre and Sidon. And behold, a Canaanite woman from that region came out and was crying, "Have mercy on me, O Lord, Son of David; my daughter is severely oppressed by a demon." (Mt. 15:1–2, 21–22)

Matthew makes a lot of sandwiches in his writings. By that I mean he often takes one story and contrasts it with a second story, setting some type of explanation in the middle. He does so with these two stories in Matthew 15.

In the first story, Pharisees and scribes come to Jesus all the way from Jerusalem. Jesus was north of Jerusalem in Galilee. This was a seventy- to eighty-mile walk, each way. Of course, that is *before* their task of finding Jesus in a somewhat large region where Jesus wandered as he taught. Jesus didn't have a permanent home where they could go knock on his door. The Pharisees and scribes didn't make this trek out of affection. They came in hostility, challenging Jesus on his rabbinical failures. In their eyes, Jesus was either failing to properly teach his disciples, or he was failing to enforce appropriate behavior.

In contrast, the other slice of bread, is the story of a woman north of Galilee, the opposite direction of all things Jerusalem. This isn't a Jewish woman, but a pagan. While the Pharisees and scribes had come to Jesus in enmity, seeking to intimidate, the woman came to Jesus in desperation, seeking his mercy. The Jerusalem contingency had defiance and indignation in their tone. The woman had worry and fear. The religious fellows boldly challenged Jesus and his teachings. The woman came with devout respect, and even good theology, recognizing Jesus as "Lord, Son of David."

The sandwich slices illustrate the importance of how I approach Jesus. The Pharisees and scribes went home embarrassed and offended. The Canaanite woman went home with her prayers answered and her daughter healed. I want to approach God with a pure heart. I want God to hear my earnest pleas. I don't want to challenge him to a religious debate. I have no place correcting God. I shouldn't be telling God how I think he should do things. That doesn't mean I don't pour out my heart to him. It doesn't mean I am not persistent in seeking his will. It comes down to attitude. At the end of the day, he is God; I'm not. And that is a good thing.

Lord, I confess I often come to you on my terms, not yours. I want that to change. Purify my heart as I learn to live in a right relationship with you. In Jesus' name, amen.

AUGUST 2

You hypocrites! Well did Isaiah prophesy of you, when he said: "This people honors me with their lips, but their heart is far from me; in vain do they worship me, teaching as doctrines the commandments of men." (Mt. 15:7–9)

Television and movies are inventions of the twentieth century, but acting goes back long before then. In antiquity, Greeks and Romans were famous for their theater. Many of the words in our vocabulary today trace their roots in the theater vocabulary of classical antiquity. Words like "scene," "pantomime," "tragedy," "drama," and "chorus" all come directly from Greek theater. In fact, even the word "theater" is from a Greek word (*theatron* in Greek was the seating place or place to see an unfolding drama). Another Greek theater word is used by Jesus in today's passage.

The English word "hypocrite" comes directly from the Greek theater. A *hypocrite* in Greek was an actor, one saying a line for affect, not in truth. A hypocrite was one who was playing a role. Jesus uses this graphic term for certain people who claimed a supreme piety, but in fact were deeply flawed. These people had turned religion into a set of rules, straying far from the heart of God in the process. The irony of this is that the religious actors were indicting Jesus for not playing their game. They wanted to embarrass Jesus and bring him to account publicly for his error-filled teaching. This wasn't a case of the pot calling the kettle black. They lived the false life of an actor. Jesus was authentic.

The British theologian F. F. Bruce is quoted as saying, "There are religious actors still, and they often play to a full house." Heaven forbid that be me! It causes me to ask myself certain questions. Do I practice religion or is my heart truly seeking God? Are my decisions based on what I want, or do I consider the desires of God? Is my public behavior a show, or does it accurately reflect my private devotion? Am I one way around my religious friends and another around my worldly friends? Does God invade all aspects of my life, or do I keep him in certain compartments? Am I content as I am, or do I see my shortcomings, prompting me to seek greater holiness?

These questions rightly gnaw at me. They challenge me. They inspire me. I don't want to be an actor. I want authenticity. I want my words to be genuine reflections of a pure heart.

In my legal practice, I have had the joy of representing a number of actors. They aren't the same in person as they are on the screen. On-screen they play a role; real life is real. I need to take that to heart.

Lord, forgive my lip service. May I diligently seek and serve you in truth. In Jesus, amen.

AUGUST 3

And he called the people to him and said to them, "Hear and understand: it is not what goes into the mouth that defiles a person, but what comes out of the mouth; this defiles a person." (Mt. 15:10–11)

Make no doubt about it, handwashing with clean water and soap is very important! Statistics show that human and animal feces are sources for the germs *Salmonella*, *E. coli*, and those that cause noroviruses. One study indicated that a single gram of human feces can contain one trillion germs! But washing hands isn't simply running your hands under water. One needs clean water and soap, which is the real germ remover/killer. Welcome to the wonders of modern science!

At the time of Jesus, certain religious zealots required handwashing before eating. This wasn't twenty seconds under clean running water with soap. It was a ritual, one where the water itself might have germs that deposit on the hands. Therefore, when the religious traditionalists came to Jesus indicting him for not insisting that his disciples wash their hands before eating, their concern wasn't hygiene. It was tradition. It was doing an outward task to make someone appear holy and devoted to God.

Jesus was all about holiness and devotion to God, but not in a showy fashion. Jesus pointed to the important difference between godliness in an outward, almost pompous sense, and holiness of heart. Jesus wanted people to understand that God isn't about outward actions only. God wanted the hearts and minds of people.

God is a God of more than the externals. Living right before God isn't found solely in what we do. God wants authenticity. Life should never be a show before God. God searches our hearts and minds, seeking devotion and the good works that flow from there.

This means that we need to rewire our brains. We need to develop new thought patterns. We need to soften our hard hearts. We need to grow in our devotion to God. We need to become disciplined in purified desires. We need to better understand right and wrong. We need to adjust our priorities.

This brain work isn't done overnight. Like getting in physical shape, it takes time. But instead of time in the gym, this means time in God's word, time with God in prayer, time with God in worship, and time with God's people. It is through both quantity and quality time that we will find God daily at work, remaking our hearts and minds in devotion to him. May God help me!

Lord, I want to be authentic. I need you to reclaim my heart and mind. Make me more like you. Give me focus and commitment. In Jesus' name, amen!

AUGUST 4

Then the disciples came and said to him, "Do you know that the Pharisees were offended when they heard this saying?" He answered, "Every plant that my heavenly Father has not planted will be rooted up. Let them alone; they are blind guides. And if the blind lead the blind, both will fall into a pit." (Mt. 15:12–14)

In my first year of high school, I was "kidnapped" one Saturday morning to be initiated into a certain school club. The junior and senior guys did the kidnapping. The initiation included things like smoking a cigarette. This was no renegade club; it was for the debate team! As the cigarette was passed around, the pressure to smoke was intense. Peer pressure can be that way.

Peer pressure doesn't end with high school. It continues through much of life. (In fairness, my ninety-year-old grandmother may not have felt much peer pressure. In her later years she proudly proclaimed those days were over! She could say whatever she wanted and do whatever she wanted.) In life, we want to fit in; we want friends; we want to be part of a larger group. This may drive part of the pressure we feel to go along with the crowd.

Jesus' disciples were not immune to this. When the Pharisees and scribes came into Galilee from Jerusalem, the local folks were likely in awe a bit. This was the big-time people from the city coming into the small local communities that rarely hosted such folks. Jesus, however, was not cowed by the city folks. Their positions were not so lofty that they impressed Jesus. What was worse, their teaching was off—dangerously off. Jesus would have none of that, whether they were from the big city or from Timbuktu.

So, Jesus challenged the Pharisees and scribes. He revealed the falsity and danger of their teaching, and no doubt embarrassed them in the process. They had come to intimidate Jesus, the country teacher, and Jesus stopped them dead in their tracks. Jesus spoke truth and revealed darkness. It left the hypocrites offended. (No one likes their hypocrisy exposed!)

When the disciples pointed out that the city leaders were offended, Jesus dismissed their concerns. Jesus wasn't worried about fitting in, he was worried about leading people to God. "Fitting in" with blind leaders means the blind leading the blind.

In high school I told the older boys I wasn't going to smoke the cigarette. I worried about the impression I might leave, but it turned out okay! In fact, they saw this as part of me being a leader. If following God doesn't make us fit in, we need not worry. Some places aren't worth fitting into!

Jesus, may I make pursuing you my highest priority today. In your name, amen.

AUGUST 5

For out of the heart come evil thoughts, murder, adultery, sexual immorality, theft, false witness, slander. These are what defile a person. (Mt. 15:19–20)

"Cause and effect" describes a relationship between two things where one thing makes something else happen. If I chew and swallow my breakfast, it makes the food more digestible and moves it into my digestive tract. If I cut my fingernails, it makes them shorter. If I hang upside down, it makes blood rush to my head. You get the idea . . .

Jesus was concerned with cause and effect. Jesus knew how it worked in the mind. Jesus knew that certain thoughts were associated with certain actions. Because of this, Jesus sought to focus on the cause and not simply the effects.

In today's passage, Jesus explains his concerns after a confrontation with some misdirected religious leaders. These leaders thought that one could be a shining example of devotion to God by performing simple external rituals. Jesus knew that their showy actions were coming from dark hearts, and as showy as the rituals might be, they were no substitute for authenticity.

Jesus used the moment to teach the important truth of cause and effect in human life. In a sense, we live inside our minds. (While the Hebrew thought system at the time of Jesus believed the heart to be the location of thinking, we know it to be the brain. So, as we read Jesus speaking to them of the thoughts of their hearts, he wasn't speaking emotionally per se, he was speaking of what we would call the "mind" in our understanding.) It is in the mind that one finds motives. In the mind one finds being and a sense of self.

Understanding this, Jesus knew that one's mind was a cause to many effects. If one's mind is stewing in evil thoughts, evil actions will flow. If one is thinking of murder, kindness is not going to be produced. If one is thinking of adultery, faithful love will be hard to come by. If one is thinking of sexual immorality, godly intimacy will be missed. If one is thinking of theft, one will not be a ready and generous giver. If one is thinking of lying, one will struggle to be honest. If one is thinking ill toward another, one will not be loving to all.

Instead of these negative thoughts, and the result they cause, think of the results of positive thoughts. How great the world would be if we thought of kindness toward all, faithfulness to commitments, godly expressions of human desires, giving to the needy, being real and honest, and wishing others the best of life.

Lord, today I want to think right! I want the effects caused by godly thoughts. Help me today in Jesus, amen.

AUGUST 6

And behold, a Canaanite woman from that region came out and was crying, "Have mercy on me, O Lord, Son of David; my daughter is severely oppressed by a demon." But he did not answer her a word. And his disciples came and begged him, saying, "Send her away, for she is crying out after us." He answered, "I was sent only to the lost sheep of the house of Israel." But she came and knelt before him, saying, "Lord, help me." And he answered, "It is not right to take the children's bread and throw it to the dogs." She said, "Yes, Lord, yet even the dogs eat the crumbs that fall from their masters' table." Then Jesus answered her, "O woman, great is your faith! Be it done for you as you desire." And her daughter was healed instantly. (Mt. 15:22–28)

Today's story is a harsh one for many. It doesn't seem to portray the compassionate, interested, helpful Jesus that we know and love. Instead, Jesus comes across a bit mean and aloof. The woman is desperate for his help, and Jesus ignores her pleas. As she persisted, knowing her daughter required the intervention of the Healer, Jesus still puts her off, seeming to insist that her genetics made her not his intended audience.

What do we do with this story? Was Matthew not writing it fairly? Was Jesus having a bad day? Was there some secret about the woman that we don't know, such that the actions of Jesus were appropriate? I believe a deeper principle is at work here.

The Bible repeatedly teaches that God tests the hearts and minds of people. Psalm 11:5 says, "The LORD tests the righteous." The prophet Jeremiah called on God as the "LORD of hosts, who tests the righteous, who sees the heart and the mind" (Jer. 20:12). Perhaps my favorite explanation of the testing of God comes from the prophet Zechariah, whose name means "God remembers": "And I will put this third into the fire, and refine them as one refines silver, and test them as gold is tested. They will call upon my name, and I will answer them. I will say, 'They are my people'; and they will say, 'The LORD is my God.'"

I think this is clearly at work with the Canaanite woman. Jesus tests her. It isn't an easy test; refining silver takes time in the fire. But from the test comes purity. It drives one to call upon God and then experience the answer. This is what the woman did. She made certain that Jesus heard her pleas. Jesus ends this story as the prophet Zechariah promised. Jesus calls this woman of non-Jewish lineage a woman of great faith, that is, one of God's own.

As I type this, a dear friend e-mailed me about his son's persistent medical problem and the doctor's inability to get it figured out and under control. We will persist in prayer, knowing our God refines us for his purposes!

Lord, hear our prayer. Help the needy. Please. In Jesus' name, amen.

AUGUST 7

And when they had crossed over, they came to land at Gennesaret. And when the men of that place recognized him, they sent around to all that region and brought to him all who were sick. (Mt. 14:34–35)

Do you know the old song, *Pass It On*? It begins with the lyrics, "It only takes a spark to get a fire going. And soon all those around can warm up to its glowing. That's how it is with God's love, once you experience it. You spread his love, to everyone, you want to pass it on."

The song isn't loaded with subtle and deep lyrics. It doesn't have some majestic melody or ear-catching hook. But the simple idea is a marvelous one. Sharing the love of God is a marvelous thing to do.

As Jesus gave his last instructions to his disciples, he included their commissioning to go into the world and share the good news of the death and resurrection of Christ (Mt. 28:16–20). But even before that, passages like today's show the naturalness of sharing the presence and work of Jesus with others.

Jesus traveled to the eastern shore of the Sea of Galilee, and people recognized him! The gospels are fairly clear that he wasn't recognized as "Jesus, the Son of God" but rather he was seen as the Nazarene fellow who had left his carpentry business to be an itinerant rabbi. But he wasn't just any rabbi. He had an ability to heal the sick, like no one had ever seen. Rabbis were teachers; Jesus was a teacher *and* a healer.

As Jesus was recognized, the people got busy. They went far and wide and found anyone who needed Jesus. They brought those folks to Jesus! Now the word used for "brought" in Greek is *prospherō* (προσφέρω); it references "bringing" someone, but it also conveys the meaning of "offering" or presenting something that was brought. In a sense, the folks were doing both. They were bringing Jesus to those who needed Jesus' touch. They were also presenting or offering those in need to Jesus. Jesus received their offering with his healing touch.

This passage motivates me. It makes me think. I know Jesus. In a real sense, I "recognize" him. He isn't just a teacher and healer; I know him also as a Savior. I need to bring to him all those who need his touch. Like a spark that starts a fire, I should spread the news of Jesus and bring in offering to him all those in need of the Savior.

Lord, give me eyes to see those who need you. Give me boldness to speak into their lives. May my words and my life invite others to you, so you might touch them and give them life. In your name, amen.

AUGUST 8

Jesus went on from there and walked beside the Sea of Galilee. And he went up on the mountain and sat down there. And great crowds came to him, bringing with them the lame, the blind, the crippled, the mute, and many others, and they put them at his feet, and he healed them, so that the crowd wondered, when they saw the mute speaking, the crippled healthy, the lame walking, and the blind seeing. And they glorified the God of Israel. (Mt. 15:29–31)

Today's passage is hugely important. Don't read past it! Take a moment and consider it. Let me first add some context.

Jesus has just had a most uncomfortable encounter with a Canaanite woman. This woman was *not* Jewish, and many religious Jews would not have even spoken with her. The woman beseeched Jesus to heal her daughter, and Jesus seems almost cold in his response. At first, he ignored her. Then, as she persisted, he told her that he was sent to the Jews and not the dogs. She wouldn't leave but reminded Jesus that even dogs got to eat scraps from their master's table. Jesus was impressed, noted her faith, and healed her daughter.

One might read from that encounter that Jesus had no regard for Gentiles, but Matthew doesn't want that misunderstanding to occur. Indeed, Jesus had other reasons for dealing so with the woman. Jesus was full of compassion for all, regardless of race, gender, age, degree of holiness, and so on. So Matthew gives today's passage as a follow up to the story of the Canaanite woman.

In today's story, Jesus sits on a mountain, giving an opportunity for loads of folks in need to get his attention. He is in Galilee, a region where a lot of non-Jews lived. As Jesus sits, "great crowds" come, and the healings are evident. The crippled are made whole, the lame walk, the blind get their sight. And Matthew adds that the people "glorified the God of Israel." In other words, these were all pagans, just like the Canaanite woman! Jesus didn't put them off. He didn't ignore them. He didn't call them dogs. He healed them and they gave God the glory.

I love to read Jesus in context, watching the stories flow one to the other. Jesus didn't live in verses, sentences, or paragraphs. He lived all day every day. Reading Jesus as his story unfolds shows layers of complexity we might miss, if we simply pull out the sections that show Jesus as we want him to be. Yet Jesus was at work for God, living according to a plan. His life and mission weren't haphazard. His actions and his words were deliberate. The end of everything he did was to bring glory to the "God of Israel," the only true God.

Lord, it is my prayer that Jesus in my life will bring you glory, forever and ever, amen.

AUGUST 9

Then Jesus called his disciples to him and said, "I have compassion on the crowd because they have been with me now three days and have nothing to eat. And I am unwilling to send them away hungry, lest they faint on the way." And the disciples said to him, "Where are we to get enough bread in such a desolate place to feed so great a crowd?" And Jesus said to them, "How many loaves do you have?" They said, "Seven, and a few small fish." And directing the crowd to sit down on the ground, he took the seven loaves and the fish, and having given thanks he broke them and gave them to the disciples, and the disciples gave them to the crowds. And they all ate and were satisfied. And they took up seven baskets full of the broken pieces left over. Those who ate were four thousand men, besides women and children. (Mt. 15:32–38)

Most everyone I know suffers a bit of an inferiority complex. Even those who say they have zero inferiorities are typically covering up deep inferiorities! We all have times of self-doubt, feelings of inadequacy, and concerns of personal value. Think of questions like: Am I good enough? Am I appreciated enough? Will people like me? Will they see me valuable? Will they want to be with me? How will they perceive me? Am I pretty enough? Handsome enough? Funny enough? Witty enough? Smart enough? These and more are questions of self-worth.

As odd as it might seem, this passage should put any such fears to rest! This is a passage where Jesus feeds four thousand-plus people *out of compassion*. Jesus specifically said, "I have *compassion* on the crowd." Now this is not the first time Jesus fed a multitude with almost nothing. In the previous chapter of Matthew, we read of Jesus feeding five thousand with just a few loaves and fish. In fact, having read that, one might wonder why the disciples so readily questioned how to feed the crowd with the little they had that day. Here it helps to read the passage a little more closely.

In this passage, the "crowd" were those whom Matthew identified as glorifying the God of Israel in the preceding story. These were Gentiles; they weren't Jews! Jesus previously had fed five thousand Jews with minimal foodstuffs, but Jews were God's "chosen people." These were the "others." Yet Jesus still expressed his compassion on them. Jesus still sought to meet their needs. Jesus still wanted to shower them with his love.

When I think about feelings of inferiority or insecurity, I like this story's message. Jesus has compassion on all people. When people come to Jesus, they find one who meets their needs, showers them with love, cares about how they are doing. Jesus is alert to our needs today and every day. He wants to help us. Right now!

Lord, thank you for your love and compassion. I certainly don't deserve it, and sometimes have trouble understanding it. But I need it! You are too good to me. In Jesus, amen.

AUGUST 10

And the Pharisees and Sadducees came, and to test him they asked him to show them a sign from heaven. (Mt. 16:1)

Politics in the United States sometimes frustrates me immensely. It often seems to me that folks on opposite sides of the political spectrum spend a great deal of time demonizing those who are not of the same political party. Yet, even with those distinctions, when the United States is attacked by others, those parties can and do unite on a common enemy.

This current reality should not surprise anyone, for so it was in the New Testament times with Jesus. Today's passage presents the Pharisees and Sadducees coming together on a common goal—discrediting Jesus. Pharisees and Sadducees were two entirely different groups of Jews at the time, and they really didn't get along on much of anything. The Pharisees adhered to the entire Old Testament as Scripture; the Sadducees followed only the first five books (the Torah or Books of Moses). This resulted in some core theological differences (e.g., the Pharisees believed in a resurrection from the dead, but the Sadducees did not). The Pharisees emphasized careful adherence to Jewish law, but the Sadducees were more centered on adhering to temple ritual. The Pharisees were exclusivists who scrupulously avoided contact with non-Jews, while the Sadducees were deeply involved with the Romans in administering law in Judea.

Yet these two widely divergent, even antagonistic parties united in one thing: Jesus was a destructive force, a problem who needed to be fixed. In this story, these two divergent groups unite to bring Jesus to account. If the old maxim, "united we stand; divided we fall" is to be believed, the Pharisees and Sadducees were going to be a formidable group contending against Jesus. But such was not the case. Today, almost two thousand years later, Pharisees have disappeared as a Jewish faction. Sadducees are nowhere to be found. But followers of Jesus are legion.

Why is that? Why did this unlikely group of bedfellows vanish, while Jesus' followers proliferated? A few years after these events, Jesus died, was resurrected, and ascended to heaven. The apostles were persecuted by Pharisees and Sadducees alike. At the hearing where Pharisees and Sadducees were deciding what to do with the apostles, a devout Pharisee named Gamaliel rose and said, "'So in the present case I tell you, keep away from these men and let them alone, for if this plan or this undertaking is of man, it will fail; but if it is of God, you will not be able to overthrow them. You might even be found opposing God!' So they took his advice" (Acts 5:34–39). Following Jesus is a worthy life choice.

Lord, please help me as I seek to follow Jesus with my life. Give me clarity of vision and a hungry heart for my Lord and Savior. In whom I pray, amen.

AUGUST 11

And the Pharisees and Sadducees came, and to test him they asked him to show them a sign from heaven. He answered them. . . . "An evil and adulterous generation seeks for a sign, but no sign will be given to it except the sign of Jonah." So he left them and departed. (Mt. 16:1-4)

When I was in college, I took a few courses at a state school. One of those was an anthropology course. I went to visit the professor during his office hours to ask about an upcoming exam. While talking to him, I made a reference to my faith in God. What happened next stunned me. Gone was the polite professorial tone, and in its place was obvious anger. The professor challenged me on my faith. In an antagonistic, almost hateful manner, he said, "You can't really believe there's a God!" I told him I did. At which point, he said, "Well, let me get a hammer and begin to smash you on the head, and if there's a God, you get him to stop me!" I told him God wasn't interested in tests like that and then immediately dropped the course!

Jesus was subjected to antagonistic testing as well. It always fascinates me that the miracle-working Jesus, who produced the unexplainable—blind people given sight, lame people walking, and so on—would be challenged to produce a "sign." How much more proof should one want than clear miracles? Yet some people with 20/20 vision were blind to the works of Jesus.

Jesus calls these questioning doubters an "evil and adulterous generation." That phrase is worthy of attention. The Greek word translated as "evil" (*ponēros*, πονηρός) can also easily be translated as "wicked," "vicious," "base," "worthless," "degenerate." Jesus recognized that these people weren't genuinely seeking God. They were ill-intentioned, to put it mildly. Theirs was antagonism, not genuine seeking of truth. Jesus also uses the term "adulterous" to describe them. Jesus is using the noun for an adulteress as an adjective. These enemies were not being faithful to their vows. While they professed an allegiance to God, they were standing against God as they challenged Jesus.

I think there is a distinction between truly seeking God and challenging God out of anger and hatred. I have met good people who are upset with God, and one reads of such even in the Psalms. That seems right and proper to me. But there is an important line where anger and frustration can turn into hatred. That line is to be avoided at all costs. These people weren't seeking God. They were bent on destroying Jesus. They were evil and adulterous!

Our motive in life should be to seek and understand God. We should do so with willing hearts. Jesus assures us that those who seek him, will find him (Mt. 7:7).

Lord, I seek you. Please show me your truth and love in Jesus, amen.

AUGUST 12

When the disciples reached the other side, they had forgotten to bring any bread. Jesus said to them, "Watch and beware of the leaven of the Pharisees and Sadducees." (Mt. 16:5-6)

For almost fifty years, following Jesus has been a goal for me. I want to have his heart and mind. I want to adopt his priorities. I want to emulate his attitudes. And so, passages like today's leave me shaking my head in amazement. In some ways, it shows Jesus as so far from me, and it inspires me to grow.

Jesus led a troupe of men who had divided up chores among them. Jesus was the leader, rabbi/teacher, healer of the masses, and the voice of the group. He gave direction, discerned the will of God, and was a man on a mission. The disciples were variously in charge of keeping the company's funds and other nitty, gritty details of daily life. It fell on the disciples to pack the necessary provisions for their excursions and journeys. Most times we read of no glitches or dropped balls, but not this time. This time the disciples in charge had forgotten to bring the food!

I have left things behind, and I can certainly identify with the disciples here. But forgetting the food is a fairly major thing, especially in an era where one didn't have credit cards or ATM access. Nor were there convenient fast food restaurants on each corner from which to buy food. This was a costly mistake, and one that is certainly worth a bit of exasperation, if not a stern, "Look, you need to get your act together and do better!" speech.

Yet for Jesus, there was no such reaction. Jesus saw this as a teaching moment. The lesson Jesus taught wasn't on how to remember things; Jesus taught a much more important lesson. Using the well-known metaphor of leaven or yeast as sin, Jesus instructs his followers to avoid the error-laden teaching of the Pharisees and Sadducees.

I would love to think of myself as a patient teacher, using even frustrating moments to a greater purpose of delivering a memorable lesson about God. My dad did this in a way when we made similar mistakes growing up. He would frequently say, "Well, if this is the worst thing that happens, we're going to be okay." He had that knack of putting things into perspective.

The example of Jesus here is something I want to follow. I want to find even life's inconveniences, the mistakes and errors of others, as chances to teach something greater about God and life. I want to see those times as teaching moments, not simply opportunities to sound off on others' errors.

Lord, give me your patience and teach me to teach! In Jesus' name, amen.

AUGUST 13

Jesus said to them, "Watch and beware of the leaven of the Pharisees and Sadducees." (Mt. 16:6)

Sin is seductive and sticky. It entices you, traps you, and then begins to chip away at you, damaging who you are and affecting who you can be. The most bizarre part is that we often don't even realize what is going on, or we realize it too late.

In the Old Testament, sin is often symbolized by leaven. Just as a little leaven infiltrates a dough, affecting the entire loaf, so sin was seen to act in people's life. The symbolism draws out some of the teaching of leaving all leaven out of bread, and even getting it out of the house during the week of Passover. Today's passage draws on some of this symbolism, but the passage goes a bit deeper.

In its fuller context, this passage is funny. Jesus and his disciples have launched into a countryside journey, but the disciples in charge of bringing their provisions forgot to bring bread. Bread was a staple of any meal in that day, especially one on the road. When Jesus became aware that his team had forgotten the bread, rather than express frustration, Jesus found a teaching moment. He told his team, "Watch and beware of the leaven of the Pharisees and Sadducees." Those were groups that had been opposing Jesus and his ministry.

The disciples thought Jesus was telling them that as they went to buy some bread to add to their provisions, don't buy bread from those groups! As they were discussing this, their conversation came to Jesus' attention, and he interrupted them. He pointed out that he wasn't talking about where they should get the bread. After all, he could feed an army on a few loaves, as he already demonstrated twice. Only then did they understand that he was using an educational moment, and he was talking about being careful of the *teachings* of the Pharisees and Sadducees.

Bad teaching is a bit like sin. It can also be seductive and sticky. It can entice you, trap you, and begin to chip away at you. It can damage who you are and affect who you can be. Bad teaching is like sin: we often don't realize it, or we realize it after its damage is done.

This is why Paul was insistent that his protégé Timothy "do your best to present yourself to God as one approved, a worker who has no need to be ashamed, rightly handling the word of truth" (2 Tim. 2:15). Paul prayed for the Philippians to abound "with knowledge and all discernment, so that you may approve what is excellent, and so be pure and blameless for the day of Christ" (Phil. 1:9–10). Teaching and *learning* God's word rightly is of great importance!

Lord, please give me a good and right understanding of your word. In Jesus, amen.

AUGUST 14

At that time the disciples came to Jesus, saying, "Who is the greatest in the kingdom of heaven?" And calling to him a child, he put him in the midst of them and said, "Truly, I say to you, unless you turn and become like children, you will never enter the kingdom of heaven. Whoever humbles himself like this child is the greatest in the kingdom of heaven." (Mt. 18:1–4)

At a legal seminar, I was on a panel with several other lawyers discussing the subject of motivation. The conversation steered into why we do what we do. What made us leave the comfort of home and office to travel to an oft distant city for sometimes up to three or four months, staying awake nearly around the clock to win a case in court. For some, it was the competitive desire to win. For others, it was a fear of losing. Hopefully for some of us there was/is a higher calling—the pursuit of justice.

The desire to win, to come out on top, is not new. Everyone who supports a football team wants to win the Super Bowl, not come in second. Kids play games like "King of the Hill" to come out on top.

Today's passage illustrates that being first isn't a twenty-first-century phenomenon. The question of who was greatest among Jesus' disciples, and who was greatest in the kingdom of heaven was a frequent issue. Over and over the disciples tried to get guarantees of their own placement at the right or left hand of Jesus, or at least of some type of prominence. On the occasion in today's devotional, the disciples were seeking insights into Jesus' state of mind on who would be where in the pecking order. Jesus' reply conveys something very important.

Jesus called a child out as a visual aid to teach a lesson. Children had a place in society that was well known to adults. The children were not society's decision makers. They weren't in positions of glory or authority in the adult world. Yet these were the illustration for Jesus to get his disciples' attitudes right. They were to be humble as to the kingdom, not self-seekers. The disciples shouldn't seek their value on being first. God's kingdom is about something much grander.

Matthew isn't simply reciting history in this story. He is teaching a lesson to those who want to follow Jesus. No one should measure her or his self-worth on status, place, or accomplishments. One's value is based on being what God wants one to be, and to do it as God wants it done. If I will spend my time seeking God's will and trying to do it, then I have all the motivation I should need. Life isn't about me winning or losing. I am not successful by coming out on top. I succeed when I do God's will, regardless of where that leaves me in the world's eyes.

Lord, teach me humility and give me a heart for serving you. In Jesus, amen.

AUGUST 15

Whoever receives one such child in my name receives me, but whoever causes one of these little ones who believe in me to sin, it would be better for him to have a great millstone fastened around his neck and to be drowned in the depth of the sea. (Mt. 18:5–6)

Growing up in church and in Christian community, one often sees children coming to faith or trust in Jesus at an early age. It is easy for adults to look at children coming to embrace Christ and the Christian message and feel like the children don't have enough experience in the world to really understand what they are doing. Yet, in the face of such skepticism comes today's passage.

Jesus speaks of the need to care for little ones and not cause them to stumble. But there is a twist. Jesus speaks of protecting those little ones "who believe in me." These are children who trust Jesus to take care of them, now and in the future. These children come to faith early, and Jesus doesn't dismiss their faith as premature. Jesus instructs his followers to look out for young believing children.

The verb translated as "receives" is the Greek *dechomai* (δέχομαι). It includes the idea of being receptive or welcoming someone. It can reference the approval or conviction that accompanies accepting someone. Jesus accepts the young faith and tells his followers to do the same. Rather than minimizing the child's faith, Jesus says that adult followers have a responsibility to build up and protect the young one's faith. Failure to do that, or even worse, acting in such a way that causes a young person to stumble in faith is very serious in God's eyes.

Everyone should take this charge seriously. The next generation of faith is not just the responsibility of the parents. Children don't rear themselves, and parents need all the help they can get. This means that churches need good ministers to youth at all ages. Programs and facilities to minister become high priorities, whether one has children in those programs or not. The investment of time, energy, and money in the faith of children is an investment in Jesus and God.

I have found myself in church challenged by music that doesn't fit my style of music, yet seems to invigorate the youth. I have listened to young teachers who seem to need a bit of ripening in the faith in ways that only time offers. What do I do in times like those? Do I wring my hands in frustration that things aren't as I like them, or do I rejoice that I have a chance to help those young ones in their faith? Do I pray for them and encourage them? These questions aren't rhetorical. This was a big issue for Jesus, and should be to me.

Lord, may I have a heart for the younger generations. May I seek to help them grow through faith in this journey. In Jesus, amen.

AUGUST 16

Woe to the world for temptations to sin! For it is necessary that temptations come, but woe to the one by whom the temptation comes! And if your hand or your foot causes you to sin, cut it off and throw it away. It is better for you to enter life crippled or lame than with two hands or two feet to be thrown into the eternal fire. (Mt. 18:7–8)

Science teaches that the brain's prefrontal cortex (found right above the eyes in the front of the skull) is the principal brain region that thinks about the future, better understands the consequences for current actions, and aids one in making better decisions. Humans have an impulsive side to the brain as well as a reflective/cautious side. Current thought is that the impulsive develops much more rapidly than the cautious. For some, the impulsive running amuck without help from the cautious is the definition of a teenager. Studies show that the prefrontal cortex, careful and contemplative of potential consequences, doesn't finish developing in some till around age twenty-five. I am far past twenty-five years old, but I think my prefrontal cortex still has a way to go!

Jesus spoke in today's passage about sin and temptation. He is speaking to inform the prefrontal cortex! The bottom line, as Jesus makes clear, is that sin has horrendous consequences, both in the here and now, and in the future. I lived long enough to see the truth in Jesus' teaching.

Sin is terrible stuff! Its consequences are long lasting. It hurts the sinner and those within fallout range. The sins of a spouse can affect the other spouse, and do damage to a marriage. The sins of parents affect their children. The sins of one friend, affect other friends. Businesses and corporations are ruined through sin, affecting the lives of employees and more. Sins of government leaders cause death in war and through bad policies. Sins of church leaders lead many astray and give the name of God a black eye in the world.

Yet sin we do. Why? Doesn't a developed prefrontal cortex tell us, "Don't do that! It leads to bad, BAD stuff!" Yet we seem to let impulse, the moment, overrule sense. Or maybe it's that we believe we are the exception. That consequences won't apply to us. We choose to ignore the teachings of Jesus and think that we can skate the negatives.

I need to take this passage to heart. I should read it daily, and maybe many times a day. I need to get it into my prefrontal cortex. Likely, I need to also cut others some slack also. Falling under the category of "people in glass houses shouldn't throw stones," I should recognize that we all need forgiveness for our sins and its affects. God has some work to do on me!

Lord, please forgive me my sins, as I forgive those who sin against me. Help me to live more deliberately, using the good sense you gave me! In Jesus, amen.

AUGUST 17

I have come into the world as light, so that whoever believes in me may not remain in darkness. (Jn. 12:46)

It was my big toe on my left foot. I smashed it good. I was sleeping in a strange hotel room and got up to use the restroom. The room was totally dark. I failed to remember, and couldn't see, the small yet heavy table that was between me and the restroom. I think I cried out loud!

Today's passage evokes that memory for somewhat obvious reasons. Jesus is the light that explodes and dispels darkness. Darkness cannot continue when light is in the same place. Light wins over darkness; it is that simple. Take a dark room, a dark box, a dark corner, anywhere dark, and put light there. The light will shine and illuminate the darkness. Wherever the light is, the darkness by definition recedes. That in itself is worthy of meditation today, but this verse has a small key to it that expands my thoughts here.

The passage has a critical word for me to consider. The word is *menō* (μένω) in the Greek and is translated here as "remain." Several translations use "abide" instead. The word could be used about one's character, one's location, or even one's relationships. This opens up several avenues of understanding and meditation on today's passage.

Consider how Jesus comes into the world and affects one's character. When speaking of one's character, *menō* conveys the idea of constancy or staying the same. In this sense, there is a darkness that changes to light as one trusts or believes in Jesus. (The Greek word translated as "believe" also means "to trust.") Now, I may not trust Jesus and his teaching and yet feel I have pretty good character. But that is akin to getting my eyes adjusted to darkness. Illumination of light still makes all the difference in the world, and I never realize how dark my space is, until I see it bathed in light.

John in his gospel frequently uses menō (or "abide/remain") in relationships. In this sense, he speaks of Jesus "abiding" in the Father (Jn. 15:10). Jesus also wishes to abide/remain in his people (Jn. 15:4–7). As we trust in Jesus, we make him the place where we abide or remain. This moves us from a place of abiding or remaining in darkness. It also changes us. We become people of the light. Our character illuminates the love and passion of God. We find greater interest in holiness and begin to grow in our distaste of darkness. We seek the better in life. We want God's will because we trust/believe it is best. We stop stumbling around in the dark and stubbing our toes. We find life in the light as different as day from night.

Lord, may I trust in you, and abide in you. Change who I am. Change how I think and live. Make me shine with your brightness in the dark world. In Jesus' name, amen.

AUGUST 18

The book of the genealogy of Jesus Christ, the son of David, the son of Abraham. Abraham was the father of Isaac, and Isaac the father of Jacob, and Jacob the father of Judah and his brothers. . . . So all the generations from Abraham to David were fourteen generations, and from David to the deportation to Babylon fourteen generations, and from the deportation to Babylon to the Christ fourteen generations. (Mt. 1:1–2, 17)

Both Matthew and Luke chart the genealogy of Jesus back to Abraham. This wasn't to lead people to do internet searches on Ancestry.com. The connection between Jesus and Abraham was important for a number of reasons.

First, that Jesus descended from Abraham, meant that Jesus was Jewish. Abraham was the Father of the Jewish nation, and God himself is often identified as the "God of Abraham" (Ps. 47:9). As a Jew, a descendant of Abraham, Jesus was one of the "chosen people" (Ps. 105:6). In Jesus, one sees a specific feature of how Abraham and his descendants were "chosen."

The second reason Jesus' descendancy from Abraham is important is that the Messiah was to be descended from Abraham. This is the specific feature of "chosen" I wrote of in the previous paragraph. God's promise, that he would bless all the peoples of the world through the seed of Abraham, was ancient (Gen. 22:18).

A third reason the genealogy from Abraham is important is that it sets the culmination point for Jewish history. It serves as a bookend of sorts. Abraham was the beginning of the Jewish people. Jesus was the peak. With the ministry of Jesus, the blessing of Abraham reached out to the world. God's favor extends beyond the Jews, and to speak of all his children across genealogical lines as "chosen people" now becomes appropriate.

Peter spoke of all believers in Christ as "a chosen race . . . a holy nation, a people for his own possession, that you may proclaim the excellencies of him who called you out of darkness into his marvelous light" (1 Pet. 2:9). This is the life of the believer. You and I are no longer John or Jane Doe. We are named and selected by God. We have a purpose and a destiny.

This happened as God had promised. From Abraham, one sees the beginning of God's holy people, but from the seed of Abraham, in the Messiah Jesus, one sees the culmination of that blessing as it explodes the barriers between Jew and Gentile. All believers have equal chosen status before God. His special love and attention flow on all his children. This is the ultimate blessing of Jesus, the son of Abraham.

Lord, thank you for your touch. Thank you for your calling. Thank you for making me special. May my life show your special love into the darkness of the world. In him, amen.

AUGUST 19

Now he was teaching in one of the synagogues on the Sabbath. And behold, there was a woman who had had a disabling spirit for eighteen years. She was bent over and could not fully straighten herself. When Jesus saw her, he called her over and said to her, "Woman, you are freed from your disability." And he laid his hands on her, and immediately she was made straight, and she glorified God. But the ruler of the synagogue, indignant because Jesus had healed on the Sabbath, said to the people, "There are six days in which work ought to be done. Come on those days and be healed, and not on the Sabbath day." Then the Lord answered him, "You hypocrites! Does not each of you on the Sabbath untie his ox or his donkey from the manger and lead it away to water it? And ought not this woman, a daughter of Abraham whom Satan bound for eighteen years, be loosed from this bond on the Sabbath day?" As he said these things, all his adversaries were put to shame, and all the people rejoiced at all the glorious things that were done by him. (Lk. 13:10–17)

In today's story, the "Godness" of Jesus is on full display. It should encourage and bless us.

A woman who was unable to stand straight for eighteen years was in bondage to her physical disorder. Jesus sees her, and without her even asking, Jesus heals her. He lays hands on her, something odd for a man to do to a strange woman in that day, and heals her to the glory of God.

As the gospels repeatedly show, some of those present got upset over Jesus performing "work" on the Sabbath. The Sabbath was meant for rest, and work on the Sabbath was taboo. But this story showed an aspect of the Sabbath that those present were missing. The Sabbath was associated with the work of God setting Israel free from the bondage of the Egyptian overlords. The Jews were to celebrate the Sabbath, in part, as a memory of God's liberating work in their life (Deut. 5:15).

Jesus as Lord of the Sabbath uses the Sabbath to "free" the woman from her bondage, the disability that kept her from standing straight. Here the Godness of Jesus as "Lord of the Sabbath" repeats the liberation of his people, albeit on an individual level. Notably, Jesus also calls the now-straightened woman a "daughter of Abraham," the only time that phrase is used. That title was always used for men, the "sons" of Abraham. Jesus was a gamechanger on every level.

This is God's lesson for us. I believe God often works in ways of liberation, meeting our needs before we ask. What is left for us is what we find in this woman. We glorify God!

Lord, thank you for repeatedly meeting my needs, often without me asking. Your mercies are overwhelming, and I glorify you for who you are! In Jesus, my Lord, amen.

AUGUST 20

And he left there and went to the region of Judea and beyond the Jordan, and crowds gathered to him again. And again, as was his custom, he taught them. (Mk. 10:1)

My wife and I have an expression, "Same old, same old." Saying it twice seems to denote the emphasis that as we do the same thing often done, we are doing it the same way. I'm rather confident that my wife and I didn't invent this expression. Many people probably use it, or some other variety of words. Regardless of how it is said, humans are frequently creatures of habit. We find ourselves doing the same things over and over, and often in the same ways.

The Greeks had a word for doing something over and over. It was the adverb *palin* (πάλιν). *Palin* was used when something was being repeated in the same manner. It could be used for the same old, same old. Mark uses the adverb twice in the passage above. It is translated as "again."

The action is pretty simple. Jesus has left Capernaum, a headquarters of sort for his ministry in the Galilee, and headed out to Judea, a southern region as Jesus made his way to Jerusalem. Crowds were coming to Jesus and Jesus was teaching them. My short rendition of the events conveys the information Mark wrote in today's passage. But I am missing a key element of Mark's story. I left out the *palin*.

Mark wants his readers to know that it was typical for crowds to follow Jesus. They followed him in this passage, but it was very much the same old thing. Mark also wants his readers to know that Jesus teaching his followers was also the same thing that typically happened.

I like the way Mark writes it. I like knowing that I am supposed to be following Jesus, and as I do so, I am following the path of many before me. I am doing what I should be doing. Similarly, I follow Jesus with the assurance that he is aware of me and is working to teach me. Jesus wants not only my presence, but he wants to make me something better than I was before I came to him.

Too often I live as if Jesus follows me, and I teach him what I want, what I like, what I perceive I need. I have that backward. I need to follow him and learn from him. I have the assurance he will teach me. It is the same old, same old. You walk with Jesus, and Jesus leads you where you should go, equipping you as you should be equipped.

Lord, I want this today—to follow Jesus and to learn from him. Teach me, please. In Jesus' name, and for his sake, amen.

AUGUST 21

Thus, when you give to the needy, sound no trumpet before you, as the hypocrites do in the synagogues and in the streets, that they may be praised by others. Truly, I say to you, they have received their reward. (Mt. 6:2)

Look carefully at today's passage. See the word "truly"? Jesus begins his sentence with "Truly, I say to you . . ." That may or may not strike you as odd. But it should!

The word translated as "truly" is actually the word "amen." In the Greek, it is written *amēn* (ἀμήν), which is the Greek way of writing the Hebrew word *amen* (אָמֵן). The Hebrew originating word for this comes from a verb referencing something that is confirmed, supported, and true. But here's the catch. The verb was used in the Old Testament as a *response* of a person or congregation to something that was said. In other words, it *followed* what was said.

For example, in 1 Chronicles 16:36, after hearing "Blessed be the LORD, the God of Israel, from everlasting to everlasting!" the people said 'Amen!' and praised the LORD." This was the pattern and form. Someone said something true and profound, and the emphasis was added by others listening with the "amen." It is still often used that way today, both in and out of church. It validates what was said and notes its binding nature.

Paul, Peter, Jude, the writer of Hebrews, and John the Revelator in the New Testament used "amen" the same way, responding to a statement to validate it and emphasize it (e.g., "To the King of the ages, immortal, invisible, the only God, be honor and glory forever and ever. Amen" [1 Tim. 1:17]).

But Jesus did something quite different. He is the one source in the Bible for using "amen" to *begin* a statement! Jesus put his "amen" before his statement. He affirmed, emphasized, and noted the permanent nature of his teachings all by himself. And he did it *before* making those statements. This is so awkward that most English Bibles don't translate the amen as "amen." Instead, they let is pass untranslated, or put it into some other English like "verily" or "truly," which is used by the English Standard Version I quote from above.

Scholars puzzle over why Jesus did this, but they readily recognize the profundity of it. Jesus was the AMEN. He was the one who could put the amen before his statements, because his statements were true. They were everlasting. They were of permanent importance. As the great amen, everyone can go to the bank on the teachings and promises of Jesus. He amened the importance of reconciliation (Mt. 5:26), of giving freely (Mt. 10:42), of humility (Mt. 21:31), and so much more.

Lord, may I put my faith and full confidence in you and your promises. In Jesus, AMEN!

AUGUST 22

But love your enemies, and do good, and lend, expecting nothing in return, and your reward will be great, and you will be sons of the Most High, for he is kind to the ungrateful and the evil. (Lk. 6:35)

"Divine generosity" is a proper phrase for describing the character of God. God is a giver. What is more, he gives with a directed focus on his people. He looks for opportunities to bless and care for his people.

God doesn't give stingily, but gives with abundance. Consider his gifts to you. As you do so, don't see the glass half-empty. Don't dwell on what is missing in your life. We will consider needs and wants in a moment, but first consider the positives given to you by God.

Are you alive? Do you have a chance to read and learn of God and his love? Do you have a moment in time right now to consider his goodness? These are gifts and blessings many have missed throughout the ages. Do you have food to eat? Are you safe? Do you have friends? Family? Can you count ten things that God has given to you? Can you think of ten reasons to be grateful to him for his abundance?

I haven't even begun to speak of his sacrifice on our behalf. That God, before the creation of the world, made the deliberate decision to become flesh and die in the stead of humanity is the ultimate demonstration of his divine generosity. Paul makes this point in Ephesians speaking of God's choosing his people before the creation of the world (Eph. 1:1–10). Paul adds that God did so because he is "rich in mercy" and loves us with a "great love" (Eph. 2:4).

Jesus tells us that we are to emulate God's giving nature. We are to seek to give mercy to those in need, provide food to the hungry, and forgive those who have wronged us. God, the divine giver, is rightly reflected in the lives of his children.

Yet what do we do with what God doesn't seem to give us? How should the Jobs in the world handle the losses, the miseries, and the sad circumstances that are part of life? Without giving a full dissertation on this, I offer the note that Jesus himself sustained those hardships yet never questioned God and his goodness. Jesus knew that the burdens he bore, he bore for God's good purposes in the overall scheme of the kingdom, and the conquering of this world and its sin. In that, Jesus found peace. For that, in some ways, shows the ultimate giving God. He will endure even difficulties to find the ultimate resolution of human history in the most positive way.

Lord, give me a grateful heart. May I praise you as the great giver, and may I illustrate your giving nature in how I interact with others. In Jesus' name, amen.

AUGUST 23

Therefore I tell you, every sin and blasphemy will be forgiven people, but the blasphemy against the Spirit will not be forgiven. And whoever speaks a word against the Son of Man will be forgiven, but whoever speaks against the Holy Spirit will not be forgiven, either in this age or in the age to come. (Mt. 12:31–32)

Jesus' injunction about blaspheming the Holy Spirit is one of those rare passages that is found in all four gospels. It is also one of the most common questions asked when the floor is opened to discussions about Bible passages. What does it mean and what are the implications?

"Blasphemy" is an anglicized word from the Greek *blasphēmia* (βλασφημία). The Greek is a compound of two words. The last word in the compound all agree on—*phēmi* (φημί). In Greek, it is stating something usually orally, but also in writing. The first word is a shortened form of one of four options: either *blaptō* (injure), *blax* (stupid), *ballō* (throw), or *blabos* (harm). At any event, blasphemy is tantamount to speaking ill or abusively of someone.

In the Old Testament, as it is used of God, "blasphemy" refers to denying God and his abilities. An instructive passage is found in 2 Kings 19. There the Assyrian king was noted to have "blasphemed" God by challenging God's ability to save the Jewish people. This Old Testament usage unplugs a good understanding of the unforgivable sin of blaspheming the Holy Spirit. One blasphemes the Spirit when one denies the Spirit's ability to save.

Jesus explained his purposes in sending the Holy Spirit, as well as the work of the Holy Spirit, in John 15–17. Among Jesus' comments is that the Holy Spirit will draw people to Christ, convicting people of sin, righteousness, and judgment (see, esp. Jn. 16:1–15). As the Holy Spirit works in people, he draws them to Christ. The Spirit stirs up faith and conviction. For those who receive this work of the Spirit, there is a born-again experience. However, for those who deny God's working in their lives, there is no forgiveness. For the forgiveness only comes from Christ who, by definition, is being rejected.

This speaks to me of two sides to a coin. First, it magnifies the importance of me hearing the call of the Spirit. I am drawn to making that commitment to belong to Christ. Second, it teaches me that in Christ, all my sins find forgiveness. I am not beyond forgiveness from any sin if I hear the cry of the Spirit and turn my heart to Christ.

Lord, thank you for the forgiveness of my sins. Thank you for the call of your Spirit, and the work in my life. All glory and praise to you. In Jesus' name, amen!

AUGUST 24

Woe to you, scribes and Pharisees, hypocrites! For you clean the outside of the cup and the plate, but inside they are full of greed and self-indulgence. You blind Pharisee! First clean the inside of the cup and the plate, that the outside also may be clean. (Mt. 23:25–26)

Occasionally the *New York Times* crossword puzzle will use the clue "woe" for a five-letter answer. The answer is then "oy vey." This is a Yiddish phrase for "woe is me." The Hebrew portion of the phrase is the "oy" part. *Oy*'s are found throughout the Old Testament, and generally are translated as "woe." It can be a reference to personal woe, as in, "Woe to us! For nothing like this has happened before" (1 Sam. 4:7), or it can be used as a curse like Isaiah 5:20, "Woe to those who call evil good and good evil."

In the times of Jesus, "woe" could be used in the same way. At times Jesus uses it to express sad personal situations. The translators in Matthew 24:19 don't even use the word "woe" in translation, instead saying, "And alas ["woe"] for women who are pregnant and for those who are nursing infants in those days!" (Jesus' language is translated into Greek in Matthew, the Greek equivalent of "*oy*" being *ouai* [οὐαί].)

But in today's passage, Jesus isn't using "woe" as merely expressing dismay, sorrow, or pity. Here, Jesus uses it as a curse, very much in the form of Isaiah. Today's passage comes amid a string of curses that Jesus pronounces on the scribes and Pharisees. In this, the fifth "woe" of that string, Jesus contrasts the inward and outward actions and attitudes of those indicted. Referencing the cleaning rituals of washing a plate or cup, Jesus draws attention to the difference between those who seek to appear holy and clean to the outward world, but were indifferent to the conditions of their hearts and minds.

The world might be impressed with our outward actions that seem holy. We might do something really impressive in the world, but when it is done for show, done so the world might be impressed, it is not proceeding from a pure heart. God is not impressed with whether we appear to others righteous. God seeks a righteous and pure heart that produces holiness in living.

I often return to Christ's metaphor of a good tree producing good fruit, of which I have written elsewhere in this devotional. If we want apples, look to a good apple tree. But don't go the grocery store, buy apples, and tape them to an oak tree. That doesn't make an apple tree. It is only an oak tree with apples taped on it. God is not impressed. That tree carries the curse of Jesus!

I want a pure heart.

Dearest Father, please purify my heart so I produce good fruit for you. In Jesus, amen.

AUGUST 25

Some people brought to him a blind man and begged him to touch him. And he took the blind man by the hand and led him out of the village, and when he had spit on his eyes and laid his hands on him, he asked him, "Do you see anything?" And he looked up and said, "I see people, but they look like trees, walking." Then Jesus laid his hands on his eyes again; and he opened his eyes, his sight was restored, and he saw everything clearly. (Mk. 8:22–25)

This story of the two-touch healing is found only in Mark. When I was in high school, I found it a bit perplexing. Why did Jesus have to touch the fellow twice? Why didn't it work right the first time? Was Jesus having a bad day on healing? Was he not concentrating the first time? I was a paper boy in my youth, and I would fling newspapers on my customers' porches each morning. Sometimes my toss would skate across the porch and land in a flower bed. I would need to go grab it and toss it again on the porch. Had something similar happened that day to Jesus?

As I got older I began to read the theological writings of others, and I came across a writer who believed that there were two-touches of God in the life of a Christian. The first touch brought salvation. The second touch brought a special gift of the Holy Spirit that heightened one's life to a new level of insight and spirituality. This story of healing was used by that author as a text to prove the theology. I didn't see that as what Jesus was teaching then, and I still don't.

There is an important lesson behind this passage. The lesson is found in the context of Mark's gospel, but also of Jewish culture at the time of Christ. Blindness was a physical sickness, but it was also a metaphorical condition for those who missed seeing the world rightly because of sin. Seeing and hearing were spiritual concerns, not simply physical ones. Jesus spoke of those who had eyes but couldn't see, and ears but couldn't hear. In Matthew 13:15, Jesus said, "For this people's heart has grown dull, and with their ears they can barely hear, and their eyes they have closed." Jesus was speaking of a condition of the heart and mind, not a physical malady.

Today's passage comes amid Mark's litany of narratives on how Jesus' disciples were dull and unable to understand Jesus' teachings about his upcoming suffering and glory. They were spiritually dull, not unlike the blind healings Mark inserts into this section.

As I grew to see these themes, metaphors, and context more fully, I began to grasp more fully the message behind this healing. In short, it is this: whatever is going on in life, stick with Jesus! Things may not be as clear to us at first, but over time with Jesus, clarity will come. We need Jesus not once, but constantly, if we are to see things aright.

Lord, give me wisdom and insight. Hold me close and teach me. In Jesus, amen.

AUGUST 26

Now as they were eating, Jesus took bread, and after blessing it broke it and gave it to the disciples, and said, "Take, eat; this is my body." (Mt. 26:26)

It is estimated that there are over one million restaurants in America. New York City alone has over 25,000 restaurants. You could eat at a different restaurant in New York City every day for over sixty years, and you wouldn't eat at them all. With so many restaurants, the variety of food is also massive. Each ethnicity has its own cuisine. There are food options you've never heard of. Beyainatu is a famous choice for food at an Ethiopian restaurant, but most non-Ethiopians likely don't know what it is.

In biblical times, I suspect that there was less diversity in food. One thing is for certain, the main staple of the typical Jewish diet in the days of Jesus was bread. It was an ordinary, everyday food, typically made with grain (ground wheat or barley), salt, water, with either leaven added (from a pre-leavened dough or one which has sat out long enough to accumulate the wild microscopic yeast that is in the air) or in an unleavened state.

Bread was so common in the diet that the word for bread (*lechem*, לֶחֶם in Hebrew) was also just the common word for "food." So passages like "Man shall not live by bread alone" (Mt. 4:4 quoting Deut. 8:3) are not a reference to adding peanut butter. They mean more than bread. They mean "food." People don't live by food alone, but by God and his teachings. Similarly, in the Lord's Prayer, to ask, "Give us this day our daily bread" isn't exclusive to the bread food group. It means our "food." Quite often "bread" was a simple synonym for "food."

In this sense, today's passage takes on a notably deep meaning. Jesus took bread, a specific reference to the actual "bread" foodstuff, but used it as a metaphor for his body, the real full sustenance of life.

People must have food. Without it, life will end. Jesus knew for his people to *really experience life*, not the dead-end existence of daily drudgery, not the hollow searching for significance or meaning, not the frenetic movement from one high in search of another, not a pain-dulling chemically induced numbness, but a *full, meaningful, purposeful, peaceful, joyful life*—for this, one would need the broken body of the Lord. Only as people are put in a right relationship with God are they truly sustained with life. Only in God's care are people fed for eternity.

We find true life in the broken death of the Lord Jesus.

Lord, thank you for the sacrifice of Jesus. May it be my daily sustenance to a full life. In him I pray, amen.

AUGUST 27

Then Peter came up and said to him, "Lord, how often will my brother sin against me, and I forgive him? As many as seven times?" Jesus said to him, "I do not say to you seven times, but seventy-seven times." (Mt. 18:21–22)

In most professional sports, there are score keepers. For many years, the score keeper for the Houston Rockets basketball team was a good friend of mine. We went to church together. He was charged with keeping track of every point, how many fouls were committed by which player, who had the next neutral ball possession, and so much more. He had a mind that didn't miss a detail.

My buddy is my reference point for today's passage, but *only if I misunderstand the passage!* Let me explain.

In the twenty-first century, numbers fill a fairly distinct role in life. Two is two. Five is five. Twenty-first-century life is loaded with math, science, identification numbers (driver's license, social security numbers, etc.). We use numbers to calculate price, balance bank accounts, Venmo for a share of dinner, and so on. Numbers are used mainly to express numerical value.

If I read today's passage with a twenty-first-century view of numbers, then I must forgive someone more than seven times. It should be seventy-seven. Like my scorekeeping buddy, I can keep track, and once we hit time seventy-eight: BOOM! No more forgiveness!!!

Yet we know instinctively that isn't the point of Jesus' teaching. What really is happening in this passage is that we see the ancient use of numbers for something beyond their numerical value. To the ancients, numbers had multiple uses. For example, the number one might mean a single item, but it also might stand for loneliness. The number four might mean the numerical value of four, but it also could stand for something physical or earthly (likely because there were perceived four corners of the earth, four winds, four elements—fire, water, earth, and air, etc.). The number seven was considered a "full number." It stood for a totality or completeness. It is in this sense that one best understands today's passage.

Peter was asking Jesus if he should forgive his brother seven times. Peter meant "fully" or "totally." The shock then is Jesus' answer. Rather than saying "Yes," Jesus says, "seventy-seven." In other words, we are called to forgive those who sin against us more fully than fully could ever be. There goes my score keeping! I have a lot of work to do!

Lord, give me a forgiving spirit. May I quit keeping score, and walk in forgiveness daily, giving out the same forgiveness you give me. In Jesus' holy name, amen.

AUGUST 28

It is easier for a camel to go through the eye of a needle than for a rich person to enter the kingdom of God. (Mk. 10:25)

Are you familiar with the term "aphorism"? An aphorism is a pithy statement that contains a general truth. It is a proverb of sorts. A common example is, "If it ain't broke, don't fix it." Or, "Integrity starts with i, not u." Typically, aphorisms are used with a bit of humor, even if the true statement has a little bite to it.

Today's passage is an aphorism. It is one of those delightful passages that illustrate the broad depth of the literature and language in the Bible. After all, the Bible is a huge collection of books that contain the full range of literary genres. In the Bible one finds poetry, narratives, teaching stories, and parables, even humor and aphorisms!

The truth behind today's passage is found in the general idea that one with great wealth will not find it easy to enter the kingdom of God. The expression "it is easier for a camel to go through the eye of a needle" is the humor in the aphorism. Of course, a camel can never make it through the eye of a needle. The idea of a camel even trying is an absurdity. I have no doubt that the disciples listening were chuckling if not outright laughing as Jesus made the comparison.

But Jesus is teaching an important and memorable point. The tendency of the wealthy is to trust in their wealth. The Christian calling is to trust in God. Compare those two. If one needs food and can't afford it, one will cry out to God for help. If one has plenty of money and food, one doesn't need to cry out for God there. One can, in essence, say to God, "I got this one. No need for you here!" Or if one needs medical care and doesn't have the money for it, one might be begging God to step into the picture. Yet to the fully insured, with money to spare, it is only a question of what medical care is available. For some, paying the bills requires divine intervention. For others, it is merely writing a check out of abundance. Which person finds it easier to rely on God, the wealthy or the needy? Clearly it's the needy. When relying on God is the basis for entry into the kingdom, then it is easier for the needy, and the wealthy are going to struggle for entry.

To some who are missing the aphorism, many attempts have been made to soften what Jesus is saying. In the ninth century, someone came up with the idea that there was a gate in Jerusalem called the "eye of the needle" that a camel had to kneel to get through. There was no such gate. Jesus was using a great illustration of an absurdity to show the importance of relying on God, not wealth. May we all heed this humorous aphorism!

Lord, all I have is yours. I am a caretaker of that which is yours, and nothing more. Please meet all my needs, I rely wholly on you! In Jesus, amen.

AUGUST 29

And when he got into the boat, his disciples followed him. (Mt. 8:23)

On September 3, 1939, Germany invaded Poland and World War II began. Two days later, England and France declared war on Germany. The world was only twenty years out from the end of World War I, the first war ever designated by the moniker of being a war of the entire world. That first war had left some twenty million dead and twenty-one million more wounded. The fresh memory of the war's savageness was on the mind of most every British military-age male as the fall term at Oxford University began in October 1939.

Undoubtedly, most people enrolled at Oxford questioned the point of college life. After all, many if not most of the young men would leave for military duty unable to complete their degree. Furthermore, the question was fairly raised of why one should spend their energy reading things like British literature when a war of the world was brewing.

To address these doubts and questions, Oxford turned to the eloquent and thoughtful C. S. Lewis to address the incoming class. Lewis mounted the pulpit at St. Mary's university church in Oxford on October 22 to deliver his address about learning in wartime. One of the big arguments Lewis gave was a recognition that young men were going to be reading *something*. It might only be the newspaper. Or it might be a dime-store novel, but in that day, when there was no television, limited radio, and no computers, reading was the media of choice. Lewis reasoned that if the young men were going to read something anyway, they ought to choose good literature or good writings on history, for example.

These events speak to me in passages like today. I believe everyone becomes a disciple in some way, to someone or to something. We choose to follow ideas, ones we find in advertisements. We choose to follow leaders as we cast our votes for one candidate or another. We choose to follow informers as we read news accounts. We choose to follower influencers as we check our Twitter feeds. We choose to follow our own appetites as we determine what to eat for lunch.

During a life where we are making choices to follow one thing or another, it seems to me the wise choice is to follow Jesus, first and foremost. Jesus becomes our teacher, informing us about life choices. He tells us to prioritize God and his kingdom. He inspires us to love our friends and enemies. He trains us to guard our minds and hearts as the fountain from which flow our actions. He teaches us kindness and mercy. If I am going to follow someone in my life, I think it ought to be Jesus!

Dear Lord, I want to follow Jesus. I want to see him better than ever before, understanding his heart and mind, and letting him transform mine. I pray in him, amen!

AUGUST 30

For God so loved the world, that he gave his only Son, that whoever believes in him should not perish but have eternal life. (Jn. 3:16)

Today's passage may be the most well-known verse in the Bible. It certainly would be in the top five. The passage has a marvelous offer: an unending life if one "believes" in the Son of God. Knowing that to be the offer, it makes me want to understand what all is involved in "believing."

The English I set out above is a translation from John's original, which was in the Greek language in use in the first century. Greek had an amazing group of words that stemmed from the *pist-* sound in Greek. In the verb form found here, the word (*pistuō*, πιστεύω) is translated as "believe." In the noun form (*pistis*, πίστις) the word is often translated as "faith" or "belief." There are other forms, but these serve to instruct us on John 3:16.

The idea of "belief" or "faith" is sometimes understood in English as accepting something as true. I might say, "I believe in UFO's," at which point I mean I think they exist. Or perhaps, "I don't believe in UFO's," meaning I don't think they exist. If this is our limited idea of the meaning in "faith" or "believe," then we are missing a huge chunk of what was meant in the Greek.

The Greek idea of faith/believe included a strong element of trust or confidence. Contemporary English uses the word a bit like the Greek in a story like this: A young teenager has a curfew of 11 p.m. The teenager comes in at 11, and the parent is hovering, upset that the child has waited until the last minute. The parent begins quizzing the child, at which point the child says, "Don't you have any faith in me?" The child is not asking whether the parent believes the child exists. This child is speaking about whether the parent has trust or confidence in the child.

This story gives the fuller concept of the Greek word used in today's passage. One is called to trust or rely on Jesus in order to have an unending, eternal life. How then do I trust in Jesus?

The first step is to make a decision that Jesus will be my all. That means that I don't stand before God because of my personal merit, but because of the merit of Jesus. This is often seen as a conversion moment, and that is good. But even after the conversion moment, I want to trust Jesus in day-to-day decisions. I can decide to trust Jesus or trust myself when faced with circumstances where his instruction teaches one thing but my desire leads differently. I want to trust and follow Jesus into a true life each day.

Lord, I put my faith, my trust, my confidence in Jesus Christ my Lord, in whom I pray, amen.

AUGUST 31

So if the Son sets you free, you will be free indeed. (Jn. 8:36)

This morning, before I sat down to write this, I went for a walk with one of my daughters and her dog. She had the dog on a leash, and he walked dutifully next to her. At one point, my daughter let go of the leash and gave the dog freedom to run. I was interested to see what the dog did with his freedom. We were near some ducks, and I have seen him chase ducks before, causing my daughter to grab his leash and ruin his freedom! But this time, he ignored the ducks. He just ran around as dogs are wont to do, sniffing this and that, all in a grand "run and smell" adventure.

Freedom is an interesting concept. Paul speaks of being set free over and over in his writings. His letter to the Romans repeatedly speaks of being set free from sin and bondage. He wrote to the Romans of sin being an enslaver of people, and the power of Jesus to break the bondage of sin. Paul, James, and Peter all speak of freedom as an important aspect of the Christian life. Surprising to some, however, Jesus and the gospels speak of freedom almost never! There is the story in today's passage and one passage in Matthew. That's it!

Yet even though the gospels use the word "freedom" or "set free" rarely, the idea of freedom is present on every page. The ministry of Jesus is both an appeal to people to recognize their bondage and a recognition that Jesus would set people free from bondage.

Recognizing one's bondage is apparent in stories like the rich young ruler who is so bound up and tied to his possessions that he can't follow the instructions of Jesus (Mk. 10:17-27). Repeatedly, one reads stories of people who are in bondage to demons, to sickness, or to an isolated and lonely life. Here we see Jesus bringing freedom.

To the man possessed by a legion of demons, living in exile among the tombs of the Gadarenes, Jesus brings freedom, sending the man back into civilized life (Lk. 8:6-39). To a woman outcast by an incessant flow of blood rendering her unclean to the Jewish community, Jesus brings freedom and release, healing her on the spot and allowing her to reintegrate into society (Lk. 8:43-48).

Jesus didn't speak so much of freedom, but he lived it. He brought freedom. Which brings me back to my daughter and her dog. My question becomes, what am I going to do with that freedom! Will I chase after sin (ducks?), and need to be reined in? Or will I live my best life enjoying God's freedom to do what he would have me do?

Lord, thank you for freedom from sin and its consequences. Let me live wisely before you. In Jesus, amen.

SEPTEMBER 1

Nevertheless, many even of the authorities believed in him, but for fear of the Pharisees they did not confess it, so that they would not be put out of the synagogue; for they loved the glory that comes from man more than the glory that comes from God. (Jn. 12:42–43)

I have been in meetings—secular meetings and religious meetings—and seen a common thread. People in those meetings are often trying to impress others. I can see it so well, because like most other problems, I readily identify with them, I have the same problem.

Where it began, I can't say. When we are young, we often try to impress others to fit in or be accepted. I know a host of young people who, when asked what they want to be in the future, answer, "Famous!" Whether as a star athlete, a famous singer, or president of the United States, young people want fame and recognition. As people grow through adolescence, they still seek to impress certain others. Many children as young adults still look to their parents to get approval or appreciation for a job well done.

So maybe it is hard-wired into our thinking patterns, such that by the time we are adults functioning in the world, we naturally want and even feed off affirmation from others. I use the term, "affirmation junkie," referring to its addictive power.

It isn't uncommon in a legal meeting for those in attendance to preen like peacocks, showing off their knowledge as if it were a colorful plume for all the world to see. It seems to fit under the idea of "letting people know I am valuable, so they turn to me for help." That may be a bit more understandable, but how about in a religious setting, when people are jostling to be recognized as important, knowledgeable, or holy? Those times make one wonder a bit about what is driving the need for recognition.

In today's passage, John puts his finger on a truth that is important in processing life. John spoke of those who believed in Jesus as the Messiah but failed to say so out loud, lest it affect how others perceived them. They would rather keep their notable seats in the community synagogue than risk losing the synagogue by professing their faith. John's point was that these were people who would rather have man's glory and approval than God's.

John makes a sobering point. I am to live, to work, and to play as one doing so to please God. Paul, who stated he would be a Greek to the Greeks and a Jew to the Jews, did so to please God (1 Cor. 9:20).

I need to live to please God, not others. This is going to take some work!
Lord, may you be my focus, first and foremost! In Jesus' name, amen.

SEPTEMBER 2

This, the first of his signs, Jesus did at Cana in Galilee, and manifested his glory. And his disciples believed in him. (Jn. 2:11)

Look at today's passage carefully. It reads a bit unusual if you don't have on your religious hat. "Manifested his glory." What does that mean? That is not a phrase I typically hear used. I have been in courtrooms where amazing things have happened—stellar arguments, witnesses caught in a lie crumbling before all watching, spectacular verdicts and awards—but I never heard someone say, "Person X manifested his glory." I have watched great sporting events on television with the best announcers, but never have I heard someone describe an athlete's accomplishment as "manifesting her/ his glory."

Are our translators just taking ancient ordinary language and making it more difficult to understand? Actually no. This phrase reads a bit unusual in normal everyday Greek. It makes sense only to those who have read the Old Testament in Greek. Then one begins to grasp what John is saying about Jesus. Let me explain.

The common Greek word translated as "glory" is *doxa* (δόξα), from which English gets the word "doxology." But to ancient Greeks, the core idea behind *doxa* was "opinion," especially used for a good opinion or reputation. If this typical usage was all that John meant, then the translators might say that Jesus "revealed his reputation." But there is still awkwardness, for how does one "reveal" or "manifest" one's reputation?

The special understanding comes from the Greek translation of the Old Testament commonly used by Jews at the time of Jesus. *Doxa* was the word selected for translating the Hebrew word *kavod* (כָּבוֹד). This was used to describe the shining, visible "glory" of a God who could not otherwise be seen. This was the "glory" of the Lord that dwelt on Mount Sinai for six days as a cloud enveloped the mountain and a devouring fire went forth (Ex. 24:16-17). It was the *kavod/doxa* glory of God that Moses asked to see in Exodus 33:18. God's *kavod/doxa* glory passed before Moses as Moses was protected by a rock (Ex. 33:22).

Jesus wasn't anything ordinary. Jesus was this same manifestation of the holy God that shown forth on the pages of the Old Testament. When Jesus wrought his miracle of turning water into wine (the source for today's passage), Jesus was revealing the otherwise unseeable glory of the very God of Israel.

No, "manifested his glory" is not an ordinary phrase. But then again, Jesus was no ordinary person!

Lord, I praise you for your glory! May the world see it in Jesus. In him I ask, amen.

SEPTEMBER 3

The Passover of the Jews was at hand, and Jesus went up to Jerusalem. In the temple he found those who were selling oxen and sheep and pigeons, and the money-changers sitting there. And making a whip of cords, he drove them all out of the temple, with the sheep and oxen. And he poured out the coins of the money-changers and overturned their tables. (Jn. 2:13–15)

I was watching television once, flipping channels to find something interesting. I came upon a "religious" channel. What I saw both amazed and disgusted me. A fellow was on the station, holding up a handkerchief. The fellow called it his "amazing prayer towel." The man explained he had prayed over the "amazing prayer towel" and if someone wanted to have their prayers answered, they needed to send him some amount of money (I don't remember the amount), and he would send them his amazing prayer towel.

The image of grandmothers concerned over their children and grand-children taking the pittance of social security they receive each month and sending money for this fellow's amazing prayer towel incensed me. Snake oil salesmen from the Wild West days couldn't outdistance this "religious man" in levels of being a charlatan.

Jesus would have had no trouble reaching through the television and tearing up this man's amazing prayer towel. It reminds me of today's passage.

Too many people see religion as a tool to make money. It wasn't right in the day of Jesus, and it isn't right today. Did Jesus charge for tickets to listen to the Sermon on the Mount? Did Moses charge folks five shekels to get to see the Ten Commandments? (Ten if they wanted to touch them?) NO!

God paid to get people to hear his message. God incarnating into Jesus wasn't a vacation, it was a step away from the glory of heaven. The Creator became a creation. That was a price Jesus paid, and it was paid *by God* so that people would hear God's message. When anyone truly believes they carry the great, life-changing, eternal news that restores someone to the right relationship with God, why do they think it should be for sale?

Now one might think this unusual, but I have a dear friend at church who has had to stop various members from using church as their business contact list, wanting to use church rolls to send out business solicitations. I don't think God's kingdom is to become a marketplace for profit.

Lord, examine my motives. Purify my love. Forgive my putting personal goals ahead of your kingdom. May I live for you alone, trusting you to meet my needs in Jesus, amen.

SEPTEMBER 4

And he told those who sold the pigeons, "Take these things away; do not make my Father's house a house of trade." His disciples remembered that it was written, "Zeal for your house will consume me." (Jn. 2:16–17)

"Zeal" is a curious word. Our word comes directly from the Greek word *zēlos* (ζῆλος). It usually speaks of an intense, positive interest in someone or something. "Ardor" is a rarer but also splendid English word that can be used in translation. At times, it can also indicate a negative feeling over another's achievements or actions. Then it is generally translated as "jealousy."

"Zeal" is used to describe God in the Bible. Two stories in contrast help. Seven hundred years before today's passage took place, Sennacherib, the king of the mighty Assyrian Empire ran roughshod over Israel and much of Judah, having surrounded Judah's king, Hezekiah, and his people seeking refuge within the walls of Jerusalem. No army alive had been able to stop Sennacherib's forces. Hezekiah, trapped in Jerusalem, sought God's intervention, praying for divine rescue. God sent Isaiah the prophet before King Hezekiah to inform him of God's answer to the prayer. God had seen all that Sennacherib had done, and God was set against the Assyrian king. God was going to set a hook in his nose, a bit in his mouth, and turn him around, driving him back the way he came. God would do this because of the "zeal" he had for his people (2 Kgs. 19:31).

The second story comes from today's passage. Jesus, the country carpenter turned roving teacher, had come into the same city, Jerusalem. This time the Romans occupied the city. Jesus came to the most holy place of the city, the temple known as the "house of the Lord." Jesus did not find a king or the people praying to God for his divine help. Instead, he found merchants who had set up to profit off those seeking to worship God. The house of God had become a common Greek marketplace. This time God's zeal wasn't to turn away a foreign invader, but embodying the words of Psalm 69:9, Jesus made a whip out of cords, and turning tables upside down, Jesus began driving the profiteers away. Jesus proclaimed, "Don't make my father's house your shopping mall!" Jesus did this because of the "zeal" he had for his Father's house. In this sense, the "zeal" of God shows God a "jealous" God. God was not proud or supportive of those abusing his house and his people for their own profit.

Two stories, two impacts on God's people, and two instructions for me. Do I come to God for help? Do I earnestly seek him and his divine rescue in my life? Or do I use God? Do I find him to be my tool for the life I want to lead? God has zeal; it can also be termed "jealousy." God doesn't smile on our placing other things in line before him.

Lord, I repent. Forgive me for putting other things before you. Be my rescue and help in Jesus, amen.

SEPTEMBER 5

So the Jews said to him, "What sign do you show us for doing these things?" Jesus answered them, "Destroy this temple, and in three days I will raise it up." The Jews then said, "It has taken forty-six years to build this temple, and will you raise it up in three days?" But he was speaking about the temple of his body. When therefore he was raised from the dead, his disciples remembered that he had said this, and they believed the Scripture and the word that Jesus had spoken. (Jn. 2:18–22)

Sometimes I have completely misunderstood God. I don't mean thinking he said 567 when he really said 568. Nothing so slight. Sometimes it's as if I think he said 567 when he really said, "Eat your vegetables!" At times I have *totally* misunderstood my God.

I am not alone in this. Today's story is a brilliant example of people misunderstanding God. After Jesus threw the moneychangers and merchants out of the temple courts, some Jews asked Jesus what right he had to take such extreme measures. They wanted Jesus to show them some sign that gave him authority to police God's courtyards. Jesus responded. His sign for authority over God's court and temple would be shown when they tore down the temple. Jesus would rebuild it in three days. The Jews thought Jesus absurd. After all, it took forty-six years to build the temple.

The people thoroughly misunderstood Jesus. The temple was a human construct where God had deemed at times to meet his people. It was where the glory of God was seen in ancient times when Israel was walking in fellowship with God. Other times, it was simply a building, often misused and abused, even at times a place to worship idols. Jesus was never referencing the human building. Jesus knew that in his bodily presence, God was meeting his people. The humanity of Jesus of Nazareth was the house of the God of Israel. The glory of God was seen in the incarnation standing before them.

When Jesus referenced the people destroying the "temple" or the abode of God, he was referencing the people's role in his crucifixion, which was upcoming. Jesus knew that his body would be killed, but that God would resurrect him in three days. This was the sign that Jesus had authority—not just over the temple courts, but over death itself! Jesus had full authority and should be followed, not challenged.

The people misunderstood Jesus, and I confess I often do myself. I have thought Jesus allowed me to act in ways where I should have known better. I have thought that things about God were really things about me. I have held bitterness over things where I should rejoice. I have turned from Jesus at times I should turn to Jesus. I have some work to do!

Lord, help me get on your wavelength. Help me hear, understand, and follow you in Jesus, amen.

SEPTEMBER 6

Now when he was in Jerusalem at the Passover Feast, many believed in his name when they saw the signs that he was doing. But Jesus on his part did not entrust himself to them, because he knew all people and needed no one to bear witness about man, for he himself knew what was in man. (Jn. 2:23–25)

The phrase, "flattery will get you nowhere," seems to have originated in the mid-twentieth century in America. The disdain of flattery, however, goes back much further. In the play *The Knights*, by the Greek playwright Aristophanes (c. 446–c. 386 BC), one main character is mocked for his efforts to win a leadership position by flattering the crowds. Yet in the same play, flattery is also seen as effective when exercised by another character, the sausage-seller Agoracritus. This alternate truth reminds one of the other mid-twentieth-century Americanism, "Flattery will get you everywhere!"

Think through flattery for a moment. One can genuinely compliment others. My wife met me for lunch recently and I told her, "You look nice!" That was no platitude, it was true. She looked great!

But there are other times when something is said for manipulative purposes. One says something to endear themselves. I suspect that at times I have been complimented or applauded, not because it was genuine, but to get in my good graces. One time I felt I was surrounded by a few "yes" people who were going to say "yes!" to anything I said. I experimented. I stated a policy that I thought was wrong, and sure enough, I heard, "Great idea!" I then did an about-face and said, "No, on second thought, I think that is wrong, and we need to do ABC instead." To this I heard, "Yes, I see that now too!" That quickly became a useless meeting.

I have also seen times when one person begins flattering another, and you could almost visibly see the head of the flattered expand in size! The person's shoulders went back, their head rose a bit higher, their chest expanded, and they seemed at least six inches taller, all because of a flattering compliment.

This brings me to today's passage. Jesus was in Jerusalem and in his love and compassion, he was healing people and meeting their needs. Those who saw him were amazed at what he was doing, and no doubt quite flattering to him. But their words, actions, and thoughts were not genuine in the sense of following Jesus. They were simply stunned by his deeds and wanted to be on his good side. Their support was an inch deep and a mile wide. One whiff of a negative, one hint of persecution, and they would drop Jesus like a hot potato. Jesus knew better. He wasn't beguiled by any flattery or superficial attention.

Lord, I want my devotion to you to be genuine. Purify my thoughts. Grow me spiritually. May my words of praise come from deep wells of true appreciation. In Jesus, amen.

SEPTEMBER 7

Again he entered the synagogue, and a man was there with a withered hand. And they watched Jesus, to see whether he would heal him on the Sabbath, so that they might accuse him. And he said to the man with the withered hand, "Come here." And he said to them, "Is it lawful on the Sabbath to do good or to do harm, to save life or to kill?" But they were silent. And he looked around at them with anger, grieved at their hardness of heart, and said to the man, "Stretch out your hand." He stretched it out, and his hand was restored. The Pharisees went out and immediately held counsel with the Herodians against him, how to destroy him. (Mk. 3:1–5)

Like it or not, you are not a computer program. Neither am I. We have choices. We make decisions that have real consequences. That's not to say that everything can make choices. Rocks are rocks. They don't decide to change, mutate into pine trees, or make a boat. But people aren't rocks. Made uniquely, we have an ability to choose between alternatives. This includes the choice to sin.

Part of the moral decisions we make involve deciding what influences to follow. Will we listen to one voice or another? Will we opt for one career or another? What will inform our decision is an individual choice. Similarly, we can choose to be stubborn or malleable. We can choose to repent our errors or stand entrenched in them, come what may.

Scripture repeatedly speaks of people with a hardened heart. These Scriptures will sometimes say God hardened one's heart; other times it will say the person hardened his/her own heart. The Pharaoh is the perfect example. In Exodus 4:21 God says he will harden the Pharaoh's heart, and then both Exodus 8:15 and 32 reinforce that the Pharaoh hardened his own heart. The Pharaoh was not a computer. He made his choices, and God reinforced those choices.

In today's passage, Jesus gets angry. The people cared more about their perceptions of religious formality and rules than the hurting and health of a fellow human being. Jesus' anger is noted, and Mark inserts a reason for the anger. Jesus grieved at the people's "hardness of heart." In Hebrew thought, the "heart" was understood as the seat of thought (like "mind" in English), as well as one's will and one's views of morality. When the people hardened their hearts, they were setting their minds, wills, and moral sensibility against the heart and compassion of God. This not only hurt their neighbors, but hurt themselves too, and that made Jesus angry.

I'm not a computer. I can have a soft or hard heart. I want a soft one!

Lord, soften my heart to your love, compassion, and will for me and others. In Jesus, amen.

And crying out with a loud voice, he said, "What have you to do with me, Jesus, Son of the Most High God? I adjure you by God, do not torment me." For he was saying to him, "Come out of the man, you unclean spirit!" And Jesus asked him, "What is your name?" He replied, "My name is Legion, for we are many." (Mk. 5:7–9)

When I was a teenager, a petrifying movie was released: *The Exorcist.* Based on a 1971 novel, this movie was downright scary! Without detailing the plot, let me just say that it kept me awake at nights. Mercy!

Fast-forward decades later. We live in an era where few people believe in demon possession. In 1942, amid World War II, C. S. Lewis published *The Screwtape Letters.* They were fictional letters from a demon named Screwtape to his demon nephew Wormwood. In those letters, Screwtape coached Wormwood on how to best ruin the life of his human charge, generally by drawing him away from God and into the world. I read the book in high school right after seeing *The Exorcist.* Wormwood was a different demon. Instead of twisting his charges head around (yes, that happens in the demon possession of Regan in *The Exorcist*), Wormwood was subtle.

I think Lewis got it right for this age, at least in the United States. Satan's goal is not to show himself big. His goal is to ruin human life and fellowship with God. Satan does that best when cloaked and unseen. Disbelief in Satan becomes the devil's best weapon.

Keith Green, in his 1977 song *Satan's Boast,* got it right singing as Satan,

> *Oh, my job keeps getting easier as time keeps slipping away*
> *I can imitate your brightest light and make your night look just like day*
> *I put some truth in every lie to tickle itching ears*
> *You know I'm drawing people just like flies 'cause they like what they hear*
> *I'm gaining power by the hour. They're falling by the score*
> *You know, it's getting very simple now. 'Cause no one believe in me anymore*

I suspect if Satan were manifesting himself in possession, people everywhere would be on spiritual alert. But when Satan works without such gaudiness, people are liable to lapse into spiritual lethargy, wondering if there is a spiritual world at all.

I want to stay on alert.

Lord, give me eyes to see the Deceiver trying to work in this world, and the strength to stop him in Jesus' name, amen.

SEPTEMBER 9

Jesus sent two of his disciples and said to them, "Go into the village in front of you, and immediately as you enter it you will find a colt tied, on which no one has ever sat. Untie it and bring it. If anyone says to you, 'Why are you doing this?' say, 'The Lord has need of it and will send it back here immediately.'" And they went away and found a colt tied at a door outside in the street, and they untied it. And some of those standing there said to them, "What are you doing, untying the colt?" And they told them what Jesus had said, and they let them go. And they brought the colt to Jesus. (Mk. 11:1–7)

Today's devotional is summed up in a simple sentence: God directs and equips. This should inform not only my day, but my life.

The story comes from the days before the Last Supper and the crucifixion of Jesus, with all that entails. As Jesus' purpose on earth is drawing to a monumental peak, Jesus sent two of his disciples on a most important errand. Jesus is not just getting to Jerusalem, but he is doing so in ways that fulfill countless messianic prophecies proclaimed over centuries and recorded in numerous biblical pages.

Zechariah, the prophet who spoke God's message about 550 years earlier, had promised in chapter 9, verse 9, "Behold, your king is coming to you; righteous and having salvation is he, humble and mounted on a donkey, on a colt, the foal of a donkey." That king was Jesus. Doubtlessly, the two disciples Jesus sent on this important errand were clueless about its true purpose. That Jesus sent them to aid in his fulfillment of this and many other Scriptures wasn't on their mind. But obedience was.

As Jesus directed the two to go, he added some important information. He told them what to do in the event someone interrupted their borrowing the colt. They were to instruct any inquisitor that Jesus needed it, and Jesus would return it. (Jesus was no thief!) Once the two found the colt set out as Jesus as said, they began to untie it. Sure enough, bystanders questioned the disciples on why they were taking a colt that wasn't theirs. They gave the explanation given by Jesus and were allowed to proceed. The Jesus who gave them direction, equipped them to accomplish their assignment.

That's the way of God. God doesn't play a short-game where things surprise him and he is in constant reaction mode. God made plans centuries before you and I were born. He instructs us in his will, most explicitly through teaching us his ways in Scripture, and then he equips us to do what we need to do for him. This gives me confidence to walk for him today. If I just seek to do his will, I am smart enough, resourced enough, to achieve what he has set out for me to do.

Lord, I want to know what you would have me do, then do it, fully supplied by you in every way to accomplish what you set before me. To your glory and in your name, amen.

SEPTEMBER 10

And he said to them, "Pay attention to what you hear: with the measure you use, it will be measured to you, and still more will be added to you. For to the one who has, more will be given, and from the one who has not, even what he has will be taken away." (Mk. 4:24–25)

An average ear of corn has 800 kernels in sixteen rows, or so says the Kansas Farm Bureau. Think about the implications of that on farmers. I can plant one kernel, get an entire cornstalk that will produce one to two more ears of corn, that is, another 800–1,600 seeds of corn. This makes for amazing math. With one ear of corn, I can plant 800 stalks. Those 800 stalks should give me 800 ears for eating, plus perhaps another 400 to replant. The 400 I replant would give me 320,000 new stalks, or almost half a million ears of corn!

Shift slightly from my corny math (pun intended) to a different farming analogy. Jesus gives an illustration to his disciples that made sense to farmers in his day. In the parable, a farmer is sowing seed. Without the modern combines and tractors, the farmers spread the seed by swinging their arms back and forth over the field. While most seeds hopefully fall into the ready field, some fall on a path where birds eat them. Some fall on shallow ground where they sprout but die quickly. Some fall into weedy beds where thorns choke them out. The seeds that fall into good ground reproduce like corn! Some thirty times, some sixty, some one hundred times.

Jesus explained his parable as one that involved the word of God. Jesus at other times used this parable to talk about the kingdom of Heaven, but here, where the word of God is the seed, Jesus makes another point. A simple one, really.

Jesus wants us asking ourselves, do we do what God says? Do we follow his words? Some ignore him. This is seed wasted on the path eaten by others instead. Some start doing what Jesus says but quickly dwindle in their ardor and obedience. Some are more interested in the words of the world than the words of God. But some hear the word of God, do the word of God, enduring through good times and bad, and are blessed accordingly.

In this sense, Jesus offered the promise of today's passage, with the admonition we should listen carefully to the word of God. As we hear *and use* the word of God, we will prosper like kernels of corn. We can grow astronomically in this life, finding God's success in God's purposes if we will only listen and do. Failing to do that will cause us to lose much rather than gain much.

Lord, I want to hear your voice, hear your instructions and directions. Then strengthen me to do them in Jesus' name! Amen.

SEPTEMBER 11

With many such parables he spoke the word to them, as they were able to hear it. He did not speak to them without a parable, but privately to his own disciples he explained everything. (Mk. 4:33–34)

One of our daughters was set to get married. I watched with amazement at the teamwork of my daughter and sweet wife. They found the venue, got a wedding planner's help, and then figured out the caterer. Once this was done, they scheduled the all-important "tasting." This was a time where my daughter, soon to be son-in-law, and my wife set aside a good bit of the afternoon to sit at a table and have the caterer bring small plates with many options for what the food should be at the wedding reception. They tasted multiple hors d'oeuvres, main courses, side dishes, and cakes. They had important decisions to make!

My future son-in-law did not get the idea at first. He thought the first plate brought was the food he was to eat, and eat it he did. It wasn't a tasting so much as a meal. He didn't nibble each dish, he consumed them leaving each plate empty. Of course, as the main dish options kept coming, he was quickly overstuffed. He ate all the steak, all the chicken, all the fish . . . He was beginning to sweat from overeating long before the cakes arrived.

This preparation work and experience comes to mind as I read today's passage. Jesus had a somewhat captive audience. People undoubtedly enjoyed seeing Jesus do the miraculous, but they also enjoyed his teaching. The people were under no compulsion to listen to Jesus. They were free to come and go as they wished. So, Jesus gave them a tasting, something to captivate them and hopefully inform them better further down the road.

Jesus used parables and stories to introduce the people to ideas and concepts that, if Jesus had hit them with full sermons, would have likely caused many to reject Jesus out of hand, caused many to leave, and left a few sweating profusely from trying to consume all Jesus offered. But by teaching people in parables, Jesus was able to teach the word "as they were able to hear it." They had stories to chew on. They could talk about them, recall them later, muse and meditate on them. Then ultimately, as the words made more and more sense, they could grow in their faith and understanding.

Some would have left the stories and done no more with them. But others would be intrigued and would even ask Jesus to explain the stories. Here there was growth. God seeks to move us from where we are to where we need to be. He does so in bite-size steps. We need to taste and see this goodness of the Lord.

Lord, give me patience and attention to learn from you as you teach. In Jesus, amen.

SEPTEMBER 12

On that day, when evening had come, he said to them, "Let us go across to the other side." And leaving the crowd, they took him with them in the boat, just as he was. And other boats were with him. And a great windstorm arose, and the waves were breaking into the boat, so that the boat was already filling. But he was in the stern, asleep on the cushion. And they woke him and said to him, "Teacher, do you not care that we are perishing?" And he awoke and rebuked the wind and said to the sea, "Peace! Be still!" And the wind ceased, and there was a great calm. He said to them, "Why are you so afraid? Have you still no faith?" And they were filled with great fear and said to one another, "Who then is this, that even the wind and the sea obey him?" (Mk. 4:35–41)

I love this story, not only for the events, but especially in the way Mark writes it up. It leaves me in awe of God and helps me with the common fears of life.

Jesus is in a small boat on a large lake. His disciples include some fishermen who knew boats, knew weather, and knew when to worry. Jesus was wiped out and fell asleep on a cushion while they rowed. A storm arose, and the waves were bringing water into the boat. The disciples were hands-on. Some were rowing, while others were bailing water as fast as they could. Jesus? He was still asleep. The disciples awaken Jesus to get him working too! Their rudeness is apparent in Mark's story. The event is clear. "Jesus, wake up! Get after it! We can die here. All hands on deck! Why are you sleeping? Don't you give a rip about whether we live or die? These waves are killing us! Row or bail, but do something other than sleep!"

Jesus awakens, and first turns to the weather concern. But Jesus doesn't offer to row. Nor does he grab a bucket to bail the water threatening to swamp the boat. Jesus rebukes the wind causing the waves to still. Interestingly, Mark uses the same word for "rebuke" that he does when describing what Jesus did to demons! Jesus speaks to the winds as if they are persons. Jesus then instructs the waves to go still. Suddenly, the wind ceased, and the sea was glass. Jesus then turned to his followers.

Jesus challenged his disciples in the boat. Jesus probed them to consider why they were filled with fear instead of faith. Just what were they afraid of while they were in the presence of Jesus? As Mark recounts the story, at this point the disciples were *really afraid*, not of the waves, but of the fellow in the back of the boat! As they discussed privately, who tells the elements what to do? That is a God thing, not a normal human thing! Of course, it doesn't help that they had awakened Jesus so rudely, accusing him of not caring about them.

This story is a blunt reminder to me. I should always choose faith over fear.

Lord, give me faith in the storms of life. I give myself wholly to you. In Jesus, amen.

SEPTEMBER 13

And behold, a woman who had suffered from a discharge of blood for twelve years came up behind him and touched the fringe of his garment, for she said to herself, "If I only touch his garment, I will be made well." Jesus turned, and seeing her he said, "Take heart, daughter; your faith has made you well." And instantly the woman was made well. (Mt. 9:20–22)

The gospels record Jesus healing many different people. Reading the English translations, the healings fall into three general categories: exorcisms, physical healings, and resurrections. Today's reading is in that second category, physical healing. But in the Greek, something more subtle is at play.

The English is plain enough; a woman has a physical ailment. No doctors have successfully helped her. She is desperate, and understandably so. She is not only having to handle the difficulties of her condition, but under Jewish law, that condition makes her unclean and unable to interact in social situations. She has spent twelve years as an outcast. The woman reaches out to touch Jesus' garment, and Jesus turns, pronouncing her healed according to her faith.

Matthew's account, which I have chosen here, is given to a readership that is considered Jewish. Mark's account differs in some of the Greek language used, and most scholars think that Matthew would have had Mark's account in his hands when writing what we call the Gospel of Matthew. So, the changes in language by Matthew are deliberate. The key change involves the healing. Mark gives a much-extended dialogue about the events, while Matthew cuts it way back. Leaving out a lot of the specifics, Matthew focuses on the woman's condition in a way that emphasized her uncleanness under Jewish law. Matthew then repeatedly uses a certain verb in his Greek version.

Matthew employs the verb *sōzō* (σῴζω) much more than Mark. This verb can mean "healing," but its usage goes much beyond that. It denotes also the idea of saving, rescuing, and preserving. Paul uses it to speak of salvation from sins in the famous Romans 10:9 passage, "if you confess with your mouth that Jesus is Lord and believe in your heart that God raised him from the dead, you will be saved [*sōzō*]." Matthew uses it to speak of Jesus saving from sin (Mt. 1:21) and saving from a storm at sea (Mt. 8:25). Jesus saved this woman, not only by healing her from her condition but also healing and saving her social situation and outcast status. He healed her socially and spiritually, not simply physically.

I see now more than three kinds of healing. Jesus performs exorcisms, medical healing, resurrections, and also restores my soul and my heart. What a Savior!

Lord, please bring me wholeness in all areas of life. Touch me in Jesus! Amen.

SEPTEMBER 14

And when he entered the temple, the chief priests and the elders of the people came up to him as he was teaching, and said, "By what authority are you doing these things, and who gave you this authority?" Jesus answered them, "I also will ask you one question, and if you tell me the answer, then I also will tell you by what authority I do these things. The baptism of John, from where did it come? From heaven or from man?" And they discussed it among themselves, saying, "If we say, 'From heaven,' he will say to us, 'Why then did you not believe him?' But if we say, 'From man,' we are afraid of the crowd, for they all hold that John was a prophet." So they answered Jesus, "We do not know." And he said to them, "Neither will I tell you by what authority I do these things." (Mt. 21:23–27)

NERD ALERT! NERD ALERT! I confess, I LOVE the game of chess. It is great! It is a game of strategy, tactics, art, and foresight! In deciding what to do, I must ask, "If I do this, what does my opponent do? Then what do I do, then what does . . ." I love the back and forth of it. Not surprisingly, I see chess in much of life, and I certainly see it here. The chief priests and elders of the Jewish nation have gathered in Jerusalem in a chess game of wits and logic with one they thought simply a country Jewish carpenter, turned troublesome country rabbi, Jesus. They were so wrong. In truth, he was a grandmaster who they couldn't come close to beating in a game of wits.

The competition begins with the chief priests/elders challenging Jesus to justify his actions. They considered themselves the Jewish authorities and so were thinking they had a winning position simply by asking Jesus where he got his authority to be walking around like some rabbi with special teaching and healing abilities. Jesus doesn't answer as they had hoped. Instead of saying, "I got it on my own." Or, "Someone gave me authority." Or even, "From God," which might have been the most dangerous answer, for even saying the name of God bordered on blasphemy, depending on how Jesus said it.

Jesus replied with his own question: Did John's baptism come from heaven or man? It helps here to know that "heaven" could be used in Jewish language as a substitute for God's name. While one couldn't say the name of God without being stoned, one could substitute "heaven." This grew out of an Old Testament practice seen in Daniel 4:26 ("your kingdom shall be confirmed for you from the time that you know that Heaven [aka God] rules"). The chess game begins to unravel for the priests. They can't see a viable answer. Finally they give up, and say, "I don't know," which isn't a particularly good look for the supposed top thinkers of the people.

We might say, "Checkmate." Or we might say, "Don't challenge Jesus to a game of wits. We can't outplay him. God is not so easily deceived, tricked, or beaten."

Lord, I am glad you are the victor today and always. I want to be on your team in Jesus, amen.

SEPTEMBER 15

After this Jesus went about in Galilee. He would not go about in Judea, because the Jews were seeking to kill him. Now the Jews' Feast of Booths was at hand. So his brothers said to him, "Leave here and go to Judea, that your disciples also may see the works you are doing. For no one works in secret if he seeks to be known openly. If you do these things, show yourself to the world." For not even his brothers believed in him. Jesus said to them, "My time has not yet come, but your time is always here. . . . You go up to the feast. I am not going up to this feast, for my time has not yet fully come." After saying this, he remained in Galilee. (Jn. 7:1–9)

Sometimes when I find I have an important task that requires I get up early in the morning, I find that I awaken before the alarm goes off. I check the time to see if I have overslept through an alarm malfunction or merely awakened early. If I awakened early, I have that dreaded decision of either going back to sleep, or going ahead and getting up anyway.

Those situations are in my mind when I read this passage because such circumstances marvelously illustrate the differences that can exist in two Greek words for "time." One Greek word for time is *chronos* (χρόνος). It generally is used to denote the lapse of time or the ordered numerical time like that kept by a clock. In my illustration above, it would measure what the actual time is; for example, I am writing this devotional at 4:23 a.m., because I got up earlier than I needed to this morning. The 4:23 is the *chronos* time. One can see the remnants of this Greek word in the English "chronology." A sample of this is found in John's gospel in John 5:6 when Jesus asks a man who had long had a debilitating illness, "When Jesus saw him lying there and knew that he had already been there a long *time [chronos]*, he said to him, 'Do you want to be healed?'"

A second Greek word for time is *kairos* (καιρός). This word is often found emphasizing a particular time that is especially fit for something. It can emphasize an opportune or appropriate moment, without any emphasis on a precise chronological time. It is the *right time*. So in my example opening this devotional, while I awoke at 4:23 a.m. *chronos* time, it wasn't the right moment, or *kairos* time for me to be where I needed to be, yet it was a fitting *kairos* moment for me to write a devotional.

Some times are more fitting than others. Jesus knew that. In today's passage, the chronology (*chronos* time) was such that Jesus should leave to go celebrate the Feast of Tabernacles or Booths in Jerusalem. Yet it was not the propitious moment (or *kairos* time) for Jesus to leave, so he stayed back. Both words translated as "time" in this passage are *kairos*. God always finds the right moments in life, regardless of the time on a clock.

Lord, I know you don't live by my clock. Give me the patience to live by yours, keeping up with the right times in life. In Jesus' name, amen.

SEPTEMBER 16

Truly, truly, I say to you, whoever hears my word and believes him who sent me has eternal life. He does not come into judgment, but has passed from death to life. (Jn. 5:24)

"Life"—what a word! Think of all its uses. You are told you have one "life" to live. Unless you're a cat, then you have nine! Someone is labeled the "life" of the party. You might ask, "What is the meaning of life?" If you are low-energy, you might be told to "show some life."

The Greek language of the New Testament had three different words for life. One (*bios*, βίος) referred to daily life and the resources one had for that life. A second, *psuche* (ψυχή) tended to be used for the self-conscious individual self. The third, *zoe* (ζωή) is typically used for the gift of God for life, especially used with the word "eternal," focusing upon the eternal life God gives to his people. It is this third Greek word that is used twice in today's passage.

Jesus draws a distinction between people who might hear his words and not believe them and those who do believe them. The ones who do not believe them may still be alive in a certain sense, but only those who believe his words are singled out for having the eternal life that God gives. This is a future life that comes at the end of time, but for the believer, that life has already started.

The gospels, especially John, work hard to teach that God's redeemed life isn't one that occurs just after death. But as Paul also emphasized in his letters, the everlasting life is already being experienced in the life of a believer. This is the import of being born again, or born anew, as John uses that phrase in John 3:16. "For God so loved the world, that he gave his only Son, that whoever believes in him should not perish but have eternal life." The word used there is also *zoe*, the eternal life to come that has already begun in the present.

There are mornings when I wake up and feel the blahs. Certain times during the day, I may feel worn out or frazzled. It isn't unusual to suffer some bodily ache or pain. During these times I wonder what it means to have eternal life now. The answer is found in the future. My current physical body is still subject to the frailties of the fallen human nature. Yet I know that even as this body ages away, even as I struggle to cope with all that this life throws my way, I have already begun the journey that will take me into eternity. I have already laid claim on being with God, with the assurance one day I will also get that new body that will catch up, bringing me into the fullness of eternal life. So I don't get down in the day. I keep looking to the one who will being me to completion!

Lord, give me faith, hope, and focus on you and your love. May your Holy Spirit confirm in my life the future you have already placed in me. In Jesus, amen.

SEPTEMBER 17

And falling to the ground, he heard a voice saying to him, "Saul, Saul, why are you persecuting me?" And he said, "Who are you, Lord?" And he said, "I am Jesus, whom you are persecuting. But rise and enter the city, and you will be told what you are to do." (Acts 9:4–6)

Nothing in Scripture indicates that Paul knew Jesus prior to this appearance of Jesus to Paul. Even though Paul had spent a good bit of time in Jerusalem from a young age, it doesn't seem that their paths crossed. But Jesus knew Paul, even if Paul didn't know Jesus. With his sovereign knowledge, the God who searches the hearts and minds of people not only knew Paul but had a mission for Paul.

Today's passage recounts Jesus meeting Paul on the road to Damascus, changing the course of Paul's life eternally. The context is important. Paul had trained at the feet of Gamaliel, the top legal expert of the day (meaning the top specialist in Jewish Torah or Law). Paul had worked for the Sanhedrin, the Supreme Court of Israel, and part of Paul's job was persecuting the Jewish Christians. Paul had participated in the stoning of Stephen, the first Christian martyr. Paul had gotten papers to go and arrest other Christians in the large city of Damascus, about 135 miles away. While on the road, Jesus makes a miraculous appearance, and the dialogue of today's passage ensues.

From here, Paul goes into Damascus, meets the fellow as instructed by Jesus, and finishes giving his life over to the Messiah. From this experience, several important lessons have strengthened my life, but the one I focus on today is timing.

Had I been around at the time of these events, I think I might have had some difficult questions for Jesus. They would center on, "Why did you wait so long?" I would be thinking if Jesus had acted a little bit sooner, Stephen might still be alive! Couldn't Jesus have appeared to Paul earlier?

God's goal in all of this was not to have Stephen live a long life in this body and world. God's goal was much greater. God's goal was to expand his kingdom, bringing life to many more than just a few. As horrible as the death of Stephen was, it clearly became an issue to help Paul in his humility, in seeing his need for forgiveness from the Lord, and it was likewise a catalyst that inspired generations of Christians who would subsequently give their lives for their faith.

God's timing isn't mine. What's worse, his priorities aren't always mine either. Yet I know whose timing is right. And I certainly know who has the right priorities. Hmm. . . .

Dear Father, teach me your priorities. Give me patience for your timing. Help me see your big picture, not the self-interested moments before me. In Jesus, amen.

SEPTEMBER 18

Whoever is of God hears the words of God. The reason why you do not hear them is that you are not of God. (Jn. 8:47)

Our daughter Rebecca has a dog Barney. She has trained that dog better than any dog I've ever seen (save the dog of Gen. John Ashcroft, but that is another story!). Barney doesn't simply sit, stay, place, shake. Barney will do almost anything you can think of. Of course, this is only when Rebecca gives the command. If someone else tells Barney what to do, they might as well speak Swahili. Barney looks at them and does whatever he chooses.

Rebecca started when Barney was a young puppy. She explained to me that puppies need something to occupy their minds, and if she as the owner/trainer doesn't give Barney focus points, then he will never develop to be as good a dog as he might be otherwise. The key is to give him lessons that he can focus on, learn, and grow through. This makes Barney the happiest, best dog he can be, as opposed to being a scared, undisciplined, and even dangerous dog.

This exemplifies the Christian walk to me. God speaks to his people. His messages are important, and I should *want* to hear them. God gives us focus points, and when we listen and learn, we become the best and happiest people we can be. But we are going to focus on something, and if we fail to focus on God and his teachings, then we can become the scared, undisciplined, and even dangerous dog.

In today's passage, Jesus explained that God does indeed speak. To the believer, his words are apples of gold. We listen to them, treasure them, live them. But to those who don't follow God, his words are meaningless. They might as well be Swahili.

Paul taught something akin to this in a letter to the church at Corinth. Paul explained it this way, "The natural person does not accept the things of the Spirit of God, for they are folly to him, and he is not able to understand them because they are spiritually discerned. The spiritual person judges all things . . ." (1 Cor. 2:14-15).

Therefore, as I meditate on this passage, I do so with a prayer in my heart, that God will open my ears to hear his words. I want to listen to God with an obedient heart. I know by faith that if I will focus as God gives me focus, if I will do as God instructs me to do, if his priorities become my priorities, if I embody his holiness, care for those he cares for, love as he instructed me to love, and so on, then I will become the best me I can be. But if I ignore my God, it is my own loss.

Lord, give me eager ears and a willing heart. May your heart be my heart, your mind my mind. May it all be to your glory. In Jesus' holy name, amen.

SEPTEMBER 19

Now there was a disciple at Damascus named Ananias. The Lord said to him in a vision, "Ananias." And he said, "Here I am, Lord." And the Lord said to him, "Rise and go to the street called Straight, and at the house of Judas look for a man of Tarsus named Saul, for behold, he is praying, and he has seen in a vision a man named Ananias come in and lay his hands on him so that he might regain his sight." But Ananias answered, "Lord, I have heard from many about this man, how much evil he has done to your saints at Jerusalem. And here he has authority from the chief priests to bind all who call on your name." But the Lord said to him, "Go, for he is a chosen instrument of mine to carry my name before the Gentiles and kings and the children of Israel. For I will show him how much he must suffer for the sake of my name." (Acts 9:10–16)

I like Ananias. I've never met him, but I still like him. He's the godly man who God uses to restore Paul's sight, and guide Paul into deeper faith. He's also the fellow who had no problem questioning God! Now that is pretty bold.

Jesus appeared in a vision and gave Ananias real specific instructions. Jesus explained that Ananias' actions were preordained by God and that Paul had already been told Ananias would come. Then comes the stunning line. Ananias begins to explain to Jesus all he knew about Saul. (Saul and Paul are one and the same. Saul was Paul's Hebrew name, but as a Roman citizen, Paul was required to have a Roman name as well, and Paul would have been his common Roman name.)

Ananias tells Jesus, as if Jesus didn't know, that Paul was the one who was persecuting the church. Paul had done a lot of evil, and Paul's purpose in coming to Damascus was not in the least friendly. Paul was there to arrest Jesus' followers.

Jesus doesn't scold Ananias at all. Jesus doesn't say, "Don't challenge me." Nor does he tell Ananias to get in line. Jesus goes to great lengths to explain his purposes to Ananias. Jesus tells him that Paul is God's instrument, and that Paul will be the one suffering in the future.

Ananias goes and does as Jesus instructed, and the rest is history. Paul does a 180-degree turn with his life trajectory. Paul is no longer the confident agent of the temple power structure and governmental Judaism. Paul loses his comfort, his "most likely to succeed" status, and more. Paul will be beaten repeatedly, arrested over and over, shipwrecked, robbed, berated, despised, impoverished, and abandoned. Yet Paul never regretted his decision. Everything Paul had and lost was garbage to him, compared with knowing Jesus. God saw all this coming; Ananias just had to trust God and obey him.

Lord, I know you can do amazing things if I will trust you. Forgive me for questioning your ways, and give me strength to follow you. In Jesus, I pray amen.

SEPTEMBER 20

Paul was occupied with the word, testifying to the Jews that the Christ was Jesus. And when they opposed and reviled him, he shook out his garments and said to them, "Your blood be on your own heads! I am innocent. From now on I will go to the Gentiles." And he left there and went to the house of a man named Titius Justus, a worshiper of God. His house was next door to the synagogue. Crispus, the ruler of the synagogue, believed in the Lord, together with his entire household. And many of the Corinthians hearing Paul believed and were baptized. And the Lord said to Paul one night in a vision, "Do not be afraid, but go on speaking and do not be silent, for I am with you, and no one will attack you to harm you, for I have many in this city who are my people." And he stayed a year and six months, teaching the word of God among them. (Acts 18:5–11)

Do you ever get down or disheartened? Try as hard as you might, be as holy as you can, pump yourself up with the greatest pep talks, but still sometimes you feel gutted. Emotional and spiritual exhaustion is just as real as physical exhaustion. It affects people differently. Some want to crawl into a shell. Others put on the television and check out. Or some might seek to drown their feelings in food, drink, or pharmaceuticals. I think it is important to know that everyone goes through these spells of doubts and discouragements. Paul did.

In today's passage, Paul, who seems at times unassailable, is worn out. He has had confrontation after confrontation with Jews who persecuted and worked to frustrate his plans, incarcerate him, and beat him senseless. Paul was fed up. Paul told the Jews that he would have nothing more to do with them. He shook out his garments, a physical expression of shaking the dust away. Paul proclaimed he would no longer be teaching Jews about Jesus. He would limit his ministry to reaching Gentiles for Christ.

Two interesting things seem to happen after this. First, the text notes that while Paul was staying with a Gentile who worshipped God in the Jewish synagogue, that the synagogue ruler became a believer in Jesus, along with his whole household. So while Paul thought he was through with the Jews, God used him to reach the leader of the Jewish synagogue.

The second interesting thing is the appearance of Jesus to Paul. This vision was at a critical time for Paul, and it was God working to bolster Paul's spirits. Jesus told Paul that Jesus was with Paul, and no harm would come to Paul. Paul was going to be just fine. That was just what Paul needed. Paul stayed there for a year and a half, teaching people of Jesus. This vision should not be for Paul alone. It is in Scripture to encourage us as well. God isn't blind to the world. He is taking care of us. Sometimes we just need to rest in that.

Lord, give me rest in my weariness, then use me as you can! In Jesus, amen.

SEPTEMBER 21

Take courage, for as you have testified to the facts about me in Jerusalem, so you must testify also in Rome. (Acts 23:11)

Bert Lahr played the role of the cowardly lion in the movie adaptation of Frank Baum's masterful book, *The Wizard of Oz*. Lions have the reputation of being the "King of Beasts," so for the lion to believe himself inadequate because of his fears is a funny contrast. He thinks he doesn't measure up. He supposes that he shouldn't be afraid of anything or anyone. As the story unfolds, the lion acts courageously over and over, even while acting fearfully at times. Ultimately, the Wizard of Oz simply recognizes the courage the lion always possessed and transforms the lion's self-image.

Courage is not the absence of fear. Courage is being resolute in the face of danger or fear. So it was in *The Wizard of Oz*, in the time of Jesus, and even today.

In the passage I have excerpted, Jesus is talking to Paul, coming to Paul in a vision while Paul is locked up in 57 AD. The Romans have wrongly arrested Paul for inciting a riot at the temple in Jerusalem. Certain people see this as a chance to get rid of their Paul problem once and for all. Notable people are plotting how to see that this is the end of the line for Paul. They plot his murder with hopes to carry out their plan. Jesus tells Paul, "take courage," explaining that God isn't done with Paul. God has his agenda, and no one is going to get in the way. "Courage" in this passage is the word *tharseō* (θαρσέω). Jesus is quoted using the word frequently in the gospels, where it is usually translated as "take heart." It is the instruction to be resolute in the face of danger, hurt, or concern.

I like this passage. I am glad Jesus appeared to Paul in this way. It gave Paul strength and direction, as the rest of the Acts narrative bears out, getting Paul into Rome, the heart of the empire where Paul hopes to have an audience with Nero himself.

But more than liking it just for Paul, I also like it for me. I face many things in life that could leave me the cowardly lion. Work fears, health fears, relationship fears, fears of inadequacy, fears of faith, and more haunt us all. Great people in the Bible were afraid: Abraham, Moses, David, and others. They accomplished much while afraid, as they leaned on God for his support.

How do we live in the face of those fears? Jesus and Paul should inspire us. They illustrate the eternal truth that God will take care of us as we walk in his will. This life doesn't end until God finishes his work in us.

Lord, give me courage. Help me face my fears with a resolute heart, courageous and confident in your love and concern. In Jesus, amen.

SEPTEMBER 22

"Saul, Saul, why are you persecuting me? It is hard for you to kick against the goads." And I said, "Who are you, Lord?" And the Lord said, "I am Jesus whom you are persecuting. But rise and stand upon your feet, for I have appeared to you for this purpose, to appoint you as a servant and witness to the things in which you have seen me and to those in which I will appear to you, delivering you from your people and from the Gentiles—to whom I am sending you to open their eyes, so that they may turn from darkness to light and from the power of Satan to God, that they may receive forgiveness of sins and a place among those who are sanctified by faith in me." (Acts 26:14-18)

Today's passage is loaded! Paul is relating his story to King Agrippa. It comes as Paul is incarcerated for creating a disturbance in Jerusalem. Paul wants to tell his story to Agrippa to bring the king to faith. As Paul tells what had happened to him, we get the fullest account of how Jesus instructed Paul on Paul's mission. Jesus laid out core fundamental truths to Paul.

Truth one: The crucified Jesus was not dead. He was alive. He was making an appearance to Paul as a risen Savior. Paul never spoke of Jesus as a dead Messiah; Jesus was alive. Jesus died but was resurrected, conquering death. This had implications for Paul, as it does for everyone.

Truth two: Paul had a divine appointment. That God would use Paul might not surprise us, but Paul will often explain that God divinely appoints all his people. God has purpose for each follower. Paul will tell the Ephesians that God has prepared good works for his children to do, even before the children come into existence.

Truth three: People live blinded to God's truth. The natural condition of everyone is alienation to God and his life. Yet God seeks to bring his truth to you and me. Then when God's truth becomes real, it is like turning on the lights. This is a turn from the control and power of Satan into God's conquering kingdom of truth and victory.

Truth four: The truth of the resurrected Messiah brings a deliverance from the power and consequences of sin. Sin is a moral and ethical rebellion against God. Just as God produces life, rebellion against him brings death and despair. Jesus cut the cords of death that would drag us deep into the sea by taking responsibility for our sins.

Truth five: God takes the redeemed, those whose sins are forgiven, and goes to work "sanctifying" them. This means that God gives forgiveness but then begins that process of growing us in our righteousness. All of this was wrapped up in Jesus speaking to Paul, who lived to explain these truths.

Lord, thank you for these truths. May I live rooted in each. In Jesus, amen.

SEPTEMBER 23

The true light, which gives light to everyone, was coming into the world. (Jn. 1:9)

When I was little, my dad had a project I found fascinating. He had a model kit to put together. It was the USS *Constitution*, also known as "Old Ironside." This was a three-mast ship launched by the U.S. Navy in 1797 and still maintained at a museum today. Dad's model was really cool to me; I loved watching as he tied knots in thread to emulate the rigging on the ship. Dad did so following these elaborate instructions that allowed him to produce a model that clearly reflected the two-hundred-year-old ship. The model was beautiful, but it made most sense understood in the light of its original.

In like manner, John wrote a beautiful passage in today's devotional. He had already called Jesus the "Word" in his opening verses, and now he added that Jesus, the Word, was also the true light who came into the world. John produced a marvelous metaphor. One which most anyone can grasp. However, this passage and metaphor become more stunning when one considers that John's language didn't originate from his pen. He is modeling it on language found in the Jewish Holy Scriptures. These are metaphors that are pregnant with meaning.

Consider Psalm 119. Over and over it speaks of God's "word." Then in verse 105, we read, "Your word is a lamp to my feet and a light to my path." John takes God's "word" and uses it as a metaphor for Jesus, hence the translators capitalize John's "Word." John is echoing from Psalm 119 that Jesus is the true lamp to our feet. We follow Jesus. He illuminates where we go and how we should live.

Over and over in his gospels, we read of Jesus telling people, both individually and in groups, to "follow" him. Jesus leads the way. Jesus is the true instructor, the true guide, the true model.

For a while, "WWJD" bracelets were in vogue. The initials stood for "What would Jesus do?" The bracelets were to serve the wearer as a reminder to behave in godly ways. One of my friends didn't like the bracelets. It wasn't because my friend hated the faith. In fact, he was very devout. His beef with the bracelets was that no one can do what Jesus did. He said the bracelet should say, "What would Jesus have me do?" But then WWJHMD doesn't quite have the same ring to it.

I am not against WWJD. I am also a fan of WWJHMD. I think both are closely related. I can't play basketball like Lebron James, but in watching him, I can learn how to be a better player. Similarly, I may not be able to live like Jesus, but he is still the true light that guides my path as I seek to follow him.

My Lord and my Light, illuminate my path as I seek to follow you. Amen.

SEPTEMBER 24

The next day again John was standing with two of his disciples, and he looked at Jesus as he walked by and said, "Behold, the Lamb of God!" The two disciples heard him say this, and they followed Jesus. Jesus turned and saw them following and said to them, "What are you seeking?" And they said to him, "Rabbi" (which means Teacher), "where are you staying?" He said to them, "Come and you will see." So they came and saw where he was staying, and they stayed with him that day, for it was about the tenth hour. One of the two who heard John speak and followed Jesus was Andrew, Simon Peter's brother. He first found his own brother Simon and said to him, "We have found the Messiah" (which means Christ). He brought him to Jesus. (Jn. 1:35–42)

This passage begins with John the Baptist pointing out Jesus to his followers, calling Jesus God's Lamb. Two of his disciples start following Jesus. It was about 4:00 in the afternoon. Jesus wheels around on them asking them why they are following him, what is it they are wanting? They call Jesus "Teacher," and then asked where he was staying. This was an indication that they were seeking to hitch their wagon to his. This seems foreign to twenty-first-century Americans, but it was not uncommon in his day.

Jesus told the young men to come with him and check it out. They stayed with Jesus the rest of the day. Then Andrew, one of the two, decided to go get his brother, Peter, telling him, "We have found the Messiah." This is stunning. Through this chain, comes Peter.

The way John wrote this story allows the reader to inject themselves into the dialogue. First, any reader is already aware of the basics about Jesus, else they wouldn't be reading the gospel. So when John points out who Jesus is, the natural reaction of the reader should be, "Will I choose to follow Jesus?" When anyone makes that choice, Jesus will turn around and pay attention to them. No one need worry that Jesus doesn't have time for his followers. Jesus will stop his journey, turn around, and devote attention to those who seek him.

A further instructive aspect to this story is the reply of the two seekers. They call Jesus "Rabbi," the word in the common tongue (Aramaic) for "Teacher." Yet by the time they have spent the rest of the day with him, and likely after a night's sleep on it, Andrew will announce to his brother that Jesus is the Messiah. This is an amazing growth in understanding in a brief period. Yet that is how it is with Jesus. As one spends time in his presence, one rapidly understands this is no ordinary man.

I also like that Jesus invited the two to "come and see." The presumption in the story is to come and see where Jesus was staying. Yet as the story is written, it appears to be much more. It is come and watch Jesus. This is for me! Watch Jesus and learn.

Lord, teach me, be with me, guide me, send me to do your work. In Jesus, amen.

SEPTEMBER 25

And Jesus came and said to them, "All authority in heaven and on earth has been given to me. Go therefore and make disciples of all nations, baptizing them in the name of the Father and of the Son and of the Holy Spirit, teaching them to observe all that I have commanded you. And behold, I am with you always, to the end of the age." (Mt. 28:18-20)

As of this writing, there are 7.9 billion people in the world. Counting to 7.9 billion would take over 250 years! When thinking of one's place in this huge number, two extremes often emerge: One is to think oneself insignificant because you are only one in 7.9 billion. The other is to live as if you are the center of all things. Both extremes miss a beautiful truth exhibited in this passage.

The truth missed by the extremes is heightened by understanding the larger book of Matthew, from which I drew today's passage. Matthew's gospel was written by a first-century Jew who wanted to write a gospel that Jews could readily grasp. For example, in Matthew, the genealogy of Jesus does not begin with Adam, as it does in Luke, but rather with Abraham, the father of the Jews. When the Gospel of Mark gives the encounter between Jesus and certain Pharisees about the ritual washing of hands, Mark explains the custom for those readers who aren't Jewish. Not Matthew. He assumes his readers know the Jewish custom. (Compare Mk. 7:1-13 to Mt. 15:1-9.)

Yet in this particularly Jewish gospel, targeted to a Jewish audience, the book ends with a major bang! Today's passage is the very end of a very long gospel. The end of the story, as Matthew tells it, has Jesus proclaiming his full authority. Jesus has all the authority of heaven, and all the authority of earth. With all that authority, Jesus instructs his Jewish apostles to go beyond the Jews, beyond Judea, to all of the world. Jesus told them of his care for all the nations. That is more than the 7.9 billion people today. It spans time. It is all people over all time!

This informs me today. It tells me of God's interest in me—ME!!! I am significant. I am loved. I am wanted. But this isn't about the world being all about me. God has this deep interest in everyone! God calls me to live out his interest in everyone. God wants me to tell of his love to everyone. God instructs me to show his interest, his kindness, and the good news of how far he went to secure a relationship with everyone for eternity. Wow.

Lord, thank you for your love. Thank you for reaching me. Thank you for using me to reach others. Give me the words and the heart to do so. In Jesus, amen.

Now while the Pharisees were gathered together, Jesus asked them a question, saying, "What do you think about the Christ? Whose son is he?" They said to him, "The son of David." He said to them, "How is it then that David, in the Spirit, calls him Lord, saying, 'The Lord said to my Lord, "Sit at my right hand, until I put your enemies under your feet"'? If then David calls him Lord, how is he his son?" (Mt. 22:41–45)

I have friends who read the first chapter of a novel and then read the last chapter, skipping to the end immediately to find out what happens. They can't handle the suspense. I think they miss a lot along the way. But sometimes I wonder if they aren't onto something.

God's unfolding of history has glimpses of what is to come. He assures those listening that Christ will return victorious, giving all the confident expectation that helps us endure the rough pages of life. Similarly, throughout the history of God's interactions recorded in the Old Testament, there were hints and prophetic promises about the coming Messiah.

In today's passage, Jesus has been cross-examined by a leading lawyer of the Pharisees. Jesus then turns the table and begins examining the Pharisees and their lawyer! Jesus asks them about the lineage of the expected Messiah. The Pharisees answer that the Messiah will be a king in the lineage of King David, Israel's greatest king. Jesus then presses his issue, to illuminate the Messiah must be more than simply David's offspring.

Jesus' follow-up question makes more sense in its original tongue. Noting that David was inspired by the Holy Spirit when he wrote, Jesus points them to Psalm 110, verse 1. David wrote, as quoted by Jesus, "The LORD said to my Lord . . ." The first "LORD" that I have put in all capitals is the actual name of God used in the Old Testament. The Hebrew will put "LORD" in all capitals to distinguish God's name from the common idea of "Lord."

Jesus is pointing out that David expected someone *greater* than he. David knew that God (the LORD) had spoken to DAVID'S "Lord" ("*my* Lord" as David wrote it) promising to put his enemies under his feet. So if the coming one was David's Lord, how could he be David's son? Or how could he be simply "king" after David's lineage? The Messiah *exceeded* King David.

Jesus is indeed the Son of David, but he is more. He is the full story. Jesus fulfills Judaism and completes it. In Jesus, we see the end of the book! We just have a few more pages to live out.

Lord, I give you all praise, honor, and glory in Jesus. May I live accordingly. Amen.

SEPTEMBER 27

Are not two sparrows sold for a penny? And not one of them will fall to the ground apart from your Father. But even the hairs of your head are all numbered. Fear not, therefore; you are of more value than many sparrows. (Mt. 10:29–31)

How good are you at memorizing Scripture? Some people have great memories. Others struggle to remember. For some it is age related, for others it is just how their brain is wired or working. Some can remember numbers but forget names. Some can remember voices but forget where they placed their keys. Some remember things they read but not so much things they hear.

Look at today's passage. Can you read it again and memorize it? Or does it seem you have it memorized, and then like water in your hands, it somehow passes through?

If you get a book on memorizing, the odds are the book will tell you to create associations in your brain, a kind of "memory palace." I always love reading the Bible because most of it was written (maybe all of it) in eras where ownership of books was uncommon. Most people learned to memorize stories and teachings, while few read and wrote.

Matthew wrote his gospel to make it easier to memorize. He wanted his readers to be informed and knew that most wouldn't have a ready copy of the gospel on their desk to turn to in reference times. In fact, desks were not even a form of furniture in Matthew's day! One way Matthew wrote memorably was through his use of numbers. Matthew would frequently write in threes. There were three messages to Joseph and three denials of Peter, Jesus prays three times in Gethsemane, and so on. Three was important not simply as a math number placed between two and four, but it was also seen as a holy number. It would help one remember the passages.

Similarly, Matthew often wrote in sevens, a number in his day that symbolized completion. Matthew clumped seven parables together in chapter 13. He gave seven woes in chapter 23. Matthew used another common number of five, the number of books of the Torah, or Books of Moses. Matthew places the bulk of Jesus' teaching into five sections. Matthew employs other devices to help readers memorize, like repeating words and patterns of language.

All of this to say, we miss out if we fail to memorize portions of Scripture. Look again at today's passage. It speaks of God's knowledge and care of sparrows, and then explains God cares even more for you and me. That is worth remembering! God cares and is paying attention. See if you can memorize today's passage and say it out loud!

Lord, engrave your word on my heart and mind. In Jesus' name, amen.

SEPTEMBER 28

When Jesus heard this, he marveled and said to those who followed him, "Truly, I tell you, with no one in Israel have I found such faith. I tell you, many will come from east and west and recline at table with Abraham, Isaac, and Jacob in the kingdom of heaven, while the sons of the kingdom will be thrown into the outer darkness. In that place there will be weeping and gnashing of teeth." (Mt. 8:10–12)

I have a lot of Jewish friends. Like most heritages, they are all over the map when it comes to what they believe. Some do not believe in God at all. Some believe in and practice normative Jewish faith. At least two of my longtime Jewish friends are "Jewish Hindu" in their faith. But a large number of my friends are Jewish, Jewish in faith and practice, and yet also, professing Christians who believe that Yeshua (Jesus' name in Hebrew) is Messiah (the Anglicized Hebrew word for "Christ"). These friends see Jesus as the fulfillment of the promises to the Jewish faith.

Matthew would fall into this last camp. He wrote his gospel with primarily a Jewish audience in mind. Yet his gospel resonates with the fact that Jesus came to bless all nations, not simply Jews. Matthew's gospel opens the eyes of its Jewish readers to Jesus as the fulfillment of that prophecy to Father Abraham that not only would his offspring outnumber the stars, but that through him, all the nations of the earth would be blessed (Gen. 22:18).

In this sense, in today's story, a non-Jewish Roman soldier seeks Jesus' healing touch for his servant who is paralyzed and suffering terribly. Jesus offers to come to the soldier's house and heal the servant. Matthew informs the reader that the soldier was a "centurion," meaning the soldier was in charge of a troop of one hundred Roman soldiers. One then understands why the soldier said to Jesus, "I'm not worthy for you to come under my roof. I know authority. You just say the word, and my servant will be healed."

Jesus marveled at the non-Jewish faith. He then makes the following pronouncement in today's passage. Non-Jews will join with the Jews (Abraham, Isaac, and Jacob) at God's table in the kingdom of heaven. Matthew's emphasis on this story challenges me.

God never abandoned the Jewish people or his promise to Abraham. Yet God has never been interested in the Jews alone. God wants all people to come into faith, regardless of age, gender, nationality, culture, skin color, and so on. Similarly, so should we. Our love should extend in all directions, reflecting God's global interest.

This story also challenges me to examine my faith. I would love for Jesus to marvel at my faith. But I have a good way to go before that happens!

Lord, grow my faith. Grow my love. Grow in me. May I better serve you. In Jesus, amen.

SEPTEMBER 29

Come to me, all who labor and are heavy laden, and I will give you rest. Take my yoke upon you, and learn from me, for I am gentle and lowly in heart, and you will find rest for your souls. For my yoke is easy, and my burden is light. (Mt. 11:28–30)

I need this. Over and over, these amazing words of Jesus are a balm for my soul. When the world is crashing around me. When events seem to crush me. When I can't find a way through the heavy issues of life. When responsibilities are greater than my resources can handle. When grief overwhelms my reasons for living. When relationships crumble like Humpty Dumpty, where all the king's horses and all the king's men can't put them together again. When all I want to do is crawl under a rock. When the cry of my heart is, "Stop the world, I want to get off." In these times and more, I need this.

Jesus was no ordinary man. Although fully human, he was also fully God. Jesus had the presence of God in him. He had the power and strength of God. Jesus could conquer disease. Jesus resurrected the dead. Jesus loved the unlovable, and did so unconditionally. Jesus had the might to accomplish any task needed.

Jesus was God as a human, made for a purpose. The purpose of God becoming human was you and me. God became flesh and lived his life to redeem us, "Bible language" for "getting us back" into a right relationship with him. Jesus became like you and me to rescue us from what this life would be without him. Jesus refrained from living his life for himself. To do so were the temptations of Satan in the wilderness. Jesus wasn't living for Jesus; he was living (and dying) for humanity.

This powerful and purposeful Jesus is the one who speaks in today's passage. He tells those who listen that we belong before Jesus. We should bring all our burdens to him and lay them upon his strong and purposeful shoulders. The gentle and serving Jesus wants to carry the burdens you and I are carrying.

So how do we do that? How do I set my weighty matters at the feet of my Lord and take up his easy yoke? It starts with coming to him. Seek him in prayer. Read of him in Scripture. As we do so, we seek to learn from him. Learn his priorities, so we can adjust our own. Learn his holiness so we can better make our life decisions. Learn his compassion so we can know how to treat others. Learn his humility so we can send our pride packing. Learn his truth so we can shed our deceit. Learn his love so we can love *all* those around us. As we come to him, and learn of him, we can trust him. He will take care of all those heavy matters we bring.

That's the promise of our holy God. I need that.

Lord, I bring all my weights to you. Teach me to live with your rest. In my Jesus, amen.

SEPTEMBER 30

Six days before the Passover, Jesus therefore came to Bethany, where Lazarus was, whom Jesus had raised from the dead. So they gave a dinner for him there. Martha served, and Lazarus was one of those reclining with him at table. Mary therefore took a pound of expensive ointment made from pure nard, and anointed the feet of Jesus and wiped his feet with her hair. The house was filled with the fragrance of the perfume. But Judas Iscariot, one of his disciples (he who was about to betray him), said, "Why was this ointment not sold for three hundred denarii and given to the poor?" He said this, not because he cared about the poor, but because he was a thief, and having charge of the moneybag he used to help himself to what was put into it. (Jn. 12:1–6)

In the days before Jesus was crucified, the gospels tell of the many different angles of human response to Jesus. Jesus was focused on what was before him. The crucifixion was not only his biggest challenge and temptation, but it was his purpose for coming to earth. All of the healing Jesus did, God could have done through others. Even Elijah had been used by God to raise one from the dead. But not so dying for sins. That had to be done by one who was perfectly suited (pun intended) to the task. Only the perfect Jesus, God made flesh, had the right to die for the sins of others. For only Jesus had no sin. Recognizing what was coming, Jesus was in the final days of his human purpose.

John records the actions of Mary during this turning point of history. Mary took an expensive ointment and anointed the feet of Jesus. Much of the significance of this ancient practice is easily lost in our modern society. Mary wasn't simply giving Jesus a pedicure or foot massage. The anointing of Jesus is an actual pun off of the word, "anoint." In Hebrew, the word "anoint" is the root for "Messiah," one who was anointed. As Jesus prepared for his work as Messiah, Mary gave testimony through anointing him. The anointing is also notable for it is given on Jesus' feet, not head. As early as the original sin drama in Genesis is God's prophetic promise that from the offspring of woman would come one who would step on the head of the enemy and crush it, even as his head was wounded in the process (Gen. 3:15).

While Mary was reacting to Jesus in faith and love, Judas had the opposite reaction. For Judas, this was a question of self-love and personal gain. Judas chastised Mary. He wanted the ointment to be sold so the money would be available for him to appropriate as he decided. Judas was so wrapped up in his own gain, that he ultimately decides to betray Jesus and set him up for arrest, all to get thirty chunks of metal.

I read of these reactions to the cross and ask myself where I land. Am I seeking to love Jesus through his mission or find out what's in it for me?

Lord, forgive when I focus on me, and not you. Thank you for the cross. Thank you for your love. May I love you in return in Jesus, amen.

OCTOBER 1

Let not your hearts be troubled. Believe in God; believe also in me. In my Father's house are many rooms. If it were not so, would I have told you that I go to prepare a place for you? (Jn. 14:1–2)

A number of marvelous Bible-believing people use today's passage to support the idea that Jesus died and ascended to heaven, at least in part, to construct heavenly homes for his followers. I grew up misunderstanding the passage that very way.

I can remember one song in particular, sung by a barbershop quartet, about Jesus leaving this earth to build a mansion in the sky. The image of Christ being hard at work with a celestial hammer and saw is decidedly NOT happening. It isn't at all what Jesus was referring to in this passage and to misread it thusly is to miss the great emphasis Jesus was making.

Carefully notice the verb tenses. Jesus states that as of the time he is talking, there already *are* (present tense) many rooms in his Father's house. There is no need to renovate heaven and make room for a slew of new move-ins. The rooms are already there. Jesus says he was going to "prepare a place" for his followers, but that isn't putting sheets on the bed, or getting the room ready. Jesus was talking about going to the cross.

This comment comes in the last few days of Jesus' life. He is getting his closest disciples ready for his crucifixion, with the added assurance that Jesus would not simply leave them, but would come again. Jesus was leaving "to prepare a place," but a close examination of John's vocabulary here gives further insight into Jesus' meaning. John says Jesus was going to prepare a "place" (*topos*, τόπος). That Greek word includes the idea of a passage from one place to another, or a possibility to do something enabled by that passage. This comes more carefully into the idea of what Jesus was saying.

The Father's house already had the rooms, but the opportunity to get there, the way or passage needed to be prepared. Jesus was going to the cross and was taking upon himself the sins of the world. It doesn't matter how many rooms God has, no sinful being is able to inhabit those rooms. They are rooms in the Father's house, and they are inhabited by the sinless. Jesus prepared the rooms for us in the sense that by taking our sin, he made us sinless. He made us able to inhabit in the presence and house of God!

The apostles didn't understand this as Jesus was talking, but time made it clear. Jesus had to prepare the way for us, or we would have no way home to God.

Father, all praise and glory to you for the loving sacrifice of Jesus, in whom I say, amen.

OCTOBER 2

And behold, there were two blind men sitting by the roadside, and when they heard that Jesus was passing by, they cried out, "Lord, have mercy on us, Son of David!" The crowd rebuked them, telling them to be silent, but they cried out all the more, "Lord, have mercy on us, Son of David!" And stopping, Jesus called them and said, "What do you want me to do for you?" They said to him, "Lord, let our eyes be opened." And Jesus in pity touched their eyes, and immediately they recovered their sight and followed him. (Mt. 20:30–34)

I was sitting with a bunch of lawyers over a dinner, discussing the question, "What is the greatest concert you ever attended?" Several saw the Rolling Stones in year whatever. I thought, meh . . . one saw the Eagles in their prime. I thought, meh . . . I was deliberating between two profound concert experiences: going with my son Will to U2 in Berlin or Bruce Springsteen on his River Tour in 1981. Then before my turn, my buddy Paul went. Paul said, "The Beatles at Shea Stadium August 15, 1965, front row." The table went silent. The game was over. There was zero point in continuing. (We did later seek out all videos of the concert we could find on YouTube, and sure enough, one had an audience shot that showed a young Paul Hanly in the front row!)

That was memorable for Paul. Heavens, it was memorable for me, and I just *heard* about it! It comes to my mind as I read today's passage. Jesus heals two blind men. It makes me think, how cool would it be to see a direct, unquestionable miracle of God? To see him moved in pity, reach out and touch someone's eyes, and see him heal. I would have loved to have been present the day this occurred. I am sure the air was electric. After all, Jesus touched the eyes of two blind men, healing them both. Jesus only had two hands, and they both had two eyes. That tells me that Jesus must have healed one first, and then the second. As the first one received his sight, I am confident he was shouting and rejoicing, and the anticipation of the second, who was still blind, must have been excruciating. I also suspect the first one got to have his first visible experience seeing Jesus, the Son of God, reach out and touch his compatriot's eyes, giving him vision.

Oh, I would have loved to have been there! But now, look at the passage again. These two blind men, before Jesus stopped to talk to them, were shouting for Jesus to have mercy on them. They didn't see Jesus but had heard he was passing by. And his reputation had gone before him. He was their hope. He was their chance for a better life. The stunning part is that the crowd tried to get the men to shut up! If the crowd had had their way, the crowd would have missed the chance to behold these two amazing miracles! This makes me wonder how much I might miss in God's working by living my agenda and not caring properly for others.

Lord, open my eyes to the needs of others and let me help them, not be an obstacle, so I can see your hand at work. In Jesus, amen.

OCTOBER 3

And if I go and prepare a place for you, I will come again and will take you to myself, that where I am you may be also. And you know the way to where I am going. Thomas said to him, "Lord, we do not know where you are going. How can we know the way?" Jesus said to him, "I am the way, and the truth, and the life. No one comes to the Father except through me." (Jn. 14:3–6)

A frequent cartoon shows someone on a deserted island sitting under a palm tree with the ocean lapping at the sand below them. The image is so powerful, Tom Hanks made a movie, *Cast Away*, where he played the role of Chuck Noland, the sole survivor of a plane wreck who washes ashore on a deserted island.

No one likes isolation, at least for long. No one wants to live through the thought that they may not have a future. The U.S. Marines have as their motto, "Until they are home, no man left behind." The idea isn't novel to the current age or culture. It is at the root of today's passage.

Jesus was in his final night talking to his apostles before his arrest. Jesus explained to them that their three-year journey was about to change. No longer would they awaken together, eat their meals, determine their day's agenda, and then go out as a unit teaching, serving, handling confrontations with sinners, pagans, religious zealots, the sick, the lame, blind people, demons, and even the unsuspecting person going about daily life. The apostles' time with Jesus explaining the profundities of life, teaching them the priorities of God, or prodding them to grow in spirituality was about to change.

Jesus was about to leave the apostles and go the last mile, a journey only he could take. This was Jesus about to journey to the cross, bearing the sins of the apostles along with those of the rest of humanity. He explained this to them, although they clearly didn't understand the full implications of what Jesus meant. Jesus wanted them to know and remember that even as he was going, he would return for them. Jesus was leaving so that he could spend eternity with his followers, including them.

Thomas was one of the clueless. He told Jesus, "We don't know the way you are going; we don't know *where* you are going!" Jesus responded with the core truth. Jesus is the way. As assuredly as they knew Jesus, they knew the way to where he was going, for Jesus himself was the way. Jesus was going to be with the Father, and Jesus was the way for his followers to be with the Father.

Jesus doesn't leave anyone behind or alone. Jesus is coming again. That was his whole point behind his life and death.

Father, I await the coming of the Lord. Come quickly, Lord Jesus. Amen.

OCTOBER 4

If you had known me, you would have known my Father also. From now on you do know him and have seen him. Philip said to him, "Lord, show us the Father, and it is enough for us." Jesus said to him, "Have I been with you so long, and you still do not know me, Philip? Whoever has seen me has seen the Father. How can you say, 'Show us the Father'?" (Jn. 14:7–9)

"I want to see God!" That isn't a new plea. It is as old as humanity, save for Adam right after his sin! He did *not* want to see God, and even hid from him. The atheist and agnostic cry, "Show me God, if he is real." But they are not alone. Even Moses, who certainly believed in God, asked God to show himself. God responded that no man could see his face and live, instead passing his glory before Moses. But even there, Moses could only see the back of God's glory, and not the full glory head on (Ex. 33:19*ff*).

Philip asked Jesus to do what Moses had been unsuccessful at achieving. Philip wanted Jesus to show the apostles God the Father. In Philip's language, "You do that for us, Jesus, and we will be complete! That will be enough!"

I wonder if Jesus chuckled, at least under his breath, as he responded to Philip and the other apostles. John noted Jesus saying, in effect, "Really??? After all the time we've spent together, you still don't get it? When you see me, you see the Father."

In Colossians 1:15, Paul wrote of Jesus as the *eikōn* of the invisible God (spelled in Greek εἰκών, but pronounced like the English word derived from the Greek word "icon"). When one saw Jesus, one saw God. But many who saw Jesus, never saw God. The simple truth is that eyesight does not open the heart to truth. Seeing is not always believing. Paul explained to the Corinthians that "the god of this world has blinded the minds of the unbelievers, to keep them from seeing the light of the gospel of the glory of Christ, who is the image of God" (2 Cor. 4:4).

I would love to see God, but not in some desperate effort to validate his existence. Nor do I want to see him so that I can have bragging rights of having seen that which other people long to see. My desire to see God is rooted in a desire to become more like him. I want to sing his praises more readily. I want to be able to tell the world about his nature and goodness.

With those as my reasons for wanting to see God, I return to today's passage. I need to see Jesus! I need to spend time in the gospels and time thinking about Jesus' actions, teachings, and prayers. As I do this, I am seeing God. I will grow more into his nature. I will have greater praise of his greatness. I have more to tell the world of God.

Father, show me Jesus, revealing yourself to me in the process. In Jesus' name, amen.

OCTOBER 5

Truly, truly, I say to you, whoever believes in me will also do the works that I do; and greater works than these will he do, because I am going to the Father. (Jn. 14:12)

Today's passage troubled me for a good bit of my life. It is one of those passages I would read quickly moving on to something else without wanting to think about it too long. That was my loss!

The word I found most troubling was "greater." The idea that those who truly believe in Jesus would do greater things than he did was a stumper for me that made me question my personal faith and level of commitment. After all, Jesus healed the blind; I haven't. Jesus gave hearing to the deaf; I haven't. Jesus cast out demons; I haven't. Jesus healed the sick; I haven't. Jesus walked on water; I sink in every swimming pool. Jesus commanded the weather; I check the weather. Jesus resurrected the dead; I mourn the dead. Jesus dies for the sins of humanity; I am one of those sinners. Greater? I couldn't see it.

Then one day, my lawyer brain kicked into gear. I was getting someone ready to testify in court and was asking certain questions to see how the witness would answer. I asked about whether something involved a "great bit of effort," and the witness had me define "great." The witness was right. What is or isn't "great" depends on who is speaking.

I really don't think that the greatest deeds we can do are to give sight to the blind. That is a good and worthy deed, without a doubt. My nephew Jack is an eye doctor, and he is doing God's work. But Jesus spoke about two things: (1) his followers doing as he did, and (2) his followers doing even greater things. I think the best understanding of this is found in the chapters and verses of the book of Acts, the earliest church history book.

In Acts, one reads of the apostles healing the sick and even raising the dead, all in Jesus' name. But that is Jesus' first point. The second point is the greater issue. That is also found in Acts. Through the power of the Holy Spirit, God used the apostles and others to bring people to saving faith in the death, burial, and resurrection of Christ. This is a greater thing that Jesus hadn't yet done in his incarnation, for the underlying work on which salvation is based had yet to be done. Jesus had to go to the cross, be buried in the grave, and experience the resurrection before his followers could believe in that.

This passage forces me to refocus my life and vision. Healing the sick is marvelous and a great achievement in God's name. But the greater thing is bringing people to Jesus!

Father, give me a heart for the lost. Help me to see them and influence them for Jesus, by my words as well as my love and actions. May your Spirit use me to reach others in Jesus, amen.

OCTOBER 6

Whatever you ask in my name, this I will do, that the Father may be glorified in the Son. If you ask me anything in my name, I will do it. (Jn. 14:13–14)

Hardly a day goes by that I don't have to fill in one form or another with my name. In school, I had to put my name in the heading atop each written assignment. When I first started practicing law, the firm where I practiced expected the attorneys to use their middle initial in letters. Since I went by my middle name ("Mark") instead the firm used my first initial, "W." for "William." For the longest time in legal circles I was known as "W. Mark Lanier."

One's name in twenty-first-century American life typically means one's label, a legal identifier that is on a birth certificate, driver's license, and passport. If one doesn't like their name, for a filing fee, one can go to the courthouse and get a new one. It is just a label, after all.

That was not the case in biblical times. The Greek word for "name" (*onoma*, ὄνομα) and the Hebrew word for name (*shem*, שֵׁם) both stand for more than a person's label. *Onoma/shem* not only referred to a label but also to one's character. This word was a statement of who a person truly was and what that person had done. It reflected a resume of one's life. If life events demonstrated that one had a different reputation or character than one's name, the name was changed! (See "Jacob" becoming "Israel" in Genesis 32:28.)

When Jesus instructed his apostles to ask in his name, Jesus wasn't simply saying, "pronounce my name as if it is a magical formula so you get what you want." Jesus was saying, when I seek God's intervention, I should do so based upon the character and work of Jesus, not my own. It is why my prayers are offered in Jesus' name, not my own.

Part and parcel of asking in Jesus' name, is asking in line with his priorities and desires. I don't invoke his character to help me get something that isn't in his will. His character and power are invoked for the things he desires. I am to seek his help in matters that meet his agenda, his priorities, his mission. That is integral to asking in his name.

Within this framework, Jesus taught that asking in his name would achieve the aims of Jesus. As I ask, I will receive. I need to be asking in Jesus' name. If I don't receive as I ask, I can rest assured that it wasn't in the will of Jesus. As I seek to ask, pray, and live in Jesus' name, that also means that I am at peace when I don't receive or see that which is outside his will. This can radicalize faith and prayer!

Father, in Jesus' name, I ask your will in my life today. Help me to demonstrate your love to a lost world and woo people to you. Help me to demonstrate forgiveness and teach people your love. Give me your grace to live under your authority, amen.

OCTOBER 7

If you love me, you will keep my commandments. (Jn. 14:15)

Love is such a misused and misunderstood word. Think about it. Here are some ways I have used the word in just the last month: I love my car. I love my wife. I love my daughters. I love my son. I love their spouses. I love my grandchildren. I love chess. I love apple pie and pizza. I love certain shows. I love my dog. But I have a much different feeling toward my dog than I do my wife!

With this overused, if not ambiguous value of "love," I read today's passage. Jesus is getting ready to be arrested, tried, convicted, and killed. He is giving his last colloquy to his twelve assembled closest disciples. Jesus tells them that their love for him will be shown by their behavior.

The writer of the passage is the apostle John. He was present when Jesus declared this important truth. Writing in Greek, John had a number of words for "love" available to use. John chose the verb *agapao* (ἀγαπάω), from which comes the commonly known noun *agape*. This verb includes the idea of a warm caring or cherishing for another. But additionally, it contains the idea of practicing or expressing one's love. It is the verb one would use if one wanted to talk about how to prove one's love.

Jesus knew that lip service is easy and transient. I can say I love. That is easy. The proof, however, comes in how I live. Similarly, while I can say I love, circumstances and time could change my heart, if I am only speaking of how I feel.

The type of love of which Jesus spoke was a decision love. This doesn't minimize the affection and caring aspect of the love, but it puts primary focus on deciding to show love and care. This goes hand in hand with the spiritual truth Jesus taught his followers about the human heart following the human mind and its decisions. Jesus said that wherever one invested their time, energy, service, and resources (one's "treasure") is where one will find their heart.

I find if I don't feel the love I'd like toward another, my best solution is to work on this *agapao* love Jesus called out. I need to decide and act on doing best for others. Jesus has room to talk on this point. He gave this instruction as he was on the brink of *doing* the greatest act of love he could.

So where does this leave me today? Is my lip service about loving God, or is it real? My actions will show the truth.

Father, thank you for your love. I pray that I will see it, receive it, appreciate it, and model it for those around me. May my life show my love to you. In Jesus, amen.

OCTOBER 8

And I will ask the Father, and he will give you another Helper, to be with you forever, even the Spirit of truth, whom the world cannot receive, because it neither sees him nor knows him. You know him, for he dwells with you and will be in you. (Jn. 14:16–17)

On August 6, 1965, the Beatles released their fifth album, *Help!*. One of the singles, also entitled "Help!," reportedly was one of John Lennon's most "honest" songs; one that grew out of his depressed feelings and stress handling the fame of being a Beatle. His lyrics are blunt and to the point, "Help, I need somebody; Help, not just any body; help, you know I need someone—HELP!"

Jesus knew he was about to depart from his physical life on earth. Once he left, the warm intimate fellowship of the band of apostles would be missing its leader. Jesus promised that they would not be bereft, however. He would ask the Father to send *another* helper. This means someone who would fill the role Jesus had been filling in their lives.

The word "helper" is an interesting one that has caused some challenges to translators. The Greek word *parakletos* (παράκλητος) is a compound word for "one called alongside." It was used for an advocate, a lawyer, a mediator, an intercessor, a helper, and sometimes even an adviser. Early English translators often used the word "comforter," but that doesn't quite grasp the idea of helping one's cause, implying instead that this one would bring one comfort. Now one might get comfort knowing one is arguing on their behalf, but the core idea in the word used is one who is bringing help or aid.

Who would this coming Helper be? Another like Christ! Jesus says, "another" because Jesus himself has been the constant help, aid, guidance, and counsel for the apostles. Jesus was leaving in physical form but was not leaving his followers to go it alone. The Helper was no less than God's Holy Spirit. The Spirit of God makes his earliest debut in the first chapter of the Bible, where he was present at creation and moved over the surface of the deep.

God's Spirit was present in the midst of the apostles, for Jesus was full of God's Spirit. Even as Jesus was in their midst, helping them in life and understanding, so the Spirit in Christ had been helping them as well. The apostles didn't realize it, but they "knew" the Spirit as they knew Christ. The promise of Jesus, however, was that the Spirit would come as Helper and be *in* the believer. This indwelling Spirit would be able to help in ways no outside person can.

John Lennon needed help. We all do. God wants to be our help.

Father, I welcome your helping presence in my life, your Holy Spirit. In Jesus, amen.

OCTOBER 9

I will not leave you as orphans; I will come to you. (Jn. 14:18)

Way back in the 1970s a television show called *Welcome Back Kotter* aired for four seasons. The show shot John Travolta to fame and featured a number of talented actors. One was Ron Palillo, who played the role of Arnold Horshack. Horshack was famous for raising his hand in class (the sitcom was built around a high school classroom), while shouting "Ooh Ooh Ooh!!!" Horshack reminds me of the apostle John writing his gospel.

John wrote in Greek, which has a word "*ou*" (οὐ), pronounced just like Horshack's exclamation when raising his hand. John used *ou* more than any other gospel writer, basically as much as Luke and Mark put together!

Ou is a word that means a negative. It can be "no" or "not" or something similar. In today's passage, John uses ou as Jesus says, "I will *not* leave you as orphans." (In this case, the ou has a -k at the end here because the next word starts with a vowel. . . . Sorry, Horshack!) As John used *ou* repeatedly, he often used the negative to introduce an important positive statement, as he has above. Those times John employs that technique serve as the devotional thoughts today:

Not . . .	*But . . .*
Jn. 3:17 For God did not [ou] send his Son into the world to condemn the world . . .	But in order that the world might be saved through him.
Jn. 3:36 Whoever believes in the Son has eternal life; whoever does not obey the Son shall not [ou] see life . . .	But the wrath of God remains on him.
Jn. 4:14 Whoever drinks of the water that I will give him will never [ou] be thirsty again . . .	The water that I will give him will become in him a spring of water welling up to eternal life.
Jn. 8:12 And Jesus spoke to them saying, "I am the light of the world. Whoever follows me shall not [ou] walk in darkness . . ."	But will have the light of life.

Horshack used his pleas to get attention to what he had to say. John did the same!

Father, may I embrace your positives and learn from your negatives. In Jesus, amen.

OCTOBER 10

I will not leave you as orphans; I will come to you. Yet a little while and the world will see me no more, but you will see me. Because I live, you also will live. In that day you will know that I am in my Father, and you in me, and I in you. (Jn. 14:18–20)

The apostle Paul wrote most of the New Testament, if you are counting books, not words. He preached Christ crucified to the exclusion of everything else (1 Cor. 2:2). Yet Paul never spoke of a dead Jesus. Jesus was crucified, but Jesus was still alive. That was the importance of the resurrection. Jesus is no longer dead.

Jesus explained it in today's passage. In its larger context, Jesus is in Jerusalem. He is having a last dinner with his chosen twelve, his closest followers. They have left their jobs, sculpting their lives around Jesus for the last three years. In their minds, Jesus was their future, but not a dead Jesus. They thought that Jesus was going to be physically present as he brought the new kingdom of God to Israel. With that would come release from Roman occupation. Jesus would be on an earthly throne, and they would be in the important positions overseeing things as Jesus directed. One of the twelve, Judas Iscariot, had already begun deciding this wasn't going to be. He somehow decided they were on a fool's errand, and he was none too happy about it. He was getting ready to cash out.

Jesus was explaining things a bit more fully, but mission blindness had already set in. His disciples didn't understand what Jesus was saying until after the huge pending events. Even after the resurrection, they needed proof of Jesus, as well as an explanation of what God was about. Nevertheless, Jesus was setting out important truths, knowing in time they would come to understand.

Jesus wanted to assure them that even after his resurrection and ascension, although they wouldn't physically be seeing Jesus, they would see him. Jesus would be in them. In the same way that Jesus was in the Father, even though he was physically on earth, so they would be physically on earth, yet have Jesus in them.

This is my faith. Jesus is not dead. He died, was buried, but then was resurrected. He ascended to the Father where he reigns in victory, and he promises to come again. Until that day, however, Jesus resides in me. He guides me; he teaches me; he encourages me; he is ever present. When I take my eyes off him, when I fail to take quiet time to nourish my relationship with him, when I live simply by sight, and not by faith, I lose track of him, but he never loses track of me. I come back and he is there. I am glad I am not alone. I need Jesus in my life, every day and every hour.

Father, I need the presence of Jesus right now. Help me to know his presence. Strengthen my faith and awareness. I am nothing without you. In dear Jesus I pray, amen.

OCTOBER 11

Abide in me, and I in you. As the branch cannot bear fruit by itself, unless it abides in the vine, neither can you, unless you abide in me. (Jn. 15:4)

When my son was little, I had the joy and honor of coaching his basketball teams for about eight years. The boys seemed to automatically know they had to get the basketball in the basket. They were doing that at home. But playing defense was a whole different matter. Defense must be taught. They learned defensive posture, position, and more. But when it was all put together, the most important thing they learned was to stick to whomever they were covering. I reminded them how glue worked and wanted them to stick to their opposing player like glue.

If I was using a Greek word, I might have used the one in today's passage. The word translated as "abide" (*meno*, μένω) conveys the idea of staying, remaining, and persisting with Jesus. Sticking to Jesus like glue! The assurance Jesus gives is that abiding in him will produce fruit. This brings up two important considerations: How do I abide in Jesus? What is the fruit produced?

One can abide in Jesus by making him the center of one's life. Here is what that means practically. When you awaken, you thank him for your day. You take time to pray through your day, acknowledging what lies ahead, and asking his presence to aid and help you. You spend some time in his word, prayerfully asking him to speak to you in the process. I even like to journal what I am learning. Then as you go through the day, you evaluate and try to make your decisions as if Jesus is on your shoulder. In fact, Jesus is present, and that is his promise. As we abide in him, he abides in us.

The fruit this produces is tasty and nourishing. In our day, most of us get our fruit from a grocery store, but Christ is talking about fruit that comes straight from the vine or tree. This is the tastiest and freshest. As we abide in Christ and he in us, we get some of the sweetest things life can offer. We get peace in the midst of turmoil. We get purpose in place of bewilderment. We get comfort in our grieving. We get strength in times of weakness. We get courage in the face of fear. We get joy replacing sorrow. We get light conquering darkness. All this and more comes from abiding with Jesus.

There is an old hymn we sang growing up, "Abide with Me." The lyrics include, "Swift to its close ebbs out life's little day; Earth's joys grow dim, its glories pass away. Change and decay in all around I see; O Thou who changest not, abide with me. I fear no foe, with Thee at hand to bless. Ills have no weight, and tears no bitterness. Where is death's sting? Where, grave, thy victory? I triumph still, if Thou abide with me." This is where I want to stay—abiding in Jesus.

Father, I abide with you. I need you. Thank you for your love. In Jesus, amen.

OCTOBER 12

As the Father has loved me, so have I loved you. Abide in my love. (Jn. 15:9)

Growing up, and often still today, my kids and I have had an ongoing debate of sorts. When leaving, one of us would be first to say, "I love you!" Most people answer that with, "I love you too!" but not me or the kids. If they said, "I love you!" I would answer, "I love you more!" They would then reply, "I love you most!" To which I would respond, "I love you more most." And on it would go.

I am not sure love has a meter that allows one to say who loves one more or less. But I do know one thing. God has the greatest love of all.

Realizing that, break down today's passage. God exists in a Trinity or as a "three-ness" within the Godhead. The Father, Son, and Holy Spirit doubtlessly have infinite love for each other within that Godhead. What makes this remarkable is that when the Son wants to put into words how he loves us, he does so by comparing it to the love within the Godhead; now that is amazing.

Jesus speaks plainly that he loves you and me just as the Father loves the Son. This should transform our day. We can watch the love of the Father and Son and embrace what it means for God's love for us. Consider the intimacy of the Father and Son, this closeness seen in the united purpose they shared. This united purpose and intimacy is what Jesus seeks for us. Or think about how the Father lived his will out through the Son. In the same way, Jesus seeks to live his will out through us. Jesus walked through temptation, and God walked with him. So God does with us as we experience temptation. God the Father was the power behind the Son's miracles, and so Jesus seeks to empower us.

This overwhelming love that God has for his children should not be missed. Nor should it be missed how this love should stir up his children in a loving response. When Scripture says, "We love because he first loved us" (1 Jn. 4:19), it is speaking of the way we learn love and the proper response to the love of Christ.

Paul added that "the love of Christ controls us" (2 Cor. 5:14), emphasizing that as we learn and understand the overwhelming love of Jesus, it affects the way we act and behave.

I am often amazed at God's amazing love. Sometimes I unconsciously think God "tolerates" me more so than loves me. This is a trick of the human mind. After all, God's love is much more than I can understand.

Father, your love stuns me. May I grow in my responding love to you. In Jesus, amen.

OCTOBER 13

Do you not say, "There are yet four months, then comes the harvest"? Look, I tell you, lift up your eyes, and see that the fields are white for harvest. Already the one who reaps is receiving wages and gathering fruit for eternal life, so that sower and reaper may rejoice together. For here the saying holds true, "One sows and another reaps." (Jn. 4:35–37)

Courtroom work can be fulfilling and a lot of fun. When a jury returns a verdict, giving justice to the litigants, it is exhilarating. The verdict is often the culmination of years of work. Some of my cases have taken over ten years to meet resolution. The work before the first day of trial can involve more time than you can imagine.

Contrast that to mowing the lawn. When you get a lawn mower and cut a row of grass, you can stop, look back, and see what you've accomplished. I find a sense of satisfaction in starting and finishing a task. But tasks don't always work out that way.

In today's passage, Jesus is explaining to his disciples that the time was ripe for Jesus and the kingdom of God to reap a harvest of new followers. Jesus had had an encounter with a Samaritan woman while his disciples were off buying some lunch. The disciples were in the dark about what Jesus had been up to. The disciples were not involved in the work of bringing the woman to faith (or those that were soon to follow her). Jesus used the lunch hour and the recent food bought by the disciples in a farming analogy appropriate for the season and surroundings. Jesus explained that sometimes the one who plants the seeds is not the one who harvests them. The chore for the disciples is to do the work at hand, not to worry or fret over the larger story line of history.

I need this passage in my life. I know people who are extremely important to me that don't know God, and they need to. I know things that God needs accomplished in this world. I try to get these things done, I try to reach the lost for God, but too often I am not successful. These verses today are the ones I need.

God has a big scheme. All of history is a snapshot to God. He sees tomorrow as easily as yesterday. He has tools that exceed my greatest comprehension. God's plans surpass my ability to fathom. My biggest dreams can't touch what he will do.

I am left like the disciples. My job isn't to decide where to sow and reap. My task is relatively simple. I am to do the tasks God sets before me and trust him with the consequences. I can't be God's vessel to bring the gospel to everyone. For some, I may only plant seeds. Then I may get to be the harvester for others where I was not involved before. This is God's big plan, not mine. As a trial lawyer, I should understand this, but I still need reminding!

Lord, use me in your plan to bring your kingdom to those around me. In Jesus, amen.

You did not choose me, but I chose you and appointed you that you should go and bear fruit and that your fruit should abide, so that whatever you ask the Father in my name, he may give it to you. (Jn. 15:16)

I do love a well-set buffet. Not only does the food come fast but I also love that I can choose what I want and in what proportions. Yes, I tend to do dessert first, but I try to get all the basic food groups. Sort of.

Choice is a big thing in America. We choose our leaders, choose our careers, choose our mates, choose where we live, what we drive, and so forth. We choose the names of our children. Choice is a preference that is expressed, which brings us to today's passage.

Jesus was reminding his disciples that he had chosen them. Jesus was walking along the way when he came across some fishermen and told them to follow him. Jesus found the tax collector and bade him to leave what he was doing and follow Jesus. Nathaniel was brought to Jesus, but Jesus was the one who asked him to follow. The disciples being reminded of this must have felt confirmed and special. To be chosen by Jesus is no small thing. Yet that is the important part of this passage to you and me.

Jesus selected you! Jesus selected me. You might say, "Well, in reality I selected Jesus. I asked him into my heart. I asked him to be Lord of my life." Yes, that is true, but he was the one who came to your door knocking. He was the one who first chose you. We chose Jesus in the same way his original apostles did. They were chosen by Jesus and responded to his choice, making it their own.

How does being chosen by Jesus make my life different today? First of all, I feel confirmed and special. Jesus didn't choose me because I was the superstar for his basketball team. This wasn't a playground selection of one team member over another based on talent and skill. Jesus chose me in love with the promise to make me a superstar. This wouldn't make me a superstar in the world's eyes, but one in God's eyes. It makes me a forgiven child of the King. He takes my talents and gifts (or lack thereof!) and uses me to produce fruit for his kingdom.

The key for me is to abide in him. I am to stay with my Jesus. I am to seek his heart, do his will, and follow his path. As I do so, I am assured God will bear fruit in me, do the very things he seeks to do, and do them through me. That is an amazing feat.

Buffets are nice. Choice is nice. But it's even nicer being chosen. God has chosen me to be his hands and voice today. I want to do it right!

Father, may my life be lived for you today. Thank you for choosing me. In Jesus, amen.

But when the Helper comes, whom I will send to you from the Father, the Spirit of truth, who proceeds from the Father, he will bear witness about me. And you also will bear witness, because you have been with me from the beginning. (Jn. 15:26–27)

Each day in this devotional I begin with a Scripture from the words, teachings, or life of Jesus. These words weren't written by Jesus, nor were they simply memories of his followers. Scripture is "Scripture" as opposed to an ordinary biography because they are first and foremost works of the Holy Spirit. This was Jesus' point in today's passage.

Jesus assured his apostles that they had a future calling. They were to bear witness to Jesus. But this wasn't something they would do on their own. It was really the work of the Holy Spirit, and the Spirit would be using the apostles. This was a way in which God would be securing for the ages the life and teachings of Jesus.

This makes a lot of sense in light of certain fundamental truths about you and me. First of all, we are hardwired for language. Deep in the structures of the human mind is an ability to communicate. Even for those few who are mute, the ability to communicate is built into their brains. Helen Keller (1880-1968) could neither see nor hear, yet she went on to earn a B.A. degree from Radcliffe College at Harvard University. Like all people, she was hard-wired to communicate.

Take the truth of our innate communication ability and consider that God knows it, being the creator and architect of this universe and its inhabitants, and it isn't surprising God would communicate to the ages through words. Add to this another fundamental truth. God loves us and seeks a relationship with us.

As God loves us, as he seeks a close relationship with us, it should come as no surprise he would use words to communicate that love. Those words are "Scripture." God has ensured that we would have words of comfort as needed. We have instructions to help us navigate life. We have stories of his mighty works to inspire and give us confidence. We have examples to demonstrate his love. God has ensured for his people food for each day and all circumstances.

This makes it so important to me to spend time each day chewing on those words that have come from his Holy Spirit, through the pens (quills?) of his chosen apostles. These are words of life. These are words that transform you and me. This is the work of God himself.

Father, thank you for your words. I need your encouragement, inspiration, support, direction, and love. I praise you as a providing God. In Jesus' name, amen.

OCTOBER 16

When the Spirit of truth comes, he will guide you into all the truth, for he will not speak on his own authority, but whatever he hears he will speak, and he will declare to you the things that are to come. He will glorify me, for he will take what is mine and declare it to you. (Jn. 16:13–14)

Have you been hodegeo'ed today? Oh, you're thinking you just found another typo in this devotional. You're thinking "Hodegeo isn't a word!" Yes, I am notorious for typos, but this is no typo. I am just using the English spelling of an important Greek word—ὁδηγέω. Perhaps I should give you the English translation found in today's passage. It is "guide."

Jesus sent the Holy Spirit to *hodegeo* his people. This speaks to how God's Spirit works in us. Now it isn't the way I would necessarily pick for God to work. After all, I would love to have God speak audibly to me, or at least e-mail/text me, especially to tell me what to do on big important decisions. Yet that isn't how God has chosen to be with me. Something deeper is at work here.

God gave you and me the ability to choose. We have limits to our choices, but we are thinking people, not puppets. When God made Adam, he gave Adam the responsibility of giving names to all the animals; but God didn't tell Adam what to name them. Genesis 2:19 says, "And whatever the man called every living creature, that was its name." God works with us as a guide. Our role is to follow his lead.

If one were to look up *hodegeo* in a lexicon (a Greek/English dictionary) the key word would be "assist." As a leader or guide, the verb expresses one assisting another in reaching a desired destination, or assisting another in acquiring information or knowledge. This is what the Holy Spirit does for us. The Holy Spirit assists us getting where we need to go, learning what we need to learn, and knowing what we need to know.

What does this mean for me practically? If I am to live by the Spirit, to use Paul's terminology from Galatians 5:25, how do I do that? A good starting point is found in the teachings of Scripture. The Scriptures are a product of the Spirit. So as we read and follow these teachings, we follow the Spirit. Beyond that, there is still a need to be still and quiet, to prayerfully consider situations and discern God's will thoughtfully.

This is the role of humans in the process. God teaches us to hear his voice, discern what he says, and make wise choices. This includes prayerfully living in his Scriptures, asking him for his guidance. We can be assured he will answer those prayers.

Father, purify my heart to discern your will. Help me discern your Spirit. In him, amen.

OCTOBER 17

I have said these things to you, that in me you may have peace. In the world you will have
tribulation. But take heart; I have overcome the world. (Jn. 16:33)

This is a tough world. Admittedly, "tough" is relative, and I readily
admit that even my worst days are sunnier than the existence of many
others. I have food, I have relative safety, I have family and friends. Yet
even with all these blessings, everyone experiences times of struggle and
challenge. In those times, Jesus' words in today's passage are especially
meaningful to me.

A host of things can and do go wrong. We find a world of broken
health, with sickness, disease, and injuries all too frequent. We know broken relationships, some seemingly beyond repair. We experience anger and
hurt. We struggle with personal failure, sometimes on an epic scale. We
worry about things we can't control. We feel the pressure of expectations.
Our brains don't always function as we need them to. Our resources seem
to dissolve as our finances deplete. I could write on and on, but you get the
idea. So did Jesus!

In today's passage, Jesus spoke to the many issues that would confront
his team in their coming days. Having explained a number of problems,
Jesus summarizes that they would have tribulation in the world. *Thlipsis*
(θλῖφις) is translated as "tribulation" but could just as easily be translated
as "distress," "affliction," "trouble," or "turmoil." Jesus knew firsthand the
human experience. But Jesus isn't all doom and gloom over what they were
going to experience.

Jesus gave the apostles the answer to their coming tribulation. Jesus is
overcoming the world. Jesus never came just to die. Jesus came to die and
be resurrected! Jesus sets aright creation. Jesus becomes the new Adam,
ushering in a new age. The followers of Jesus are joining in his victory. In a
real sense, we know the end of the story and the victory we have.

In Jesus, the overcomer, everyone can face each struggle with confidence that Jesus is at work. Jesus can bring health, either in this life, or by
ushering one into the life to come. Jesus can repair any relationship, and
promises that one day, even the lion and lamb will lie together in peace.
Jesus takes hurt and teaches people to forgive and heal. Jesus takes personal
failure and redeems it for his good purposes. Jesus is in control even when
we aren't. Jesus empowers us to achieve far beyond our own abilities. Jesus
is our intercessor, our defender, and our source for all good things.

We can take heart knowing the resurrected Jesus and his work for us.
Father, praise Jesus, my overcomer! May I live in his peace! In him I pray, amen.

And when he got into the boat, his disciples followed him. And behold, there arose a great storm on the sea, so that the boat was being swamped by the waves; but he was asleep. And they went and woke him, saying, "Save us, Lord; we are perishing." And he said to them, "Why are you afraid, O you of little faith?" Then he rose and rebuked the winds and the sea, and there was a great calm. And the men marveled, saying, "What sort of man is this, that even winds and sea obey him?" (Mt. 8:23–27)

Do you know the word "querulist"? It is a rare word used a bit more in England than the United States, but it refers to someone who complains a lot. Querulist is not easy to say, and complainers are not easy to be around! At times, I have been querulent, but I hope to never be a querulist!

Today's passage has the apostles not only complaining, but also somewhat panicked! They were in a boat crossing the Sea of Galilee and feared the boat was going to be swamped. Waves were coming over the boat's sides, and faster than the experienced fishermen could bail water out, it was coming in. Jesus wasn't helping the bailing effort. He was fast asleep after a grueling day of being "on" for everyone, healing, preaching, explaining, and so forth. The cry "save us" was a cry to help bail water, or do anything else Jesus could do to aid the effort. They never dreamed Jesus would just rebuke the winds and waves, just as he rebuked demons in the earlier chapter. After Jesus rebuked the winds, the waves stopped, and calmness was on the face of the lake. This story isn't only an homage to the power of the Messiah, but it also speaks metaphorically to my life.

Bethel Music took a well-known hymn and added a modern set of verses and melody to the older chorus and produced a twenty-first-century version of the song "It Is Well." The genesis of the original by Horatio Spafford is well known. He was a Chicago lawyer in the 1800s who sent his family on to England, planning to follow them shortly. His wife and children died in the crossing when the ship sunk. He wrote verses reminding the singer and listener that "when sorrows like sea billows role," he had learned to say, "It is well with my soul."

Then Bethel added some marvelous verses including, "Grander earth has quaked before; Moved by the sound of His voice. Seas that are shaken and stirred; Can be calmed and broken for my regard. Through it all . . . my eyes are on You. Through it all . . . It is well . . . Far be it for me to not believe; Even when my eyes can't see. And this mountain that's in front of me, Will be thrown into the midst of the sea . . . So let go my soul and trust in Him. The waves and wind still know His name." I don't need to worry or complain. The waves and winds still know his name; therefore, it is well with my soul.

Father, I need you to calm the waves and winds in life. I need you to calm the waves and winds in my heart. I need you. In Jesus' name, amen.

OCTOBER 19

I do not ask for these only, but also for those who will believe in me through their word, that they may all be one, just as you, Father, are in me, and I in you, that they also may be in us, so that the world may believe that you have sent me. (Jn. 17:20–21)

Have you ever had the conversation, "If you could dine with anyone throughout history, whom would you choose?" I have been in that conversation a lot, and typically so many people pick Jesus that you almost have to insert a rule, "You are not allowed to pick Jesus!" The idea of being able to visit with Jesus over dinner is beyond incredible.

Imagine having Jesus look into your eyes. How would one sense his immense love and caring? How would his kindness manifest itself? Heavens, I'd just like to see what he ate!

I think some of this is why I love today's passage so much. I cannot travel back in time to be with Jesus during his incarnation. But in today's passage, I see that Jesus already had me in mind. Look carefully at the passage in its context. Jesus is praying as part of his all-night vigil in the Garden of Gethsemane. From here he gets betrayed by Judas' kiss, and the cataclysmic events culminating in the crucifixion begin. Part of what was going through Jesus' mind during this time was you and me.

Jesus prays not only for his followers but also for "those who will believe in me through their word." These words of the apostles became Scripture. These are the words that we read in our Bibles. These words bring about conversion. These words grow us in the Lord. Jesus is praying for us.

Needless to say, that the Lord Jesus said a prayer for you and me, even though it was somewhat global, is extremely touching to me. It makes me want to take seriously what Jesus sought for me from God the Father. Jesus asked the Father that we (me and other believers) would be united in purpose and fellowship.

We are fulfilling Jesus' prayerful wish that we don't let the divisions of humanity work the same in our churches. One culture shouldn't set itself against another. One socioeconomic group shouldn't be deemed more or less valuable than another. The educated and uneducated should bind together. Churches should be true melting pots of unity in the midst of diversity.

I can't have dinner with the physical Jesus today, but I can still help meet his prayerful concerns for me. Jesus prayed for me. I should not take that lightly.

Father, thank you for the love and concerns of Jesus expressed in prayers for me. Give me wisdom and strength to live responsive to his prayers! In Jesus' name, amen.

So they watched him and sent spies, who pretended to be sincere, that they might catch him in something he said, so as to deliver him up to the authority and jurisdiction of the governor. So they asked him, "Teacher, we know that you speak and teach rightly, and show no partiality, but truly teach the way of God. Is it lawful for us to give tribute to Caesar, or not?" But he perceived their craftiness, and said to them, "Show me a denarius. Whose likeness and inscription does it have?" They said, "Caesar's." He said to them, "Then render to Caesar the things that are Caesar's, and to God the things that are God's." And they were not able in the presence of the people to catch him in what he said, but marveling at his answer they became silent. (Lk. 20:20–26)

I love a good spy novel. I have read plenty of them. But I have to be careful. After reading too much, I tend to start watching my rearview mirror when I drive. I want to make sure I am not being followed! It's something spies do. It is kind of creepy to think of those who actually have to live thinking they are being targeted by spies. It makes today's passage a bit weird.

The passage comes on the heels of Jesus teaching through a parable that God will destroy the temple leaders in the rise of Jesus as king in God's kingdom. Jesus will be the stone the builders rejected who will become the cornerstone in God's reign. Jesus added that those who reject the stone will be crushed by it. This sent the leaders into a frenzy. They sent spies to infiltrate Jesus' camp and catch him teaching something that could get him arrested. (The spies needed to be plural because the testimony of one man could not carry a conviction. They needed two witnesses or more.)

The spies pretended to be sincere seekers, offering flattery to Jesus to make him think they were on his side. Lying through their teeth, the spies said, "We know that you speak and teach rightly . . . you truly teach the word of God." Then came the set up, "Under the Torah, should we give tribute to Caesar?" This was a loaded problem. Tribute to Caesar could denote appreciation of Caesar as a god, something the Torah (the law of Moses) prohibited. In that event, it was wrong. Others saw it simply as a tax, and found it outside the Torah's prohibition. Where did Jesus land on this? Jesus sidestepped it in a way that neither watered down the Torah nor ran afoul of Roman law. Jesus asked for a tax coin and used the picture of Caesar to say, "Give Caesar what is his, but give God what is God's." The spies got nowhere.

Jesus gave a lesson to the spies and to me as well. The Christian walk isn't a tricky thing. It is fairly simple. We are to give ourselves to God. Christianity isn't a list of do's and don'ts. God wants me. God came for me. I am to give myself to God. Jesus taught the spies this truth, but they were looking for something else and missed it.

Father, I don't want to miss your truth. I give you all I am. In Jesus, amen.

OCTOBER 21

And in the hearing of all the people he said to his disciples, "Beware of the scribes, who like to walk around in long robes, and love greetings in the marketplaces and the best seats in the synagogues and the places of honor at feasts, who devour widows' houses and for a pretense make long prayers. They will receive the greater condemnation." Jesus looked up and saw the rich putting their gifts into the offering box, and he saw a poor widow put in two small copper coins. And he said, "Truly, I tell you, this poor widow has put in more than all of them. For they all contributed out of their abundance, but she out of her poverty put in all she had to live on." (Lk. 20:45–21:4)

I had an expert testifying in a case once, and in cross-examination, the opposing lawyer said, "You are saying ABC, but earlier in another case you said XYZ, true?" My witness said, "You are taking that out of context." The lawyer repeated with emphasis, "Sir, today you said ABC, but before you said XYZ, *is that true?*" My witness said, you have not given my whole statement. It is like quoting me for saying, "It was a beautiful day . . . ," but leaving out the rest of my sentence, " . . . until the tornado hit." My witness was right. Everything belongs in context.

So with today's passage, we miss something huge if we just read about Jesus commenting on the widow giving her two small copper coins. I have seen this passage wrongly used to get poor people to give their last few cents into someone's coffers. That isn't the passage at all, however. Jesus set up two opposing groups here. The first were religious specialists who like the pomp and circumstance of their position. They were the admired ones, the ones in power who got the primo seats and attention. They gave long prayers to impress those listening. (God doesn't answer prayers based on word count.) What's more, they "devour widows' houses" when God teaches us to take care of widows and orphans.

In contrast to those scribes, Jesus points out the poor widow who put her last two coins in the offering box. In this passage, this isn't Jesus holding her up as a model to teach people to put all their money into his coffers. Rather Jesus is illustrating the truth of what he already said, that the scribes were upholding a system that abused the poor, rather than assist them. This poor widow had put in all she had, while the scribes and rich had more than they needed.

Jesus came to preach good news to the poor. He came to help meet their needs, not set up a system to further impoverish them. God gives riches to people to use for God's purposes, including helping those in need. The scribes could have taken some of the time they were investing in long, showy prayers and used it better to help those in need. I have some work to do to better get the heart of Jesus.

Father, please open my eyes and heart to helping those in need. In Jesus, amen.

OCTOBER 22

Then Satan entered into Judas called Iscariot, who was of the number of the twelve. He went away and conferred with the chief priests and officers how he might betray him to them. And they were glad, and agreed to give him money. So he consented and sought an opportunity to betray him to them in the absence of a crowd. (Lk. 22:3–6)

U2 has a song, "Until the End of the World." The song is a dialogue between Judas Iscariot and Jesus. Bono wrote the lyrics while staying at his father-in-law's house, awakening one morning to the idea of what such a conversation might have been. I wonder the same.

What happened to Judas? He had been there to see so many of Jesus' miracles. He had heard Jesus' teaching. At some point he had made a decision to follow Jesus. Among all those following Jesus, Judas had been one of the inner twelve. He had gone out on the mission trip where Jesus sent out his disciples in groups of two to teach and heal those in the surrounding communities. Judas had seen Jesus deliver people from demonic possession. Judas had dined with Jesus in intimate settings as well as when Jesus fed thousands with a few loaves and fish. Judas sat while Jesus washed his feet, a humbling show of love by Jesus. What happened?

I think several things were at play to cause Judas to become the ultimate traitor. First, Judas was never right with money. He didn't understand that all money was God's and he was simply a steward trying to figure out how God wanted it used. Judas had been in charge of the apostles' money and was guilty of skimming off the top at times. Judas wasn't getting what was going on.

I also think that Judas wasn't flipped from an ardent disciple to a betrayer overnight. Sin rarely works that way. Rather, I see him slipping a bit here and a bit there, turning slightly awry many times, then one day waking up far from the faith he once embraced. Sin can do that. It can cause us to lose track of mission and faith. Righteous behavior and pure hearts more readily see God. The enemy enters in with sin.

A final note here: I suspect Judas was too focused on Judas to see Jesus. Anytime we turn our eyes inward, when our concerns are selfish, we fail to appreciate the most giving person to ever live. Then our mind starts making up reasons to justify ourselves. I think Judas thought Jesus had crossed a line somewhere, and Judas was getting the true mission back on track by giving Jesus up. After all, I suspect he reasoned, Jesus seemed intent on getting into deep trouble with the authorities, and who wanted to be dragged down with him? Judas was just getting some distance and letting events run their course. I don't like thinking about Judas, but like Bono, I can learn from him.

Father, I want you above all else. May it always be. In Jesus' name, amen.

OCTOBER 23

Now the Passover, the feast of the Jews, was at hand. Lifting up his eyes, then, and seeing that a large crowd was coming toward him, Jesus said to Philip, "Where are we to buy bread, so that these people may eat?" He said this to test him, for he himself knew what he would do. . . . One of his disciples, Andrew, Simon Peter's brother, said to him, "There is a boy here who has five barley loaves and two fish, but what are they for so many?" . . . Jesus then took the loaves, and when he had given thanks, he distributed them to those who were seated. So also the fish, as much as they wanted. . . . When the people saw the sign that he had done, they said, "This is indeed the Prophet who is to come into the world!" (Jn. 6:4–6, 8–9, 11, 14)

Muhammad Ali famously predicted the round in which he won his fights twelve times out of sixty-one bouts. That is amazing. I knew about it growing up, so I always tried watching Ali's fights to see if he won as predicted. Of course, it seemed every time I watched, I got one of the forty-nine out of sixty-one times Ali was wrong!

God doesn't miss. He would have been sixty-one out of sixty-one. In today's passage that is apparent, but only with a careful reading! In this story of feeding the five thousand, John built his gospel around the Books of Moses. Genesis, the first Book of Moses begins, "In the beginning, God . . ." John begins, "In the beginning was the Word . . ." Over and over John explains how Jesus was like Moses, yet greater. Moses parted the Red Sea; Jesus walked on the sea. Over and over John provides this comparison.

In this light, today's passage takes on special significance. Jesus feeding the multitudes is found in each gospel, but John not only included the story, but also set it in the time of the Passover. The Passover was the Jewish celebration of remembrance for when Moses brought the Israelites out of Egypt and into the Promised Land. In the Passover story, the people were desperate and begging for food in the Wilderness. Moses asked God and God rained manna from heaven. Here the people are hungry, and Jesus provides the food. Jesus gives bread and fish. The comparison to Moses is not to be missed.

At the end of the story, the people noted Jesus was "the Prophet who is to come into the world." This is a reference to Moses' prophecy, "The LORD your God will raise up for you a prophet like me from among you, from your brothers—it is to him you shall listen" (Deut. 18:15). God had Jesus meet all of the Messiah's prophecies. Jesus showed it. And in the process, Jesus demonstrated he came to meet our needs, to rescue us from the slavery of this world, and to bring us into the true Promised Land.

Father, I praise your love and provision and live in hope for tomorrow. In Jesus, amen.

OCTOBER 24

Then they said to him, "What must we do, to be doing the works of God?" Jesus answered them, "This is the work of God, that you believe in him whom he has sent." (Jn. 6:28–29)

Two early Jewish rabbis active in the decades before Jesus' ministry were named Hillel and Shammai. The story is recorded of a Gentile who was interested in converting to Judaism but didn't have the time or patience to learn all the intricacies of Jewish law. The Gentile came to Shammai and said he would convert if Shammai could teach him the entirety of the law while the Gentile stood on one foot. Shammai thought the pagan disingenuous or not worth the trouble and chased him away with a stick.

The Gentile then went to Hillel and posed the same offer/request. Hillel responded, "That which is hateful to you, do not do to another; that is the entire Torah. The rest is interpretation. Go study." It is noteworthy that Jesus took Hillel's view and taught it, albeit in a positive reference rather than negative. So while Hillel said, "Don't do to others what you don't want them to do to you," Jesus put it, "Do to others what you would have them do to you." The thought is the same.

In today's passage, Jesus wraps up the commandments of God into an even shorter recitation. The fellow approaches Jesus with a fairly broad question: "What must we do to be doing the works of God?" Notice the plural? The fellow is looking for a list. He wants to know how to do the works—plural—of God.

Jesus answers in the singular. Jesus doesn't catalogue the works of God, but says there is a singular "work" of God—to believe in him whom he has sent. This is powerful! To "believe" in the sense of the first-century word John chose (*pisteuo*, πιστεύω) is to consider something to be true and therefore worthy of one's trust. It includes the idea of entrusting oneself to another with confidence in the outcome.

This is the culmination of all the Law of the Torah. This is the ultimate command of our God. The follower of God is to trust in Jesus with life and death. This means that I look to Jesus to give me meaning in life. Jesus teaches me my priorities. Jesus is my example of how to treat others. Jesus exposes my shortcomings and sins and gives me full forgiveness. Jesus gives me access to God in prayer. Jesus is my Lord as well as my Savior. Jesus gives me comfort. Jesus is my blessed assurance that all will be okay. Jesus is the one I worship and proclaim! He is my life.

Jesus gave an answer that one could hear and understand while standing on two feet. But it takes a lifetime of walking to experience all that comes from that answer.

Father, I give myself wholly to you in Jesus, the Lord and Savior of humanity. Amen.

OCTOBER 25

As he passed by, he saw a man blind from birth. . . . Jesus spit on the ground and made mud with the saliva. Then he anointed the man's eyes with the mud and said to him, "Go, wash in the pool of Siloam" (which means Sent). So he went and washed and came back seeing. . . . The Pharisees again asked him how he had received his sight. And he said to them, "He put mud on my eyes, and I washed, and I see." (Jn. 9:1, 6–7, 15)

John, chapter 9, tells a fascinating and detailed story about Jesus healing a man who had been blind since birth. Jesus anointed the man's eyes with mud and told him to wash the mud off in the pool of Siloam. At what precise moment the man received his vision, we aren't told, but the man left for Siloam with mud on his eyes. Once he washed the mud off, as directed by Jesus, the man could see.

This miracle did not sit well with the Pharisees. The Pharisees wanted to know if the man had truly been born blind, or if this was a made-up show. They sought out the blind man's parents, who confirmed his malady since birth. Over and over again, the Pharisees summoned the healed man to their interrogation, trying to get him to disaffirm Jesus.

With each trip to the Pharisees, and as the time to contemplate their inquisition grew, the man got bolder and bolder in his understanding and statements about Jesus. At the first interrogation, the man told the Pharisees that while he couldn't identify Jesus (he was blind and then had mud covering his eyes), he could affirm that Jesus was a prophet. The Pharisees weren't satisfied, and this was when they asked the parents about whether he was truly blind. Hearing that the man was born that way, the Pharisees then questioned how this was done. The parents deferred to their adult son, for fear the synagogue leaders would expel them.

This brought about the second interrogation of the once-blind man who was told by the Pharisees to strip any credit for Jesus because "he is a sinner!" (The Pharisees couldn't get over the fact Jesus had done this work on a Sabbath.) Rather than disclaim Jesus, the man responded a bit tartly. He said, "Why do you keep asking me about this man? Do you want to be his disciples, too?" This infuriated the Pharisees, and then the man let loose with the affirmation, "Never since the world began has it been heard that anyone opened the eyes of a man born blind. If this man were not from God, he could do nothing." The Pharisees expelled the man from the synagogue.

Jesus then encountered the man. This was the first time the man laid seeing eyes on Jesus, and the man proclaimed his faith. Jesus then pointed out the irony in the story. The blind man came to see Jesus. The Pharisees with physical eyes were blinded to Jesus. It's amazing what eyes can and can't see.

Father, I want to see Jesus in truth. Give me that sight, in Jesus, amen.

OCTOBER 26

The thief comes only to steal and kill and destroy. I came that they may have life and have it abundantly. I am the good shepherd. The good shepherd lays down his life for the sheep. (Jn. 10:10–11)

I don't know where the idea came from, but so many people seem to have an image of God as an old man on a rocking chair, looking down on earth and wagging his finger, trying to keep people from having fun. Billy Joel encapsulated this view in his song, "Only the Good Die Young." He sings, "And they say there's a heaven for those who will wait. Some say it's better, but I say it ain't. I'd rather laugh with the sinners than cry with the saints. The sinners are much more fun." The song has a catchy tune. It also has deplorable lyrics.

Joel is wrong. God's interest isn't in making people miserable. God is interested in bringing real life to people. Joel's enticement to walk a path away from God, finding the joys of this world "much more fun," is not only short-sighted, it is foolish.

I have seen the "joys" of this world. I have seen the destruction of families from sexual indiscretions. I have seen the sickness and disease arising from gluttony. I have handled the cases of devasted families destroyed over the loss of a loved one who was killed by a drunk driver. I have kicked in a door of one lying on the floor unconscious from a stupor, calling an ambulance to save his life. I have seen children trying to recover from exploits of older people.

Sir Isaac Newton (1643-1727) was a smart fellow. He was accomplished in math, physics, astronomy, chemistry, and even theology. He was a published author, taught at Cambridge, built the first notable reflecting telescope, calculated the speed of sound, and more. Newton's third law of physics stated that to every action, there is an equal and opposite reaction. While this law would centuries later be used to produce jet engines, it explains far more than mechanics. It explains that all this worldly fun has consequences. Not just eternal consequences, but consequences in the here and now.

Jesus came to give life. This isn't a life devoid of fun. It is a life of great joy. Just as sin has negative consequences, so Jesus' life has positive ones. I have seen broken families healed by God's love. I have seen discipline restore health to those with ailing bodies. I have seen peace come into the lives of those bereaved. I have seen alcoholics set free from the bondage of addiction. I have seen people find forgiveness that releases them to live a full life, as they modeled the forgiveness of Jesus.

Jesus is not the destroyer of a good life. He is the source of a good life.

Father, thank you for my life. May I always seek your will. In Jesus, amen.

OCTOBER 27

Now there are also many other things that Jesus did. Were every one of them to be written, I suppose that the world itself could not contain the books that would be written. (Jn. 21:25)

I am thankful for today's passage, which is the very last verse in John's gospel. While in a sense it may seem hyperbole, or an exaggeration to make a point, I believe it isn't. This is a core truth. Let me explain.

John began his book with a comment on Jesus. In his first verse he wrote, "In the beginning was the Word, and the Word was with God, and the Word was God." He then made it unequivocally clear that the Word he was referencing was none other than Jesus. In chapter 1 verse 14, he wrote, "And the Word became flesh and dwelt among us, and we have seen his glory, glory as of the only Son from the Father, full of grace and truth."

Then with Jesus already in existence at the beginning of this universe, John explained, "All things were made through him, and without him was not any thing made that was made" (Jn. 1:3). In other words, the works of Jesus include all that went into the creation of over two trillion galaxies, each with countless stars, and innumerable planets. This doesn't include the creation of nonvisible matter and antimatter, and so many other things that make up the universe.

Add to this Jesus making all people, past, present, and future. Further, Jesus holds together all structures of space and time. All of these matters are "things Jesus did." Which brings me to the devotional impact of this passage.

Yes, without a doubt one impact of the passage is the rightful response of praising, glorifying, and magnifying the greatness of the Lord. But beyond that is an incredible aspect of this, as related to the stories John chose to include in his gospel. John makes reference to all of creation being made through Jesus, but that isn't where he spends his ink. John's time is spent showing this awesome Jesus who made all there is and still cares enough about a wedding embarrassment to turn water into wine. He cares enough about the fright of his friends that he stills the sea storm. He cares enough about comfort and hunger to feed five thousand. He cares enough about people to heal, and even to bring the dead to life.

This inexpressible working Jesus, who has done more than writing could contain, cares about you and me. He is working in our life. We are not alone, and we are not without indescribable power in our lives. This is a great passage and truth!

Father, I entrust myself to and seek the amazing workings of Christ. In him I pray, amen.

OCTOBER 28

And he said to them, "Truly, I say to you, there are some standing here who will not taste death until they see the kingdom of God after it has come with power." (Mk. 9:1)

When I was young, I would read this verse and not understand. It sounded to me like Jesus was saying some of his people would live until his second coming! I knew that wasn't right. I wondered if Jesus got it wrong, or if I just misunderstood the passage. It wasn't until much later that I learned the mercy apparent in this passage.

Our English Bibles put this verse at the start of a new chapter, chapter 9. We might forget that in Mark's original gospel, there would not have been any such divisions, and this verse came at the end of what one had already read in chapter 8. It is plugging this into those other verses that gives it meaning.

Jesus has told his followers that they are to deny themselves, take up their crosses, and follow him. For some, that would mean a violent death. (History did show this to be the case for many of Jesus' followers.) Jesus assured them that those who lost their lives for his sake would gain their true eternal lives. Jesus then contrasted his true followers with those who were "ashamed" of Jesus and his words. These were those who did the opposite of following Jesus. These folks might have been attentive while it was safe, and it pleased them. But when trouble came knocking, they were not holding fast to Jesus. They shamefully abandoned him.

Into this contrast between the two, Jesus gives this verse. Jesus speaks of those who would not "taste death," an interesting phrase. This is a "Semitism" or Hebrew expression that tracks the prior concept of a harsh and violent death. Jesus was affirming that while his followers were called to walking in faith, come what may, it wouldn't necessarily be a call to martyrdom.

This sets up an interesting paradigm. It says that I am to follow Jesus, period. It may lead me to a violent death. It may lead me to embarrassment. It may lead me to personal challenge. I may lose money in the process. I may not be as popular as I'd like. I may not have all the possessions I want. I may not . . . fill in the blank! But if I am following my Lord, I am right where I need to be.

I also can know that as I follow him, I can have times of blessing and joy. He gives good gifts and meets my earthly needs. I will have unspeakable joy and peace. He takes my heavy burden and exchanges it for a light one. My God holds the future. My job is to walk in it faithfully.

Lord, give me strength to be yours, today and every day. In Jesus, amen.

OCTOBER 29

One who is faithful in a very little is also faithful in much, and one who is dishonest in a very little is also dishonest in much. (Lk. 16:10)

Today's passage is a simple lesson. So simple, in fact, that it is easy to read over, and hard to truly live.

The passage follows Jesus telling a parable of a rich man who has a business manager who has been wasting the rich man's resources. This is *not* a parable intended to use earthly characters to represent God and humanity. This is a simple, everyday life story of people that Jesus uses to drive home a point. The manager enjoys a high social position because of his job. He was likely a slave, or a freedman who sold himself to the rich man for the high societal role of managing the rich man's affairs as his agent. Without that job, the manager would likely be reduced to a slave position of manual labor, or even begging.

The manager gets news he is getting fired, and before being booted from the house, he starts cutting deals to make friends with others. He reduces the debt of various people who owed his master oil, wheat, and the like. The hope was that the manager would make friends who would help him once he was discharged from his prior job. The rich man commended the shrewdness of the manager, even while Jesus labeled the manager dishonest.

Jesus gives insight into his parable, noting that "sons of this world are more shrewd in dealing with their own generation" than the "sons of light" are in dealing with the kingdom of God. This is followed by Jesus' admonition to use the wealth of this world and age (which Jesus terms "unrighteous wealth") wisely. It should be used by children of the light with an eye toward the future kingdom of God.

Following on the heels of this real-world parable, comes the comment of Jesus found as today's passage. Jesus assures the truth that as children of God are faithful in little amounts, they are faithful as the amounts increase. In other words, faithfulness breeds faithfulness. But similarly, dishonesty breeds dishonesty.

God expects his people to be faithful in what they have. This is a stewardship issue. As God's people are faithful, God entrusts them more and more. But unfaithfulness never results in God increasing one's responsibility. God wants his children to live in this corruptible world with a love for God's better world to come. It puts money and opportunities into perspective. We live for God.

Father, I want to be a good and wise steward. I want my life to reflect a love for you, not for money or things of this world. May I live in this way, in and for Jesus. Amen.

OCTOBER 30

One Sabbath, when he went to dine at the house of a ruler of the Pharisees, they were watching him carefully. (Lk. 14:1)

People are watching! They watch you and they watch me. They watch to see what we will do. They watch to see if we practice what we preach.

In today's passage, Jesus is dining at the house of a leader of the strictest religious order of the day. Some would see this as an opportunity for Jesus. If Jesus could persuade this man, and those guests he would have in attendance, then Jesus would be well on the road to religious acceptance. All Jesus had to do was be on his best religious behavior. Jesus needed to mind his pey's and qoph's! (The Hebrew letters for p's and q's.)

Jesus, however, wasn't bent on impressing the religious leaders of his day. He was interested in doing his Father's business. If that coincided with the priorities and concerns of the religious folks, then all well and good. But if it didn't, Jesus was always going to side with the Father.

With all of that, however, Jesus certainly wasn't trying to repel the religious. He wanted them to find the truth of God just as much as the disinterested people. So Jesus went about the Father's business at this dinner, but not as the religious would have thought.

At the dinner was a man with dropsy. Healing this man would normally be a good thing; however, this dinner was a Shabbat dinner. With it being the Sabbath, the religious zealots and religious lawyers didn't think it appropriate to "work," and that included being a doctor and healing the sick.

So Jesus quizzed the lawyers and leaders, "Is it lawful to heal on the Sabbath or not?" Jesus put the question front and center. Hearing no answer, Jesus healed the man and sent him on his way. Jesus knew he was being watched and didn't want to leave it there. Jesus wanted those present to understand God better and to grow in appreciation for God's priorities. Jesus asked whether the leaders would pull a son or ox from a well on the Sabbath, if either had fallen into the well. The people still had no reply, but I have no doubt they thought about it long after the dinner was over.

People do watch us. That doesn't mean we live to please others. It also doesn't mean we pretend to be something we aren't. We don't practice our piety for show, as Jesus warned against in Matthew 6. But we also don't needlessly offend people. We should live right before God in genuine ways, so that those who watch are drawn to God.

Father, give me wisdom and discretion to live before the watching world in ways that bring glory to your name. In Jesus, amen.

OCTOBER 31

Now he told a parable to those who were invited, when he noticed how they chose the places of honor, saying to them, "When you are invited by someone to a wedding feast, do not sit down in a place of honor, lest someone more distinguished than you be invited by him, and he who invited you both will come and say to you, 'Give your place to this person,' and then you will begin with shame to take the lowest place. But when you are invited, go and sit in the lowest place, so that when your host comes he may say to you, 'Friend, move up higher.' Then you will be honored in the presence of all who sit at table with you. For everyone who exalts himself will be humbled, and he who humbles himself will be exalted." (Lk. 14:7–11)

When our children were young, we began a game, of sorts, we would play over dinner. The game involved the accumulation of "munits." This made-up word was explained as a combination of "manners" and "units." It was where we all used our best table manners, and anyone caught talking with their mouth full, or with elbows on the table, and so forth, would be assessed a "munit." Then at the end of the meal, the one of us with the least munits didn't have to help clear the table or clean the dishes.

Teaching manners is one of parenting's greatest challenges in the day-in-day-out of rearing children. I find it fascinating to read Scripture with an eye toward how Jesus taught his followers religious manners. These are lifestyle manners that are appropriate for followers of God. They are also appropriate for good living.

Today's passage is an excellent instruction in religious manners. Jesus placed a short story before those listening about how to approach a special event. Rather than choosing the place of honor, Jesus taught his followers to choose the lowest place. This approach to life is one where one can get the blessing of being elevated to somewhere better. It is much better than someone asking you to move away from a place of honor to somewhere less prestigious!

Jesus then linked this everyday mentality/manner to something much broader. Jesus linked it to life in general.

We are not to live in ways that exalt or indicate our self-importance. Those manners belong to the narcissist, not the followers of God. The follower of God is to live in humility, according all people as important image bearers of God. No one has more or less value in God's eyes, and neither should they in ours. Furthermore, we are here to serve other people, as Jesus modeled, not to be served. This is our manners lesson from the Lord!

Father, may I grow in my manners, following your lead and instruction. In Jesus, amen.

NOVEMBER 1

When the days drew near for him to be taken up, he set his face to go to Jerusalem . . .
(Lk. 9:51)

Have you ever met people who were particularly persistent? These are the people who make good long-distance runners. They are people who set their mind to something and see it through. Obstacles become merely humps, or as my dad used to say when facing a challenge, "That's no hill for a stepper!" Determination is invaluable at times in this life. Thankfully it is a trait of our God.

Today's passage is a simple verse about a third of the way into the gospel of Luke. But it is a verse that fits into a larger narrative theme of Luke on at least three levels. Seeing those three themes gives tremendous blessing to followers of Jesus today.

One theme found throughout the writings of Luke, which include his gospel as well as the book of Acts, is the motif of travel. Over and over in the gospels, the travels of Jesus are emphasized. Again, in Acts, Luke recounts the apostles' travels as well as the mission trips of Paul. Only Luke records the walk to Emmaus by the resurrected Jesus, when Jesus explains the Old Testament's prophecies about Jesus to two of his disciples. In similar fashion, Luke records the Ethiopian eunuch traveling when Philip joins him and explains the Old Testament's prophecies about Jesus. Luke saw life as a journey, and it comes through in his writings. Jesus was on a journey in his life. Jesus' journey is set out in today's passage as one where he would be "taken up."

"Taken up" is a second theme for Luke. Luke records Jesus being taken up at four critical times. Jesus goes "up" to Jerusalem (Lk. 19:28). Jesus is put up on the cross, and his body is subsequently "taken down" by Joseph of Arimathea (Lk. 23:53). Jesus arises from the dead, and in Acts Luke details the final ascension of Jesus.

A third theme is Jesus' conscious decision to be in Jerusalem to bring his life on earth to its successful conclusion. Luke says Jesus was teaching while "journeying to Jerusalem" (Lk. 13:22). For "it cannot be that a prophet should perish away from Jerusalem" (Lk. 13:33).

All three of these themes are expressed in this one verse with an important add, "Jesus set his face" for this journey. This expresses determination. Jesus knew he was on God's mission. God decided the road for the journey of life. Jesus was determined to follow God's road, confident of God's desired outcome.

I travel a road in my life. I want God's road. I want to follow it with determination.

Lord, make clear your path for me and give me strength to follow it in Jesus. Amen.

NOVEMBER 2

When I saw him, I fell at his feet as though dead. But he laid his right hand on me, saying, "Fear not, I am the first and the last, and the living one. I died, and behold I am alive forevermore, and I have the keys of Death and Hades." (Rev. 1:17)

John was on a small island off the coast of Turkey. The isle of Patmos was supposed to be a punishment for John, because John put his worship of Jesus on a level that outstripped any allegiance to the Roman emperor. But what the government planned as a punishment to stop an old man from influencing a younger generation backfired. God appeared to John and gave him a revelation on Patmos that would not only influence people in his day but has influenced people for almost two thousand years, far outlasting the Roman emperor as well as the Roman Empire.

Today's passage is one that still influences me. John was on Patmos and it was the Lord's day. While worshipping the Lord, John heard a loud voice, like a trumpet, telling him to write down a message for seven churches. (Seven was a number that represented the whole, so this was a message not only for the seven specified churches, but also for the church as a whole.) John turned to see who was speaking and it was a frightful sight!

Like the Roman emperor, the speaker wore a long robe with a sash around the chest, but this man was more than the emperor. His hair was full and white, his eyes aflame, his feet like bronze, and the roar of his voice was like the ocean's waves pounding the surf. His face was like the sun, he held stars in his hands, and a sword came from his mouth. John was stunned. He fell down petrified. This was not how he expected to spend that Sunday!

As John lay on the ground like a corpse, the man reached out and touched him. So now one can picture the man holding stars—yes STARS—in his right hand, setting down those stars so he can use that right hand to gently touch John. With this touch, the man identifies himself to John. The man is the "first and last." He is a resurrected man, one who *is* living, even though he has died once before. He can never die again, but he is alive for eternity. This man holds the keys to death and Hades. John sees that this is no ordinary man. This is Jesus, the Son of God.

What I find remarkable in this story is that Jesus begins his explanation of who he is with the phrase, "Do not fear, for I am . . ." The very fact that Jesus is these things instills a bit of fear in me! But it shouldn't. I should only fear this Jesus if I am his enemy. But Jesus told this to John all while giving him a gentle touch. This is a loving Jesus who sets down the stars to tend to his scared friend. I worship this same awesome, powerful, universe maker. He calls me friend, and he will set down the stars to comfort and assure me. I have no need to fear anything today!

Lord, I need your touch of love. Drive out fear and give me your peace. In Jesus, amen.

And as he entered a village, he was met by ten lepers, who stood at a distance and lifted up their voices, saying, "Jesus, Master, have mercy on us." When he saw them he said to them, "Go and show yourselves to the priests." And as they went they were cleansed. Then one of them, when he saw that he was healed, turned back, praising God with a loud voice; and he fell on his face at Jesus' feet, giving him thanks. Now he was a Samaritan. Then Jesus answered, "Were not ten cleansed? Where are the nine? Was no one found to return and give praise to God except this foreigner?" (Lk. 17:12–18)

Our daughter Gracie has a knack for being thankful. She is one of those people who sees and expresses gratitude in the smallest situations. I readily confess, I struggle at times to be as thankful as I should; to quote the platitude, I need an attitude of gratitude. It isn't that I am ungrateful; it's often that I am too busy, or too preoccupied to be still, appreciate what is there, and express thanks for it.

How much has God done for you and me that we fail to acknowledge, fail to thank him for, and for which we fail to give praise and credit to God? I never want to be the ungrateful recipient of the Lord's bounty. I want to have a thankful heart.

James, the brother of Jesus, wrote a letter that touched on this. Early in the letter James was clear, "Do not be deceived, my beloved brothers. Every good gift and every perfect gift is from above, coming down from the Father of lights" (Jms. 1:16–17).

So today, nothing it too profound in this devotional. It is a simple time to thank God for his many gifts. I will write out my prayer and ask you to join me in it, adding your own words where appropriate.

Dear Lord, I give you all the praise for this incredible life you have given me. Thank you for nature—the trees, birds, air, sky, storms, sunsets—the beauty all around me. Open my eyes to see it better.

Thank you for my life. For each breath you give me, each beat of my heart. Thank you for the seconds, minutes, hours, and days. Help me to live them all for you.

Thank you for my family and friends. For [list them!]. May I help all of them see Jesus.

Thank you for my church family and other believers you have put in my life. May I never take for granted a chance to worship you with others.

Lord, I give you praise and adoration as the great providing God. Thank you especially for your attention to me, your giving love, the sacrifice of Christ and the forgiveness that flows from his cross. I repent of ingratitude and seek to bless your name. In Jesus, amen.

NOVEMBER 4

Yet this you have: you hate the works of the Nicolaitans, which I also hate. (Rev. 2:6)

"Hate" is a strong word. It evokes ideas of an intense or even passionate dislike for someone. "Hate" is an emotional word that stems from feelings and attitudes. These modern ideas of hate can make it a bit startling to read passages like today's where Jesus applauds the church at Ephesus for hating the works of the Nicolaitans, adding that Jesus also hates them.

This is a splendid verse for bringing reflection to the biblical idea rooted in the word "hate." The biblical notion of this word is not so much about personal animosity. Rather it is rooted in God's wrath for things that are sinful, evil, and destructive to people.

My Greek professor Dr. Harvey Floyd explained it this way: He saw two cars at an intersection paused for a red light. The light turned green. The first car sat there, and the second car lightly tooted his horn. Car 1 didn't move but blew his horn back. Then car 2 blew his longer. Then car 1 blew his longer. They both sat on their horns the entire green light. Dr. Floyd called this road rage, getting mad, temporary insanity. That is *not* the wrath of God. God doesn't fly off the handle or have an issue with his ego.

Only one thing incites the wrath of God: evil. This is the other side of God's holiness. Apart from sin, there is no wrath of God. This is why God spoke through the prophet Isaiah, "For I the LORD love justice; I hate robbery and wrong" (Isa. 61:8). This is why Jesus got angry in Mark 3 when he healed a man with a withered hand and the Pharisees tried to stand in the way.

No one should have a problem reconciling the love of God with the wrath of God. Having been a child, and having had five children, I can affirm that if a parent has never been displeased with a child, it means one of two things. Either the child is perfect, or the parent doesn't care. God must get angry with sin or else it means he is indifferent to sin. That isn't God! God is a moral being.

As Dr. Floyd said, "If you see some great big burly fellow kicking the teeth of a small kid, and you walk by as cool as a summer breeze saying, 'Some like chocolate, some like vanilla, some like cruelty . . . ' then you have no moral values!" God has wrath because he is a moral God who cares about right conduct. So, the wrath of God is against the sin, and against those sinners tied to the sin. But God always wants the sinner to repent, and God stands ready to forgive the sin based on the substitutionary death of Jesus as just punishment for the sin.

Lord, I am sinful. Grow my distaste for sin. Thank you for forgiveness in Jesus, amen.

NOVEMBER 5

And to the angel of the church in Smyrna write: "The words of the first and the last, who died and came to life. I know your tribulation and your poverty (but you are rich)." (Rev. 2:8–9)

My mom and dad worked hard. Dad was a railroad man, and Mom spent most of her working life in non-profits. Growing up we were far from wealthy, with Mom and Dad counting pennies, but we were well fed, had good clothes, and were all given great educations. After Dad retired, I can remember on more than one occasion, he would exclaim with wonderment in his voice, "I am rich." Now we knew he didn't mean economically, but I never probed him on what he meant until one day he said, "I think I'm the richest man alive!" and then added the question, "Mark, do you know why?" I asked why, and he told me, "Because of the love in our family. There could be no greater riches for any man."

As I type this lesson, Dad passed over sixteen years ago, but I still remember his understanding of true riches as if he was dictating this devotional to me. Dad was right.

Today's passage is a letter that Jesus had John write out to send to a church in Smyrna (ancient Turkey). This church was enduring difficult times. They were experiencing *thlipsis* (θλῖφις), often translated as "tribulation," "affliction," "trouble," or "oppression." One of my Greek professors gave us the picture associated with the word. He said take a rope and turn it into a C shape. Then take a second rope and turn it into a backward C. Lay one over the other such that you have made a loop. Whatever is in that loop, as someone pulls both C's experiences *thlipsis*. It is like the tightening of a noose around the neck, as one is pulled two directions at the same time. The stress and pressure can become too much for many to bear.

The church at Smyrna was enduring this constriction. The pressures of life were tremendous. The church was also impoverished. Money can help alleviate a lot of affliction, but the church didn't have economic resources at its disposal.

Yet in the midst of this tribulation and lack, Jesus told the church, "you are rich." What of this? The church had Jesus. The church had the rock that sustains anyone who stands upon it, throughout all of life's storms and tribulations. These believers could sing the Hillsong verse, "So I'll stand with arms high and heart abandoned, in awe of the one who gave it all . . . All I am is yours." This is riches like my dad understood. These are the family riches of those who know God as Father. Life in Christ is an abundant life, whether it contains worldly goods or not, whether life is calm or raging. Every believer can say, "I am rich!"

Lord, thank you for your grace and mercy. Guide me through this life in Jesus. Amen.

NOVEMBER 6

Do not fear what you are about to suffer. Behold, the devil is about to throw some of you into prison, that you may be tested, and for ten days you will have tribulation. Be faithful unto death, and I will give you the crown of life. (Rev. 2:10)

This one verse is packed with important ideas that each need to be examined. Jesus is giving John instructions for a letter to go to the believers in ancient Smyrna (modern Izmir, Turkey). Smyrna was an impoverished church that had already undergone noticeable tribulation and affliction. Jesus told John to inform the believers that it was about to get worse.

Jesus warned the believers that the devil would soon be throwing some of them into prison. Because John's revelation frequently uses symbolism and metaphors, it is not clear whether the imprisonment is literal or a figurative. Either way, it was not something anyone would want! Prison was not then what it is today. (Not that today it's a vacation spot!) In the Roman era, prison was frequently a hole in the ground, inhabited by rats and darkness-loving bugs. There was little to no sunlight, no exercise opportunity, and not even any food. A prisoner was only fed if family and friends brought them food. Frequently, the imprisonment process itself led to death from hunger and disease.

So, whether the imprisonment was going to be real or a metaphor for what was coming, most people would be in dread or abject fear of it happening to them. But here Jesus preempted the suffering by affirming that the believers should *not* fear what was coming. The devil could throw his worst at them, and he might indeed do so, but by walking in faith, by trusting in God, the believers would make it out of the suffering and receive the crown of life.

This suffering was set to last "ten days." Again, most likely this isn't to be read as a literal ten days, for ten was a symbolic number that represented a completeness. As one typically has ten fingers and ten toes, so the ancients viewed ten as a full number. Jesus' point was that the suffering was coming, that it would last or run its entire course, and that it would then end.

The key for the believers in Smyrna is no different than the key for me today. The devil is still at work. He still seeks to make life difficult and even miserable for believers. His tools include not only sin and its consequences but also the stifling effect of fear. Fear is not my companion of faith; it is the enemy. Jesus wanted the church to hear this message. The believer should face the reality of the world as a place of difficulty and suffering. And the believer shouldn't fear that. Faith in the Lord is the walk to the crown of life.

Lord, give me faith in the midst of difficulty. I repent of fear and whining! In Jesus, amen.

NOVEMBER 7

And to the angel of the church in Pergamum write: "The words of him who has the sharp two-edged sword. I know where you dwell, where Satan's throne is. Yet you hold fast my name, and you did not deny my faith even in the days of Antipas my faithful witness, who was killed among you, where Satan dwells. But I have a few things against you: you have some there who hold the teaching of Balaam, who taught Balak to put a stumbling block before the sons of Israel, so that they might eat food sacrificed to idols and practice sexual immorality." (Rev. 2:12–14)

Today's passage may be one of the most relevant passages found in Christ's letters to the churches placed in Revelation. The passage was to the church in Pergamum. The church had done some good things, remaining faithful to God even though persecution had already visited the church. Yet there was a significant issue brewing that needed the church's attention.

Pergamum was the center of the imperial cult in Asia. The city not only had a temple built to the Roman emperor as a god but the proconsul in Pergamum as Caesar's representative held the "right of the sword." He was empowered to put to death anyone for any reason. But the proconsul was eclipsed in power by Christ, who held the double-edged sword, able to execute on the world!

The church had maintained their faith, even in the face of persecution, but the storm that was brewing on the horizon was of an entirely different nature. The letter describes the spiritual equivalent of locking the front door but leaving the back door open wide. The key to understanding this is the reference in the letter to the "teaching of Balaam, who taught Balak to put a stumbling block before the sons of Israel." This story is found in the Old Testament in Numbers. Balaam was hired to put a curse on Israel, but God protected Israel. So instead of a direct curse on Israel, Balaam placed Midianite women before Israel to seduce the men into licentiousness. The men chose the sexual immorality and God brought judgment on Israel.

Sexuality is not something to be treated lightly. Many a believer, strong in their faith, locking the front door against a frontal attack by the enemy, falls into a seductive trap of the pleasures of life. This can take forms that are a blatant rebellion against God. Of course, the nature of such a trap convinces the believer that the sin isn't *that bad*, or maybe isn't even sin at all.

Christ warned against these traps. Believers need to be about the business of the kingdom not the business of this world.

Lord, please help me direct my efforts and energies into serving you and your kingdom. May I not wander in eyes, mind, or life. May I seek you above all else. In Jesus, amen.

NOVEMBER 8

Therefore repent. If not, I will come to you soon and war against them with the sword of my mouth. He who has an ear, let him hear what the Spirit says to the churches. (Rev. 2:17)

Sometimes I want to cling to a simple faith. I have become a Christian. I know Jesus loves me. I know God is love. I know I make mistakes, but that I am forgiven by God's grace because of Jesus' death. I pray before my meals and before going to sleep. I love my wife and children. I try to be honest in my work and before the world. I will die one day. Then God's gift of eternal life will enable me to be in his kingdom forever. That seems simple enough.

Then into my simple faith comes a passage like today's. This passage disturbs my simple faith. It is found in a letter Christ dictated for John to send to the church in Pergamum. This church had a lot on the ball! They were believers. When persecuted by authorities, the church held firm to their faith even to the point of death. Their testimony was amazing. But all was not as it should have been. The church had some members who were holding onto practices and beliefs that were contrary to God's instructions. So, Jesus told the church to repent! If the church failed to repent, tough consequences were coming. The need to repent and the consequences that would follow in the event repentance wasn't forthcoming were in spite of this being a faithful church! This jolts me in my simple faith.

I know I do things and think things that I shouldn't. I also fail to do things that I should. The list of sins given in various places of the Bible include many with which I don't struggle—sorcery has never been on my secret sin list. But when Paul lists sorcery as a sin, he doesn't leave it there. He includes "sexual immorality, impurity, sensuality, idolatry, sorcery, enmity, strife, jealousy, fits of anger, rivalries, dissensions, divisions, envy, drunkenness, orgies, and things like these" (Gal. 5:19-21). Some of those hit close to home! Or how about Paul's list to Timothy: "lovers of self, lovers of money, proud, arrogant, abusive, disobedient to their parents, ungrateful, unholy" (2 Tim. 3:2). I suspect I am covering most everyone right now.

So back to the command to repent. The word "repent" includes not only the idea of feeling remorse but also the decision to turn or change one's mind. Jesus told the church to repent of their sins. The church was to feel remorse and to change its mind. This call to repentance includes a confessional prayer to God. Failure to repent places one before the disciplining sword of Jesus. Like a parent, God will train us in holiness, even if he has to use discipline to teach us right from wrong.

Lord, I confess to you my sins [think about them and list them!]. I repent and seek your help to do better. In Jesus' name, amen.

NOVEMBER 9

Now the tax collectors and sinners were all drawing near to hear him. And the Pharisees and the scribes grumbled, saying, "This man receives sinners and eats with them." (Lk. 15:1-2)

Studies indicate that people subconsciously assess others incredibly fast. The human brain has shortcuts to make quick decisions on whether someone is safe, likeable, worthy of attention, to be wary of, or even not worth one's time. All too often, people lapse into the bad trait of labeling others as "in" or "out." Maybe not consciously, but unconsciously people often find those who they like, and seek to be with them, while those who are deemed different or even unlikable are avoided.

Jesus was never a respecter of persons in the sense most people are. The gospels never show Jesus looking at people as who was the most fun, who was the most popular, who was the most successful or had the most money, who was the best looking, who was the most engaging, who had the strongest education, who stood highest in society, or who would boost his career.

Jesus looked at people as individuals in need of God, people with a heart for God, people with burdens looking for relief, people crushed under concerns of life needing support, people hungry for a meaningful existence, people wounded and needing a salve, people lost wanting a shepherd to find and guide them, and people curious about life willing to seek out answers. These types of people got Jesus' time and attention. Jesus sought to meet the needs of these folks. These people needed the kingdom of God, and Jesus worked to bring it to them.

Jesus also saw people who were in quite a different category. These people included those who were arrogant, stuck on their own perceived self-worth, those who scorned and even mocked others, those whose minds were bent to the base things of this earth with no care or regard for something better, those who trampled on others to get what they wanted, those who were complacent to others' pain or needs, those who lived for the moment with no care or regard for the morrow, those who were harsh judges of others, seeking to justify their own lives by criticizing others, and those who were disposed to argue, with no real regard to truth. These people needed the kingdom of God, but most had no use for it. Jesus brought the kingdom. It stared them in the face and most spurned it.

I know which category I want to be in. I want the kingdom; I need the kingdom! I want to be in a relationship of peace with God. I want his unconditional love. I need to change how I see people and how I see God.

Lord, give me your eyes to see others in this world. Let me live your love in Jesus, amen.

Or what woman, having ten silver coins, if she loses one coin, does not light a lamp and sweep the house and seek diligently until she finds it? And when she has found it, she calls together her friends and neighbors, saying, "Rejoice with me, for I have found the coin that I had lost." Just so, I tell you, there is joy before the angels of God over one sinner who repents. (Lk. 15:8–10)

In 1980, a jazz and soul band named Kool & the Gang, had their first number one hit. The song went on to become an international anthem of joy and happiness. The song was titled "Celebrate," and its refrain heard over and over was simple: "Celebrate good times, come on! (Let's celebrate); Celebrate good times, come on! (Let's celebrate)." The verses were repetitive as well, generally along the lines of "There's a party goin' on right here. A celebration to last throughout the years. So bring your good times and your laughter too. We gonna celebrate your party with you." By my count, which could be wrong, the three minute, thirty-nine-second song has the word "celebrate/celebration" in it forty-three times, or basically every five seconds.

Celebration is a time of rejoicing. It is a time of joy. Celebrations occur when something marvelous is happening. The idea can be an international anthem because everyone seeks the elation of times when something marvelous happens. This celebration is not only on earth. It is in heaven!

Luke spends chapter 15 recounting stories Jesus told about the lost being found. The chapter begins with Jesus telling a parable of a shepherd who had one hundred sheep, lost one, and left the ninety-nine to find the lost lamb, bringing him back on his shoulders. The shepherd called his friends and neighbors for it was time to "celebrate!" Then, Jesus told the parable in today's passage, of a woman who had ten coins, lost one, worked to find it, and then declared "celebrate!" The chapter then ends with the story of the prodigal son. This son who took his inheritance, rebelled from his father, squandered his money, living like a hog until he was literally living with the pigs, finally came to his senses and returned to his father in repentance and shame. His father readily forgave him and held a massive party for all to "celebrate."

The theme to each of these stories is the same. God seeks out the lost. God values people, and he wants these people to live in a healthy, thriving, loving, nurturing, protected, and meaningful relationship with him. People often rebel, however, and God goes to work bringing the lost lambs, the lost coins, the missing child, back home. And every time a lost soul returns to the fold, Jesus said, heaven itself was singing "Celebrate!" I want to be home with the Lord, rejoicing over those lost that return.

Lord, give me your heart for the lost. Use me to help bring them home. Then may I join in heaven's celebration! In Jesus' holy name, amen.

NOVEMBER 11

He entered Jericho and was passing through. And behold, there was a man named Zacchaeus. He was a chief tax collector and was rich. And he was seeking to see who Jesus was. . . . And Jesus said to him, "Today salvation has come to this house, since he also is a son of Abraham. For the Son of Man came to seek and to save the lost." (Lk. 19:1-3, 9-10)

Social scientists indicate that the average person can see a stranger, and within seconds, immediate impressions are formed about whether the stranger is interesting, important, scary and dangerous, or innocuous. As one meets and interacts with the stranger, those initial, sometimes unconscious, impressions can change. Any changes still generally accord around certain values and ideas. God doesn't judge people in the way most humans do, however. That is a subtle, yet important, underlay to today's passage.

The story behind today's passage is well known. Many young people who grow up in churches hear the child's song, "Zacchaeus was a wee little man, and a wee little man was he. He climbed up in a Sycamore tree for the Lord he wanted to see. And when the Lord passed by that way, he looked up in that tree. And he said, 'Zacchaeus, you come down from there! For I'm going to your house today.'" The song gives a great summary of the story, but beyond the narrative, consider one of the underlying themes.

Luke describes Zacchaeus in three ways: physical appearance, occupation, and social status. Physically, Zacchaeus was short. His job was that of a tax collector (not a popular job among the masses for tax collectors spent too much time interacting with the authorities and often cheating those who were taxed). His social status was that of a rich man.

Having identified Zacchaeus as the world saw him, Luke narrates the story with a preview line. Zacchaeus was in Jericho, and he wanted to see Jesus. He wanted to see Jesus so badly that he found a tree he could climb. Before entering Jericho, Jesus had just healed a blind man begging by the side of the road (Lk. 18). No doubt for this and many other reasons, Zacchaeus wanted to see who this Jesus was.

Jesus not only walked by the tree where Zacchaeus was but stopped and called out to Zacchaeus. Jesus was going to his house. Jesus didn't describe Zacchaeus as a short, rich tax collector. Jesus saw Zacchaeus as one spiritually sick who needed healing. The Great Physician healed Zacchaeus and the story ends with God's view of Zacchaeus. God didn't see a short, rich tax collector. God saw a son of Abraham (who was the paragon and patriarch of a Jew believing and trusting in God) who had been lost but was now saved. God sees truly what I am and what I can be if I seek Jesus.

Lord, I would see Jesus. Change me and make me yours. In him I pray, amen.

NOVEMBER 12

And he was seeking to see who Jesus was, but on account of the crowd he could not, because he was small in stature. So he ran on ahead and climbed up into a sycamore tree to see him, for he was about to pass that way. (Lk. 19:3–4)

One of my most valuable employees for decades has been a marvelous woman who on paper never had the qualifications to work in the role she has held. Yet Jan has a quality that not only allowed her to be in that job but to excel in it. This woman has persistence.

Webster's defines persistence as the act of going on "resolutely or stubbornly in spite of opposition, importunity, or warning." In over thirty years of working together, I have trouble remembering any assignment I gave to her that she didn't figure out some way to get done. She found the unfindable witnesses. She appeased the unappeasable. She figured a way around or through any obstacle that came her way. She reminds me of Zacchaeus.

Today's passage falls in the narrative of Zacchaeus, that "wee little man" who *really* wanted to see Jesus. He tried to jostle through the crowd but to no avail. After all, Jesus had been popular for several years at that point, and right before entering the town of Jericho, Jesus had miraculously healed a blind beggar. This was all occurring before computers, Netflix, or even television! This was BIG TIME excitement unlike any of these folks had seen before. Who was this famous miracle-working carpenter from the hills, turned rabbi?

Zacchaeus might have gone home or gone back to work. Having tried to see Jesus, he could have written off his dismal luck as another result of being unduly short. But not Zacchaeus. He had "persistence." Zacchaeus predicted the route Jesus was taking in Jericho, ran ahead, found a tree that he could climb, and then climbed that tree so he could see Jesus as Jesus walked by. In the language I grew up hearing in West Texas, Zacchaeus "got 'er done!"

The persistence of Zacchaeus paid off handsomely. Jesus not only went the direction Zacchaeus predicted, allowing Zacchaeus to be seen, but Jesus saw Zacchaeus! Jesus stopped under the tree, called Zacchaeus by name, and then invited himself to lunch at Zacchaeus' house! Through persistence, Zacchaeus got to see Jesus, be seen by Jesus, dine with Jesus, talk with Jesus, and be changed by Jesus.

I want persistence. Each day, I want a Zacchaeus attitude. I want to see Jesus in every moment of my day. In struggles and in good times, I want to see Jesus. In joyous and sad times, I want to see Jesus. I am going to try and be persistent in seeing Jesus!

Lord, open my eyes to see you in my moments today. Through Jesus I pray, amen!

And when Jesus came to the place, he looked up and said to him, "Zacchaeus, hurry and come down, for I must stay at your house today." So he hurried and came down and received him joyfully. (Lk. 19:5–6)

My pastor and friend for over a decade and his marvelous wife have a "life verse." Their family life verse is from the writings of Paul to the church at Ephesus. Paul wrote to the Ephesians that God "is able to do far more abundantly than all that we ask or think, according to the power at work within us" (Eph. 3:20). Pastor David and Beverly even had this verse engraved on a stone that sits outside their home bearing witness to God's bountiful graciousness.

Zacchaeus could have had the same stone! Zacchaeus at least had the same testimony after his experience with Jesus. Consider the well-known story. Here was this diminutive fellow who desperately wanted to see Jesus. Jesus had just finished healing a blind man right outside the gates to Jericho. Then entering Jericho, Jesus had a massive crowd all around him. Zacchaeus couldn't see Jesus, try as he might. So, as a final effort to see the Lord, Zacchaeus found a sycamore tree on the path Jesus was walking, ran ahead, climbed the tree, and waited for his chance to lay eyes on the miracle worker.

One shouldn't be surprised that God ensured that Zacchaeus would get that chance to see Jesus. After all, this is the same God who has assured people that those who seek God will find him (Mt. 7:7). But in true Ephesians fashion, Zacchaeus got so much more than he ever dreamed of. He didn't just get a glimpse of the Lord. Jesus stopped and spoke with Zacchaeus. More than that, Jesus invited himself to Zacchaeus' house for a meal! The Lord put Zacchaeus on his agenda, called him by name, gave him personal attention, and brought salvation into his house.

This is the amazing God we serve. God at work is an awesome spectacle to behold. When we walk in his will, seek first his kingdom, and prayerfully serve him, God showers us with his blessings.

I want to live in these blessings of God. I want the thrill of seeing his hand work in my life for the glory of his kingdom. I don't want this to be selfish. This isn't about me getting things I want. This is about God using me for his good purposes. As Keith Green sang, "and when I'm doing well, help me to never seek a crown, for my reward is giving glory to you!" ("Oh Lord, You're Beautiful"). Then with my friends, with Paul, with the Ephesians, with Zacchaeus, I can proclaim the wonders of my bountifully gracious God!

O Lord, I seek your face. Shine your light through me into the dark world for your glory. Let my life bring you honor. Through the marvelous Lord Jesus I pray, amen.

NOVEMBER 14

And when they saw it, they all grumbled, "He has gone in to be the guest of a man who is a sinner." (Lk. 19:7)

The well-known adage, "Do you see the glass half empty or half full?" reveals something deeply rooted in human nature. Are people optimists or pessimists? Life's experience (and maybe even a bit of DNA) has left some folks always thinking the best of situations, while others are more wary of what might go wrong. There is nothing wrong with being an optimist nor with having a healthy degree of skepticism. Humanity needs those who dream of things that never were and ask, "Why not?" as well as the realists who see things as they are and ask, "Why?" But there is a subtle difference between being a realist, or even a pessimist, and being one who finds disdain in the good in this world.

Some people, confronted with good, will insist on finding the bad. This is not a good trait, but it is one on display in today's text. Understand the context behind today's verse. A crowd of people had gathered around Jesus in Jericho. Jericho was a notable town. This was the first battle for the Israelites after crossing the Jordan River in their conquest of the Promised Land. It was at Jericho that God miraculously caused the walls to fall down without so much as a stone being thrown by the Israelites. Jericho, a town that got its start by observing the miracles of the Lord, is visited by Jesus.

Jesus begins his entry into Jericho by healing a blind beggar. One mustn't gloss over that. This man had been begging for years from the people of Jericho. Everyone saw him, many gave him money, and he struggled for a subsistent living. Then comes Jesus and BAM!, just like that, the man has 20/20 vision. This was unheard of, amazing, and full of incredible ramifications. The crowd around Jesus is intense! What else will this man do? What other miracles might he perform? What a day to be in Jericho! What good fortune to be around when this happened! None of the Jews had been in Jericho that fateful day of the invasion some 1,200 years before, but they were there now!

Then the next miracle occurs. Jesus takes an interest in a short, rich tax collector named Zacchaeus who is despised by the community. Jesus decides to go eat lunch at Zacchaeus' house. One mustn't gloss over this either. Zacchaeus might not have seen Jesus absent great effort and persistence. Jesus could have chosen to eat anywhere, but he went where there was a searching soul, ripe for the harvest in God's kingdom. Jesus taught that the angels in heaven rejoice when a lost soul enters the kingdom. So here it happened.

Yet someone always grumbles. Yes, on this amazing day of miracles, these people were grumbling. That isn't optimism, pessimism, or realism. That is disdain for the hand of God.

Lord, forgive my grumbling. May I always find pleasure in your works. In Jesus, amen.

NOVEMBER 15

For the Son of Man came to seek and to save the lost. (Lk. 19:10)

John Newton (1725–1807) made his money trafficking in human flesh. Working on ships, in his own words he was "exceedingly vile." In his autobiography he wrote, "I not only sinned with a high hand myself, but made it my study to tempt and seduce others upon every occasion." Newton describes in lucid, but not lurid, detail his life as a sinner. Over and over God was calling out to him, and he profanely ran from God. Finally, Newton gave in to God's call.

Newton found grace in a number of passages in the Bible. It was paramount to him that Jesus come to save him, the chief of sinners. Today's passage says it succinctly. Jesus' mission, his reason for incarnating as a human, for spending his life among people, for teaching those who would learn, for healing those who were sick, for feeding those who were hungry, for consoling those hurting, and for dying for all sinners, for resurrecting unto a new life, and for promising to come again to complete the good work he began in his children is all wrapped up in this passage: The Lord Jesus became a Son of Man in order that he might seek and save those who were lost.

This reality moves many to song. When young, we sang a song in church proclaiming, "Blessed assurance, Jesus is mine. O what a foretaste of glory divine. Heir of salvation, purchase of God, born of His Spirit, washed in His blood. Perfect submission, all is at rest. I in my Savior am happy and blessed. Watching and waiting, looking above, filled with His goodness, lost in His love. This is my story, this is my song, praising my Savior all the day long."

Newton had a song too. He wrote one of Christendom's most well-known and deeply moving songs: "Amazing Grace." The song is so frequently sung that one can easily overlook the lyrics. But the lyrics make the song brilliant and are worthy of careful and prayerful reflection.

Amazing grace, how sweet the sound,
That saved a wretch like me.
I once was lost, but now I'm found,
Was blind, but now I see.

The third verse proclaims my hope this day and each day. "The Lord hath promised good to me. His word my hope secures; he will my shield and portion be as long as life endures." I grieve over Newton's life of sin, but it brought a brightness to God's grace that shines through the ages for me and many others since.

Lord, with humble gratitude, thank you for seeking and saving me. In Jesus, amen.

NOVEMBER 16

As he said these things, a woman in the crowd raised her voice and said to him, "Blessed is the womb that bore you, and the breasts at which you nursed!" But he said, "Blessed rather are those who hear the word of God and keep it!" (Lk. 11:27–29)

When driving a car, one is generally kept headed properly by the system of roads. As long as I drive on the right road, I am assured I am headed the right direction. But directions are a bit different in boats and airplanes. There are no lanes that keep your boat or airplane on course. You can drift right or left without a curb or shoulder insisting you keep going the right way. GPS and guidance systems become extremely helpful with these vehicles. Typically, a screen will show the captain or pilot when the vessel of aircraft is moving off target.

Ethical choices, values that sculpt our actions and priorities, are like boats and planes. The path for life isn't always marked out by clear roads. Some external instruction is needed, and often a need for correction is there.

Jesus and the word of God are like the GPS and guidance systems of boats and planes. We set our course, and Jesus guides us gently moving us back on course when we wander or stray. Consider in this sense, today's passage. Jesus has just explained an important truth to a crowd that is divided. Some of the crowd were in amazement that Jesus had cast out a demon. Others in the crowd were thinking that Jesus commanded demons only because Jesus was in cahoots with the Prince of Demons. Jesus illustrated the illogic of the skeptics, causing a woman to shout out a proverb, likely in general use, "Blessed is your mom for bringing you into this world!"

Now without a doubt, Jesus' mother was blessed. Luke has already gone into great detail about the blessedness of Mary in the beginning of his gospel. But the woman's statement was a little off course. She could have stated the truth more profoundly. So like a GPS, Jesus nudges the woman back on course. The true blessed ones are those who hear the word of God and keep it! That, by the way, did include Mary the mother of Jesus, but it also includes you, me, and anyone else who follows the Lord and his teaching.

I love this picture of Jesus. It is one of the teachings that trigger in my mind the song lyrics of Keith Green's "Lord, You're Beautiful": "I want to take your word and shine it all around. But first help me just to live it, Lord. And when I'm doing well, help me to never seek a crown; for my reward is giving glory to you." That is squarely on course with where I want my life headed.

Lord, please continue to guide me in life. Help me see and understand where my course needs correcting. Help me to follow you carefully and purposefully. In Jesus, amen.

NOVEMBER 17

Now the tax collectors and sinners were all drawing near to hear him. And the Pharisees and the scribes grumbled, saying, "This man receives sinners and eats with them." (Lk. 15:1–2)

Today's passage strikes me as odd. Think about it for a moment. You have three types of people in the passage: Tax collectors and sinners count as one type. The Pharisees and scribes count as a second type. And Jesus is the third one in the group.

To the righteous Jews of Jesus' day, tax collectors were among the worst of sinners. After all, they worked for the Roman Empire, the occupiers of God's holy land that was given to Abraham and his offspring. The Romans didn't belong there, and any Jew who worked for them was a collaborator or traitor. Furthermore, these tax collectors took money from good Jews and gave it to the Roman authorities. On top of all this, the tax collectors were having to deal with all sorts of people from all walks of life, all nationalities, and all ethnic backgrounds. This put the tax collector in a constant state of impurity, as the Pharisees understood the law. Of course, no one likes to pay taxes, and it is not surprising that almost everyone believed every tax collector was overcharging and skimming money from the collection process. Tax collectors were hated and despised.

The second type were the Pharisees and scribes. Pharisees had descended from the pious Jews who fought and gave their lives to stop Judea from becoming a Greek religious outpost. After Alexander the Great took Greek religion and culture throughout the Mediterranean world, including Judea, efforts were made to bring Greek religion into Judea. Even the Jewish temple was used to sacrifice offerings to Greek gods. A righteous set of Jews arose that stood firmly for the law of Moses, rebelling against the governing powers and refusing to let the nation worship idols. From these pious leaders arose the Pharisees who viewed themselves the watchdogs of proper Judaism. Because they would stand firm for righteousness under the law, they trusted God would protect their nation. The scribes were scholars who knew the law and copied the law for others to access. Spending their days writing out and working through the law letter by letter, they knew the holy writings extremely well. Hence, they were often hand in hand with the Pharisees who were enforcing the law.

Then there was Jesus. Jesus was the Holy One, God Incarnate. Jesus was approached by the sinners and tax collectors who held Jesus in fascination. Jesus spent his time with them, seeking to reach their hearts for the kingdom. This is why this is odd to me. I would think the Pharisees and scribes would rejoice over God reaching the lost. But I don't think they saw Jesus for who he was. I think they distrusted him and his motives. Without faith, we are blind to what God is about.

Lord, give me faith. Let my heart align with yours for the lost. For Jesus' sake, amen.

NOVEMBER 18

And he said to his disciples, "Temptations to sin are sure to come, but woe to the one through whom they come!" (Lk. 17:1)

At the root of today's passage are several seminal truths about true spiritual living. Four that stand out are: (1) the reality of sin; (2) the reality of temptation; (3) the influence one can have over another, and (4) the responsibility everyone has to those around her or him.

"Sin" as a concept is often reduced to a list of do's and don'ts. While do's and don'ts certainly exist, and many of them can comprise a list, at the root, sin is something much more insidious. Sin is an infection that causes death. Sin is destructive to the human spirit. Sin is also something that bears bad fruit in this life. Sin might produce momentary happiness, but sin destroys joy. Sin might make life's road seem easier or more interesting, but the road always leads to something destructive. Sin isn't an arbitrary list of do's and don'ts; sin is behavior and attitudes that lead to bad consequences. In a simple definition, sin is ungodliness. Because humanity was made in God's image, ungodliness by definition runs contrary to what is best for people.

Temptation to sin seems built into the human DNA. Inherent in the human condition after the fall is a bent toward sin. Even reading the last paragraph about the truth of sin's mighty destruction, many will read to try to think of "exceptions." God didn't make humanity with a bent toward sin. This tendency came as a core negative fallout from the first sin. That sin, as God had warned, led to death. That death included death of human purity. I will be tempted to sin today. That is a fact. How I handle that temptation will require me to stay focused on God and living by his power.

Not only will the temptation to sin come my way, but it will come to yours as well. One question each person must make daily is how one lives around others. I can choose to help people walk in righteousness. I can choose to be indifferent to how others act. Or I can even choose to tantalize others with the allure of sin. It might seem strange to think that anyone would tempt another to sin, at least after entering adulthood, but it happens. This isn't just offering an alcoholic a drink or suggesting one pocket a candy bar at a store. This includes asking another to tell a lie to cover for this or that. This includes getting someone to join in overindulging at a meal (yes, gluttony is a sin!). This includes many things that, at first blush, might seem innocuous.

This leads to the final truth. Everyone has a responsibility to others. By my words, actions, and choices, I will influence those around me. I want to influence them for good!

Lord, please give me the presence of mind to live with love for others. In Jesus, amen.

NOVEMBER 19

The apostles said to the Lord, "Increase our faith!" And the Lord said, "If you had faith like a grain of mustard seed, you could say to this mulberry tree, 'Be uprooted and planted in the sea,' and it would obey you." (Lk. 17:5–6)

Today's passage sounds alarm bells in my trial lawyer mind. Had this interchange happened in court, a lawyer would be very tempted to stand up and say, "Objection, your honor. Nonresponsive!" In other words, the apostles made a request that Jesus increase their faith. Jesus doesn't say yes or no. Jesus seems to give a response that is not necessarily a valid response to the request. Yet Jesus wasn't deflecting the question. Jesus' response may be subtle, but it is directly on point.

I have a level of faith in God. By "faith," the Greek word is used in its fuller meaning than simply our English idea of "belief." The Greek word (*pistis*, πίστις) references not only an intellectual knowledge but also an experiential trust. The word also includes an idea of commitment. The apostles, then, are asking that Jesus increase their level of trust and commitment to God and his work. This is a good request, one that I should also be making of the Lord.

How does Jesus respond? Jesus responds by motivating them to grow in faith. Jesus tells them the great value of faith. Trusting in God, committing oneself to God's plans and purposes, is greatly desirable. It enables one to do things that are not possible by human effort. Jesus uses expressions that were common in his day to make the point that with a trusting commitment to God, the impossible will become possible.

Knowing this to be true in and of itself gives me a greater level of trust (or faith) in God. I can safely rely upon God in the face of anything, knowing that God isn't limited as I am. What I could never do isn't the issue if I am trusting in God. The issue is simply what God can and will do.

Jesus gave the apostles an answer that was on point. The answer was one that in itself increases faith as one understands the value of faith. It makes one want to live a more trusting and committed life. When I live my life by my own objectives, when I trust in my mind, my willpower and drive, my money and resources, or anything at my command, I will always be limited. But when I put my trust and commitment in God, there is no limit to what can be done in and through me.

With this greater understanding of the passage, I realize that if this had transpired in court, when I said, "Objection, nonresponsive!," a wise judge would say, "Overruled!"

Lord, please increase my faith. Help me to more fully trust and commit my life to you. In Jesus, amen.

NOVEMBER 20

Will any one of you who has a servant plowing or keeping sheep say to him when he has come in from the field, "Come at once and recline at table"? Will he not rather say to him, "Prepare supper for me, and dress properly, and serve me while I eat and drink, and afterward you will eat and drink"? Does he thank the servant because he did what was commanded? So you also, when you have done all that you were commanded, say, "We are unworthy servants; we have only done what was our duty." (Lk. 17:7–10)

Among the many sayings of Jesus, today's passage cries out for one to transport into the culture of Jesus' day. For many today, at least in Western cultures, the passage seems harsh. But two thousand years ago, the teaching would have made good sense.

If one understands the passage in its era, then one is able to interpret the passage and apply it to today's values and practices. In New Testament times, servants were quite common. The role and responsibility of a servant was not only understandable, but normal. (It is noteworthy that God set out clear instructions for how Israel was to treat servants, giving them status and rights not otherwise available in the surrounding cultures.) The servant was a worker who received wages for what he/she did. The servant was also under the protection of the "employer."

A servant/worker was paid and protected to do as the employer instructed. Hence, if a servant's job was to work for a time in the field, and then to come into the house and prepare and serve supper, then the worker was expected to do that. The employer wasn't unfairly expecting the laborer to labor. In fact, getting to serve at the master's table was a job of honor for a servant. Food preparation and service involved a great deal of trust. One could easily poison another in the process. One could also use old or spoiled food, and make those who ate it quite sick. The servant Jesus is referencing in this hypothetical story is given a job of high honor.

Within that frame of reference, one can better understand the point Jesus is making, and then apply that teaching to today. Jesus made the point that when a position of honor is given to a servant, then that servant should be blessed by getting to perform the job.

Here is what this story means to me on a personal level in today's language. I gave my life to God. I told God that I was his; everything I have, everything I hope for, I pledged to his service. God will take that from me, protect me, and put me to work for his kingdom. I shouldn't expect God to say, "Thank you, Mark. I am in your debt!" That God would use me is a blessing beyond measure. Heaven forbid I should seek a pat on my shoulder for the service I am giving to the Lord. That I get to serve him is such an honor in itself.

Lord, THANK YOU for letting me serve you. It is my pleasure and honor! In Jesus, amen.

NOVEMBER 21

Being asked by the Pharisees when the kingdom of God would come, he answered them, "The kingdom of God is not coming in ways that can be observed, nor will they say, 'Look, here it is!' or 'There!' for behold, the kingdom of God is in the midst of you." (Lk. 17:19–20)

The United States of America does not have a king. The U.S. was formed after a rebellion against a king, and the government was set up as a republic. A number of countries still have kings, but the form of government that gives a king control over the lives of subjects is rare. At the time of Jesus, things were quite different.

Rome was an empire with an emperor who ruled with an iron fist. Other lands still had kings who presided over kingdoms, but most countries in the Mediterranean world were subject to Rome.

Israel had an interesting history with kings. As the law was given to Moses on Sinai, Israel wasn't going to have an earthly king but were to consider God as their king. Over time, Israel sought and finally got an earthly king, with all the negatives as well as pluses that brought. Eventually the kingdoms of Israel and Judah were conquered by foreign kings, and the nations/people of Israel and Judah were subject to foreign powers. Judah and the Jews lived in constant hope and assurance that God would send a Messiah who would restore the kingdom that rightly belonged to God.

In today's passage, one sees the Pharisees thinking one thing, while Jesus knew something different. The Pharisees wanted to know when the kingdom of God would come, thinking that God was going to restore Judah as a kingdom, with God ruling, perhaps through his earthly designated king.

Jesus knew the kingdom of God was something far greater than the Pharisees imagined. The true kingdom of God is ruled by the King of kings—Jesus the Messiah, the Son of God. Just as King Jesus was in the midst of the people at that moment, the "kingdom" was in the midst of them as well. The kingdom would be populated not with subjects forced to live within certain geographic boundaries. The kingdom would be without geography and would be comprised of all who entered of their own free choice. This kingdom wasn't something anyone would see, in the sense of an earthly government or location.

The Pharisees didn't understand the kingdom, and they didn't understand Jesus the King. Two thousand years later, I am in a better position to see this. I can see that God does reign, he does have a kingdom, and I am honored to be a part of it.

Lord and King, may my service in your kingdom bring you glory! Through Jesus, amen.

NOVEMBER 22

The kingdom of heaven is like treasure hidden in a field, which a man found and covered up. Then in his joy he goes and sells all that he has and buys that field. (Mt. 13:44)

If you were to take the time to think through and make a list of things you want, what would the list look like? Just because you're reading a devotional book, don't think merely devotional thoughts. Be real world. Do you want a new car? New clothes? A new place to live? A new job? A new relationship? Better health? Peace of mind? Out of trouble you find closing in on you? Release from commitments you wish you hadn't made? Out from under the weight of economic woes? Success at work or school? Respect from others? Deeper or stronger friendships? More talent in one area or another? Truthfully, a lot of people will find a lot of the above on their lists.

Into that real world of desires comes a profound teaching of Jesus. Jesus compared the kingdom of heaven to a treasure hidden in a field. A fellow finds the treasure, covers it so others don't see it, and then goes to buy the field, even though it takes everything the man has to get it. This man isn't miserable through all this. He is filled with joy. He does so gladly.

This teaching fits into my thinking on several levels. First, it established the great value of God's kingdom. Experiencing life with God is of the greatest value. It should be number one on my want list. Life with God is of greater worth than anything else I can imagine. It produces the deepest joy, the warmest peace, and the greatest fruit.

On another level, however, I see this teaching as helping to make sense of the rest of my want list. In this sense, there is nothing on my want list that I wouldn't gladly give up to be in a thriving relationship with God. But I also learn that when I'm in a vibrant walk with the Lord, he will inform me on the rest of my want list.

God will teach me what is valuable and what isn't. God will lead me in what I should have and what will distract me from walking with him. God will provide me what I need to produce fruit for him and his kingdom. God will heal that which needs healing. God will create what needs creating. God will have his way with me, and that will result in joy, not misery.

There isn't a thing on my want list that God will miss. If something doesn't belong on the list, he will remove it. If it does, he will see to it at the right time. This is kingdom living. It is why being in relationship with God in his kingdom needs to be my number one desire.

Lord, I would give all I have to know you, forever the hope in my heart. In Jesus, amen.

NOVEMBER 23

Then he left the crowds and went into the house. And his disciples came to him, saying, "Explain to us the parable of the weeds of the field." He answered . . . (Mt. 13:36–37)

Watching my little sister grow up, then having five children of my own along with nephews and nieces, and now with nine grandchildren, I have seen that most every child goes through the questioning stage. Sometimes it is as plain as is often displayed in the entertainment industry when a young child says, "Why?" always chasing down the next level of inquiry. ("Eat your vegetables, please." "Why?" "Because they will help your body grow!" "Why?" "Because they have vitamins that are used by your body!" "Why?" . . .)

Then I read passages like today's and I smile. I can envision the scene. Jesus is teaching crowds. He does it telling parables. The disciples, those who have been following Jesus diligently and consistently, are among those hearing the parables. One would think after following Jesus for an extended time, and after being with Jesus in the down times, that the disciples would be spot on, following and even expecting what Jesus was teaching. Yet they were often clueless. The disciples would hear Jesus teaching the masses, and then stumble around mentally together, trying to grasp what the master teacher was saying.

So, in today's passage Matthew delivers a revealing aspect of the disciples' walk with the Lord. The disciples didn't ask in front of everyone else, but listened respectfully, awaiting the moment when they could ask the Lord what on earth he was talking about!

The smaller group of those most intimate with Jesus went into a home with him. It was there they came up and asked, "Why?" (Or more specifically, "What?") They needed Jesus to explain his story about the weeds. This was a parable of wheat that was sown in hopes of a crop. Then an enemy came and threw weed seeds in the midst of the field. The weeds grew up alongside the wheat. The field workers wondered if the master had used bad seed, but the master explained that the weeds were the result of an enemy. The master then gave instructions on how to best harvest the wheat among the weeds.

The disciples didn't get the teaching. It went right over their heads. So, they waited until they had Jesus alone and asked what he was talking about. Jesus didn't laugh at them, didn't ignore them, didn't tell them to chill out, and didn't leave them on their own. He explained the teaching to them.

I like this simple truth. It tells me to take my questions to God. I need to pray for his wisdom and insight. I need to trust him to teach me when the time is right.

Lord, I do need your wisdom. I have questions about life that need your answers. Please teach me. Lead me. Make my paths straight before you. In Jesus, amen.

NOVEMBER 24

He put another parable before them, saying, "The kingdom of heaven is like a grain of mustard seed that a man took and sowed in his field. It is the smallest of all seeds, but when it has grown it is larger than all the garden plants and becomes a tree, so that the birds of the air come and make nests in its branches." (Mt. 13:31-32)

Today's parable has taken many turns in my life over the years. When I was a child, and thought like a child, I was bothered by the parable. Jesus said that the mustard seed was the "smallest of all seeds," yet my research indicated it wasn't! Similarly, mustard seeds grow into bushes, albeit tall ones (6-20 feet). Nothing like a majestic oak. Was Jesus flawed? As I grew up, I understood my immaturity in reading the passage. Jesus was telling a parable, which often used language and illustrations purposefully extreme to make a point. (Like, you see a speck in your brother's eye, but miss the plank in your own.) Furthermore, Jesus was likely using an adage popularized in his age, not unlike our maxim, "Great oaks from little acorns grow."

As I aged, I thought, "Well, if Jesus wasn't teaching botany, what was he teaching?" I realized then that I needed to read the passage in context as a parable. Matthew sets the passage into several teachings on the kingdom. This parable teaches that the kingdom grows from small, unnoticeable, inauspicious beginnings into something that can't go unnoticed, something that provides an environment to affect the world around it (where birds can nest). Then even later in life, I realized the personal aspect of this parable in my own life.

As one in the kingdom of God, I can see how it began small. I came to God contrite, and needing his touch, but my life on the whole was not that different before and after I came to him. I recognize that others have stories that are different, but for me, the kingdom started in my life in small ways. But as I have walked with God, that smallness has not continued.

As God's kingdom has thrived in my life, God has brought great changes in me as he has grown in my heart. God has renewed my mind, so I don't think the ways I did in the beginning. God has transformed my desires to more closely conform to the desires of his heart. God has chased away fears that used to dominate my thoughts and affect my actions. God has fortified my faith as I have experienced his reliability in life's most challenging moments. God has gently molded my love as he has unfolded his love more deeply in me.

I'm no longer troubled by the botany of Jesus' parable. I am merely thankful that God is at work, and I pray he will continue to grow me for service in his kingdom.

Lord, please do work in me and through me. Grow me for your kingdom in Jesus, amen.

A sower went out to sow. And as he sowed, some seeds fell along the path, and the birds came and devoured them. Other seeds fell on rocky ground, where they did not have much soil, and immediately they sprang up, since they had no depth of soil, but when the sun rose they were scorched. And since they had no root, they withered away. Other seeds fell among thorns, and the thorns grew up and choked them. Other seeds fell on good soil and produced grain, some a hundredfold, some sixty, some thirty. He who has ears, let him hear. (Mt. 13:3–9)

Whenever I read Jesus saying, "He who has ears, let him hear," I always hear a voice in my head shout out, "I have ears!!!" I want to hear and understand the teachings of my Lord. That can be difficult with some things, but this parable makes good sense, even if Jesus hadn't gone to the trouble to explain it later in the chapter.

When Jesus taught in Galilee, many listeners were directly involved in agriculture. Not surprisingly, Jesus used farming in many of his stories and analogies. It would have rung true with his listeners. Today's passage is a splendid example. The parable is about the kingdom of God, yet it centers on a farmer out broadcasting his seed. Jesus categorizes the seed into four groups.

The first group fell on the hardened path and birds came and ate it. Jesus described this seed as those who hear of the kingdom of God, but don't "understand" it. The verb translated as "understand" also means "think about." Some will hear of God and Jesus, but don't think about it. It goes in one ear and out the other. Or to keep with the agricultural metaphors, the message never gets below the surface to take root and grow.

The second group was thrown in rocky soil with no depth. They had an enthusiastic reception of the good news, but when the scorching sun beat down, without roots these withered away. There are some who will hear of God with excitement and joy, but when the difficulties of life come (and they most assuredly come to all), these wither from their faith, rather than take strength from it.

The third group are the seeds that fall among the thorns, a weed seed. These are those almost opposite the previous group. They aren't withering from the hardships of life (the scorching sun), but rather are seduced by the riches of life. The thorns are weeds that choke out the message. There is a real danger in life that money, success, and other seductions will distract one from growing in trust and reliance on the Lord!

I want to be group four. I want to think about, understand, and grow in the Lord in the good days and the bad. I have ears!

Lord, may I be fruitful in your kingdom to your glory! In Jesus, amen.

Then the disciples came and said to him, "Why do you speak to them in parables?" And he answered them, "To you it has been given to know the secrets of the kingdom of heaven, but to them it has not been given. For to the one who has, more will be given, and he will have an abundance, but from the one who has not, even what he has will be taken away. This is why I speak to them in parables, because seeing they do not see, and hearing they do not hear, nor do they understand. Indeed, in their case the prophecy of Isaiah is fulfilled that says: 'You will indeed hear but never understand, and you will indeed see but never perceive.' For this people's heart has grown dull, and with their ears they can barely hear, and their eyes they have closed, lest they should see with their eyes and hear with their ears and understand with their heart and turn, and I would heal them." (Mt. 13:10-15)

Today's long passage is quoted at length because it is a difficult one for many, especially in the versions as written by Mark and Luke (who also record this). Growing up I used to read this passage real fast and move on, because it made me so uncomfortable. I thought, my God isn't like that! He wants everyone to repent! He wouldn't hide something from someone to keep them in the dark about salvation!

As I aged, I began to realize the importance of this in context. Matthew sandwiches this statement of Jesus between the parable of the sower and Jesus' explanation of that parable. In the parable of the sower, Jesus explained four different groups who hear the message. Group one hears, but it doesn't register. It goes in one ear and out the other. Jesus' point isn't that they don't understand it because it's in a parable. Rather it is the condition of the person that they really don't care to consider it. Their heart prevents receiving the message. The second group hears, but they junk the kingdom message when hard times strike. The third group hears, but they jettison the kingdom in favor of the security and pleasures that come from riches. The fourth group hears and holds to the message.

Jesus knew people's hearts. Parables are marvelous tools for the saved to learn, savor, contemplate, and remember his teaching. So there was a great positive purpose for parables. But for many who were bad soil types, who would never embrace the message, and at best would act excited only to wither with the sun or get choked out, then the parables went right over their heads. It really wouldn't have done them any good to hear if they were to junk it later.

But for all who are to hear with good soil, listen! Jesus is God, and God would like all to be saved. What a pity that some choose not to care. I want to be good soil.

Lord, thank you for your love and care. Bless those around me with receptive hearts to your kingdom. May your word grow deep in me and those around me. In Jesus, amen.

NOVEMBER 27

But blessed are your eyes, for they see, and your ears, for they hear. For truly, I say to you, many prophets and righteous people longed to see what you see, and did not see it, and to hear what you hear, and did not hear it. (Mt. 13:16–17)

Almost everyone is familiar with the old adage, "The grass is greener on the other side of the fence." It runs alongside the maxim of "taking something for granted." It is a simple truth of people's myopic mental life. What we are used to, we too commonly think too little of. What we don't have can captivate us more than those things with which we have grown comfortable.

In today's passage, Jesus points out to his disciples the importance of appreciating the moment in a way that challenges my attitude today. The disciples were getting to experience Jesus in full ministry. They were walking daily with the Incarnate God. They saw firsthand his love for people. They saw his disdain for the proud and arrogant. They witnessed his passion for the Father and kingdom. They listened to his wise teaching. They truly experienced not once-in-a-lifetime moments, but once in the history of humanity moments. Jesus didn't want them to miss that truth.

Jesus knew that compared to even the holy prophets of the Old Testament, the disciples were getting something extremely rare. Those great Old Testament prophets, whose declarations comprise our Bibles, had longed for the fulfillment of the prophecies, but they could only speak of them. The fulfillment wouldn't come until Jesus. The disciples, however, got to see the fulfillment! What a day!

I think of this in light of my life now. Part of me laments not being present at the time of Jesus, a chance to be among those who experienced him day to day. Yet, look at today's time. People live today with the entire counsel of God's word in Scripture. A huge blessing! People get to live after many generations, inspired by the very Spirit of God, have considered, contemplated, grown, and taught about God, explaining him in ways that have taken time to understand. The church has produced the scriptural and godly doctrines of the Trinity, explained the concept of justification by faith, and so many more aspects of the Christian walk that even the apostles didn't fully have. The faith today is no longer limited to Jerusalem, Judea, or even the Roman Empire. It has spread around the world, and it continues to grow.

People today don't live in the time of Jesus' earthly ministry, but I live in a very rich time nonetheless. I need to be thankful for today, not wishing for yesterday or tomorrow. I need to serve God today, right here, right now. My grass is plenty green!

Lord, instill in me a vision for the present. Let me see you at work today in who I am and what I do. May I live to your glory, and give you all the praise possible. In Jesus, amen.

NOVEMBER 28

That same day Jesus went out of the house and sat beside the sea. And great crowds gathered about him, so that he got into a boat and sat down. And the whole crowd stood on the beach. (Mt. 13:1–2)

Some people are more gregarious than others. Some shine when exposed to friends, strangers, and audiences. Others shrink from such encounters. Whether you are an extrovert or an introvert, a lesson can be gleaned from today's passage.

The passage is simple enough, but placed into its context, it gives us something to aspire to in our lives. Jesus has been teaching in a home, and the people were lapping up his ministry. It was literally, a full house. Jesus' mother and brothers came to get him, and Jesus stayed with his Father's ministry rather than go outside immediately, as requested by his family.

At some point, however, Jesus did go outside. He left not so much to visit with his family, but to sit by the sea where "great crowds" could gather about and hear his teaching. Jesus moved on from where he was to make himself available to minister to God's people as best as he could. Here is the lesson for me.

I need to have the attitude of Jesus, which includes making myself available for the Father's business. It may be a day where I am not in the mood to socialize. I may not be the kind of person who naturally does well in conversations with others. But that is never the issue. Moses was ill-equipped to speak on behalf of God to the Pharaoh, yet God still used him. Moses was slow of speech, yet God still spoke through him. Moses was busy doing his own thing, yet God made him drop shepherding his father-in-law's herds so he could father God's sheep (Israel).

The question I need to ask and answer honestly is this: Where do I need to be, and what do I need to be doing, to be in the service for my Lord today? Would God have me listen to someone who has no one else to listen? Would God have me share the cure for sin with someone desperately in need? Would God have me comfort the bereaved? Would God have me inspire the faint of heart? Would God have me war against injustice or hatred? Would God have me be an example in a workplace rife with gossip, back-stabbing, or any host of ills?

Wherever God wants me, doing whatever God wants me to do, is my daily challenge. The life I live in this flesh, I am living on behalf of the one who saved me, called me, and set an example for me. I need to be available in God's service.

Lord, lead me on to wherever you will. Give me faith, wisdom, and stamina to follow your lead. Then bless my efforts for your kingdom. In Jesus' holy name, amen.

He went to a town called Nain, and his disciples and a great crowd went with him. As he drew near to the gate of the town, behold, a man who had died was being carried out, the only son of his mother, and she was a widow, and a considerable crowd from the town was with her. And when the Lord saw her, he had compassion on her and said to her, "Do not weep." Then he came up and touched the bier. . . . And he said, "Young man, I say to you, arise." And the dead man sat up and began to speak, and Jesus gave him to his mother. . . . They glorified God, saying, "A great prophet has arisen among us!" and "God has visited his people!" (Lk. 7:11-16)

Today's passage is touching and instructive. The story presents a compassionate Jesus who came in fulfillment of God's prophecies about the coming Messiah.

Jesus is walking and the story gives no insight that he was on mission for this, that, or the other. But while coming into a smallish town called Nain, Jesus had quite the entourage. By what almost seems coincidence, as Jesus and his followers headed into Nain, another crowd was headed out. The crowd accompanied a platform carrying a dead young man. Notably, the dead young man's mother was still alive. She was a widow, already having lost and buried her husband. That she had to then bury her son was an indescribable blow. As a widow, she would have been dependent on the son for her daily care. She not only was burdened with the grief of bereavement, but she also had the fear of survival. This was before the age of social security or other government intervention in the provision for those in need.

Jesus saw this and was moved in compassion. Jesus stopped the funeral procession and told the widow she could stop her weeping. The weeping undoubtedly turned to indescribable shouts of joy, as Jesus speaks to the dead young man, telling him to get up! The young man is resurrected and gets up immediately.

The compassion of Jesus is notable to me. Jesus wasn't asked to do anything. There is no indication the townspeople thought he was anything other than a visitor headed into their town. Jesus on his own met the deep emotional and physical needs of this woman. This is an important trait of our God. Our God answers prayers, but he also gives where he sees needs, regardless of prayer. He is a caring and compassionate God.

In describing the work of Jesus, Luke uses the precise wording of 1 Kings 17:23 that describes Elijah bringing back from the dead the son of the widow of Zeraphath. Hence, the people see Jesus as a "great prophet." Jesus was that great prophet, as well as one of great compassion. I think he can handle all my issues I will have today!

Father, I trust you with my day. I can't make it without you, but with you, there is no obstacle that can get in my way! I am blessed by you in Jesus, amen.

NOVEMBER 30

Then turning toward the woman he said to Simon, "Do you see this woman? I entered your house; you gave me no water for my feet, but she has wet my feet with her tears and wiped them with her hair. You gave me no kiss, but from the time I came in she has not ceased to kiss my feet. You did not anoint my head with oil, but she has anointed my feet with ointment. Therefore I tell you, her sins, which are many, are forgiven—for she loved much. But he who is forgiven little, loves little." And he said to her, "Your sins are forgiven." Then those who were at table with him began to say among themselves, "Who is this, who even forgives sins?" And he said to the woman, "Your faith has saved you; go in peace." (Lk. 7:44–49)

Today's passage comes at the end of a fascinating story. Jesus had been asked to dine at the house of a righteous Pharisee. Pharisees were the strictest among the Jews when it came to following the law of Moses. The dinner would have had a careful guest list, for dining carried social statements. One wouldn't dine with someone deemed inappropriate for company. This made it more notable that somehow a woman of disrepute came into the home, bringing with her an alabaster jar of ointment.

Dinners like this took place on benches typically shaped in a U around a table. The guests would recline on the benches to eat, lying on their sides. Thus, the feet of Jesus would be elevated. The woman came from behind Jesus, so on the side where his feet were, rather than tableside. The woman began weeping, pouring the ointment on Jesus' feet, which she was covering with her tears and kisses, all while wiping the feet clean with her hair. It was undoubtedly quite the sight.

This must have created quite the stir. The Pharisee started mumbling to himself that Jesus was clearly no prophet, for if Jesus had prophetic abilities, he would have known the woman was a prostitute. Only then in the story do we learn the Pharisees' name, for Jesus uses it. Jesus turned to Simon and we read today's passage.

Jesus knew who the woman was. Jesus knew her sins were real. Jesus forgave the sins openly and totally. This stunned Simon and his other guests. They wondered what right Jesus had to forgive sins. "Sins" (*hamartia*, ἁμαρτία) in this sense are a departure from divine righteousness. The guests wondered how Jesus could ever forgive someone's sins.

The answer, of course, is found in the person and work of Jesus. Jesus was and is God. As such he could forgive sins, although even God as a just God would have to forgive sins only based upon some righteousness. That righteousness would be the sacrificial death of Jesus on behalf of sinners. In a real sense, only Jesus could forgive sins. But he did so readily for her, and he does so for you and me also.

Father, I need the forgiveness of Jesus, and I thank you for it. In him, amen.

DECEMBER 1

Now a centurion had a servant who was sick and at the point of death, who was highly valued by him. When the centurion heard about Jesus, he sent to him elders of the Jews, asking him to come and heal his servant. . . . And Jesus went with them. When he was not far from the house, the centurion sent friends, saying to him, "Lord, do not trouble yourself, for I am not worthy to have you come under my roof. Therefore I did not presume to come to you. But say the word, and let my servant be healed. For I too am a man set under authority, with soldiers under me: and I say to one, 'Go,' and he goes; and to another, 'Come,' and he comes; and to my servant, 'Do this,' and he does it." When Jesus heard these things, he marveled at him, and turning to the crowd that followed him, said, "I tell you, not even in Israel have I found such faith." And when those who had been sent returned to the house, they found the servant well. (Lk. 7:2–10)

I hope there are people you value in your life. These are people you will look after, people whose well-being you care about, people whom you will go the extra mile for.

Today's passage teaches us about how we can help others. Most often, the healings of Jesus are performed on people who ask for Jesus' help. Blind people cry out, and Jesus heals them. The lame seek his touch, and Jesus heals them. The deaf ask Jesus, and he gives them hearing. Yet in today's passage we have one of several where the sick person isn't the one asking for Jesus' help. It is someone who cares for that person.

Interceding on behalf of another isn't new in the time of Jesus. Moses frequently interceded on behalf of Israel, seeking God's blessing over God's judgment. Jesus himself lived a life of intercession. Isaiah prophesied of Jesus saying, "he bore the sin of many, and makes intercession for the transgressors" (Isa. 53:12). The writer of Hebrews noted that Jesus "is able to save to the uttermost those who draw near to God through him, since he always lives to make intercession for them" (Heb 7:25). Repeatedly Paul would write of the Spirit interceding for the saints (Rom. 8:26, 27). Paul urged his protégé Timothy to see that the church pray and intercede for all people (1 Tim. 2:1).

God's people are to be people of intercession. This is part of the "great faith" Jesus noted that the Gentile centurion had, seeking Jesus to heal his servant.

I want to be an interceder. I want to seek God on behalf of those in need. To do this, I need to learn and discern those needs. I then need to pray about the needs. A final step, as God's hands and feet, I need to do all I can in the name of God to meet those needs of others. In this way, as God's instrument, I can be an intercessor in deed as well as words.

What a marvelous chance to serve God and people!

Lord, give me eyes and voice to intercede for those in need! In Jesus' name, amen.

DECEMBER 2

He said therefore to the crowds that came out to be baptized by him, "You brood of vipers! Who warned you to flee from the wrath to come? Bear fruits in keeping with repentance. And do not begin to say to yourselves, 'We have Abraham as our father.' For I tell you, God is able from these stones to raise up children for Abraham. Even now the axe is laid to the root of the trees. Every tree therefore that does not bear good fruit is cut down and thrown into the fire." (Lk. 3:7–9)

Some people are indirect communicators. When dealing with them, you must ferret out what they are trying to say by body language, context, and reading between the lines. Not so with John the Baptist. He spoke directly and forthrightly. With John the Baptist, you knew right where you stood. Ultimately this would cost him his head, but it is still refreshingly nice to read and see.

In today's passage, John is preaching to the masses who have come to hear this compelling prophet. John had been baptizing many people, calling on them to repent of their sins and turn over a new leaf before God. In his ministry teaching, he assured people that their birth status did nothing to ensure their situation with God. The Jews were descended from Abraham, and John didn't disparage that ancestry, for he shared it too. But for John, lineage didn't dictate relationship with God. As he explained to the Jews who came to him, God can make a Jew out of a rock. The issue is what is each person doing with their life, not who was their mom and dad!

I've always appreciated the biblical truth that God has children, but never does the Bible reference God having grandchildren. I am not right before God because of what my parents did. My parents may have had me baptized as an infant, but that wasn't my decision. It has nothing to do with what I decide to do with my life. I may have had a preacher as a father, but it doesn't mean I am a child of God.

Everyone needs to come to God individually. Everyone makes a choice of whether to give their lives to the Lord or not. Then beyond that, people choose how to live. Even among those who have given their lives to God they can engage in the struggle for holiness, or give up and go with the flow. Going with the flow for most is a walk in sin.

As I individualize this blunt teaching, I try to do a blunt assessment of my life. Have I truly given my life to Jesus? Have I addressed his call on me and answered with faith, seeking his forgiveness merited by his death at Calvary? Then having done that, do I live with him as my Lord? While I am not perfect, and while sin still tempts me, do I wage that fight seeking his strength? When I succeed do I praise him? When I fail, do I repent?

Lord, I do repent of sin, and ask you to be my Lord! I seek you through Jesus, amen.

ADVENT

Advent is the church season that occurs late in the modern calendar. Yet in the Western church's calendar, Advent signals the start of the year.

The term "Advent" comes from the Latin *adventus*, which signifies the idea of "arrival." Advent begins on the fourth Sunday before Christmas and ends on Christmas Eve. During this time, the church is expecting the arrival of Jesus.

Historically the Advent season celebrates the arrival of Jesus in three different aspects. First, Advent focuses on the common aspect of Jesus coming in the manger as the Christ child. The church contemplates the incarnation.

A second focus of the Advent season is the coming of Jesus into the lives of believers, an event that is constant and daily. Each day, we are to focus on how Jesus comes into our hearts, bringing light to darkness, uniting us to the Father, and giving us the tools to live daily in holiness.

A third focus of Advent is the prophetic promise that Christ will return again to this earth to finish making things right. He will claim his church as a bride and promises that the dark days of sin will be ended.

Advent is a season of beginning, a season of hope, a season of dedication, and a season of watchful anticipation. Each year the date Advent begins changes. This devotional book was written off the calendar year 2023, hence Advent devotionals begin with November 29 and run through Christmas Eve, when the next season of the church's calendar begins.

DECEMBER 3 (ADVENT 1)

There was a man sent from God, whose name was John. He came as a witness, to bear witness about the light, that all might believe through him. (Jn. 1:6–7)

Everyone—emphasize that word when reading—EVERYONE has a purpose before God. No exceptions. That means YOU have a purpose before God and I have a purpose before God. You may think your life is a wheel in a cage and you are the mouse. You might think your days go by while you run fruitlessly to no real purpose. Scripture teaches otherwise. We don't always see it because when we read of God's purposes brought to fruition through people, we think that those were the special ones. We are right that they were special because God purposed them in life. But you and I are no less special. He purposes EVERYONE.

Today's passage begins the season of Advent, at least for the year 2023. Advent is the season in the church calendar when people begin "expecting the arrival" of the Messiah. The incarnation of Jesus. In today's passage, John explained that Jesus didn't simply explode on the scene. God had people in place to prepare the way for him. That was a purpose in John the Baptist's life. John came as a witness to testify that Jesus was indeed the Messiah. Even John's life was not an accident, however. John was the result of a chain of events that God had in place to make him who he was, where he was, when he was. Seven hundred years before John was born, the prophet Isaiah wrote of him that he would come to "prepare the way for the Lord" (Isa. 40:3).

As I am writing this, I received a text from a friend. I had recently used my friend as an example in a book, calling him by his first name only. I pointed it out to my friend and his reply just texted to me read, "The way I feel about the Lord this day you can use my ss# and I am fine with it. Also after my bankruptcy it's not worth much." Sometimes we question our value and the lot we have in life. When we do, we need to remember this devotional lesson.

EVERYONE has value. EVERYONE has something to do with and for God. This is true today, it will be true tomorrow, and it will be true every day we live. God's world is a massive chain of events, all interconnected in a way that brings his kingdom to completion. We have roles in that. Our role today may be no more than being nice to the person who checks us out at the store. But when we are godly to that person, it can change that person's day. That person may be set on a better path that precludes them from doing something horrible that might have set off a cataclysmic chain of events. Or that person may simply be kinder to someone else. We don't know how all of time unfolds, but we can be sure, EVERYONE has a purpose before God.

Lord, teach me to walk holy before you today. May I show others your love and mercy. May I walk in the paths you have laid out for me, trusting you in Jesus' name. Amen.

DECEMBER 4 (ADVENT 2)

In the days of Herod, king of Judea, there was a priest named Zechariah, of the division of Abijah. And he had a wife from the daughters of Aaron, and her name was Elizabeth. And they were both righteous before God, walking blamelessly in all the commandments and statutes of the Lord. But they had no child, because Elizabeth was barren, and both were advanced in years. (Lk. 1:5–7)

Life without God leaves people to fend for themselves. One may have family and friends who assist in life, but ultimately, folks personally work to get what they want in life. Maybe we want a certain level of schooling, a certain job, a particular spouse, life here or there, children, and so forth. Beyond that we may be after less tangible things that are just as important, if not more so. We want good relationships with our families, good friends, a sense of satisfaction in life, joy underlying what we do each day, and more. We also work to avoid certain things. No one wants poor health, anxiety, depression, or those negative things that bring us down.

Life with God is one where we don't need to fend for ourselves. We have the assurance that when we are seeking God's will and when we put his kingdom first, then he will see to our lives being what they should be. Paul was able to write about the Christian's peace that passes understanding, even though he was imprisoned at the time of his writing (Phil. 4:7). Similarly, Paul wrote that the Lord had taught him how to thrive when life's resources were plentiful and also how to thrive when they were sparse (Phil. 4:10–14).

Sometimes we might wonder why, when we are God's, we don't seem to thrive in ways we think we should. In today's passage, we read of a godly priest named Zechariah who along with his godly wife Elizabeth, had walked in service to God for many years. The couple were past childbearing age without ever having a child. Children were a great want for them, but in spite of "doing everything right" before God, they had nothing to show for it . . . yet.

" . . . Yet," because God was at work in God's good timing for God's good purposes. A child was coming to this couple, and not just any child. John the Baptist was coming. Elizabeth was soon to be pregnant with the herald of God. John was the prophetic promise of Isaiah 40:3, "A voice cries: 'In the wilderness prepare the way of the LORD; make straight in the desert a highway for our God.'"

We need to take this story to heart. We need to be reminded that God has his plans and we are his people. The agenda is his, and his timing is not our timing. We need to not grow weary in well doing but trust that God has all things under control. If we ever feel we are doing everything right to no avail, we need to wait for the "yet."

Lord, give us patience in living for you. Keep our focus on you. In Jesus, amen.

DECEMBER 5 (ADVENT 3)

Now while he [Zechariah] was serving as priest before God when his division was on duty, according to the custom of the priesthood, he was chosen by lot to enter the temple of the Lord and burn incense. And the whole multitude of the people were praying outside at the hour of incense. And there appeared to him an angel of the Lord standing on the right side of the altar of incense. (Lk. 1:8–11)

Amazing things happen when you serve the Lord—especially while people are praying.

Consider today's passage. Zechariah was one of thousands of priests in his day. His job involved serving in the temple, offering sacrifices, burning incense, and dealing with the matters of Judah's faithful community. His particular assignment would differ day to day, but his work was normal for a priest. Two weeks a year, the priests would rotate and do their service in the temple. The events about to explode into Zechariah's life occurred while he was on temple rotation.

Priests had done the same jobs for centuries, without anything extraordinary happening. Zechariah and his wife, Elizabeth, had no reason to believe that when he left for work that particular day their world was going to turn upside down. Lots were cast for service assignments, and Zechariah's role was to enter the temple and offer incense. Some might say that the "luck of the draw," gave Zechariah the assignment to enter the temple and burn incense that day, but the Bible doesn't speak of "luck." By casting lots, the people believed that God granted the decision, not humans.

The incense was offered inside the temple itself. People weren't allowed in this inner room, only priests. Inside the room was a curtain that set apart another innermost room, called the Holy of Holies. That interior room was entered only once a year, and then only by the high priest. For Zechariah to enter into the temple was a responsibility of honor, but still not one where anything unusual was expected. Incense was offered every morning and evening, day in, day out, week after week, while months, years, decades, and centuries rolled by. It was service. It was a normal occurrence.

Yet this particular day was a turning point in history. Since before this temple had been built, the promise had been that God would send a prophet to prepare the way for the Messiah (Isa. 40). Little did Zechariah know that this would be the day of announcement! The Lord's long-awaited plans were rapidly unfolding, and Zechariah and Elizabeth were in the thick of it. The consolation of Israel was coming!

We never know what today will bring. It might be the expected—but beware! Amazing things happen when we serve the Lord!

Lord, use us today for your glory! We eagerly await your work in us. In Jesus, amen.

DECEMBER 6 (ADVENT 4)

And Zechariah was troubled when he saw him, and fear fell upon him. But the angel said to him, "Do not be afraid, Zechariah, for your prayer has been heard, and your wife Elizabeth will bear you a son, and you shall call his name John." (Lk. 1:12–13)

Most everyone remembers staying up late cramming for an exam. If not in school, then at some point in life most people have tried to remember certain things. I try hard to remember names of people when I meet them. I fail frequently, their names slipping my mind like water through my fingers. I wish my memory was flawless, but it isn't. God's memory is flawless, however, and that can be a huge blessing!

In today's passage, the story of Zechariah and Elizabeth is unfolding. Both righteous people, serving and honoring God with their lives, they had gone through their fertile years unable to have children. It was a constant prayer, perhaps turned into a lament in their old age. Zechariah had gone into the temple one day, doing his priestly duties of offering up incense on behalf of God's people. Suddenly, an angel of the Lord appeared, scaring Zechariah and turning a normal day into something extraordinary. The angel urged Zechariah to move from fear to faith because God had heard his prayers.

Zechariah had an interesting name, and the angel used it when speaking with him. The name is a Hebrew phrase composed of two Hebrew words. *Zechar* is from the Hebrew word often translated as "remember" (זָכַר). The *iah* comes from the Hebrew abbreviation for the name of God (יְהוָה) or "Yahweh" as modern English speakers reference it. So the angel calls out Zechariah, a name that can be understood to literally remind him (and us) that God remembers! God is not some forgetful God who struggles to remember who we are, what we need, what we want, or what our role is in his kingdom. God remembers and God takes action.

This passage speaks to the expectations of God's people who go to him in prayer. Our prayers may get an immediate answer (and sometimes that answer may be "No"). Or our prayers may get a delayed answer. If we are praying God's will, as Jesus taught us to do, then we can be confident God will answer that prayer, but it is God's timing, not ours.

Before the prayer is answered, we may, like Zechariah, be fearful. The unexpected can happen rather than what we prayed for or dreamed of. Yet we should work to turn that fear into faith. The unexpected to us is part of the plan of the God who remembers.

I have some exciting work to do in my life.

Lord, give me excitement over watching your work unfold daily in my life. As I go about my routines, teach me to be confident in your memory, secure in your love, and faithful through my fear. In Jesus' name, amen.

DECEMBER 7 (ADVENT 5)

And you will have joy and gladness, and many will rejoice at his [John the Baptist's] birth.
(Lk. 1:14)

I live in the United States of America. We have a calendar year that begins January 1 and runs through December 31. Ours is the same calendar year used the world over. We have Julius Caesar to thank for much of it. In 45 BC, Julius Caesar implemented January 1 as the beginning of the year. Over time (pun intended), various changes in the calendar occurred and the January start of the year wasn't official in England, and hence America, until 1750. From antiquity, Jewish civil calendars began with the month of Tishri, which generally lands in the September to October range on the Western calendar.

The church has also developed a calendar of the centuries. This season of the church calendar is the season of "Advent." "Advent" is from the Latin word *adventus*, typically translated as "arrival." Advent is the season before Christmas when the church is looking forward to the arrival of Jesus, which is celebrated on Christmas Day. On the church calendar Advent begins the fourth Sunday before Christmas, so it moves from the calendar date each year.

As a child, I did not keep a daily calendar, but that didn't leave me unaware of dates. I eagerly looked forward to my birthday, to Christmas, Thanksgiving, and other notable days. I looked forward because those days were important. They were days of joy, food, fun, family, and celebrating. As a Christian, Advent is a season of looking forward, of anticipation. We anticipate the birth of Jesus recognizing passages like that of today.

Today's passage spoke of Zechariah and Elizabeth's joy and gladness that would accompany the birth of John the Baptist. Looking back, we know that John the Baptist was the herald of Jesus. He was the one who came first, proclaiming Jesus and preparing the world to receive Jesus as Messiah God. In this we all experience joy. John the Baptist was a sort of "Advent" event himself. John was part of the train or procession of those who were coming before the Incarnate One. When the world saw and listened to John, they should have known that Jesus was behind him in the procession of God's train.

As this Advent season unfolds, we should all live in anticipation of the effect of the coming of Jesus. The birth of Jesus is not one where we were in attendance, taking a baby gift or giving presents to God (although the wise men showed up soon after with gifts). Jesus coming into the world is God giving a gift to us. God gave us the supreme gift. God gave us his very presence in a way that gives life and salvation to all who are accepting. I don't want the expectation of Jesus' arrival to get lost in my calendar!

Lord God, sometimes I get lost in my schedule and my list of "to do's." Please direct my attention to your work in this world and in my life through Jesus, amen.

DECEMBER 8 (ADVENT 6)

He [John the Baptist] will be great before the Lord. And he must not drink wine or strong drink, and he will be filled with the Holy Spirit, even from his mother's womb. And he will turn many of the children of Israel to the Lord their God. (Lk. 1:15–16)

Often when children hit middle school and even in high school, their dreams include one day being "great." For some that might mean becoming a sports star, for others a singer. Some might think about being president, while others want to be rich. Youth is a time of dreaming about what might be. As we age, some people change and lose the grandiose visions of childhood, while others continue to live in hopes of finding greatness in the world.

"Great" is a relative term, however. It means one thing to one person and can mean something entirely different to another. For some, great references fame and fortune. For others, it means being happy and content. Some are great based upon their family and friends. Others are great if they have the job of their dreams.

Today's passage speaks of John the Baptist as one who was going to be "great before the Lord." An angel of God was telling John's father about John's coming birth and life. This is an important story leading up to the birth of Jesus. The coming of John the Baptist is integral to the Advent season as part of the preparation and anticipation of the coming Messiah.

If we see John's purpose and mission as set out by the angel to his father Zechariah, we understand what it means to be great before the Lord. It isn't fame or fortune. It isn't comfort or leisure. It isn't a great family or social circle. "Great" before the Lord is living a life dedicated to God, walking by God's Spirit, and letting God work to bring about faith in others.

In this season of Advent, as we build up to the time of celebrating the Savior's birth, it is appropriate that we seek to become great before the Lord. We can dedicate ourselves to God, putting him above our desires and comfort, just as John chose to serve God and turn from the wine and strong drink that others enjoyed. We can pray for his Spirit to lead and guide us, as John was filled with the Spirit from his earliest days. We can live telling others, through our words and our deeds, about the marvelous God who came to earth to seek and save the lost. We can live as lights set on a hill, showing faith in the midst of life's stormy seas. People will watch us. People will hear us. People will be drawn to the Savior.

Greatness is achievable by everyone, if we understand true greatness before the Lord.

Lord, I give myself to you. May I put you above all other desires. May I gladly sacrifice for you. Fill me with your Spirit and use me to draw others to you, for Jesus' sake, amen.

DECEMBER 9 (ADVENT 7)

He [John the Baptist] will go before him in the spirit and power of Elijah, to turn the hearts of the fathers to the children, and the disobedient to the wisdom of the just, to make ready for the Lord a people prepared. (Lk. 1:17)

How do you react when you see something out of place? I was eating dinner with our daughter Rachel in a restaurant when a woman at the table next to us became visibly and audibly agitated because a picture on the far wall was slightly crooked. The woman was unable to eat until the picture was straightened. Her pleas to her husband to get up and straighten the picture went unanswered, so the woman finally got someone to straighten the picture. I wonder what that woman would think of today's passage.

Luke is writing about John the Baptist's work and mission and it makes good sense. A little, however, seems out of place. John is going to go before the Messiah "in the spirit and power of Elijah." Elijah was an Old Testament prophet who sought to unite Israel in worshiping the true God, rather than the idols of the day. It makes sense that John would do such in anticipation of the Messiah's arrival. The angel also declared, and Luke recorded, that John would turn the hearts of the disobedient to the wise, making them ready for the Messiah. Again, something that seems to fit. Likewise, it makes sense that John would "make ready for the Lord a people prepared." That seems right and fitting before the arrival of the Messiah. But what about turning "the hearts of the fathers to their children"? That seems not to fit so well. Were the fathers in John's day set against their children? Certainly not Zechariah. Nor, it seems, was Joseph, betrothed to Mary. This clause of John's ministry doesn't make sense unless one gives it a bit of attention.

The Hebrew Bible was divided into sections (and still is today). One section was "the Prophets." This section begins with the book of Joshua and ends with the book of Malachi. The very last verses of the final book in the Old Testament prophet section and the final verses in the Christian Old Testament are verses that prophesied about the coming Messiah. These verses kept Israel looking to God for centuries between the time the Old Testament ended and the birth of Jesus. They were God's final prophecy in the Old Testament. These last two verses in the Old Testament read, "Behold, I will send you Elijah the prophet before the great and awesome day of the LORD comes. And he will turn the hearts of fathers to their children and the hearts of children to their fathers, lest I come and strike the land with a decree of utter destruction" (Mal. 4:5-6).

This phrase is not out of place. It is spot on! It is a signal that John was heralding the long-awaited Messiah. John would tell the people, "He is coming!" I read this and find it not out of place, but inspiring. Let's get ready for Jesus!

Lord, stir up in my heart a readiness for Jesus. May Jesus invade every aspect of my life, today and every day! Amen.

DECEMBER 10 (ADVENT 8)

And Zechariah said to the angel, "How shall I know this? For I am an old man, and my wife is advanced in years." And the angel answered him, "I am Gabriel. I stand in the presence of God, and I was sent to speak to you and to bring you this good news. And behold, you will be silent and unable to speak until the day that these things take place, because you did not believe my words, which will be fulfilled in their time." (Lk. 1:18-20)

The stories of Sherlock Holmes have had an enduring popularity. In the stories, Sir Arthur Conan Doyle combined good mysteries with strong and fascinating characters. The central character is the detective Sherlock Holmes, known for his peculiar abilities to perceive details others miss. Then through powers of deduction, he solves the mystery. I have read every Holmes story but must admit to often being blind to the most obvious things before me. I wish I could be more observant.

Zechariah might join me in that wish, if he were still alive today. Here is a godly man, whose life's work is serving God as a priest. He is aware of the Bible and the stories of God interacting with people. He undoubtedly knew of Daniel, the Old Testament figure who wrote of the angel Gabriel who had been entrusted with revealing God's mysteries to key people (Dan. 8 and 9). Zechariah went to work one day and was assigned the job of entering into the holy place at the temple to offer incense on behalf of the people of Israel. Only priests were allowed in this temple area. Yet on this day an angel appeared! The angel clearly knew Zechariah, calling both him and his wife Elizabeth by name. Furthermore, the angel knew about their childlessness and proclaimed that the Messiah's forerunner was going to be born to them.

These events in the temple were miraculous, plain and simple. The angel was quoting Old Testament prophetic Scriptures and gave clear details about what would unfold in the life of this coming child. In spite of all this, Zechariah asked for a sign! As if an archangel appearing bearing knowledge that no one could have was not enough of a sign! Zechariah was no Sherlock Homes! Gabriel identified himself as the angel known from the book of Daniel and then gave an additional sign, albeit one that was also a punishment and reminder for Zechariah. Zechariah was mute (and apparently deaf—see verse 62) and would remain so until the prophecies were fulfilled.

I read this in the advent season thinking about God's Messiah. God has provided for me in every way he could, to bring me into a whole and holy relationship with him. This is God's fulfilled promise of an unrelenting care for me. Yet I still have times in my life where I want a sign of his love and trust. Silly me. I need to see the obvious!

Lord, thank you for your love. Forgive my feeble faith. In Jesus, amen.

DECEMBER 11 (ADVENT 9)

After these days his wife Elizabeth conceived, and for five months she kept herself hidden, saying, "Thus the Lord has done for me in the days when he looked on me, to take away my reproach among people." (Lk. 1:24–25)

I have a friend whose job situation is terrible. Absolutely horrific. He works for people who on their best days are unpredictable, but on their worst days seem downright evil. The work atmosphere is toxic and the employees seem to come and go (fired or quitting) like a revolving door. My friend is doing the work of several employees and is wondering why on earth God has him at that place. He has looked for another job, but his search thus far has been fruitless.

Everyone experiences ups and downs in life. Some days are easy sailing. The sun is out, the wind is behind us, sending us smoothly through life. Other days are stormy with waves beating us up, leaving us sore and adrift with no real purpose or direction. One learns early in life that there are good days and bad days. Life and death go hand in hand. We can go to the hospitals and find the maternity ward loaded with people rejoicing. We can also find those barely alive, where death is a countdown.

Into this reality of life, we find today's devotional passage. For a long time, Elizabeth had lived with the stigma of being barren. She lived in a day where there were no fertility clinics, no medical tests to determine why she was infertile, and no one who could offer her hope for a cure. She also lived in a day when infertility deemed a wife a failure. The main responsibility and role for a wife was to provide offspring that would tend to the parents as they aged (no social security or government programs then). Children were important for holding onto the family assets. In this, Elizabeth had failed.

Yet, in spite of Elizabeth's advanced age, in spite of her husband's advanced age, in spite of their history of barrenness, God intervened with a miracle. Elizabeth was pregnant! For five months, she held onto the secret of her pregnancy, no doubt amazed, likely a bit worried, and counting down the days.

Some things are too good to be true, and that is a good thing! We need to hold onto that truth when experiencing the downs in life. Ups are coming! They may not be immediate. They may not be when we wish. But God has set a time—his time—when we will see life turn around. We can be assured that he desires for us blessings, not curses. He wants for us to walk in a fulfilled life to his glory. Knowing this gives us a confidence that while we are experiencing trials and tribulations, those will pass. We can walk through those with our hand firmly in the hand of the one who will lead us through the difficulties to a place of joy and promise. That is our God.

Lord, give me strength and eyes of faith. Lead me in your way for Jesus' sake. Amen.

DECEMBER 12 (ADVENT 10)

In the sixth month the angel Gabriel was sent from God to a city of Galilee named Naza-reth, to a virgin betrothed to a man whose name was Joseph, of the house of David. And the virgin's name was Mary. And he came to her and said, "Greetings, O favored one, the Lord is with you!" But she was greatly troubled at the saying, and tried to discern what sort of greeting this might be. (Lk. 1:26–29)

Mary was young by today's standards, likely twelve or thirteen. Girls were engaged to be married as they came into childbearing age. We know from reading later in the story that Mary was a godly young woman. Still, she was undoubtedly disturbed when out of the blue she is visited by the angel Gabriel. That was not a normal occurrence by any means! Of course, Mary's circumstances were not normal either.

Gabriel appeared by name in the Old Testament writing of Daniel. Gabriel was God's messenger sent to Daniel to help Daniel understand his visions (Dan. 8:16). Unknown to Mary at the time, Gabriel had also come to her relative Elizabeth to inform her of God's miracle for Elizabeth and Zechariah. The miracles were from two perspectives. Elizabeth and Zecha-riah were too old to have a child. Mary hadn't yet known a man such that she could have a child. Yet neither obstacle stood in God's way, and Gabriel came to announce such news.

Mary's reaction is interesting. She was "troubled" at the greeting. This was *before* Gabriel told her exactly what it meant that "the Lord" was with her. It seems just the news that God was paying attention to this young lady such that he sent an angel to speak with her was in itself "troubling." The Greek word Luke used for "troubled" carries the idea of being confused or perplexed.

Perhaps Mary was perplexed because Gabriel had come to greet her, but Luke says she was confused/perplexed/troubled "at the saying." It is *what* Gabriel said she found disturbing. Gabriel told her that she was "favored" and that God was "with her." In the Greek, "greetings" and "favored one" both come from a family of words that have a core meaning of "joy." Mary was confused because God had noted her, sent his messenger to her, and greeted her with a message of joy. Mary was told God knew her, cared for her, and had plans for her. That was surprising to this young lady.

Now you and I should not be expecting to miraculously bear a child, but we should see in this story the greeting to Mary was a statement to the world. What God was doing in Mary he was doing because *he knows us, he cares for us, and he has plans for us*! We should not find that troubling, confus-ing, or perplexing. We should rejoice and live expectantly, knowing God's message in Jesus is one of joy for all of us.

Lord, thank you for caring about me. Let me walk in your will with joy! In Jesus, amen.

DECEMBER 13 (ADVENT 11)

And the angel said to her, "Do not be afraid, Mary, for you have found favor with God. And behold, you will conceive in your womb and bear a son, and you shall call his name Jesus. He will be great and will be called the Son of the Most High. And the Lord God will give to him the throne of his father David, and he will reign over the house of Jacob forever, and of his kingdom there will be no end." (Lk. 1:30–33)

Recently our college-age daughter was home for the holidays. Over the break, one morning she told us, "I don't know if y'all realize it or not, but Lauren (a friend of hers) spent the night here!" My wife and I said, "Oh that's good," and our daughter responded, "Yes, her mother was supposed to get home last night but had car trouble. So at eleven p.m. Lauren texted me and said it turned out she was more scared about staying alone than she had thought she would be. So she came over for the night." We were glad.

Fear is a powerful emotion. It can affect you, cause you to see and think things that you wouldn't normally find persuasive. It can cripple you and make you too frightened to act. Or it can remove your careful thinking and cause you to make poor choices. Today's passage and the entire Advent season speak to our fears.

Mary was a young teenage girl when she found out she was pregnant. She hadn't had any sexual relations, and the news was frightful. It didn't help that an angel was delivering the news as a message from God Almighty. Mary was frightened, and understandably so.

What was happening to Mary, however, was nothing to fear. It was unexpected. It was uncharted territory. It would bring shame on her. It would be misread by others. Mary would be subject to gossip and innuendo. People wouldn't understand. But Mary had no reason to fear. God was in control.

When God controls our lives, we needn't fear anything. Of course, this doesn't mean we live imprudently, but it does mean that as we walk in God's will, we can walk with confidence that he will be there with us. God paves the road before us. God knows where we are going, and he has purposes for us. We can walk in faith knowing that our God goes before us, behind us, and hand in hand with us.

Advent is the church's season building up to celebrating the birth of Christ. In the coming of Christ we see the biggest promise of why we have no fear. God came in flesh. The "Son of the Most High" who holds the throne for ever and ever has come to move our fears into faith. We can be confident that the God who loves us that much isn't going to let anything get in the way of his will for us. We can walk without fear!

Lord, we confess we are fearful people. Please turn our fear into faith in Jesus. Amen.

DECEMBER 14 (ADVENT 12)

And Mary said to the angel, "How will this be, since I am a virgin?" And the angel answered her, "The Holy Spirit will come upon you, and the power of the Most High will overshadow you; therefore the child to be born will be called holy—the Son of God . . . For nothing will be impossible with God." (Lk. 1:34–37)

Let me be personal today: I can't figure God out. Oh, I get some things about him. I know his love and I am convinced he works out his kingdom for the good of his children. But I don't get how he always does it. He is constantly surprising me.

I don't believe God is inherently unpredictable. I don't have any reason to suspect that he takes joy out of throwing me a curveball. But I stand amazed in his presence, and I watch his hand work with wonder. I don't think I'm alone in that. I think Jesus stunned his friends and foes alike. Who predicted he would feed five thousand with a few loaves and fishes? (Mt. 14:15–21). Who thought he would raise Lazarus from the dead? (Jn. 11:1–44). Who ever dreamed that he would spit and touch a blind man twice before he fully healed him, when every other time he healed the sick on the first go around? (Mk. 8:22–26).

I also know that God stunned Israel and others in the Old Testament. The Pharaoh never expected the plagues. Who would? Moses was stunned over the manna, as were the rest of the Israelites. As for sending a fish to deal with the recalcitrant prophet Jonah, that one was from left field!

Perhaps nowhere was anyone as stunned as Mary when she was told that she, a virgin, would be giving birth to the Son of God. Mary knew that was an impossibility. Mary was right. It was impossible for anyone other than God. But God is unpredictable, as Mary found out.

I like this about God. I like that God isn't bound by my "range of possibilities." I like that something new seems to be around every corner. The key for me is two-fold. One, I need to remember to trust him. That means set aside worry and fear, move away from fretting, and trust in his goodness and vision. It also means that I can be excited about what is coming, even if I am in trouble and the rest of the world is worried. I have a deliverer who will come in due time, in his way, and on behalf of his children (including me).

So I can't figure God out. But I am okay with that. More than okay, I am thankful.

Lord, I commit my life to you. Work in, through, and around me to your glory. Let me not lose sight or fear what you have in store. I live eager to see you at work. In Jesus, amen.

DECEMBER 15 (ADVENT 13)

And Mary said, "Behold, I am the servant of the Lord; let it be to me according to your word." And the angel departed from her. (Lk. 1:38)

Have you heard the slogan, "Let go and let God"? It is a good aphorism that reminds us how we are to walk in faith. I need reminders like that because, if I am honest, I am a bit of a control freak. (Likely my sweet wife and others close to me would take issue with that . . . unless I deleted the words "a bit of.")

In our world and in our lives, certain things are under our control. We decide where to work, when to wake up, what to eat, and so on. We decide what clothes to wear. We decide how we are going to treat people. We decide how we are going to respond to God's invitation to walk with him. But there are other things that we do not control. At the top of that list is: God.

God doesn't exist under your thumb or mine. He is not our servant to do as we beck and call. He is not a hotel concierge who hears our requests and delivers on them. I fear that sometimes because God revealed himself to us as a Father as well as through the Savior Jesus, we tend to think of him as existing to serve our needs. We have it wrong.

God is our Father and Savior, but he is something far beyond that as well. God is the King of kings and Lord of lords. He is the only wise God who exists from eternity to eternity. God reigns on high and oversees all that is. God has a kingdom that he will bring to fullness on earth as it is in heaven. God saved us, yes, but not so God could play on our team or be our personal trainer and coach. God saved us so we could play on *his team*. This is all about him. Not us.

As someone with a controlling nature, I need to confront this head-on. I need to know that God is about something large, and my question should be simple: How do I best plug in? God has given me a number of instructions and I need to be serious about following them. He has told me to love those around me. He wants me to be honest and forthright. He wants me to grow in love, kindness, peace, patience, goodness, gentleness, self-control, humility, service, and more.

Today's passage emphasizes Mary's response to the news of her role in the salvation saga. Mary was to bear the Christ child. Though society wouldn't approve, Mary didn't urge God to find someone else. She knew God's will and responded, "Behold, I am the servant of the Lord; let it be to me according to your word." I have a lot to learn from Mary.

Lord, I confess I often make life about me, even in my walk with you. I don't want that to be the case. Please forgive me and let it be to me according to your word. In Jesus, amen.

DECEMBER 16 (ADVENT 14)

In those days Mary arose and went with haste into the hill country, to a town in Judah, and she entered the house of Zechariah and greeted Elizabeth. And when Elizabeth heard the greeting of Mary, the baby leaped in her womb. And Elizabeth was filled with the Holy Spirit, and she exclaimed with a loud cry, "Blessed are you among women, and blessed is the fruit of your womb!" (Lk. 1:39–42)

Do you share the works of God in your life? Do you fear that doing so might make people think you are a bit nutty? Let's rewrite that program in our brain using today's Advent passage.

Mary had been told she was pregnant with the Christ child. Mary immediately "went with haste" into the hill country to find her relative Elizabeth. Unknown to Mary, because Elizabeth had yet to tell folks, Elizabeth was also pregnant with the child who would be John the Baptist. Elizabeth didn't recoil at Mary's news. Elizabeth confirmed it! Yes, Mary was pregnant, and this was a blessing! Elizabeth knew it was God's work.

I like that Mary went "with haste." She was in a hurry. She had news to share.

This passage does not mean that one speaks with haste without an awareness of one's audience or purpose. Indeed, Mary wasn't telling everyone she met on her journey about what God was doing. Furthermore, the godly Elizabeth had sat silently on her news of her pregnancy for six months. But the passage does give us an example of how one should be compelled to speak of God and what God is doing. Mary didn't waste any time.

I think through the chances in my life to share God's hand with others. I see that sometimes I have done so with joy and openness. I also see sometimes when I have been hesitant, staying silent lest people take it wrongly. A few friends have actually come up to me in life and asked me why I never talk to them about God, since God is obviously important to me and it is equally obvious that they know nothing about God.

I need to do better about this. I need to have that burning desire to share the greatest news that anyone could receive. I need to readily tell folks of the ways God works in my life, and how he wants to work in theirs. When good things happen, I need to make sure people know the credit goes to God, not to me or anyone else. I should be president of God's fan club, not a silent member attending an occasional club meeting!

Lord, I confess this is an area where I need to grow. May I never fail to proudly proclaim your hand at work in my life and in our world. May all glory for all goodness come to you alone. Forgive my failures and make me bold to be your biggest fan among others, so they can see your greatness. In Jesus, amen.

DECEMBER 17 (ADVENT 15)

For behold, when the sound of your greeting came to my ears, the baby in my womb leaped for joy. (Lk. 1:44)

When was the last time you leapt for joy? I think mine was at a Houston Rockets basketball game. Some of you can relate to that. Some can relate if we change the team or sport. Some of you likely think me a bit off my rocker for leaping at any sporting event. But you should have seen that play!!!

In today's passage Mary comes into the presence of Elizabeth for the first time in months. Unknown to Mary, Elizabeth is roughly six months pregnant with John the Baptist. Unknown to Elizabeth, Mary is newly pregnant with Jesus. When Mary first said her hello to Elizabeth, inside Elizabeth's womb, John the Baptist "leapt for joy." I love this.

The events described in today's passage are a testimony to the consistency of God. This truth is rooted in understanding a teaching of Jesus more than thirty years later. When Jesus was getting ready for his crucifixion, he had a last opportunity to tell his closest friends and apostles that in the future God would send the Holy Spirit to indwell them, something apart from the fact the Holy Spirit had been with them in the form of Christ (Jn. 14:15–17). Jesus said that the Holy Spirit would come to bear witness to Jesus (Jn. 15:26). The Holy Spirit would also bring glory to Jesus (Jn. 16:14). Here we see the marvelous consistency of God. In a special way, the Holy Spirit was already indwelling John the Baptist. That we know from reading the story line up to the point of Mary's and Elizabeth's interaction. Then, even as an unborn infant, simply at the presence of Jesus in the womb of Mary, undoubtedly unseen, and certainly not yet spoken of to Elizabeth, the unborn John leaps for joy, bearing witness and bringing glory to the unborn Christ child.

This makes me want to leap for joy! It also makes me want to bear witness and bring glory to the Lord. I want to let the Holy Spirit fully loose in my life to glorify the arrival of Jesus, God made man.

Because Jesus the Messiah came into existence as a human, I am set free from the eternal consequences of my sin. I am in a relationship with the Almighty God with an intimacy that can only come with a purity I had lost through sin. Because Jesus came, I am aware of God's love in ways that I might have suspected before, but never experienced. God's love isn't something simply discussed. It is shown. Because Jesus came, I am instructed in the importance of loving others in a kind and humble way. Jesus did not regard his heavenly status something he needed to keep. Out of love, he set it aside and took on the lowly form of a human. He then let humans treat him like garbage all to win the eternity of those he loves. What a model he is for me! I want to leap for joy!

Lord, I praise you and what you've done, with great joy in my heart! In Jesus! Amen!

DECEMBER 18 (ADVENT 16)

And Mary said, "My soul magnifies the Lord, and my spirit rejoices in God my Savior, for he has looked on the humble estate of his servant. For behold, from now on all generations will call me blessed; for he who is mighty has done great things for me, and holy is his name." (Lk. 1:46–49)

Have you ever been so joyful you broke out in song? Maybe you made the song up on the spot, or more likely you sang a few bars of a song you associated with happiness. Maybe you are a singer, but you have had a level of joy where you let out a whoop or holler. However you express joy, sometimes life unfolds and events collide where our joy overflows into something others can see and hear (if they are nearby).

If you are reading this and thinking, "Well, that hasn't happened to me in a long time," then think again! Today's passage is a good place to start. Mary, pregnant with Jesus, has come to see her much older relative Elizabeth who was also pregnant, but with John the Baptist. John leapt in Mary's womb praising the presence of the unborn Christ. When Elizabeth told Mary, Mary was excited. Mary hadn't known Elizabeth was pregnant and had yet to tell Elizabeth her own news of Jesus. Mary was so excited she broke out into song. We have a few bars of what she likely continued to form as her song over the years to come.

One might think, "Well of course *she* did. She was carrying the Christ child!" If you think like that, then hit the pause button! Yes, she was carrying the Christ child. God had descended his heavenly throne and embedded himself incarnate into a young unmarried virgin. But the miracle of Christ coming wasn't simply something Mary received. Christ came into the world for you and me too!

In the Advent season, we celebrate the coming of Christ into the world in three different ways. He came into the world at Bethlehem to bring to completion the earthly actions necessary to redeem us from the death of sin. We also celebrate the fact that Christ still come into the hearts of all his children today. We don't carry Christ in our bodies in the sense that Mary did, but we still have Christ alive in each of us today. A third way we celebrate the coming of Christ during Advent is in his promise to return to earth again at the end of days.

These three comings of Christ should be enough for all of us to break out into song! Is it any wonder that the Christmas season is one of song? Find your favorite Christmas hymn/song and break out into voice now! Christ has come, and he will come again!

Lord, we celebrate your presence in our world, in our lives, and in our future! Lord, come quickly! In Jesus we sing and pray, amen.

DECEMBER 19 (ADVENT 17)

And his mercy is for those who fear him from generation to generation. (Lk. 1:50)

My friend Weston speaks English as his primary language, but he also has taught biblical Greek for many years, speaks modern Hebrew, reads and works in ancient Hebrew, and switches between these languages with dexterity. Once he was proofing something I'd written, and he came across my saying that an old Hebrew or Greek word "meant" and then I used an English word. Weston gently showed me my error. One ancient word doesn't turn into one modern word. I would be more accurate to note the ancient word had a "semantic range." In other words, among the modern ways of expressing that ancient concept is our modern word . . .

Weston is right. Usually it is quite difficult to translate one word from an ancient language into one contemporary English word while capturing all the meaning of the older word. Translation doesn't work like math, where things are quite definite. In math, we can say if $2 + x = 3$, then x must equal 1. We can do the math and confidently exchange the x for the "1," knowing we got it right. In translating old languages (and many modern ones) into English, however, it isn't so simple.

So in today's passage, there is an ancient Greek word *eleos* (ἔλεος). It is translated "mercy." Those who fear God receive God's "mercy." I know what "mercy" means in English, but this passage makes me want to know the "semantic range" of the Greek word's meaning. In other words, beyond the simple word, "mercy," what does the Greek mean?

One of the most commonly used authoritative dictionaries of ancient Greek defines the Greek word giving the fuller range of meaning beyond the simple "mercy." It defines the word as "kindness or concern expressed for someone in need, mercy, compassion, pity, clemency" (*A Greek-English Lexicon of the New Testament and Other Early Christian Literature*). This definition rightly captures my attention.

In the passage, Mary is singing her praise of God. She sings that God is kind and concerned, that God expresses that kindness and concern for those in need when they fear him. God has compassion and pity on those who fear him. I want that. I *need* that! I pray for that!!! "Lord, please have kindness and concern, compassion and pity on me!"

This takes me to the phrase, "those who fear him." What is the range of meaning for "fear"? Beyond the one word "fear" is the idea of "a profound measure of respect or reverence." I need to respect, revere, and fear God, and he will show me mercy, kindness, and compassion. What an amazing God we serve.

Lord, I am in awe of you. I need your compassion and mercy daily. In Jesus, amen.

DECEMBER 20 (ADVENT 18)

He has shown strength with his arm; he has scattered the proud in the thoughts of their hearts; he has brought down the mighty from their thrones and exalted those of humble estate. (Lk. 1:51–52)

Several of my nephews are quite strong. They go work out together and have these lifting contests. They can bench press more than I ever could. They curl weights worthy of Arnold Schwarzenegger. They didn't start out this way. I held them when they were babies. But something happened along the way and they got stout!

God didn't grow into his strength. He has always had it. He created this cosmos and all that is in it, so he is certainly strong enough to deal with the inhabitants of this dirt clod we call earth rotating around an average sun out in a borderline galaxy.

If God wanted to show off how strong he is, I would think it would best be done by parting the Red Sea. Bringing Lazarus back would certainly be a big display of strength too. But those "change the rules of the universe" ways of showing God's strength are not what Mary chose to sing about in today's passage. Mary chose to sing about how God "scatters the proud in the thoughts of their hearts," and how God brings down the mighty while exalting the humble. Those are the mighty works worthy of Mary's praise.

Of course, the context of Mary's song is the coming virgin birth of Jesus, itself another huge display of God's strength. But Mary isn't touting that as making her case. Still, the overlay of that coming of the Messiah is tied closely to what Mary is saying. In coming to earth, Jesus was dealing with the proud and the humble.

The incarnation of Christ destroys the proud. Jesus displays the inherent greatness of God in ways that should bring even the most arrogant and haughty to their knees. No one stands up to the greatness of God. If any are haughty enough to think they might, the day will come when they learn otherwise. As Paul assured the Philippians, the day is coming when *every knee shall bow and every tongue confess* that Jesus is Lord (Phil. 2:10–11).

The coming and presence of Christ also exalts the humble. Mary knew this firsthand. Mary was not a haughty snob lifting herself above others in her community. She was a humble servant of the Lord seeking to serve him in her own way. God lifted her up and chose to come into our world through her. This is worthy of song.

I read today's passage and I commit myself again into wanting to be humble, not proud. I want to see God's strength in lifting up the works of my hands, not bringing me down!

Lord, grow me in humility to better serve you. In Jesus' name, amen.

DECEMBER 21 (ADVENT 19)

He has filled the hungry with good things, and the rich he has sent away empty. (Lk. 1:53)

I really like today's verse. The verse gives a glimpse into God's character that brings me joy. God "fills" the hungry, and he fills them with "good things." I have been hungry. Now I've never had hunger to the point of endangering my health if I don't eat, but I know hunger. My problem with getting hungry is that I tend to eat too much to satisfy my hunger. I binge. I also tend to use my hunger as an excuse to eat the bad food I ordinarily work so hard to avoid.

Perhaps this is why today's passage speaks to me as it does. God doesn't overfill the hungry person. Nor does God let the hungry person stay hungry. God "fills" the hungry, giving them just the right amount. What's more, God doesn't give the hungry junk food. God gives the hungry "good things."

Note carefully Mary's proclamation in her praise song. Mary didn't say that God fills the hungry with good "food." Food isn't mentioned at all. In Mary's time, as in our day today, "hunger" serves as a metaphor for a longing or desire. Some people hunger for attention. Some hunger for knowledge. When we "hunger," we have a yearning or want that we seek to have filled. God fills those hungers, but only with good things.

Understanding hunger as a metaphor makes it even more important to realize that God fills with "good things" and not garbage. If we hunger for knowledge and we seek that from God, he will fill us up with good knowledge, not bad. If we hunger for righteousness, we can be assured he will fill us up to be righteous. If our hunger is for immorality or some selfish desire, we can be confident that God won't be filling up and satisfying that hunger.

Clearly today's message should move us to a conviction that we will hunger for good things, but we leave today's verse too early if we fail to look at the last clause. God sends the "rich" away. Why is that? The rich, in the sense of this verse, are those who satisfy their own hungers. If I seek to fill myself and believe I have the resources to do that, then I will not be getting the good and filling things that come from the Lord. God will leave me to my own devices.

I do like this passage. I like the idea of finding God as the satisfaction of my needs, rather than being left to myself. This is nowhere more apparent than in the Advent season. The coming of Jesus is God filling my greatest need—forgiveness.

Lord, I am hungry for you. I need your love, your righteousness, and your mercy. Please fill me with these good things to your glory. In Jesus, amen.

DECEMBER 22 (ADVENT 20)

And Joseph also went up from Galilee, from the town of Nazareth, to Judea, to the city of David, which is called Bethlehem, because he was of the house and lineage of David, to be registered with Mary, his betrothed, who was with child. And while they were there, the time came for her to give birth. (Lk. 2:4–6)

Some people are really good at waiting. They don't mind standing in line too much. They can sit in a restaurant with a slow waiter without breaking out in hives. They are patient in the face of delay. They can even drive below the speed limit because they are in no hurry to get wherever they are going. Some people enjoy the calm that comes when things seem to be on hold. I am none of the above—not even close.

I am always trying to figure out the most efficient way to do something, meaning to me the fastest way to accomplish whatever is before me. If it is driving from A to B, I want the fastest route. I try to figure out which lane will accelerate from the light the quickest. I grumble at those who choose to go slow in the fast lane, thus clogging up traffic. When I get to a restaurant, I am ready to order even before getting the menu. I've been thinking about what to order since the decision was made to go to the restaurant. Why waste more time? (I should add that I drive my family crazy over this last example.)

One thing that people like me need to learn is that God has his own timing. God's timing isn't dictated by your personality type or mine. God's timing is dictated by the reality of this world and his plans for its future. God's timing operates at his pace. It may seem rapid or it may seem to take forever, but it is always right.

In today's passage, Luke writes that Mary and Joseph got to Bethlehem when *"the time came for her to give birth."* Luke chose a word for time (πίμπλημι, *pimplēmi* in the Greek) that isn't referencing a clock or calendar's time. Nor does it mean the time of day. The Greek word references when something is "full" or "fulfilled." Luke wants his readers to know that a convergence of things was happening at that moment. God's prophetic promises were being fulfilled. For millennia, God had promised that one would come forth from woman to set right the havoc and tragedy brought about by Satan and sin (Gen. 3:15). That time was fulfilled. Also converging on that moment was the fulfillment of Mary's pregnancy term. She was at the point where her body was ready to give birth to a healthy child. The moments were converging with society being where it would provide the necessary environment for Jesus to grow into ministry and manhood.

God's timing isn't my timing. He has the larger view. He has the grander purpose. He has the patience to wait for the time to be ripe. I need to trust him and his timing and not let my impatience rule the day.

Lord, give me greater patience and confidence in you and your timing. In Jesus, amen.

DECEMBER 23 (ADVENT 21)

The true light, which gives light to everyone, was coming into the world. (Jn. 1:9)

John spoke of the coming of Jesus as the coming of light into a world of darkness. John did not conjure up these themes anew. The themes were deeply embedded in God's Scriptures for centuries.

In Psalm 36, for example, darkness is contrasted with light. The "wicked" live in darkness, oriented to sin, proud of their own insight and without fear of God. God, on the other hand, is full of light shining in his steadfast love and righteousness. God provides in abundance for his children, sheltering them and providing a refuge. The psalmist wrote, "For with you is the fountain of life; in your light do we see light" (Ps. 36:9).

John saw in the coming of Jesus, the coming of God, the fountain of life and the light by which we all of that life will be enlightened. Jesus reveals sin for what it is and points the willing to God's way of life. Jesus evidences the steadfast love of God that gives eternal security to those of faith.

With the coming of Jesus into the world, no one need fear sin, wickedness, and darkness. Anyone who has been in a dark room and turned on a light has seen that in a battle, light always triumphs over darkness. Darkness never wins that contest.

Our goal is to walk in the light that is Jesus. We should take what he illuminates and make it our path. We are to live faithfully trusting in the truth of who Jesus is. We confess our sins and receive forgiveness. We do not parade as ones who are perfect on our own. We are not the light; we reflect the light.

Christ has brought the believer out of the dominion of darkness into the kingdom of light, which is the kingdom of the Son. This deliverance comes with redemption, with the forgiveness of sins. Christ was not merely coming to earth to point the way from darkness to light, he came to make the way, redeeming people from darkness to light (Col. 1:11–14).

In the Advent season, as Christmas approaches, I need to let the light of God change me. The light that shows sin should move me to confession and repentance. The light that shows holiness beckons me to follow. The light that lifts my life should be reflected by me into the dark world so others would see Jesus and through that, come into the kingdom of light. I have some work today and every day that God gives me from here out.

Lord, thank you for your light. I confess that I often play in the darkness and I repent. Teach me to better walk in your light and to share that light with others. In Jesus, amen.

DECEMBER 24 (ADVENT 22)

So all the generations from Abraham to David were fourteen generations, and from David to the deportation to Babylon fourteen generations, and from the deportation to Babylon to the Christ fourteen generations. (Mt. 1:17)

Remember the biblical character Abiud? Zerubbabel's kid? Remember how he grew into such an interesting fellow. His education at a young age was mediocre at best, but he tried hard. He was okay at sports. Until his parents found him a bride, no one was certain he would ever get married. It wasn't his looks. His looks were normal, sort of. But for the longest time, marriage didn't seem to interest him. He had a quirky sense of humor and loved the taste of good food, especially carbohydrates! One must admire the way Abiud handled pressure. His tendency was to worry, but he learned to put his trust in the Lord, letting prayer bolster his strength to stand under the crush of life's concerns.

If you are wondering how and where you missed the biblical story of Abiud, you need to set your wonders aside. I made up everything about the fellow other than his father was Zerubbabel. Abiud is mentioned in the Bible only once, in Matthew. Matthew begins his gospel recounting the genealogy of Jesus. In the middle of the genealogy, at verse 13, we read, "and Zerubbabel the father of Abiud, and Abiud the father of Eliakim, and Eliakim the father of Azor." That's it for Abiud. That is his only mention in the Bible.

Does that mean all my story about Abiud is false? We simply don't know. He had some kind of education—everyone does. It might have been through life rather than school, but we all learn as we live. Was he athletic? We will never know how his hand/eye coordination was, but he must have had some degree of ability. Perhaps when he threw a rock it went where he aimed, or perhaps he missed his targets. We don't know his looks, his personality, his sense of humor, or lack thereof. But he, like all of us, possessed these things in varying degrees. How he handled the stresses and strains of life, we have no clue. But we can be assured that he had problems. Everyone does.

So here we have this relatively unknown fellow, who over two thousand years after his death has a devotional written about him and distributed around the world in a language he never knew to lands he never dreamed about. He was and is a relatively unknown guy, yet I find him incredibly inspirational. He was a link in the genealogy of Jesus. He was a critical part of the chain that brought forth the Savior. We know nothing else about him, but we know he was crucial in God's plans. I wonder if he knew that?

You and I are Abiuds. We may never have fame or fortune, and the world will likely soon forget we were here. But God has a purpose for us. We are links in the chain of his kingdom. We fit where he wants us. We should smile today, knowing God is using us!

Lord, use us as you will. We are yours. In Jesus, amen.

CHRISTMASTIME

Many people think of Christmas as December 25, followed by shopping and New Year's Day celebrations. People may sing the song, "The Twelve Days of Christmas," but think of it as applying to twelve days *before* Christmas. This is a common misperception among people who are not active in a liturgical church that adheres to the church calendar.

The twelve days referenced in the song refer to days *after* Christmas, not before. The church celebration of Christmas centers on the incarnation of Christ, and that didn't end on the day of his birth. On subsequent days, the wise men came and other events happen around the infancy narratives.

So in the Western calendar, as the New Year begins, the focus in the church calendar is still on the infancy of Jesus, the incarnate God. This lasts until the day of Epiphany (January 6).

DECEMBER 25 (CHRISTMAS DAY)

And the angel said to them, "Fear not, for behold, I bring you good news of great joy that will be for all the people. For unto you is born this day in the city of David a Savior, who is Christ the Lord." (Lk. 2:10–11)

Different times of the day are especially important in the life of my wife. Each morning, she likes quiet time to pray, study, and drink coffee. Also at five o'clock each evening, there is a five-minute block where she really doesn't want to be disturbed. A news show comes on then. It begins with the mantra, "Happening now! Breaking news!" Then for five minutes the show recaps the day's most important events. Becky likes to catch how various news sources prioritize the last twenty-four hours of world events.

On the morning we celebrate as Christmas, it was the "Happening now! Breaking news!" story of the day . . . of the year . . . of the century . . . of eternity! It was the biggest news since the fall of Adam and Eve! This news was "good news." It was news of "great joy." The news wasn't isolated to one group or another, but it was for "all the people." Born that day was "Christ the Lord" and "Savior" for the world! Announcing this news wasn't a cable or a network personality but an actual angel sent by God in heaven.

What made this breaking news so great? The world desperately needed a Savior. Not because the world was about to be hit by a meteorite or some epidemic worthy of a Hollywood script. But because the world and its people suffered from the true, life-altering reality of sin. Sin is the worst disease before a just and perfect God because sin brings death. Sin ruins lives and relationships. Sin destroys us from the inside out and from the outside in. Sin is sticky and we can't escape it on our own. Sin also breeds itself rapidly and prodigiously. Sin begets sin begets sin begets sin. What can save us from sin and the death that follows in its wake? Jesus Christ the Lord! God made flesh to come into the world as a human and take care of the human problem of sin.

Jesus was anointed to do this very thing. Jesus was set aside and marked as the one to do this. In his day, the Jews would anoint kings, prophets, and priests. Jesus was anointed for all three purposes. (The Greek word for anoint is translated as "Christ." The Hebrew word equivalent is "Messiah.") Jesus is Christ/Messiah, anointed the King of kings, the Supreme Ruler, the One before whom all will eventually bow. As King, Jesus saves his people from sin as surely as any earthly king could lead his people into battle and vanquish the enemy. Jesus is anointed prophet, speaking life on God's behalf, bringing salvation to people entrapped in sin. Jesus is anointed priest, bridging the gap between God and humanity, giving us entrance before the very throne of God.

Happening now! Breaking news! God is made flesh to save his people. REJOICE!

Lord, I rejoice in your salvation with a humble and grateful heart. In Jesus, amen.

When the angels went away from them into heaven, the shepherds said to one another, "Let us go over to Bethlehem and see this thing that has happened, which the Lord has made known to us." And they went with haste and found Mary and Joseph, and the baby lying in a manger. (Lk. 2:15–16)

Christmas is almost always a busy event in our home. We have lots of people in our home: five children, their extended families and friends, our siblings, nieces, nephews, grandparents, and a few dear friends who might not legally be family but who really are part of the family. Along with those people are traditions built up over the years, including gift-giving, certain food events (homemade yeast donuts for Christmas morning along with a full feast at some midpoint between lunchtime and dinnertime).

Christmas is so busy, that for us, the day after Christmas is one of recovery. The events surrounding the birth of Jesus, however, were not over on the second day of Jesus' life. In some ways, Jesus coming into the world was like a snowball rolling down a hill, gaining size and significance each successive day. Once the angels announced the birth to shepherds in the field, the shepherds didn't delay reacting. They realized that the Savior was born, and they "went with haste" to find him! They didn't want to miss that unique opportunity in world history.

In each of our lives, we can celebrate Christmas, but if we celebrate with family and friends, if we go to candlelight services, if we tell the Christmas story, only to spend the next day recouping and returning to "normal life," then we have missed something important. The Christmas miracle wasn't a one-time event that opens up a wonderland of giving, Christmas carols of world peace and drummer boys, feasts of gluttonous proportions, and days off from work with sporting events on television. The Christmas miracle sets up the real miracle of life—Jesus coming into our hearts to transform us into his image.

The incarnation shows God made human in Jesus, and it is the prelude to God inhabiting each of us. The goal is for us to meet Jesus, as the shepherds hastened to do, for in meeting Jesus, we find our lives transformed. The meeting and transformation aren't done in a holiday. Transformation comes from a lifetime relationship that begins with meeting Jesus, but doesn't stop there. We want Jesus in our lives each day, working for the Father and teaching us how to live.

So on the day after Christmas, as we seek to recover and get back into normal life, I want a "new normal." I want to seek to have Christ in me, growing me into what I need to be for him. May Jesus dwell in our hearts today and every day, to his glory.

Lord, I live today for you. Teach me what that means and grow me up in Jesus, amen.

DECEMBER 27

And suddenly there was with the angel a multitude of the heavenly host praising God and saying, "Glory to God in the highest, and on earth peace among those with whom he is pleased!" (Lk. 2:13–14)

Rick is a dear friend of mine. He is Jewish by genetics and was curiously looking at whether or not Jesus (*Yeshua*) might indeed be the long-awaited Messiah. Rick explained to me that growing up, he was taught that Jesus could not have been the Messiah because the Messiah would usher in peace. Yet the world hasn't been at peace at any time since the advent of Jesus. The lights went off in Rick's eyes when he realized for the first time that the promised peace might be something greater than world peace. It might mean personal peace.

Humanity lives in rebellion to God. We are what Paul called "children of wrath" (Eph. 2:3). God has a purity that we don't have. He isn't tainted by the selfishness that pollutes our best intentions. God doesn't dabble in sin. God's purity sets him apart from us and stands in the way of our intimacy with him. As sinners, we are cancers that need to be destroyed. We can't make ourselves good enough. We can't fix our sin problem.

As a result, we have a distance that exists between us and the pure God. That distance comes from the fact that God hates evil and sin. Sin is a corruption that rightly earns not only God's disfavor, but God's wrath. That means that we, as children of sin, have a problem with God's wrath. It is the reason that few people can find true inner peace.

Yet when Jesus was coming, the angels "praised God" as they said that the birth of Jesus marked not only glory to God but also peace among people. This peace was not a community peace. It didn't mean that one group quit fighting another. Jesus' birth marked the advent of the true peace that people need with God. The problem of sin is erased. We have a true and just forgiveness of that sin with its penalty paid in full. Jesus paid that in full.

What does that mean to me in this Advent season? Advent celebrates the coming of Jesus in three ways: the coming in the flesh at Bethlehem, the coming into my life each day, and the coming again at the end of time. The peace we enjoy is intimately recognized and celebrated in all three ways. We sing for joy with the angels at the coming of the Jesus baby, the fulfillment of God's long-awaited promise. We also rejoice each day as we experience the peace we enjoy with God, one based not on our own good deeds, but based on the finished work of Jesus. Finally, we also live with joy viewing our future through the lens of Jesus returning to finish our restoration to the Lord. We have peace upon peace upon peace! Glory to God in the highest!

Lord, we give you glory as we rest peacefully in the care of our Savior Jesus, amen.

DECEMBER 28

And she gave birth to her firstborn son and wrapped him in swaddling cloths and laid him in a manger, because there was no place for them in the inn. (Lk. 2:7)

I grew up and live in the United States of America. We view ourselves as "the land of opportunity." I was brought up with the common idea that anyone can become anything in America. America's capitalism burns on the fuel of hard work producing good results for those who "earn" it. In the American system of government, everyone gets to participate. As Abraham Lincoln explained in his Gettysburg address, ours is a government of the people, by the people, for the people.

This approach to life, government, and economy has great results in propelling people and society to great accomplishments. However, a problem can also lie at its roots. We can easily become a proud people. The idea of "self-made" can produce a subtle, or not so subtle, arrogance. Such haughtiness has no place in light of today's passage.

Jesus was NOT born into existence in the manger, having only existed for the nine months he inhabited Mary's womb. Jesus is God and has always been God. Jesus existed before the incarnation. Paul explained that Jesus "existed in the form of God" (Phil. 2:6). In becoming the Christ child, Jesus "emptied himself, taking the form of a servant, being made in the likeness of men" (Phil. 2:7).

Take a deep breath and consider this anew. God set aside the perfection and completion of heaven to become a human creature in an imperfect and shattered world. In doing so, God didn't just descend, take on the sins of humanity, die, and resurrect from the dead. He came as an infant more than thirty years before those events. Nor did God come into the human palaces, born as a king to the worship and adoration of the nations, placed in the finest luxuries that humans could muster. He came to an impoverished family without a place to stay, born into the ancient equivalent of a barn.

God's act of incarnation was an act of utter humility. God modeled humility in a way that should alter our lives. Paul used this example to urge the believers to have the same attitude of humility, the same willingness to go to the extremes in order to help and lift up others. Paul explained that as we reflect on what God did as Jesus, we should "do nothing from selfish ambition or conceit, but in humility count others more significant than yourselves. Let each of you look not only to his own interests, but also to the interests of others" (Phil. 2:3–4).

America is a great nation and a land of opportunity. But the believer doesn't take that as a basis for pride. It gives us the tools to help others.

Lord, may I walk humbly in service to you, following your example in Jesus, amen.

DECEMBER 29

He has helped his servant Israel, in remembrance of his mercy, as he spoke to our fathers, to Abraham and to his offspring forever. (Lk. 1:54–55)

How good is your memory? Some people have a near photographic memory, while some have a memory a bit more like swiss cheese (with big holes). Memory is important, especially when we give our word on something. If we make other promises that last days or weeks, we need to remember to keep them. Some commitments are life-long, till death do us part, which again we need to remember and keep. Even our longest commitments and memories, however, are necessarily limited by our lifetime. Not so for God.

God has always been and always will be. He is not limited to a span within the space-time continuum. God isn't here today but gone in a few generations. Because of that, God's commitments transcend a human lifetime. His stretch is forever.

Consider Abraham, a man of God who lived some two thousand years before Jesus. If we measure a generation as twenty-five years, then eighty generations or lifetimes had passed between Abraham and Jesus.

But God made some promises to Abraham, and they were promises God said he would keep even through Abraham's children. What were the promises? They included that Abraham's "faith" or "belief" would be "counted to him as righteousness" (Gen. 15:6). Abraham believed that God would fulfill a promise of offspring more numerous than the stars. God also promised Abraham that through him, all the nations of the earth would be blessed (Gen. 12:3). This was an affirmation that the Messiah, the Savior of humanity promised to Eve at the fall in the garden, would come through Abraham.

By the time of Jesus, Abraham was long gone. Neither he nor his children nor his grandchildren for eighty generations would be in a position to criticize God for failing to keep his promise to Abraham. But God is not bounded by time, and his word is good for eternity. So through the offspring of Abraham, at the right moment, God brought forth the Christ child, the Savior of the world.

It was because God knew what would come that God had been able to forgive the sins of Abraham. Paul makes the point that the death of Christ had to happen, even if the world had ended at that moment. Because God had passed over sins of the Old Testament–era saints, knowing that their faith could be counted as righteousness because Christ would die for their sins (Rom. 3:25 and chapter 4). Jesus is our assurance God keeps his promises, even the ones that are eighty generations old.

Lord, forgive me for ever doubting you. I trust you with all that I am. In Jesus, amen.

DECEMBER 30

And on the eighth day they came to circumcise the child. And they would have called him Zechariah after his father, but his mother answered, "No; he shall be called John." And they said to her, "None of your relatives is called by this name." And they made signs to his father, inquiring what he wanted him to be called. And he asked for a writing tablet and wrote, "His name is John." And they all wondered. And immediately his mouth was opened and his tongue loosed, and he spoke, blessing God. (Lk. 1:59–64)

When I was young, one of the punishments I most dreaded was "time-out." This punishment was used when my parents needed me to quiet down, get out of the heat of the moment, and think about what I had done or was doing. Little did I know, but timeout became a useful lifetime tool for learning the importance of slowing down and quieting myself when life around me is going haywire.

Zechariah had a good timeout from God. The punishment came some nine months earlier when the angel Gabriel appeared to Zechariah and told him that his wife Elizabeth would be pregnant and give birth to the Messiah's precurser, John the Baptist. In spite of the miracles involved in the manifestation of the angel, of the angel's perfect display of knowledge, of the clear assurance that the angel had come from God and spoke on God's behalf, Zechariah doubted and wanted a sign that God would keep his word and the angel was telling the truth. At this, God put Zechariah in timeout.

For the better part of a year, Zechariah lost the ability to speak, and evidently to hear as well. (Today's passage indicates that the people had to sign to Zechariah to ask him what to name the child.) Zechariah followed the angel's instructions and assigned the name "John." Once Zechariah saw the truth of the angel and responded in obedience, trusting that the child would indeed be who the angel said he would, the timeout ended.

I still need some timeout periodically. Sometimes life is frantic, the pressures mount up, the worries accumulate, sleep is lost, blood pressures rise, tempers flare, impatience rules the day, minds can't stop racing, self-discipline lags . . . the list goes on and on. In those days, I need to pause and remember, God is God. God has sent messengers to me (isn't that what the Bible is?) to assure me of his love, his purpose in the midst of aimlessness, his presence in the midst of chaos, his strength in the midst of weakness, his supply in the midst of need, his teaching in the midst of immaturity, and his forgiveness in the midst of sin. A good timeout with prayer to the Lord can change the way I face life. In a real sense, my quiet devotional time is part of that timeout. It sets me aright.

Lord, thank you for timeouts. I need these times to reflect on who you are and what you do. Forgive me for losing sight at times. Bolster my faith in Jesus, amen.

DECEMBER 31

And his father Zechariah was filled with the Holy Spirit and prophesied, saying, "Blessed be the Lord God of Israel, for he has visited and redeemed his people and has raised up a horn of salvation for us in the house of his servant David, as he spoke by the mouth of his holy prophets from of old, that we should be saved from our enemies and from the hand of all who hate us." (Lk. 1:67-71)

Zechariah was looking for the Messiah. He knew that God had promised to send one from the house of King David to redeem his people. This promise was about one thousand years old, but Zechariah, a priest of God, hadn't lost sight of it.

The promises of God are irrevocable. God doesn't make them and then change his mind. The all-knowing God knows what will unfold before he makes promises. I like the Advent season as one that testifies to our God keeping his promises. This is a good time to remember promises God has made that apply to us today. Like Zechariah, we can praise God for holding firm to his assurances. We can live in faith that God will do as God has promised.

God promises:

- that he will work all things out for good for those that love him (Rom. 8:28-29).
- that he will stand up for us when people accuse us wrongly (Isa. 54:17).
- that he will give strength to the weary and those who trust him (Is. 40:29-31).
- that he will give wisdom to those who ask (Jm. 1:5).
- that he will go before us in life in love and protection (Deut. 31:8).
- that he will bless what we give to him (Mal. 3:10).
- that he will meet all our needs (Phil. 4:19).
- that he will give us comfort in the midst of crisis and grief (Ps. 23:4).
- that he will bless our paths as we walk them in faith (Prov. 3:5-6).
- that he will give us good gifts (Mt. 7:9-11).

God's word contains many other promises, too numerous to list in today's devotional. But going through some of these promises needs to stir up in us the same reaction of Zechariah. We should be blessing his name and proclaiming aloud what he has done for us. Our faithful God has not lost a single promise made!

Lord, we pause to bless your name. We tell all who will listen of your goodness and love. Your faithfulness to your own word, exhibited in your love to us, defies our understanding, but we are amazed nonetheless. May we never fail to proclaim your goodness to the world around us. In Jesus' holy name, amen.

ACKNOWLEDGMENTS

Special gratitude goes out to the many people over my six decades who have contributed, albeit unknowingly, to these devotionals. I often name them in the pages, but a few times I grant them anonymity. I would be remiss without mentioning my family, without whom my life would be a shell of what it is.

So my gratitude begins with my wife, Becky, Mom, my children, Will, Gracie, Rachel, Rebecca, and Sarah, their spouses Nora, J.T., Lee, and Daniel. Even our grandchildren get credit for some of this as they served to motivate me on a number of the devotionals, so I give thanks to Ebba, Francis, John Henry, Lydia, Abigail, Chloe, Mia, Violet, and Caleb. My sisters, Kathryn and Hollie, have always inspired and encouraged me, and I am thankful to them and their husbands, Kevin (BIL) and Randy.

Outside of my family many gave me direct insight and help, and I wish to thank my class at church, the Biblical Literacy class, Pastors Brent Johnson, David Fleming, and Jarrett Stephens, as well as Dale Hearn, David Capes, and Janet Siefert, class members who went above and beyond in their help. A special shout out to Harvey Brown and Charles Mickey who helped proofread a number of these.

I believe Lois Chaney was right when she wrote that we are made up of bits and pieces of the people with whom we have come into contact. Many of those bits and pieces are found in these pages. Many of my friends (Rick, Kevin, Tim, Mark, and more) and mentors will find their stories lace these pages. Thank you for sharing your life with me.

Also great thanks to the folks at Baylor University Press for making this publication a reality. David, Dave, Cade, Lisa, Jenny, and Harry, thank you all!

Of last note, the church calendar begins with Advent, those four Sundays before Christmas that anticipate the coming Christ child. This book begins with January 1, the Western start of the year. Therefore, this book begins toward the end of the Christmas season, then rapidly moves through the rest of the church calendar before "starting" in Advent.

To God be the glory.